THEORY OF
HARMONY

THEORY OF
HARMONY

ARNOLD
SCHOENBERG

Translated by
ROY E. CARTER

UNIVERSITY OF CALIFORNIA PRESS

BERKELEY   1978   LOS ANGELES

Originally published in 1911
by Universal Edition, Vienna as Harmonielehre
This translation, based on the Third Edition (1922),
first published in 1978
by University of California Press
Berkeley and Los Angeles, California

ISBN 0-520-03464-3
Library of Congress Catalog Card Number 77-73502

Printed in Great Britain

TO THE HALLOWED MEMORY OF

GUSTAV MAHLER

CONTENTS

TRANSLATOR'S PREFACE

Shortly after the revised edition of Arnold Schoenberg's *Theory of Harmony* was published, his pupil and friend, Erwin Stein, assembled a *Practical Guide to Schoenberg's THEORY OF HARMONY: A Handbook for Teachers and Pupils.*[1] In his Preface, Stein stated the purpose of his *Guide* as follows:

> This *Guide* is designed to facilitate instruction from Schoenberg's *Theory of Harmony.* In view of the abundance of ideas and the great amount of space taken by theoretical derivations and justifications of harmonic phenomena, by polemical arguments, and by criticisms of the usual system of instruction, the use of that book may have been inconvenient for many a pupil who wanted merely to learn or review the handicraft of harmony, and for many a teacher who only wanted a facile survey of the material to be taught. This *Guide* should remedy that inconvenience. It leads through the course of instruction and indicates only those things the pupil must unquestionably learn.[2]

Schoenberg introduced the *Guide* with a few comments of his own (appearing at the head of Stein's Preface). He himself had instigated the writing of the *Guide*; yet he could not gladly approve its stated purpose. His comments, characteristically sardonic, include the following:

> My *Theory of Harmony* is obviously much too long. Once its author is out of the way – the living obstacle to judicious cutting – three quarters of the text must then surely go by the board.
>
> For my part, this *Guide*, written at my own behest, is an attempt to make even the remaining quarter unnecessary. . . . One need only work diligently through this *Guide*, forthrightly taking what little is worth keeping; that way one can leave my entire *Theory of Harmony* alone, unchanged.[3]

The *Guide*, in outline form, cites page and line of Schoenberg's text where the pupil or teacher may find the names of chords, instructions for building and connecting them, pertinent examples, and suggested exercises. These things the pupil 'must unquestionably learn'; he may, if he chooses, ignore all the rest. He may ignore the prefaces, the first three chapters, and the first section of the fourth, as well as the last chapter and many sentences, paragraphs, and pages from other chapters. Roughly estimated, the unessential portions make up at least one third of Schoenberg's treatise.

Yet, Schoenberg insisted throughout his *Theory of Harmony* that the pupil

---

[1] *Praktischer Leitfaden zu Schönbergs Harmonielehre: ein Hilfsbuch für Lehrer und Schüler* (Vienna: Universal-Edition, n.d.). Stein's Preface is dated March, 1923.

[2] *Ibid.*, p. 3.   [3] *Ibid.*

must unquestionably learn more than mere chords and rules for manipulating them. It is true, his chief aim was to present the *craft* of harmony, the harmonic usage that had evolved prior to 1900, and to present it as systematically as possible, leading the pupil step by step toward mastery of that craft. Nevertheless, Schoenberg could not be satisfied with showing the pupil *how* something is done; the teacher and pupil should search behind and beyond the 'how', trying to find what it is, and why it is so, and indeed, whether it need be so.

Schoenberg used his harmony text as a vehicle for publishing his views, not only on the origins, evolution, and implications of harmonic practice, but also

. . . on more complex relationships . . . on the similarities and relationships between artistic creation and other human activities, on the connections between the natural world outside ourselves and the participating or observing subject.[1]

Indeed, practically every topic, be it the major scale or the minor, be it parallel fifths and octaves, non-harmonic tones, modulation, or the minor subdominant, leads him into wide-ranging speculations on nature, art, and culture, and vigorous attacks upon ossified or irrational aesthetics. This preface to a translation of the *Harmonielehre* is hardly the place to discuss Schoenberg's speculations, but it is perhaps not amiss to mention here one of the many writers who have done so. In his essay, 'The Speculative Content of Schoenberg's *Harmonielehre*',[2] Professor John F. Spratt has ably summarized a number of Schoenberg's main ideas and addressed himself in particular to Schoenberg's attitudes toward nature and culture. Professor Spratt views Schoenberg

. . . as a determinist with respect to nature, a relativist with regard to culture, a Spinozan naturalist in the sense of regarding nature as an exemplary system and regarding inference from nature as a vital force in culture,[3]

and concludes that, in his considerable reverence for nature and natural law, and in spite of his cultural relativism, Schoenberg clearly remained within the Platonic tradition of rationalism. 'No law is eternal except as it removes itself from the world of transient phenomena.'[4]

All these digressions from the strictly practical aim of his textbook Schoenberg justified on grounds that he was searching, as the pupil should search, for explanation. That the pupil should learn so to search – this Schoenberg considered his most important teaching. Hence, he could not give his unqualified blessing to the *Practical Guide*.

From the first chapter to the last, Schoenberg explicitly renounced any claim that he was writing a 'theory' of harmony or a 'theory' of anything at all – at least, not a systematic theory. But even if he did aim at a systematic pedagogical presentation rather than a systematic theory, his presentation is nevertheless saturated with theory, with speculation (the roots of both words denoted 'looking' and 'seeing', and Schoenberg indeed exhorts us to 'search'); thus the only English translation of the *Harmonielehre* available heretofore, that of

---

[1] *Infra*, p. 17.   [2] *Current Musicology*, XI (1971), pp. 83–8.
[3] *Ibid.*, p. 84.   [4] *Ibid.*, p. 88.

Robert D. W. Adams, is entitled *Theory of Harmony*,[1] as is the present translation. Yet Professor Adams, intending his translation as a practical student
edition, followed Erwin Stein's *Guide*, included only 'the essentials – explanations, directions, examples' – and thus omitted from the *Theory of Harmony*
virtually all of Schoenberg's theoretical commentary.[2]

This new, complete translation grew out of the conviction that the abundance
of Schoenberg's theorizing, speculation, and polemics is no less 'essential' than
the purely technical material. In fact, he so interwove the practical with the
theoretical that the one is incomplete without the other. For example, he de-
cried the usual exercises by which a pupil is supposed to learn harmony: the
realization of given figured basses and the harmonization of given melodies. If
we would understand why he objected to such exercises, what alternatives he
recommended, and why he recommended these, we must read his theoretical
commentary together with his instructions on how to proceed.

Schoenberg's *Theory of Harmony* is indeed his seminal theoretical work. In
his later textbooks[3] he was able to keep his theoretical commentary to a minimum by simply referring the reader back to his earlier work. Moreover, he gave
expression in his *Theory of Harmony* to a number of the notions that have most
excited the twentieth-century musical world. Most obviously, there is the proposition that the system of major-minor tonality is no necessity of music, no
natural law – even if it is partially founded upon the natural laws of harmonics;
it is rather a convention, once viable, now exhausted, now undoubtedly to be
modified or replaced by other conventions, perhaps by 'tonalities' of twelve
tones. Then there is the fascination with 'tone colour' (see the last two pages of
the text); there is the notion that musical order may be manifest in many previously inconceivable ways; and there is the very questioning of the need for
order in music.

[1] (New York: Philosophical Library, 1948). The title *Harmonielehre* has been variously translated as 'Treatise on Harmony', and 'Manual', 'Textbook', or 'Theory of
Harmony'. A *Lehre* can be a theory; it is, essentially, the collection of facts, laws,
opinions, and theories *taught* within a certain field of learning. Textbooks of harmony
in German generally bear the title, *Harmonielehre*, as those in English are quite often
simply entitled *Harmony*. This, the most general title, would perhaps be the most
accurate translation of Schoenberg's title; but since the book is far more theoretical
than the usual textbook of harmony, and since it is commonly cited in English as
Schoenberg's *Theory of Harmony*, it was deemed appropriate to retain that title for this
new translation. Within the text, however, the word 'Harmonielehre' has been variously translated, according to its context, as 'instruction' or 'course in harmony' and
the like, or 'harmonic theory'.

[2] Adams, *ibid.*, p. xi.

[3] *Models for Beginners in Composition*, New York: G. Schirmer, 1942; *Structural
Functions of Harmony*, New York: W. W. Norton, 1954; *Preliminary Exercises in
Counterpoint*, London: Faber and Faber, 1963; and *Fundamentals of Musical Composi-
tion*, London: Faber and Faber, 1967. See also his *Style and Idea* (Leonard Stein, ed.,
London: Faber and Faber, 1975): this volume of selected essays (written by Schoen-
berg between 1909 and 1951) contains many references to topics discussed in *Theory of
Harmony*.

This translation is based on the third, revised (improved) and enlarged edition, completed in 1921 and published in 1922. The first edition was published in 1911.[1] Since the appearance of the revised edition, it has been reprinted a number of times. The last copyright date is 1949. The latest reprint was edited by Josef Rufer, whose Preface is dated Autumn, 1966. As noted in his Preface to the seventh edition,[2] Rufer made a few minor alterations following Schoenberg's marginal notes (dated March, 1922) in a 'Handexemplar mit Fehlervormerkungen' (author's copy, indicating *errata*) and in addition deleted four of Schoenberg's footnotes. These alterations were not made in the present translation, but they are cited at the pertinent places by translator's footnotes. Rufer also corrected typographical errors in the examples and made a few minor revisions in their figuration. The examples here have been revised according to Rufer's corrections and revisions.

It is noteworthy that Schoenberg wrote the original edition of his *Theory of Harmony* during approximately the same years in which he composed such works as the Three Piano Pieces, Op. 11, 'The Book of the Hanging Gardens', Op. 15, the Five Pieces for Orchestra, Op. 16, and *Erwartung*, Op. 17 – his first 'atonal' works. Moreover, the revision of his book coincided approximately with the composition of the Five Piano Pieces, Op. 23, the Serenade, Op. 24, and the Suite for Piano, Op. 25 – the first pieces in which he ventured his 'Method of composing with twelve tones which are related only with one another.' Thus, it is perhaps not amiss to say that these two editions mark the beginning and the end of the most critical period in Schoenberg's artistic career, the period in which, having finally asserted his independence from the old laws of tonality, he sought the stability of a new law.

The facts cited above can quite naturally arouse one's curiosity as to what changes he may have made in revising his *Theory of Harmony*. Here it must suffice, first, to affirm that Schoenberg's general statements in his Preface to the third edition[3] accurately summarize the differences between the two editions, and secondly, to cite a few of the more important changes.

The changes range from substitution of other words, or even merely other punctuation, to the extensive revision of whole chapters (e.g. Chapters XI, XVII, and XXI). Schoenberg enlarged various sections substantially, in addition to the 'Guidelines' he specifically mentioned in the Preface. As is perhaps to be expected, the changes he found necessary were most often in the speculative or polemical passages, many of which are longer in the later edition. Many of his ideas were of course clearer to him in 1921 than they had been in 1911; hence, they are more clearly expressed. A few passages, it must be admitted, seem less clear in the revision. The essentials, the principles set forth in the first edition, remain intact in the third. One might describe the edition of 1921 as merely a polished and expanded version of that of 1911. The earlier might even be viewed as a rough draft of the later.

However interesting the changes Schoenberg saw fit to make, we should of

---

[1] Both editions were published in Vienna by Universal-Edition.
[2] (Vienna: Universal-Edition), p. IX.   [3] *Infra*, pp. 4–5.

course also take note of those portions that remained unchanged. For example, in the last chapter, 'Aesthetic Evaluation of Chords with Six or More Tones', and in the third, 'Consonance and Dissonance', he made only a few minor revisions. In Chapter IV, on the other hand, Schoenberg so extended his footnote on the more minute subdivision of the octave that it is now almost a chapter in itself.[1] In the revised edition he went on in this footnote to deny that further subdivision of the octave was necessary as the next step beyond the tonal (diatonic-chromatic) system. He went on to argue for the use of twelve tones, elaborated polyphonically, as preferable, at least for some time, to further proliferation of tones within the octave. Finer subdivision of the octave Schoenberg did not accept as, at that time, technologically feasible or culturally necessary.

Section 8 of Chapter XIX, entitled 'The Chromatic Scale as a Basis for Tonality', was added to the first edition as an afterthought, 'after completing the book.' In the first part of this section, in both editions, Schoenberg summarized the principles of his *Theory of Harmony*. Then he went on to discuss some minor chords that are remote from the key and suggested two ways one can relate, for example, minor triads on $d\flat$, $e\flat$, $f\sharp$, $a\flat$, and b to the key of C major. He then continued (page 434 of the first edition, page 387 of this translation):

A third and more significant way, however, would be to work out an idea already mentioned in this book: to base our thought, not on the seven tones of the major scale, rather, on the twelve of the chromatic scale.

Then, in the first edition, having thus arrived at the topic indicated by the title of this section, he simply dismissed the topic by saying that 'a future theory will undoubtedly follow that course; it would thereby reach the only correct solution to this otherwise difficult problem.' The chapter then ended with a short paragraph merely repeating a point he had made earlier, that all chords can be 'vagrant', even triads.

The title of this section therefore seems unjustified in the first edition. Whatever the reason for the lame ending in 1911, he did continue in the revised edition. Instead of the hasty appeal to some future theory, Schoenberg now pursued the topic indicated in his title, at which he had just arrived in 1911, by outlining how 'such a theory could begin.'[2]

Now, after that outline Schoenberg concluded the chapter by stating two of the assumptions that underlie both his book and his music: that the evolution of harmonic theory had reached a frontier it could not cross, at least not for a while; and that, therefore, music now stood at the door to a new polyphonic era, in which, as in past times, 'harmonies will be a product of the voice leading: justified solely by the melodic lines!'[3]

In the edition of 1911, again in Chapter IV (p. 31), he wrote:

It should not be said that order, clarity, and comprehensibility can impair beauty,

[1] *Infra*, Appendix, pp. 423–5.   [2] *Infra*, pp. 387–9.
[3] *Infra*, p. 389.

but they are not a necessary factor without which there would be no beauty; they are merely an accidental, a circumstantial factor. For nature is also beautiful even when we do not understand her, and where she seems to us unordered.

He rewrote this passage as follows:

This is not to say that some future work of art may do without order, clarity, and comprehensibility, but that not merely what we conceive as such deserves these names. For nature is also beautiful. . . .[1]

Schoenberg seems to have said in 1911 that order in music is unnecessary, at least as far as beauty is concerned, and in 1921 that it is necessary but can be conceived much more variously than is commonly assumed. Perhaps the latter statement merely makes clear what he had intended to say in the first edition. However that may be, he maintained in both editions that the listener's interest in order and beauty surpasses that of the composer, and that order and beauty may be attributes, not of the music, but of the listener's perception. Yet, his efforts during those years (c. 1909–21) to define the order, or to create order, in his 'atonal' works led him to devise a method which, pursued to its logical conclusions, could perhaps create total order in a piece of music. Of course this possibility of total order, theoretically attainable by rigorous application of serial methods to all aspects of music, did not seem to interest Schoenberg as it has some subsequent composers. He did, nevertheless, invent the 'Method of composing with twelve tones which are related only with one another' and thereby demonstrated that Schoenberg, the composer, was, after all, looking for some explainable 'order, clarity, and comprehensibility' in his music.

Schoenberg undoubtedly referred to such statements as that quoted above from the original edition when he wrote (in 1949) of exaggeration in his *Theory of Harmony*, of the intoxicating

enthusiasm of having freed music from the shackles of tonality. . . . In fact, I myself and my pupils Anton von Webern and Alban Berg, and even Alois Hába believed that now music could renounce motivic features [as well] and remain coherent and comprehensible nevertheless.[2]

For the edition of 1911, toward the end of Chapter XXI, 'Chords Constructed in Fourths', Schoenberg wrote a long footnote attacking aesthetic dogma and the aestheticians and theorists who try to preserve that dogma. In the revised edition this footnote, thoroughly reworked and greatly expanded, appears as text, as the last section of the chapter; and for the revised edition he also wrote a new footnote,[3] discussing and denouncing the use of the word 'atonal' and its implications. In fact, he mentioned that word only twice in his *Theory of Harmony* (the other instance is on page 128). This is after all a textbook of traditional, tonal harmony and has nothing to do with his 'atonal' and twelve-tone music. Nothing to do, that is, explicitly. But with this book (and

[1] *Infra,* pp. 29–30.
[2] 'My Evolution', *Musical Quarterly,* XXXVIII, No. 4, October, 1952, pp. 524–5. The article was completed in August, 1949.
[3] *Infra,* Appendix, p. 432.

his initial essays in 'atonal' composition) he cleared and prepared the ground; in his *Theory of Harmony* he recorded the premises and the reasoning that were expressed musically in his 'atonal' and twelve-tone works.

Schoenberg added several examples in the revised edition, especially in the later chapters. A number of other revisions (but by no means all) are also indicated here and there in the translation by translator's footnotes.

Schoenberg himself provided some direction for any would-be translator of his works. In a letter of 27 October 1932, he wrote of the likelihood that his *Harmonielehre* would be translated into English; but he feared that the result would hardly be 'on a level above the colloquial and the journalistic'. He recalled that German translations of Strindberg's works did not confirm the Swedish author's reputation as an 'outstanding stylist'.[1] And Schoenberg severely reprimanded a translator of some of his articles (in a letter from Los Angeles, 3 December 1947), chiding that translator, 'a civilized European', for having

so little respect for another man's intellectual work as to expect him to permit changes such as those you are making in my articles.

You put bits in, leave things out, make something long-winded out of what was said clearly and concisely, choose uncharacteristic expressions to replace pertinent ones, and even go so far as to change the structure of paragraphs. . . .

. . . Your changes go beyond the limit of what even my Americanised conscience can permit.[2]

Always acutely conscious of Schoenberg's *caveat*, I have tried to observe the following rules (which are to some extent self-evident, thus, should be stated): (1) above all, the sense of the original should be at least as clear as it is in the original, including the subtleties of emphasis, of connection and contrast of ideas, etc.; (2) as implied by the first rule, the translation should be idiomatic in the new language – that is, the reader should not be reminded, at least not too often, that he is reading a translation; and (3) so far as is consistent with the first two rules, the author's manner of expression should be reflected in the translation. If any of Schoenberg's strictures quoted above have been violated here (Alas! they have), then I can only plead in my defense the truism that translation requires change, a putting-into-other-words. It is an imitation of the original in a different language; and by virtue of the differences between the languages, not to mention cultural and generational differences, the imitation can never be a duplicate. I do, however, assume full responsibility for all shortcomings of translation.

Certain idiosyncrasies of Schoenberg's style have been retained in the translation wherever they could be accommodated; for example, his use of the colon and the frequent ellipses and incomplete sentences. The bracketed interpolations represent efforts to clarify the author's meaning where ellipsis or an incomplete sentence could create ambiguity or obscurity; and since the antecedent

[1] *Letters* (ed. Erwin Stein and trans. Eithne Wilkins and Ernst Kaiser; New York: St. Martin's Press, 1965), p. 168.

[2] *Ibid.*, pp. 250–1.

of many a relative or demonstrative pronoun is vague in the original, I have often taken the liberty of replacing such a pronoun with the noun or phrase to which it most likely refers. In a few particularly obscure passages, the interpolations and the translation represent my best guess as to Schoenberg's intent.[1] Certain lengthy paragraphs of the original were divided here into two or more paragraphs, where the original paragraphs were clearly divisible. Schoenberg's chapter divisions and subdivisions have been retained, although one or two chapters are quite long and one or two quite short. The numbering of chapters has been added for the sake of convenience. In the examples, the letter 'j' was not used in the original (perhaps to avoid confusion with the letter 'i'), nor is it used here.

Schoenberg did not consider it worth his while to document his occasional references to the writings of others or even his quotations of examples from the musical literature (see p. 16 below). He 'did not collect his knowledge by reading'; however original or unoriginal, what he had to say was what he had learned largely from his own experience in teaching, composing, and studying the masterworks. Nevertheless, for the convenience of the reader who wishes to consult the works mentioned or cited by Schoenberg, I have endeavored to document them as unobtrusively as possible. A few of the books were simply unavailable; most of those that I was able to consult are not generally available.

Translator's footnotes are designated by Arabic numerals and are enclosed in square brackets. Schoenberg's are designated by the asterisk. A number of Schoenberg's footnotes have been transferred to an Appendix, particularly those that extend to several pages. Where I have taken this liberty, it is indicated in a translator's footnote on the pertinent page of the text.

As names of keys or tonalities small letters indicate minor, capitals indicate major (e.g. *a* minor, *A* major).

It is a duty and a pleasure to acknowledge here my debt to those who have facilitated the preparation of this work: to Dr. John F. Spratt – like Schoenberg, a searcher – for the constant stimulus of his insight; to Mrs. Gertrud Schoenberg for permission and encouragement to undertake the translation and to Mr. Lawrence Schoenberg for smoothing the way toward publication; to Mrs. Sylvia Fitzmaurice and Miss Rose Barber for their generous assistance with typing and research; to Mr. Donald Mitchell, who set the work on its way toward publication, and to Miss Judith Osborne, who guided it through publication and refined many details; to my wife and children, who endured certain sacrifices occasioned by this work; and to all others who have lent suggestions, criticism, or simply encouragement. To Arnold Schoenberg himself, whose work so richly rewards study – but how can we describe our debt to him?

To the following publishers and journals, my thanks for permission to quote from the works cited: W. W. Norton – C. P. E. Bach, *Essay on the True Art of Playing Keyboard Instruments* (trans. William J. Mitchell); Faber and Faber – Herbert Read, *The Meaning of Art*; Universal Edition – Erwin Stein, *Praktischer*

[1] For some instructive comments on the problems of translating Schoenberg's prose, see Leo Black's Translator's Preface in the new (1975) edition of Schoenberg's *Style and Idea*.

Leitfaden zu Schönbergs HARMONIELEHRE, and the first and seventh editions of *Harmonielehre*; St. Martin's Press – Arnold Schoenberg, *Letters* (ed. Erwin Stein, trans. Eithne Wilkins and Ernst Kaiser); *The Musical Quarterly* – Arnold Schoenberg, 'My Evolution'; *Current Musicology* – John F. Spratt, 'The Speculative Content of Schoenberg's *Harmonielehre*'.

Finally, I should like to thank Universal Edition, Vienna, for permission to reproduce Schoenberg's music examples.

Roy E. Carter

PREFACE TO THE FIRST EDITION

This book I have learned from my pupils.

In my teaching I never sought merely 'to tell the pupil what I know'. Better to tell him what *he* did not know. Yet that was not my chief aim either, although it was reason enough for me to devise something new for each pupil. I labored rather to show him the nature of the matter from the ground up. Hence, I never imposed those fixed rules with which a pupil's brain is so carefully tied up in knots. Everything was formulated as instructions that were no more binding upon the pupil than upon the teacher. If the pupil can do something better without the instructions, then let him do so. But the teacher must have the courage to admit his own mistakes. He does not have to pose as infallible, as one who knows all and never errs; he must rather be tireless, constantly searching, perhaps sometimes finding. Why pose as a demigod? Why not be, rather, fully human?

I have never tried to talk my pupils into believing me infallible – only a 'Gesangsprofessor' (professor of singing) finds that necessary. On the contrary, I have often risked saying something that I had later to retract; I have often risked giving instructions that, when applied, proved to be wrong and so had to be corrected. Perhaps my mistakes did not benefit the pupil, but they hardly caused him much harm. Indeed, the fact that I openly acknowledged them may have set him to thinking. As for myself, since the instructions I gave were untested products of my own thought, I was compelled by my errors, which were quickly exposed, to examine my instructions anew and improve their formulation.

This, then, is the way this book came into being. From the errors made by my pupils as a result of inadequate or wrong instructions I learned how to give the right instructions. Successful completion of assignments by the pupils established the soundness of my efforts without luring me into the fallacy that I had solved the problem definitively. And I think neither the pupils nor I have fared badly that way. Had I told them merely what I know, then they would have known just that and nothing more. As it is, they know perhaps even less. But they do know what matters: *the search itself*!

I hope my pupils will commit themselves to searching! Because they will know that one searches for the sake of searching. That finding, which is indeed the goal, can easily put an end to striving.

Our age seeks many things. What it has found, however, is above all: *comfort*. Comfort, with all its implications, intrudes even into the world of ideas and makes us far more content than we should ever be. We understand today better than ever how to make life pleasant. We solve problems to remove an unpleasantness. But, *how* do we solve them? And what presumption, even to think we have really solved them! Here we can see most distinctly what the prerequisite of comfort is: superficiality. It is thus easy to have a 'Weltan-schauung', a 'philosophy', if one contemplates only what is pleasant and gives no heed to the rest. The rest – which is just what matters most. In the light of the 'rest' these philosophies may very well seem made to order for those who hold to them, whereas, in that light, the tenets which constitute these philoso-phies are seen to spring above all from the attempt at self-vindication. For, curiously enough, people of our time who formulate new laws of morality (or, even more to their liking, overthrow old ones) *cannot live with guilt*! Yet com-fort does not consider self-discipline; and so guilt is either repudiated or trans-formed into virtue. Herein, for one who sees through it all, the recognition of guilt expresses itself as guilt. The thinker, who keeps on searching, does the opposite. He shows that there are problems and that they are unsolved. As does Strindberg: 'Life makes everything ugly.' Or Maeterlinck: 'Three quarters of our brothers [are] condemned to misery.' Or Weininger and all others who have thought earnestly.

Comfort as a philosophy of life! The least possible commotion, nothing shocking. Those who so love comfort will never seek where there is not definitely something to find.

There is a mechanical puzzle that consists of three small metal tubes of differ-ent diameters sealed in a glass-covered box. The problem is to get the smaller tubes inside the larger. Now one can try to do it methodically; then it usually takes quite a long time. But it can also be done another way. One can just shake the box at random until the tubes are inside one another. Does that happen by chance? It looks that way, but I don't think so. For an idea lurks behind this method. Namely, that movement alone can succeed where delibera-tion fails. Is it not the same with the learner? What does the teacher accomplish through methodology? At most, activity. If everything goes well! But things can also go badly, and then what he accomplishes is lethargy. Yet lethargy pro-duces nothing. Only activity, movement is productive. Then why not start moving right away? But comfort!? Comfort avoids movement; it therefore does not take up the search.

Either [tentative, perhaps random] movement generates searching or else searching generates movement – one or the other way must be taken. It does not matter which. Only action, movement, produces what could truly be called education or culture (*Bildung*):[1] namely, training (*Ausbildung*), discipline and cultivation (*Durchbildung*). The teacher who does not exert himself, because he tells only 'what he knows', does not exert his pupils either. Action must start with the teacher himself; his unrest must infect the pupils. Then they will search as he does. Then he will not be disseminating education (*Bildung*), and

[1 'Bildung' connotes 'education' and 'culture' in the most profound sense of the words, i.e. extensive, *active* knowledge that yields understanding and wisdom. How-ever, like the English words, it is commonly used to denote extensive schooling and erudition, even though these do not necessarily impart understanding.

'Ausbildung' means development of skill, and 'Durchbildung' adds the notion of thoroughness.]

that is good. For 'education' means today: to know something of everything without understanding anything at all. Yet, the sense of this beautiful word, *Bildung*, is entirely different; and, since the word now carries a derogatory connotation, it should be replaced by *Ausbildung* and *Durchbildung*.

It should be clear, then, that the teacher's first task is to shake up the pupil thoroughly. When the resultant tumult subsides, everything will have presumably found its proper place.

Or it will never happen!

The activity which in such manner emanates from the teacher comes back again to him. In this sense also I have learned this book from my pupils. And I must take this opportunity to thank them.

Some I have to thank in yet another respect. Those who have supported me in this work through proofreading, etc.; through approval, which was gratifying to me; and through criticism, which roused me, but also brought my attention to a number of shortcomings: Alban Berg (who prepared the topical index), Dr. Karl Horwitz, Dr. Heinrich Jalowetz, Karl Linke, Dr. Robert Neumann, Josef Polnauer, Erwin Stein, and Dr. Anton von Webern. Some of them will soon be heard from in better circumstances.

And so perhaps this activity, too, will eventually return to me.

Vienna, July 1911.

ARNOLD SCHOENBERG

PREFACE TO THE THIRD EDITION

This new edition does not differ essentially from the first, although I have made quite a lot of changes. Noteworthy improvements are to be found in the structure of many sections and chapters and in many a stylistic detail. Enlargements include in particular the number of examples in the first half of the book. As for what is new, the 'Guidelines' are especially worthy of mention. These are given in the form of summaries at various points in the book to aid in the use of material already presented. This improvement springs from my pedagogical experiences, as does yet another: a number of my instructions, which originally left up to the pupil choices that could be undesirable to the teacher, are now more binding and more exclusive. In individual details can be found yet very many, sometimes extensive additions, a number of them even dealing with matters of principle. In general, I am happy to note, I was able to leave the book unchanged, even where I have come one step or several closer to the truth since the writing of the first edition. For they have been steps in the same direction.

Many typographical errors which in the first edition eluded the most painstaking correction, especially in the examples, have been culled out, thanks to the help of numerous friends and pupils. And I earnestly hope, nevertheless, that this edition will be at least as well corrected as the first, if not better.

Let me take this opportunity to extend warmest thanks to my former pupil, Erwin Stein, who has not only done a most conscientious job of correction but has also taken this opportunity to induce me, through astute and unsparing criticism, to remove many grave shortcomings. If this book is on the way toward becoming what I can require of myself, then much credit must go to him for his initiative.

The sentences which in the first edition accompanied the dedication to Gustav Mahler are now omitted as superfluous.[1] They were words written in

---

[1 Mahler died in 1911 shortly before the first edition of the *Harmonielehre* was published. Schoenberg's dedication read as follows:

'This book is dedicated to the memory of GUSTAV MAHLER.

'The dedication was intended, while he yet lived, to give him a little pleasure. It was to express veneration for his work, his immortal compositions. And it was to bear witness to the fact that his work, which the educated musicians pass over with a superior shrug of the shoulders, even with contempt, is adored by one who perhaps also understands a thing or two.

'Gustav Mahler had to do without pleasures greater than that which this dedication intended for him. This martyr, this saint passed away before he had established his work well enough even to be able to entrust its future to his friends.

'I should have been content just to give him a little pleasure. But now that he is dead, profound grief directly after Mahler's death. They trembled with the pain of bereavement and with anger over the disparity between his worth and the recognition that he had found. They were agitated, impassioned words, fighting words, which now seem almost to detract, since the younger generation has almost fulfilled its duty in placing his work beside that of our greatest. The declaration that 'He was an altogether great man', being unproved, thereby won very nearly the power and the repute of a prophecy. But this declaration, which indeed was intended to win in order to give, won more than it gave: to him, who has everything, it can give as much but no more.

Mattsee bei Salzburg, 24 June 1921

ARNOLD SCHOENBERG

---

it is my wish that this book bring me such recognition that no one can pass over my words lightly when I say: "He was an altogether great man." '

Cf. Schoenberg's essay on Mahler in Arnold Schoenberg, *Style and Idea* (London: Faber and Faber, 1975), pp. 447–72, and the letters to Mahler included in the English edition of Schoenberg's *Letters*, pp. 293ff.]

I THEORY OR SYSTEM OF PRESENTATION?

Someone who teaches musical composition is called a theory teacher;[1] but if he has written a book on harmony, he is called a theorist. Yet a carpenter will never think of setting himself up as a theory teacher, although of course he, too, has to teach his apprentices the handicraft. He may very well be called a master carpenter, but this is more a designation of his proficiency than a title. Under no circumstances does he consider himself anything like a scholar, although he, too, undoubtedly understands his craft. If there is a distinction, it can only be that the technique of musical composition is 'more theoretical' than that of carpentry. This distinction is not easy to grasp. For if the carpenter knows how to join pieces of wood securely, this knowledge is based no less on fruitful observation and experience than is the knowledge of the music theorist who understands how to join chords effectively. And if the carpenter knows which types of wood are required by a particular job and selects accordingly, he is thus taking natural relationships and materials into account, just as does the music theorist when, appraising the possibilities of themes, he recognizes how long a piece may be. On the other hand, whenever the carpenter introduces flutings to enliven a smooth surface, he exhibits bad taste equal to that of most artists, and almost as little imagination; even so his imagination and taste equal that of all music theorists. If, therefore, the carpenter's teaching, just like that of the theory teacher, rests on observation, experience, reasoning, and taste, on knowledge of natural laws and of the requirements of the material – is there then really any essential distinction?

Why then do we not also call a master carpenter a theorist, or a music theorist a master musician? Because there is a small distinction: the carpenter could never understand his craft in a merely theoretical way, whereas the usual music theorist has no practical skill at all – he is no master. And still another distinction: the true music theorist is embarrassed by the handicraft because it is not *his*, but that *of others*. Merely to hide his embarrassment without making a virtue of it does not satisfy him. The title, master, is beneath him. He could be taken for something else, and here we have a third distinction: the nobler profession must be designated by a correspondingly nobler title. For this reason, although even today the great artist is still addressed as 'master', music does not simply have instruction in its craft, its techniques – as does painting; music has, rather, Instruction in Theory.

And the result: the evolution of no other art is so greatly encumbered by its teachers as is that of music. For no one guards his property more jealously than the one who knows that, strictly speaking, it does not belong to him. The harder it is to prove ownership, the greater the effort to do so. And the theorist, who is not usually an artist, or is a bad one (which means the same), therefore

[1 Note that Schoenberg viewed instruction in harmony, counterpoint, and form as constituting instruction in composition, or rather instruction preparatory to composition (*Infra*, p. 13).]

understandably takes pains to fortify his unnatural position. He knows that the pupil learns most of all through the example shown him by the masters in their masterworks. And if it were possible to watch composing in the same way that one can watch painting, if composers could have *ateliers* as did painters, then it would be clear how superfluous the music theorist is and how he is just as harmful as the art academies. He senses all this and seeks to create a substitute by replacing the living example with theory, with the system.

I do not wish to quarrel with honest efforts to discover tentative laws of art. These efforts are necessary. They are necessary, above all, for the aspiring human mind. Our noblest impulse, the impulse to know and understand (*erkennen*), makes it our duty to search. And even a false theory, if only it was found through genuine searching, is for that reason superior to the complacent certainty of those who reject it because they presume to know (*wissen*) – to know, although they themselves have not searched! It is indeed our duty to reflect over and over again upon the mysterious origins of the powers of art (*Kunstwirkungen*). And again and again to begin at the beginning; again and again to examine anew for ourselves and attempt to organize anew for ourselves. Regarding nothing as given but the phenomena. These we may more rightly regard as eternal than the laws we believe we have found. Since we do definitely know (*wissen*) the phenomena [as facts] we might be more justified in giving the name, 'science' (*Wissenschaft*), to our [direct] knowledge (*Wissen*) of the phenomena, rather than to those conjectures that are intended to explain them.

Yet these conjectures, too, have their justification: as experiments, as results of efforts to think, as mental gymnastics – perhaps sometimes even as preliminary steps to truth.

It art theory could be content with that, if it could be satisfied with the rewards afforded by honest searching, then one could not object to it. But it is more ambitious. It is not content to be merely the attempt to find laws; it professes to have found *the eternal* laws. It observes a number of phenomena, classifies them according to some common characteristics, and then derives laws from them. That is of course correct procedure, because unfortunately there is hardly any other way. But now begins the error. For it is falsely concluded that these laws, since apparently correct with regard to the phenomena previously observed, must then surely hold for all future phenomena as well. And, what is most disastrous of all, it is then the belief that a *yardstick* has been found by which to measure artistic worth, even that of future works. As often as the theorists have been disavowed by reality, whenever they declared something to be inartistic 'which did not with their rules agree' ('was nicht nach ihrer Regeln Lauf'),[1] they still 'cannot forsake their madness' ('vom Wahn nicht lassen'). For what would they be if they did not at least have a lease on

[1 If ye by rules would measure
   What doth not with your rules agree,
   Forgetting all your learning,
   Seek ye first what its rules may be.
      —Hans Sachs in Richard Wagner, *Die Meistersinger*, Act I, Scene 3 (trans. Frederick Jameson).]

Beauty, since art itself does not belong to them? What would they be if it were to become clear to everyone, for all time, what is being shown here once again? What would they be, since, in reality, art propagates itself through works of art and not through aesthetic laws? Would there really be any distinction left, in their favor, between themselves and a master carpenter?

Someone could declare that I am going too far, that nowadays, as everybody knows, aesthetics does not prescribe laws of Beauty but merely attempts to infer their existence from the effects of art (*Kunstwirkungen*). Quite correct: almost everybody does know that nowadays. Yet hardly anyone takes it into consideration. And that is just the point. Let me illustrate. In this book I believe I have succeeded in refuting some old prejudices of musical aesthetics. That these prejudices have remained with us right up to the present would in itself be proof enough of my contention. But when I say what it is that I do not consider a necessity of art; when I say: tonality is no natural law of music, eternally valid – then it is plain for everyone to see how the theorists spring up in indignation to cast their veto against my integrity. Who today would want to admit that [my statement about tonality is true] even if I proved it still more incisively than I shall do here?

The power that the theorist has to have to fortify an untenable position comes from his alliance with aesthetics. Now aesthetics deals only with the eternal things, thus always comes too late in life. People call that 'conservative'. But this is just as absurd as a conservative express train. The advantages that aesthetics assures the theorist are too great, however, for him to worry about this absurdity. There is so little grandeur in the sound of it, if the teacher tells the pupil: One of the most gratifying means for producing musical form is tonality. What a different impression it makes, though, if he speaks of the principle of tonality, as of a law – 'Thou shalt . . .' – adherence to which shall be indispensable to all musical form. This word 'indispensable' – one can detect a whiff of eternity! Dare to feel otherwise, young artist, and you have them all against you, those who claim that I am merely saying what everybody knows. And they will call you 'Neu-Junker-Unkraut'[1] and 'charlatan' and will slander you: 'You fake! You thought you could put something over on us!' And when they have finished smearing you with their vulgarity, they will pose as those courageous men who would have thought it cowardly not to risk something in behalf of their views – something, that is, which only hurts the other. And in the end you are the clod!

To hell with all these theories, if they always serve only to block the evolution of art and if their positive achievement consists in nothing more than helping those who will compose badly anyway to learn it quickly.

What one could reasonably expect of them [the theorists], they do not fulfil. The form in which they practice aesthetics is indeed extremely primitive. It does not amount to much more than some pretty talk; yet the main thing the theorists have borrowed from aesthetics is the method of apodictic assertions

[1 Wagner, *Die Meistersinger*, I, 3. Beckmesser's epithet, expressing his hatred for Walther, may be paraphrased as 'meddlesome upstart', 'disgusting pretender', and the like.]

and judgments. It is asserted, for example: 'That sounds good or bad' (beautiful or not beautiful would be more correct and forthright). That assertion is first of all presumptuous; secondly though, it is an aesthetic judgment. If it is put forward unsupported, why then should we believe it? Should we trust in the authority of the theorist? Why then? If he offers no support for what he says, it is then either just something that he knows (that is, not what he himself has discovered, but rather what he has learned [secondhand]), or what all believe because it is experienced by all. Yet, beauty is not something in the common experience of all, rather, at most, in the experience of individuals. Above all, however, if that sort of judgment could be accepted without further justification, then the justification would have to follow so necessarily from the system itself that to mention it would be superfluous. And here we have hit the theorists' most vulnerable spot: Their theories are intended to serve as practical aesthetics; they are intended to influence the sense of beauty in such a way that it will produce, for example, harmonic progressions whose effect can be regarded as beautiful; they are intended to justify the exclusion of those sounds and progressions that are esteemed not beautiful. But these theories are not so constructed that the aesthetic judgment follows as a consequence of their first principles, of the logical development of these principles! On the contrary, there is no coherence, absolutely no coherence. These judgments, 'beautiful' or 'not beautiful', are entirely gratuitous excursions into aesthetics and have nothing to do with the logic of the whole. Parallel fifths sound bad (why?). This passing note sounds harsh (why?). There are no such things as ninth chords, or they sound harsh (why?). Where in the system can we find logical, mutually consistent answers to these three 'why's'? In the sense of beauty? What is that? How is the sense of beauty otherwise related to this system? To this *system* – if you please!!

These systems! Elsewhere[1] I will show how they have really never been just what they still could be: namely, systems of presentation (*Darstellung*). Methods by which a body of material is coherently organized and lucidly classified, methods derived from principles which will assure an unbroken logic. I will show how quickly this system fails, how soon one has to break into it to patch up its holes with a second system (which is still no system), in order even halfway to accommodate the most familiar facts. It should be quite different! A real system should have, above all, principles that embrace all the facts. Ideally, just as many facts as there actually are, no more, no less. Such principles are natural laws. And only such principles, which are not qualified by exceptions, would have the right to be regarded as generally valid. Such principles would share with natural laws this characteristic of unconditional validity. The laws of art, however, consist mainly of exceptions!

Nor have *I* been able to discover such principles, either; and I believe they will not be discovered very soon. Attempts to explain artistic matters exclu-

[1 *Infra*, Chapter XVII ('Non-harmonic Tones'), for example. The entire book is a critique of musical systems in general and the major-minor harmonic system in particular.]

sively on natural grounds will continue to founder for a long time to come. Efforts to discover laws of art can then, at best, produce results something like those of a good comparison: that is, they can influence the way in which the sense organ of the subject, the observer, orients itself to the attributes of the object observed. In making a comparison we bring closer what is too distant, thereby enlarging details, and remove to some distance what is too close, thereby gaining perspective. No greater worth than something of this sort can, at present, be ascribed to laws of art. Yet that is already quite a lot. The attempt to construct laws of art from common attributes should no sooner be omitted from a textbook of art than should the technique of comparison. But no one should claim that such wretched results are to be regarded as eternal laws, as something similar to natural laws. For, once again, the laws of nature admit no exceptions, whereas theories of art consist mainly of exceptions. What we do achieve can be enough, if it is given as a method of teaching, as a system of presentation – a system whose organization may aim, sensibly and practically, towards the goals of instruction; a system whose clarity is simply clarity of presentation, a system that does not pretend to clarify the ultimate nature of the things presented.

I have aspired to develop such a system here, nothing more; I do not know whether I have succeeded or not. But it seems to me as if I have at least managed to escape those straits where one has to concede exceptions. The principles of this system yield possibilities in excess of those that have actually been realized [in music]. Those systems that do not account for all the facts also have this shortcoming. Thus, I have to make exclusions, just as they do. However, they do it through aesthetic judgments: something sounds bad, harsh, not beautiful, etc. They do not take the much more modest and truthful way: to affirm that the exclusions simply have to do with what is *not common usage*. What is really not beautiful could hardly be made to sound beautiful, certainly not in the sense these aestheticians intend. But what has merely not been common usage can very well become so, although it does not have to. And, with this [change in viewpoint], the teaching of composition is relieved of a responsibility that it could never have fulfilled, and can restrict itself to that which is really its task: to help the pupil attain such skills as will enable him to produce something of *established effectiveness*. It does not have to guarantee that what he produces will be new, interesting, or even beautiful. It can give assurance, however, that through attention to its directions the pupil can produce something which in its materials and techniques resembles older compositions – that is, up to the point where, even in the technical, mechanical aspects, the creative mind forsakes every [conventional] control.

However much I may theorize in this book – for the most part, in order to refute false theories, I am compelled to expand narrow and confining conceptions to include the facts – however much I may theorize, I do so with constant and full awareness that I am only presenting comparisons, in the sense indicated above; symbols, which are merely intended to connect ideas apparently remote from one another, to promote intelligibility through coherence of presentation, and to stimulate the pupil to productive work by showing him the wealth of ways in which all facts relate to an idea. But not to set up new eternal laws. If I should succeed in teaching the pupil the handicraft of our art as completely as a carpenter can teach his, then I shall be satisfied. And I would be proud if, to adapt a familiar saying, I could say: 'I have *taken* from composition pupils a bad *aesthetics* and have *given* them in return a good *course in handicraft.*'

II THE METHOD OF TEACHING HARMONY

The materials involved in the teaching of musical composition are commonly divided up into three subjects: Harmony, Counterpoint, and Form. These are defined as follows:

Harmony: the study of simultaneous sounds (chords) and of how they may be joined with respect to their architectonic, melodic, and rhythmic values and their significance, their weight relative to one another.

Counterpoint: the study of the art of voice leading with respect to motivic combination (and ultimately the study of the 'contrapuntal forms').

Form: disposition [of the material] for the construction and development of musical ideas.

This division is advantageous; for it is thereby possible to study separately the factors which together constitute the technique of musical composition. Nevertheless, the necessity for training in each division of the material, apart from the others, creates excessive separation. The separate subjects then lose their relationship with one another, that affinity which should reunite them in the interest of their common goal: courses in harmony and counterpoint have forgotten that they, together with the study of form, must be the study of composition; and the pupil, who in his harmony course has presumably learned to think and invent harmonically, in counterpoint, polyphonically, is helpless before the task of combining these individual abilities he has acquired and making them serve that common purpose [composition]. Therefore, here – as in all human endeavors – a middle way must be chosen; the question is, what viewpoints should guide us in determining it?

It will lighten the task of both teacher and pupil if everything presented is so clearly coherent that one thing grows out of another. The first necessity then is: to restrict attention to the matter at hand, freeing it from all that is more remote. Therefore, it will surely benefit us here, in the study of harmony, to derive the nature of chord connections strictly from the nature of the chords themselves, putting aside rhythmic, melodic, and other such considerations. For the complexity that would arise, if all possibilities of harmonic functions were compounded with all rhythmic and motivic possibilities, would surely overwhelm the teacher as well as the pupil. Nevertheless, it will occasionally be necessary even at the most elementary stage to give directions whose application will not be fully realized until a higher stage is reached. After all, this work is supposed to be preparation for the study of composition. But only such directions should be given as can really serve that ultimate purpose; and others are to be avoided if they contribute nothing to that purpose: namely, those that develop certain skills which exist only as ends in themselves, merely because they grow out of the system.

In this sense all harmony courses that, following the old thorough-bass method, require the pupil to write out the other voices over figured basses are inappropriate; for there he learns mere voice leading, which might be, to a limited extent, a secondary task of harmony teaching. To expect that the pupil will automatically acquire a sense for good chord progressions from realizing figured basses is no more defensible than to expect that he will learn them through studying masterpieces, where indeed these and better progressions also appear. Then the teacher is relying on the talent of the pupil, by all means the best thing to do, especially wherever the teacher is not able to influence the pupil's awareness deliberately, wherever he cannot apply explicit methods to produce explicit, predictable knowledge and abilities in the pupil. It is clear at least that with this [the figured-bass] method the pupil is not practicing the primary, but rather a secondary matter. It is furthermore clearly wrong to assign the pupil, without preparation, the task of harmonizing chorales; for he has spent most of his time merely writing parts over harmonic progressions whose effectiveness was determined by someone else. Chorale harmonization requires him to devise chord progressions himself, and he has to be responsible himself for their effectiveness. This task was neither explained nor drilled by the thorough-bass method. Of course gifted pupils may be able to do it moderately well; for these are already equipped, through listening to music and remembering it, with a certain instinct for the right harmonic progression. With them the teacher has to do little more than touch up minor instances of roughness, weakness, or monotony. The less gifted or those gifted in other ways are helpless, since their training dealt merely with voice leading; and they never learn to design a piece of music whose harmonic construction succeeds by virtue of logical progressions.

The realization of a thorough bass may have had value formerly, when it was still the keyboard player's task to accompany from figured basses. To teach it today, when no musician needs it any more, serves no purpose and is a waste of time, hinders more important work, and fails above all to make the pupil self-reliant. The principal aim of harmony instruction is to connect chords with an ear to their individualities, to arrange them in such progressions as will produce an effect suitable for the task at hand; and to achieve this aim, not much skill in voice leading is required. The little that is necessary to deal with forbidden parallels, dissonances, and the like can be mastered rather easily. Besides, courses in counterpoint and form deal in a much more appropriate way with the construction of parts, which is really inconceivable without motivic activity, whereas for chord connection not much more is required than to avoid unmelodic voice leading. On the other hand, the 'melodizing' so commonly encountered[1] ruins the pupil's taste and evokes in him false notions concerning composition.

Therefore, I prefer the older method, which from the outset required the pupil to determine the sequence of chords himself. I start with simple phrases whose purposes grow along with the pupil's skill, from the simplest cadences, through modulation, to some exercises in applying the skills acquired. This procedure has the advantage that from the very beginning the pupil is himself,

[1 'das gewisse Melodisieren,' i.e. the use of passing tones and the like wherever possible merely to dress up the part writing. See Chapters XVI and XVII.]

in a certain sense, composing. These phrases which, guided by the instructions, he sketches out himself can lay the foundation upon which his harmonic sense of form can develop. They will be put together at first without any pretense at 'effect'; the pupil's aims can become more ambitious as the means at his command increase. Thus he learns not merely to understand the means, but also to apply them correctly. As soon as possible a definite purpose will be given to each assignment: to establish, to express the key – i.e. the cadence; and then the contrary: to leave the key – i.e. modulation. To the latter I devote the utmost care; for in modulation as in the cadence, the architectonic, the structural functions of harmony, of chord connection, are indeed most intensively expressed. Here, also, I go back to older methods, in that I do not allow the abrupt modulation that is found in most harmony texts, where to modulate means simply to juxtapose a few unprepared, modulatory chords. On the contrary, it will be our aim to modulate gradually, to prepare the modulation and make it evolve, so as to form the basis for motivic development. Analysis of masterworks shows that modulation (say that from the principal theme to the secondary) occurs almost exclusively in this manner; and, since the teacher's task can only be to impart the technique of the masters to the pupil and to stimulate him thereby wherever possible to go on to composing on his own, every other purely theoretical method is then clearly irrelevant. We can pass over the question whether such modulations as Richter[1] recommends could ever form the basis for motivic development. It is certainly doubtful. It is probable that, in such abrupt modulations, these, the only modulatory chords recommended (dominant seventh or diminished seventh chords), would be much too artless and primitive. A piece in which such an intense harmonic crisis is manifest surely needs richer and more complex means of modulation. For my part, I have tried to show as many different means for modulation as possible and to demonstrate, or at least indicate, the wealth of possible combinations. Again, the first exercises in modulation aim merely at the quickest and simplest solution of the problem; but with every newly mastered means the aim must be extended accordingly. If, for example, the deceptive cadence is being used, it should guard the final cadence against the monotony of a repetition, yet assure the final cadence the heightened intensity of this repetition. Thus the pupil learns from the outset to use the means at his command to the greatest possible advantage, that is to say, he learns to exploit his means fully and not to use more of them than necessary. Here we are teaching composition, as far as it can go in a harmony course. Yet it should surely go that far.

I have omitted harmonic analyses in this book, because I consider them superfluous here. Were the pupil able to extract from the musical literature what he needs for composing, then no one would have to teach harmony. And it is

[1 Ernst Friedrich Richter, *Lehrbuch der Harmonie* (Leipzig: Breitkopf und Haertel, 1853). The twenty-fifth German edition of 1907 was translated into English by Theodore Baker and published under the title *Manual of Harmony* (New York: G. Schirmer, Inc., 1912).

For Richter's recommendations concerning modulation, cited here by Schoenberg, see p. 95 of Baker's translation.]

indeed possible to learn everything this way. I myself have never formally studied harmony and am therefore one of the many who prove that possibility. But most pupils do need instruction; and I say: if you do teach, then say all that can possibly be said. Generally, though, analysis is more a test the author uses for the correctness of his theory than an advantage for the pupil. I do not deny that it would benefit the pupil to account for the harmonic procedure in master-works. But to do this the way it should be done, i.e. by examining the harmonic structure of an entire work and the significance of the individual chords and chord progressions, would be impossible within the limits of a harmony course. Yet, anything else is relatively pointless. Those usual analyses which show through what keys a theme modulates, or more correctly, show how many chords, however foreign to the key they may seem, a musical idea can contain without its leaving the key – this is to show something which it is not necessary to show. For whenever the pupil has the means to do it himself, he will understand it so much better, just by doing it, than he could by analysis – that is, he will understand the harmonic aspect of music. The balanced relation of motives to harmony, rhythmic elaboration, in short, what really pertains to composition, if it indeed can be explained at all, does not belong in a harmony course. The pupil is again being shown what is unessential! And I cannot understand how he is ever to grasp the essential if the unessential is always given first place in his study.

In general I do not intend to name individual methods and engage in pole-mics against them. I will confine myself to explaining things as I understand them. Only when I begin what I believe to be a new interpretation do I find it necessary first to refute the older, usual one. The same reason that leads me to this new interpretation frees me from the obligation to specify which of the ideas presented I consider new. As a musician who did not collect his knowledge by reading, but who may rather characterize what he offers as the results of his own thought about his experiences in teaching and composing, I presumably have the right not to be fettered by the citation of sources customary in scholar-ly works. Such unfruitful and time-wasting labor may be left to those indivi-duals whose ties to the living art are weaker than their ties to the theoretical. Instead, I would rather just acknowledge my obvious debt to the existing systems for many ideas. How many ideas and which ones I no longer know. Because of the way I have assimilated them, it has long since escaped my power to be so specific. But I must say, it is mostly to bad books and wrong ideas, which forced me to think and find out what is right, that I owe the best of this book. Other things came of their own accord from my working through the traditional system. Everything, however, is based on a steady contemplation of art, hence, is firsthand. I think that some of the ideas presented here can lay claim to novelty, and that others may to some extent depart from the familiar at least in their precision of statement or in the breadth of perspective afforded by the presentation. I shall gladly renounce the reputation for novelty, however, if I may then be spared the chore of wading through the most important harmony texts.

I should like this book to be, wherever possible, a textbook, thus to serve practical ends: that is, to give the pupil a dependable method for his training. But I cannot on that account forego the opportunity to make known my views, through an occasional hypothesis, on more complex relationships (*Zusammenhänge*) – on the similarities and relationships between artistic creation and other human activities, on the connections between the natural world outside ourselves and the participating or observing subject. To repeat: what is said in this regard is not to be considered theory, but rather a more or less detailed comparison, in which it is not as important that it holds in every respect as that it gives rise to psychological and physical exploration. It is possible that this book will therefore be a little hard for the ordinary musician to grasp, since even today he still does not like to exert himself in thinking. Possibly it is a book just for the advanced student or for teachers. In that case I should be sorry, for I should have liked it above all to be of use to beginners. But I cannot change the way things are, and so I must wait. I hope, however, that it will not be too late for the ideas I have to offer when the average musician reaches the point where one may write for him, too, in a manner other than 'abridged', other than in untearable picture-book style.

III CONSONANCE AND DISSONANCE

Art in its most primitive state is a simple imitation of nature. But it quickly becomes imitation of nature in the wider sense of this idea, that is, not merely imitation of outer but also of inner nature. In other words, art does not then represent merely the objects or the occasions that make impressions, but above all these impressions themselves, ultimately without reference to their What, When, and How. Inference of the original, external object is here perhaps of only secondary importance due to its lack of immediacy. In its most advanced state, art is exclusively concerned with the representation of inner nature. Here its aim is just the imitation of impressions, which have now combined, through association with one another and with other sense impressions, to form new complexes and new motives, new stimuli (*Bewegungen*). At this stage, inference of the external stimulus is almost certain to be inadequate. At all stages the imitation of the model, of the impression, or of the complex of impressions is only relatively faithful. This is true, on the one hand, because of the limits of our abilities; on the other, because, whether we are conscious of it or not, the material [the medium] in which the imitation is presented differs from the material or materials of the stimulus, so that, for example, visual or tactile sensations might be represented in the material of auditory sensations.[1]

If, then, perhaps even the simplest imitation of nature is based on a complex, on manifold combinations and recombinations, and if it is understandably difficult to identify the external objects which were the models, then unsurmountable difficulties lie in the way of analysis if the impression on the observing subject is now taken as the point of departure for inquiry. As Schopenhauer shows in his theory of colors, however, a real theory should start with the subject. And, just as he considers the colors physiological phenomena, 'conditions, modifications of the eye',[2] so one would have to go back to the subject, to the sense of hearing, if one would establish a real theory of tones. Now it is not my aim to present such a theory or even a theory of harmony, nor do I possess enough ability and knowledge to do so; I am rather simply trying to present the harmonic means of music in such a way that they can be directly applied in practice. It could happen, nevertheless, that in this way I achieve

[1 I.e. the imitation cannot be absolutely faithful to the object imitated, if for no other reason, because of the translation from one medium to another.]

[2 Arthur Schopenhauer, *Sämtliche Werke: Schriften zur Erkenntnislehre* (Zweite Auflage; Wiesbaden: Eberhard Brockhaus Verlag, 1948), p. 21.

The *Subjekt*: the observer (including the listener); the *Objekt*: the observed. Schopenhauer developed his theory of the relation between *Subjekt* and *Objekt* in his *World as Will and Idea*.

At the time he was writing the *Theory of Harmony* Schoenberg was a remarkably productive painter. Some of his paintings are reproduced in Josef Rufer, *The Works of Arnold Schoenberg – a catalogue of his compositions, writings and paintings*, trans. Dika Newlin (London: Faber and Faber, 1962).]

more than I am actually striving for, since my goal is just clarity and compre-
hensiveness of presentation. But however little that would displease me, it is
still not my purpose. Therefore, whenever I theorize, it is less important
whether these theories be right than whether they be useful as comparisons to
clarify the object and to give the study perspective.

So, for two reasons I may reject the subject as the basis for my study: first,
because I do not intend to give a theory of tones or of harmony, but merely a
presentation of certain artistic means; secondly, because this presentation does
not claim any right to be taken for a theory. Thus I may devote my study to
the object, the material of music, if I succeed in bringing what I want to show
into accord with what is known or surmised concerning this material.

The material of music is the tone; what it affects first, the ear. The sensory
perception releases associations and connects tone, ear, and the world of feeling.
On the cooperation of these three factors depends everything in music that is
felt to be art. Nevertheless, even if a chemical compound does have characteristics other than those of the elements from which it was formed, and if the
impression a work of art makes does display characteristics other than those
which could be derived from each single component, it is still justifiable for
many a purpose, in analyzing the total phenomenon, to bring up for consideration various characteristics of the basic components. Indeed, the atomic weight
and valence of the components permit a conclusion with respect to the molecu-
lar weight and valence of the compound. Perhaps it is indefensible to try to
derive everything that constitutes the physics of harmony from one of the
components, say, just from the tone. Some characteristics can be derived from
the tone, however, for the very reason that the constitution of the ear, the organ
predetermined to receive tone, at least relates to the constitution of the tone
somewhat as do well-fitting concave to convex parts. One of the three factors,
however, the world of our feelings, so completely eludes precisely controlled
investigation that it would be folly to place the same confidence in the few conjectures permitted by observation in this sphere that we place in those conjectures that in other matters are called 'science'. In this sense it is of little consequence whether one starts with a correct hypothesis or a false one. Sooner or
later the one as well as the other will certainly be refuted. Thus, we can only
base our thought on such conjectures as will satisfy our formal necessity for
sense and coherence without their being considered natural laws. Should someone succeed in deriving the phenomena solely from the physical properties of
tone and explaining them solely on that basis, should the problems be thereby
successfully clarified and solved, then it would hardly matter whether our
physical knowledge of the nature of tone is correct or not. [For] it is entirely
possible that in spite of an observation falsely construed as fundamental we
may, by inference or through intuition, arrive at correct results; whereas it is
not at all a proved fact that more correct or better observation would necessarily yield more correct or better conclusions. Thus, the alchemists, in spite of
their rather poor instruments, recognized the possibility of transmuting the
elements, whereas the much better equipped chemists of the nineteenth century
considered the elements irreducible and unalterable, an opinion that has since

been disproved. If this view [of the nineteenth-century chemists] has now been superseded, we owe this fact, not to better observations, nor to better perception, nor to better conclusions, but to an accidental discovery. The advance, therefore, did not come as a necessary consequence of anything; it could not have been predicted on the basis of any particular accomplishment; it appeared rather in spite of all efforts, unexpected, undeserved, and perhaps even undesired. Now if the correct explanation must be the goal of all inquiry, even though the explanation does almost always turn out to be wrong, we still do not have to allow our pleasure in searching for explanation to be spoiled. On the contrary, we should be satisfied with this pleasure as perhaps the only positive result of all our trouble.

From this point of view it is thus of little importance for the explanation of harmonic problems, whether science has already refuted the function of overtones or only raised some doubts. Should one succeed, as said, in defining the problems sensibly and presenting them intelligibly, even though the overtone theory be false, then the goal could still be reached – even if it turned out after some time that both, overtone theory and explanation, were false (but this outcome is by no means inevitable). I can make the attempt with so much the more confidence since, as far as I know, no one has yet refuted the theory beyond all doubt; and since no man is able to examine and prove everything himself, I, too, have to get along with the existing knowledge as long as I may and can believe in it. Therefore, I will proceed in my study from the possibly uncertain overtone theory because what I can deduce from it seems to agree with the evolution of the harmonic means.

Once again: the tone is the material of music. It must therefore be regarded, with all its properties and effects, as suitable for art. All sensations that it releases – indeed, these are the effects that make known its properties – bring their influence to bear in some sense on the form of which the tone is a component, that is, on the piece of music. In the overtone series,* which is one of the most remarkable properties of the tone, there appear after some stronger-sounding overtones a number of weaker-sounding ones. Without a doubt the former are more familiar to the ear, while the latter, hardly perceptible, are rather strange. In other words: the overtones closer to the fundamental seem to contribute more or more perceptibly to the total phenomenon of the tone – tone accepted as euphonious, suitable for art – while the more distant seem to contribute less or less perceptibly. But it is quite certain that they all do contribute more or less, that of the acoustical emanations of the tone nothing is lost. And it is just as certain that the world of feeling somehow takes into account the entire complex, hence the more distant overtones as well. Even if the analyzing ear does not become conscious of them, they are still heard as tone color. That is to say, here the musical ear does indeed abandon the attempt at exact analysis, but it still takes note of the impression. The more remote overtones

* The pupil can partially demonstrate the phenomenon of overtones for himself by silently depressing the keys *c'*, *e'*, *g'* and then forcefully striking *C* once, staccato, or the lower octave contra *C* (all without pedal). Then he can hear the tones *c'*, *e'*, *g'*, the overtones, whose sound is similar to that of the harmonics of stringed instruments.

are recorded by the subconscious, and when they ascend into the conscious they are analyzed and their relation to the total sound is determined. But this relation is, to repeat, as follows: the more immediate overtones contribute *more*, the more remote contribute *less*. Hence, the distinction between them is only a matter of degree, not of kind. They are no more opposites than two and ten are opposites, as the frequency numbers indeed show; and the expressions 'consonance' and 'dissonance', which signify an antithesis, are false. It all simply depends on the growing ability of the analyzing ear to familiarize itself with the remote overtones, thereby expanding the conception of what is euphonious, suitable for art, so that it embraces the whole natural phenomenon.

What today is remote can tomorrow be close at hand; it is all a matter of whether one can get closer. And the evolution of music has followed this course: it has drawn into the stock of artistic resources more and more of the harmonic possibilities inherent in the tone.

Now if I continue to use the expressions 'consonance' and 'dissonance', even though they are unwarranted, I do so because there are signs that the evolution of harmony will, in a short time, prove the inadequacy of this classification. The introduction of another terminology at this stage would have no purpose and could hope for little success. Since I still have to operate with these notions, I will define consonances as the closer, simpler relations to the fundamental tone, dissonances as those that are more remote, more complicated. The consonances are accordingly the first overtones, and they are the more nearly perfect the closer they are to the fundamental. That means, the closer they lie to the fundamental, the more easily we can grasp their similarity to it, the more easily the ear can fit them into the total sound and assimilate them, and the more easily we can determine that the sound of these overtones together with the fundamental is 'restful' and euphonious, needing no resolution. The same should hold for the dissonances as well. If it does not, if the ability to assimilate the dissonances in use cannot be judged by the same method, if the distance from the fundamental is no measure of the degree of dissonance, this is even so no evidence against the view presented here. For it is harder to gauge these differences precisely, since they are relatively small. They are expressed by fractions with large denominators; and as it requires some thought to say whether $8/234$ is larger or smaller than $23/680$, because a mere estimate can lead one astray, the mere estimate made by the ear is just as undependable. Efforts to make use of the more remote consonances (today called 'dissonances') as artistic means thus led necessarily to many an error, to many a detour. The way of history, as we can see it in that which has actually been selected by practice from the practicable dissonances, hardly leads here to a correct judgment of the real relations. That assertion is proved by the incomplete or unusual scales of many other peoples, who have, nevertheless, as much right as we to explain them by appeal to nature. Perhaps their tones are often even more natural than ours (that is, more exact, more correct, better); for the tempered system, which is only an expedient for overcoming the difficulties of the material, has indeed only a limited similarity to nature. That is perhaps an advantage, but hardly a mark of superiority.

The most nearly perfect consonance (after the unison) is the first tone of the overtone series, thus the one that occurs most frequently, consequently the strongest: the octave. The next most nearly perfect are the fifth and the major third. The minor third and the major and minor sixths are, in part, not relations of the fundamental, in part, not relations in the ascending direction. That explains why it used to be questioned whether they are consonances at all. On the other hand, the fourth, known as an imperfect consonance, is a relation of the fundamental, but in the opposite direction; it could, therefore, be counted with the perfect consonances, in the same sense as the minor third and the major and minor sixths, or simply with the consonances, as indeed often happens. But the evolution of music has gone a different way here and has given the fourth a peculiar position. Only the following are designated as dissonances: the major and minor seconds, the major and minor sevenths, the ninths, etc.; in addition, all diminished and augmented intervals, thus, diminished and augmented octaves, fourths, fifths, etc.

IV THE MAJOR MODE AND THE DIATONIC CHORDS

Our major scale, the series of tones *c, d, e, f, g, a, b*, the tones that also provided the basis for the Greek and church modes, we can explain as having been found through imitation of nature. Intuition and inference (*Kombination*) assisted in translating the most important characteristic of the tone, the overtone series, from the vertical (as we imagine the position of all simultaneous sounds) into the horizontal, into separate, successive tones. The natural model, the tone, exhibits the following characteristics:

1. A musical sound (*Klang*) is a composite, made up of a series of tones sounding together, the overtones; hence, it forms a chord. From a fundamental, *C*, these overtones are:

$$c, g, c^1, e^1, g^1, (b\flat^1), c^2, d^2, e^2, f^2, g^2, \text{etc.}$$

2. In this series the *c* is the strongest sound because it occurs the greatest number of times, and because it is actually played or sung itself, as a fundamental.

3. After the *c* the next strongest tone is *g*, because it occurs earlier in the series, therefore more often than the other tones.

If we think of this *g* as a real tone (as indeed occurs when the overtone series is realized horizontally, when, for example, the fifth of a horn tuned in *c* is played), it then has overtones itself (as a tone actually played); these are:

$$g^1, d^2, g^2, b^2, d^3, \text{etc.};$$

and at the same time this *g*, together with its overtones, presupposes the *C* (fundamental of the horn). Thus it happens that the overtones of the overtones also contribute to the total sound.

Consequently:

4. An actual tone (the *g*) appears as dependent upon a tone a fifth below, the *C*.

The conclusion that follows from the foregoing:

This tone, *C*, is likewise dependent upon the tone a fifth below it, *F*.

Now if the *C* is taken as the midpoint, then its situation can be described by reference to two forces, one of which pulls downward, toward *F*, the other upward, toward *G*:

Here the dependence of *G* on *C*, with which, strictly speaking, the force of the *C* is exerted in the same direction as that of the *F*, may be considered like the force of a man hanging by his hands from a beam and exerting his own force against the force of gravity. He pulls on the beam just as gravity pulls him, and in the same direction. But the effect is that his force *works against* the force of gravity, and so in this way one is justified in speaking of the two opposing forces.

I will often speak of this characteristic and will draw a number of conclusions from it. What is important for the moment is to establish that these tones are very closely related to one another, that they are next of kin. *G* is the first overtone (after *c*) of *C*, and *c* the first of *F*. Such an overtone bears the closest similarity to the fundamental (after the octave), therefore contributes most to the quality (*Charakteristik*) of the sound, to its euphony.

If one is justified in assuming that the overtones of the *G* can become real tones, then this assumption may be applied analogously to those of *F*. After all, *F* is to *C* as *C* is to *G*. And thus it is explained how the scale that finally emerged is put together from the most important components of a fundamental tone and its nearest relatives. These nearest relatives are just what gives the fundamental tone stability; for it represents the point of balance between their opposing tendencies. This scale appears as the residue of the properties of the three factors, as a vertical projection, as addition:

Funda- mental	Over- tones								
F	f	. . c	. . f	. a					
C		c	. . . g	. .	c	. e			
G		g	. . .	d	. . . g	. b			
	f	c	g a	d e	b				

Adding up the overtones (omitting repetitions) we get the seven tones of our scale. Here they are not yet arranged consecutively. But even the scalar order can be obtained if we assume that the further overtones are also in effect. And that assumption is in fact not optional; we must assume the presence of the other overtones. The ear could also have defined the relative pitch of the tones discovered by comparing them with taut strings, which of course become longer or shorter as the tone is lowered or raised. But the more distant overtones were also a dependable guide. Adding these we get the following:

Funda- mental	Over- tones			
F	f . . . c . . f . a . c . (e♭) f g a b c etc. f etc.			
C	c . . . g . . c . e . g . (b♭) c d e f etc.			
G	g . . . d . . g . b . d . (f) g a b c d			
	(e♭) (b♭)			
	c d e f g a b c d e f g a b c d			

our *C*-major scale.

An interesting by-product appears here:

The two tones *e* and *b* appear in the first octave, but *e* is challenged by *e♭*, *b* by *b♭*. That explains why it was once questioned whether the third was a consonance, and shows why *b* [*b♭*] and *h* [*b*] appear in the German tone alphabet.

It could not be decided (because of the first octave) which tone was correct.* The second octave (in which the overtones of *F* and *C* necessarily sound more faintly) resolved the question in favor of *e* and *b*.

Whether the pioneers of music arrived at this scale through intuition or through inference (*Kombination*) we cannot judge. It is unimportant anyway. We may nevertheless take issue with theorists who set up complicated doctrines (*Lehren*); for, contrary to those doctrines, we have to give the discoverers credit not only for instinct, but for the ability to reason as well. It is then not at all impossible that the right thing here was discovered by reason alone, that therefore credit is due, not to the ear alone, but in part to inference. We are not the first who can think!

The discovery of our scale was a stroke of luck in the development of our music, not only with regard to its success, but also in the sense that we could just as well have found a different scale, as did for example the Arabs, the Chinese and Japanese, or the gypsies. That their music has not evolved to such heights as ours does not necessarily follow from their imperfect scales, but can also have to do with their imperfect instruments or with some other circumstance which cannot be investigated here. Moreover, it is not to our scale alone that we owe the evolution of our music. And above all; this scale is not the last word, the ultimate goal of music, but rather a provisional stopping place. The overtone series, which led the ear to it, still contains many problems that will have to be faced. And if for the time being we still manage to escape those problems, it is due to little else than a compromise between the natural intervals and our inability to use them – that compromise which we call the tempered system, which amounts to an indefinitely extended truce. This reduction of the natural relations to manageable ones cannot permanently impede the evolution of music; and the ear will have to attack the problems, *because it is so disposed*. Then our scale will be transformed into a higher order, as the church modes were transformed into major and minor modes. Whether there will then be quarter tones, eighth, third, or (as Busoni[1] thinks) sixth tones, or whether we will move directly to a 53-tone scale that Dr. Robert Neumann has calculated,[2] we cannot foretell. Perhaps this new division of the octave will even be untempered and will not have much left over in common with our scale. However that may be, attempts to compose in quarter or third tones, as are being undertaken here and there, seem senseless, as long as there are too few instruments available that can play them. Probably, whenever the ear and imagination

---

* Perhaps that also explains why there were church modes: The effect of a fundamental tone was felt, but since no one knew which tone it was, all of them were tried. And the accidentals are perhaps accidents in the mode chosen, but not in the natural, the basic one.

[1 Ferrucio Busoni, *Sketch of a New Esthetic of Music* in *Three Classics in the Aesthetic of Music* (New York: Dover Publications, 1962), pp. 93–4. Originally published in Leipzig, 1906, Busoni's work was reprinted in this anthology from Theodore Baker's translation, published by G. Schirmer, Inc., c. 1911.]

[2 Important (and long) footnote by the author. See Appendix, pp. 423–5. In Chapter XIX (p. 384) Dr. Neumann is identified as 'a young philosopher'.]

have matured enough for such music, the scale and the instruments will all at once be available. It is certain that this movement is now afoot, certain that it will lead to something. It may be that here again many digressions and errors will have to be overcome; perhaps these, too, will lead to exaggerations or to the delusion that now the ultimate, the immutable has been found. Perhaps here, once again, laws and scales will be erected and accorded an aesthetic timelessness. To the man of vision, even that will not be the end. He recognizes that any material can be suitable for art – if it is well enough defined that one can shape it in accordance with its supposed nature, yet not so well defined that the imagination has no unexplored territory left in which to roam, in which to establish mystical connection with the universe. And since we can still hope that the world will long continue to be a riddle to our intelligence (*Verstand*), we can say in spite of all Beckmessers that the end of art is not yet at hand.

If the scale is imitation of the tone on the horizontal plane, that is, note after note, then chords are imitation on the vertical, notes sounded together. If the scale is analysis, then the chord is synthesis of the tone. It is required of a chord that it consist of three different tones. The simplest of such chords is, obviously, that one which most closely resembles the simplest and most evident aspects of the tone, that one which consists of fundamental, major third, and perfect fifth – the major triad. It imitates the euphony of the single tone by omitting the more distant overtones and reinforcing the more immediate. The triad is without doubt similar to the tone, but it is no more similar to its model than, say, Assyrian reliefs are to their human models. Such triads might have come into use harmonically, as it were, when someone discovered it was possible to sing, at first, the fifth with the fundamental, later, the third as well; or it might have happened by the singing of parts in such a way that they came together on none other than such chords as these. Neither way, however, can today be proved with any certainty. It is probable that simultaneous sounds of this kind were already felt to be euphonious before the polyphonic manner of writing was able to use them. Yet the possibility is not to be excluded that, conversely, monophonic melody and scales existed before the chords, and that the step from monophonic to polyphonic music did not occur through the setting of chords as accompaniment to tones or melodic progressions, but rather through the singing of two or three melodies at the same time, one of which eventually became the principal melody. However it may have been in the earliest days of music, both methods, harmonic and polyphonic, have cooperated equally for at least four hundred years in promoting the evolution of our present-day music. It is therefore hardly appropriate to formulate chords on only one of the two principles. It is hardly appropriate, on the one hand, to present chords as if they had germinated and developed spontaneously, as they are usually presented in the teaching of harmony; nor is it appropriate, on the other hand, to explain polyphony as nothing else but voice leading that merely follows certain conventional rules and does not consider the chords resulting from the coincidence of parts, as usually happens in the teaching of counterpoint. It is much more correct to say that the development of harmony was not only essentially influenced by melodic principles, that the development of the possibility of voice leading was not only essentially influenced by harmonic principles, but that in many ways each was actually determined by the other. Every treatment, however, that uses the one or the other principle exclusively will run into facts that will not fit into its system. Hence the numerous exceptions. Hence the numerous places where the teacher has to lift a prohibition, carelessly given, with a concession, grudgingly given. And the numerous places where the teacher has to say: 'Well, that's just the way it is; nothing else is possible,' without being able to give any reason why. Where the pupil must accept as given whatever the teacher imposes on him and may surely ask 'for its name', but not 'about its kind'.

At first glance it looks as if what I say here would contradict what I say in the introduction about the scope of harmony teaching and in the later chapter about 'Non-harmonic Tones'. But the contradiction is only apparent. For if I show that this or that chord progression is to be *explained* on melodic grounds, it is in fact far different from assigning the pupil to work out something melodically because its origin is melodic – as happens with passing tones, changing tones, and the like, which would long ago have been regarded as chord components if the system of non-harmonic tones were not so much more convenient.

The consideration and judgment of harmonic events necessitates an intelligible classification. This classification will be so much the more complete, the more it satisfies legitimate claims. Now I find that the long-established method of instruction is adequate for most of the demands we may make, with the reservations that it is no system, and that it can only take us to a certain point. Therefore, my treatment, too, is so constructed. This method, by taking up first the diatonic triads, does in fact start with the simplest structures and builds up this system in a practical manner: after these triads come the other diatonic chords, the four and five-part chords; then, after showing in the cadence an application of these diatonic chords, the method goes on to nondiatonic chords and here, too, shows applications in modulation, etc. My objections to this method I will reveal later on. It is usable, however, up to a certain point, and I will follow it that far.

The harmonic sense of the key (*Tonart*) in all its ramifications is comprehensible only in relation to the idea of tonality, which should therefore be explained before anything else. Tonality is a formal possibility that emerges from the nature of the tonal material, a possibility of attaining a certain completeness or closure (*Geschlossenheit*) by means of a certain uniformity. To realize this possibility it is necessary to use in the course of a piece only those sounds (*Klänge*) and successions of sounds, and these only in a suitable arrangement, whose relations to the fundamental tone of the key, to the tonic of the piece, can be grasped without difficulty. Subsequently, I shall be compelled to take issue with various aspects of tonality and can therefore confine my remarks here to just two points: (1) I do not, as apparently all theorists before me have done, consider tonality an eternal law, a natural law of music, even though this law is consistent with the simplest conditions of the natural model, that is, of the tone and the fundamental chord; all the same, however, (2) it is essential that the pupil learn thoroughly the basis of this effect [tonality] and how to attain it.

Whenever all chords of a complete piece of music appear in progressions that can be related to a common fundamental tone, one can then say that the idea of the musical sound (*Klang*) (which is conceived as vertical) is extended to the horizontal plane. Everything following it springs from this fundamental postulate, refers back to it, even when antithetical to it, elaborates and complements it, and finally leads back to it, so that this fundamental is treated in every respect as central, as embryonic. The value of such a method of composition cannot be overlooked, even by those who do not believe it is indispensable to all composition whatsoever. Thus, for example, not every biography has to begin with the birth of the hero, or indeed farther back with his ancestors, nor end with his death. Such completeness is not indispensable and may be forthwith discarded if one has some other aim, say, to present a certain characteristic period in the life of the hero. It is likewise doubtful whether the aggregate of events in a piece of music must inevitably refer to the fundamental postulate, to the fundamental chord, just because – as I have said – such reference assures good results through formal completeness and agrees with the simplest attributes of the material. It is doubtful, once the question is raised, whether such reference does not agree *just with the simpler* attributes, and especially, whether it still agrees with the more complicated. To reach a conclusion in this matter it is not necessary, nor is it enough, to think of the development sections of sonatas and symphonies or of the harmonic relations in operas whose music is continuous (*durchkomponiert*). Nor does one even have to consider present-day music. It is enough just to look at a piece, say, by Wagner, Bruckner, or Hugo Wolf to raise doubts: whether obstinately maintaining a common fundamental at the beginning and end of a piece, just on principle, is really organic any more, where there are so many details that can just as well point elsewhere; whether this traditional device is not used here merely because it is tradition; whether here a formal advantage has not given rise to a formalistic conceit; whether tonality here means perhaps more the purely external recognition of a law established by custom, thus does not spring from a structural necessity.

As for laws established by custom, however – they will eventually be disestablished. What happened to the tonality of the church modes, if not that? It is easy for us now to say that 'the church modes were unnatural, but our scales conform to nature'. That they conformed to nature was undoubtedly also believed of the church modes in their day. Besides – just how far do our major and minor conform to nature, since they are, after all, a tempered system? And what about those parts that do not conform? It is precisely these that foment revolt. In the church modes there were those elements that pressed toward dissolution of the modal system. We can easily see that today. For example, the final chords were almost always major chords, even though the Dorian, Aeolian, and Phrygian modes indicated minor final chords. Does that not look as if the fundamental freed itself at the close from the unnatural force that had been imposed upon it, as if, since it substituted its own overtones, it sensed its natural euphony? Perhaps it was this phenomenon that removed the distinctions among the modes to such an extent that only two types remained, major and minor, which contained everything that made up the individual character of each of the seven modes. We have similar phenomena in our major and minor: above all, under the pretense of modulation we can introduce into every key almost any property of other, quite distant keys (such is called 'extended tonality'). Indeed, the key may be expressed exclusively by chords other than its own diatonic chords; yet we do not then consider the tonality cancelled. But does then the tonality in effect still exist? 'In effect, that is, effectively', effected by the fundamental? Or has it not actually been cancelled already?

It is nevertheless necessary, as I said before, that the pupil learns to manipulate the devices that produce tonality. For music has not yet evolved so far that we can now speak of discarding tonality; moreover, the necessity for explaining its requirements arises also from the need to recognize its functions in the works of the past. Even if the present allows us to envision a future freed from the restrictive demands of this principle, it is still, even today, but much more in the past of our art, one of the most important musical techniques. It is one of the techniques that contribute most to the assurance of order in musical works – that order, consistent with the material, which so greatly facilitates the untroubled enjoyment of the essential beauties in the music. One of the foremost tasks of instruction is to awaken in the pupil a sense of the past and at the same time to open up to him prospects for the future. Thus instruction may proceed historically, by making the connections between what was, what is, and what is likely to be. The historian can be productive if he sets forth, not merely historical data, but an understanding of history, if he does not confine himself simply to enumerating, but tries to read the future from the past.

Applied to our present concern, that means: Let the pupil learn the laws and effects of tonality just as if they still prevailed, but let him know of the tendencies that are leading toward their annulment. Let him know that the conditions leading to the dissolution of the system are inherent in the conditions upon which it is established. Let him know that every living thing has within it that which changes, develops, and destroys it. Life and death are both equally present in the embryo. What lies between is time. Nothing intrinsic, that is; merely a dimension, which is, however, necessarily consummated. Let the pupil learn by this example to recognize what is eternal: change, and what is temporal: being (*das Bestehen*). Thus he will come to the conclusion that much of what has been considered aesthetically fundamental, that is, necessary to beauty, is by no means always rooted in the nature of things, that the imperfection of our senses drives us to those compromises through which we achieve order. For order is not demanded by the object, but by the subject.[1] [The pupil will conclude], moreover, that the many laws that purport to be natural laws actually spring from the struggle of the craftsman to shape the material correctly; and that the adaptation of what the artist really wants to present, its reduction to fit within the boundaries of form, of artistic form, is necessary only because of our inability to grasp the undefined and unordered. The order we call artistic form is not an end in itself, but an expedient. As such by all means justified, but to be rejected absolutely wherever it claims to be more, to be aesthetics. This is not

[1 Cf. *supra*, p. 18, fn. 2 and corresponding text.]

to say that some future work of art may do without order, clarity, and comprehensibility, but that not merely what we conceive as such deserves these names.
For nature is also beautiful where we do not understand her and where she
seems to us unordered. Once we are cured of the delusion that the artist's aim
is to create beauty, and once we have recognized that only the *necessity to produce* compels him to bring forth what will perhaps afterwards be designated as
beauty, then we will also understand that comprehensibility and clarity are not
conditions that the artist is obliged to impose on his work, but conditions that
the observer wishes to find fulfilled. Even the untrained observer finds these
conditions in works he has known for some time, for example, in all the older
masterworks; here he has had time to adapt. With newer works, at first strange,
he must be allowed more time. But, whereas the distance between the onrushing,
brilliant insight of the genius and the ordinary insight of his contemporaries is
relatively vast, in an absolute sense, that is, viewed within the whole evolution
of the human spirit, the advance of his insight is quite small. Consequently, the
connection that gives access to what was once incomprehensible is always
finally made. Whenever one has understood, one looks for reasons, finds order,
sees clarity. [Order, clarity] are there by chance, not by law, not by necessity;
and what we claim to perceive as laws [defining order and clarity] may perhaps
only be laws governing our perception, without therefore being the laws a
work of art must obey. And that we think we see [laws, order] in the work of
art can be analogous to our thinking we see ourselves in the mirror, although
we are of course not there. The work of art is capable of mirroring what we
project into it. The conditions our conceptual power imposes, a mirror image
of our own nature (*Beschaffenheit*), may be observed in the work. This mirror
image does not, however, reveal the plan upon which the work itself is oriented,
but rather the way we orient ourselves to the work. Now if the work bears the
same relation to its author, if it mirrors what he projects into it, then the laws
he thinks he perceives may also be just such as were present in his imagination,
but not such as are inherent in his work. And what he has to say about his
formal purposes could be relatively inconsequential. It is perhaps subjectively,
but not necessarily objectively, correct. One has only to look in the mirror from
another point of view; then one can believe that mirror image, too, is the image
of the work itself, although that image, too, is actually projected by the observer,
only this time the image is different. Now even if one can assume with certainty
that the observer will not see in the work of art something entirely different
from what is actually in it – since object and subject do indeed interact – even
so the possibility of misapprehension is still too great to allow us to say with
absolute confidence that the presumed order is not just that of the subject. All
the same, the state of the observer can be ascertained from the order he sees.

It is, indeed, not to be maintained that compliance with such laws, which
after all may correspond merely to the state of the observer, will assure the
creation of a work of art. Moreover, these laws, even if they are valid, are not
the only ones the work of art obeys. Yet, even if adherence to them does not
help the pupil attain clarity, intelligibility, and beauty, they will at least make it
possible for him to avoid obscurity, unintelligibility, and ugliness. The positive

gain of a work of art depends upon conditions other than those expressed by the laws and is not to be reached by way of the laws. But even what is negative is gain, since through avoiding such particulars as presumably hinder the realization of artistic values the pupil can lay a foundation. Not one that promotes creativity, but one that can regulate it, if it will allow itself to be regulated! Instruction that proceeds this way accomplishes something else, as well. It leads the pupil through all those errors that the [historical] struggle for knowledge has brought with it; it leads through, it leads past errors, perhaps past truths as well. Nevertheless, it teaches him to know how the search was carried on, the methods of thinking, the kinds of errors, the way little truths of locally limited probability became, by being stretched out into a system, absolutely untrue. In a word, he is taught all that which makes up the way we think. Such instruction can thus bring the pupil to love even the errors, if only they have stimulated thought, turnover and renewal of intellectual stock. And he learns to love the work of his forebears, even if he cannot apply it directly to his own life, even if he has to translate it in order to put it to very different use. He learns to love it, be it truth or error, because he finds in it necessity. And he sees beauty in that everlasting struggle for truth; he recognizes that fulfilment is always the goal one yearns for, but that it could easily be the end of beauty. He understands that harmony – balance – does not mean fixity of inactive factors, but equilibrium of the most intense energies. Into life itself, where there are such energies, such struggles – that is the direction instruction should take. To represent life in art, life, with its flexibility, its possibilities for change, its necessities; to acknowledge as the sole eternal law evolution and change – this way has to be more fruitful than the other, where one assumes an end of evolution because one can thus round off the system.

I proceed, then, to present harmonic relations by pursuing attentively the errors of the past, step by step, confident that the thorough treatment even of such ideas as are now fading into the background of practice will benefit the pupil in the sense indicated above. I will set tonality, for example, as my goal, and strive to reach it with all conceivable means; and I hope I shall be able to present some means that perhaps have not been mentioned before.

THE DIATONIC TRIADS

We begin by building on each tone of the scale a triad similar to the fundamental triad [the tone with its closest overtones]. In doing so – to set down immediately a principle that will find manifold use in what follows – we transfer to other cases, we imitate, what we have seen in a precedent. These triads, however, are not to be fundamental triads, as is the prototype, but, for the sake of tonality, free imitations of the idea: fundamental, third, fifth, i.e. the intervals 1–3–5. As the third and fifth of these triads we do not write (if we may say it this way) the *tone's own* intervals; thus, on the second tone of the *C*-major scale, *d*, we do not write *f*♯ and *a*, but rather the *scale* tones, *f* and *a*, to make sure that in our very first exercises the tonality will be felt. In other words, in the seven chords that we build on the seven tones of the major scale we use no tones other than these same seven – the tones *of the scale*, the *diatonic* tones.

In *C* major, then, the diatonic triads are as follows:

The individual tones of the scale may act as roots, that is, each may serve as the lowest tone of a triad; in this function they are called degrees. Thus, *C* in the triad *c–e–g* is the first degree, *D* in the triad *d–f–a* the second degree, *E* in *e–g–b* the third degree, etc. The structure of the triads differs. We find those that, counting from the lowest tone, build up to the perfect fifth by way of a major third followed by a minor third; in others the perfect fifth results from the opposite arrangement, first the minor, then the major third; and there is one triad whose diminished fifth is formed from two intervals of equal size, from two minor thirds. Triads of the first type, *major triads*, are found on the degrees I, IV, and V; those of the second type, *minor triads*, on the degrees II, III, and VI; the third type, the *diminished triad*, is found only on the VIIth degree. An important distinction should be noted at once. The triad on I is of course a major triad, for it is the triad from which the corresponding major key gets its name. The other two triads that are constructed the same way, those on the IVth and Vth degrees, are also customarily called major triads. The expressions '*F*-major triad' and '*G*-major triad' are used in this sense. This terminology is actually false and misleading. In *C* major there is only one triad that may be known as the 'major triad', the one on the Ist degree. The other two, on IV and V, should never be called '*F* major' or '*G* major', because one could mistakenly think the expressions refer to a key, to a tonality, namely, to the keys of *F* major or *G* major. It is likewise false to speak of the triads on II, III, and VI as of '*d*-minor', '*e*-minor', or '*a*-minor' triads. It is most appropriate to use the expressions 'first, second, third degrees', etc., or to say 'triad on *G* or *A* with major or minor third'. Whatever the names, which of these degrees have the major third and which the minor is quickly learned. The following names are also used: tonic for the Ist degree, dominant for the Vth, subdominant for the IVth, mediant for the IIIrd, submediant for the VIth, and diminished triad for the VIIth. The IInd degree also has a name that is used in certain circumstances. It will be mentioned at the proper time.

The application of the expression, dominant, to the Vth degree is not entirely correct. 'Dominant' means 'dominating' or 'governing' and would thus imply that the Vth degree 'governs' another or several others. Of course this is only a metaphor, but even so it does not seem right to me; for obviously the fifth tone, the *Quint*, appears later in the overtone series than the fundamental and has therefore less significance for the total sound than has the fundamental, which appears earlier, hence, more often. Consequently, the relationship is characterized by a dependence of the fifth on the fundamental, rather than the converse, where the fundamental would be governed by the fifth. If anything dominates, it can only be the fundamental tone; and every fundamental can in turn be governed by a tone a fifth below it, in whose overtone series the former fundamental now takes second place, as the fifth. So if the metaphor is correct, then 'dominant' would be another name for the fundamental, since something of secondary importance should not be designated as governing something of primary importance. I will keep the expression, dominant, however, in order not to cause confusion with new terminology and because this chord, while not the sovereign of the key, is still a part of the key, of its upper region, of its *upper dominant region*. It should be mentioned now, however, that much of what I will say in evaluating the degrees, i.e. in showing their capabilities for forming progressions, chord progressions, is based on this notion: that the tonic is the governor and the dominant is the governed.

The name, dominant, is usually justified by saying that the Ist degree appears by virtue of the Vth degree. The Ist would then be a result of the Vth. But it is not possible that something can be the cause of a phenomenon and simultaneously the effect of the same phenomenon. And I is in fact the cause, the origin of V, since V is an overtone of I. To be sure, I follows V. But here we are confusing the two meanings of the word 'follow'. 'To follow' means 'to obey', but also 'to come after'. And if the tonic follows the dominant, it happens only in the same sense as when a king sends his vassal, his herald or his quartermaster on ahead to make appropriate preparations for his arrival. Then the king does in fact follow his man. The vassal is there, however, because of the king, as his follower, and not the other way around.

SPACING THE CHORDS

The chords could of course be connected in a purely schematic way, whereby each chord is regarded as a mass that is followed by another such mass, by another chord, as sometimes happens in piano pieces:

The most important principle of harmonic connection, good progression, is not affected by this type of connection. However, as I mentioned earlier, since many chord connections are not of purely harmonic origins, but rather of melodic, it is necessary to connect the chords in such a way that the melodic influences have a chance to become evident. Therefore the chords are presented as entities resulting from the concurrent movement of parts; but in so presenting them one should not forget that the *Motor* that drives this movement of voices, the motive, is absent. For presenting chord progressions through the movement of parts, since most harmonic events require an average of four parts, we use a combination of the four principal types of the human voice: soprano, alto, tenor, and bass. With these we obtain the so-called four-part writing.

This combination of human voices is just as practical as it is natural, as we shall see both now and later. Not only does it assure those acoustical distinctions that help to distinguish the parts clearly from one another, but it also affords that acoustical uniformity that at the same time makes it easy to hear the parts as a coherent whole, as chords. Even in the limitations of the individual voices, in their relative incompleteness, there are advantages.* The necessity for utilizing them within the narrow range of their effectiveness demands characteristic usage and treatment consistent with the material. Thus the pupil learns by this simple example to heed an important principle of handicraft: to make characteristic use of the strengths and shortcomings of the material at hand. The properties of the human voice relevant to our present task are as follows (most instruments, moreover, reveal similar properties): There is a register in which every normal, healthy voice sings easily and without strain, the middle register; and there are two registers that demand more effort and cause more fatigue, the high and the low. The middle register sounds less expressive and less impressive than the high or low registers. Since, however, the presentation of harmonic connections is not so much concerned with these effects as with those that are purely harmonic, the following principle can be given for the treatment of the voices (this principle even conforms to a certain extent to common practice): In general each voice is to sing in its middle register; only as other conditions require (difficulties in voice leading, avoiding monotony, etc.) will we seek out the higher or the lower register. The range of the voices is, as far as this purely schematic treatment is concerned, approximately that indicated by the half notes:

---

* I am taking such pains with these things, not so much out of concern that the pupil might, if they were not explained, thoughtlessly accept and mechanically apply them, as to establish explicitly that these principles are not derived from aesthetics but from practical considerations. If what is known as aesthetics does in fact contain much that is merely practical handling of the material, and if what is known as symmetry is perhaps often not much more than an organization of the material that reveals a sensible regard for its properties, yet I consider it worthwhile to set down these observations. For the conditions of practicality can change, if we take a different view of the material and if the purpose changes. But aesthetics alleges it has discovered eternal laws.

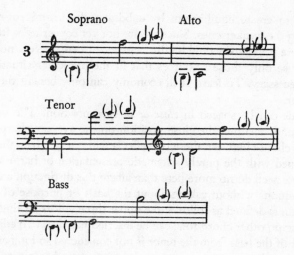

The quarter notes in parentheses indicate those tones at each extreme of the ranges that may be used in case of necessity. Obviously the range of solo voices, yes, even of choral voices, is in reality larger than, perhaps different from, that indicated here, which only aims at a fairly correct average. The middle register, which should be the one chiefly used, lies a fourth or a fifth from the highest and lowest tones, so that we have:

Of course the pupil cannot get along with just the tones of the middle register and will have to use some from the higher or lower registers – naturally, at first only the adjacent tones, but then also on occasion the highest or lowest, if there is no other way. In general, however, he should seldom overstep to any significant degree the bounds of an octave; whoever wants to write parts comfortable for the voice will avoid, even in actual composition, extended passages exclusively in one of the outer registers. The pupil should therefore enter these registers only for a short time and leave them as soon as possible. Whenever the treatment of solo or choral voices in practice indicates otherwise, it is because the composer sought some compositional or acoustical effects irrelevant to our present aims.

The characteristics of the voices indicate the requirements, supported by experience, for their combination in choral writing. If no voice is to stand out, then all voices will seek out registers whose acoustical potential is approximately the same. For, were a voice to sing in a more brilliant register, while the others move in a duller register, that voice would naturally be quite noticeable. If this voice is intended to stand out (for example, when an inner voice has the melody), then it is well that it sing in a more expressive register. But if it is inadvertently conspicuous, then the director would have to rely on shading, he would have to create equilibrium by subduing the prominent voice or by strengthening the weaker ones. Since we are not yet concerned with motives or melodies, these problems would hardly be relevant here, were it not inherent in our task to use only those resources that fit the particular situation, that are absolutely necessary. To learn such economy can only benefit the pupil, both now and later.

The chords can be spaced in *close or in open* position. The open position generally sounds mellow, the close position on the average sharper. The task of having to choose between these two effects will not be given the pupil while he is concerned with the purely schematic presentation of harmonic relations. Therefore, we need do no more here than affirm this distinction and proceed to use both positions without asking about the basis or purpose of their effects. Close position is defined as follows: the upper three voices all sing chord tones so spaced that no other chord tone can be inserted between two adjacent voices. The distance of the bass from the tenor is not considered so long as it is not too great. If among the three upper voices the tones sung by two adjacent voices are far enough apart that one or more chord tones can be inserted between them, then the chord is in open position.

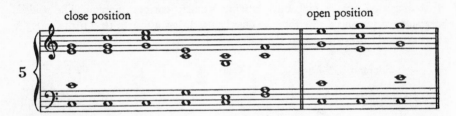

Experience teaches that an average balance in a chord is best achieved when no two [adjacent] voices of the upper three are separated by more than an octave at most; but the bass and tenor can be even farther apart. Of course, if other than this balanced effect is desired – a circumstance irrelevant to our present task – then the voices can and must be spaced differently.

In the distribution of three chord tones among four voices it becomes necessary to double one of the tones. The first to be considered is the root, also called fundamental, next the fifth, and only then, lastly, the third. This order of preference comes from the nature of the overtone series. If we want to imitate by synthesis the sound of the natural tone, that is, if we want to obtain a sound whose euphony recalls the euphony inherent in the material, then we must do something similar to what nature does. The sound is most similar to nature when the root, the tone that appears most frequently in the overtone series, also appears more often in the actual chord. For the same reason the fifth is less suitable for doubling than the octave [root], though more suitable than the third. The last-named will be doubled less often, moreover, because it already stands out prominently as the determiner of the mode – major or minor. Since acoustical effects and others not exclusively harmonic do not come under consideration here, we will always construct our chords with just that doubling which is necessary. Therefore, since here, at first, the doubling of the fifth and third is superfluous, we shall restrict ourselves to *the doubling of the octave* [root].

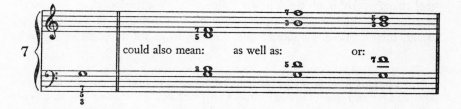

In Example 6 the triad on the Ist degree of *C* major is presented in various forms of open and close position. The pupil's first exercise is to write, in the same manner, the triads on II, III, IV, V, and VI (VII is omitted for the time being), adhering to the suggested voice registers; he should then repeat this procedure in some other keys. The exercises are to be notated on two staves with the treble and bass clefs. It is best for the pupil to write the soprano and alto parts on the upper staff (treble clef), the tenor and bass on the lower (bass clef). Often, or depending on individual circumstances, the tenor may be included on the upper staff,* in which case the bass stands alone on the lower. The examples will be given here largely in *C* major; nevertheless, the pupil must always do an exercise, once mastered in the original key, in other keys as well. Otherwise these will remain foreign to him.

Here we should mention also the method of the so-called thorough bass, or figured bass, a kind of musical shorthand that was formerly used to give the harpsichordist the harmonic skeleton of the work. This skeleton he translated into sound by improvisation, filling in and filling out the harmonies indicated. For this purpose figures were written below the bass line which expressed schematically the intervals between the lowest tone, the bass, and the other tones of the chord, but without indicating whether the interval lay in the same or in a higher octave. Thus, for example,

* The range of the tenor is that notated in Example 3 in the bass clef. The adjacent notes in parentheses (in the treble clef) refer to the manner of notation generally practiced in *Lieder*, operas, choral music, etc., where the notes in the treble clef are read down an octave. The notation in our exercises approximates that used in piano scores, where the tenor notes, whether they appear in the bass or the treble, always sound as written, that is, as if they were written for the piano rather than for voice, *without the octave transposition.*

The figures 3–5–7 merely indicated the schematic order of the chord components in their closest position, but one or more octaves could be added to 3, 5, or 7. The figure '3' meant there was a third above, in some octave or other; '5' meant there was a fifth above, '7' a seventh, '9' a ninth, '6' a sixth, etc., in some octave or other. Whether in performance the tones had the order 3–5–7, 5–3–7, or 7–3–5, or yet another, was left to the judgment of the harpsichordist, whose decision was based on necessities of voice leading. The chords were formed from tones of the scale corresponding to the key signature, unless there was a special sign (♯, ♭, or ♮) beside a figure. A triad in root position, whose symbol would have been ⅝, was left unfigured.* If, however, a figure 8, 5, or 3 appeared with a bass note, it meant that the highest voice (in our case the soprano) should take the 8, 5, or 3. The chord is then said to be in octave position, fifth position, or third position.

CONNECTION OF THE DIATONIC PRIMARY AND SECONDARY TRIADS

The satisfactory solution of the problem of *connecting chords with one another* depends on the fulfilment of certain conditions. These conditions are not set up here in the form of laws or rules, but rather as directions (as I have already intimated and will repeat on many occasions). Laws or rules ought to hold always, unconditionally; and the saying that 'exceptions prove the rule' is true only of those rules whose very exceptions constitute their sole proof. Directions, however, serve merely to impart means by which a certain goal can be reached. Therefore, they do not hold eternally, as laws, but are changed as soon as the goal changes. Although the following directions do correspond, in part, to the practice of composers, they nevertheless do not spring from aesthetic aims; rather, their purpose is a limited one: namely, to guard the pupil against mis-

---

* The figured bass, as a sensible shorthand, aimed at making do with the fewest possible symbols. Therefore, only that which was not self-evident was specifically indicated. It was assumed to be self-evident (historically correct) that every bass note is accompanied by 3 and 5. Such a note need not be figured. On the other hand, everything different, but only what was different, had to be specially indicated. Taken literally, the figure 6 below a bass note could also mean that 3 and 5 remain and 6 is added. But a supplementary principle takes over here to indicate the position of the dissonance ⅝; thus the figure 6 could be used in place of the more complete ⅝ by applying the single figure exclusively to a single position, the six-three chord, and designating all other positions that contained a sixth by at least two figures. [This footnote was added in the revised edition.]

takes that cannot be explained and described until later. The first of these directions requires that in the voice leading, at first, *only that be done which is absolutely necessary for connecting the chords*. This means each voice will move only when it must; each voice will take the smallest possible step or leap, and then, moreover, just that smallest step which will allow the other voices also to take small steps. Thus, the voices will follow (as I once heard Bruckner say) the *'law of the shortest way'*. Consequently, whenever two chords that are to be connected have a common tone, this tone will be taken by the same voice in the second chord as in the first – it will be 'sustained'. Now, to simplify the task still more, we shall choose for our first exercises only such chords as have one or more tones in common (two triads cannot have more than two common tones) and shall sustain one or more of them as a *harmonic link* [*common tone*].[1] The following tables show those chords that are available for these exercises, that is, those chords that have common tones:

I	.	III	IV	V	VI	.
.	**II**	.	IV	V	VI	VII
I	.	**III**	.	V	VI	VII
I	II	.	**IV**	.	VI	VII
I	II	III	.	**V**	.	VII
I	II	III	IV	.	**VI**	.
.	II	III	IV	V	.	**VII**

Degree	has common tones with			
I	III	IV	V	VI
II	IV	V	VI	(VII)
III	I	V	VI	(VII)
IV	I	II	VI	(VII)
V	I	II	III	(VII)
VI	I	II	III	IV
VII	II	III	IV	V

The Roman numerals indicate degrees.

As can be seen, every degree [triad] has a common tone with every other degree except the one directly before and the one directly after. That is indeed obvious. The IInd degree is *d–f–a*. The roots of two neighboring degrees (for example, *c* and *d*) are one step apart from each other; therefore, the thirds (*e* and *f*) and the fifths (*g* and *a*) will likewise be one step apart. Thus, there is no common tone. On the other hand, those chords whose roots are a fifth or a fourth apart have one common tone, whereas those whose roots are a third or a sixth apart have two.

[1 'Harmonisches Band'. Schoenberg also used elsewhere the expression 'gemeinsamer Ton' (common tone); but he apparently preferred 'harmonisches Band' (harmonic link, or tie, or bond), perhaps because of its emphasis on the idea of connection. 'Common tone', the usual expression in English, seemed preferable here. Cf. *infra*, Chapter VI.]

C	C						
D		D					
E	E		E				
F		F		F			
G	G		G		G		
A		A		A		A	
B			B		B		B
C				C		C	
D					D		D
E						E	
F							F

As the table indicates, the Ist degree can be connected, assuming a common tone is required, with III, IV, V, and VI.

In these first exercises the fundamental tone should always be the lowest tone of the chord, that is, it goes in the bass. The bass voice should always be the lowest, the tenor next above the bass, then the alto, and, as the highest voice, the soprano. The pupil should completely avoid *crossing* of voices, that is, writing a lower one higher than a higher one (e.g. the tenor higher than the alto or soprano). First of all, the pupil should write under [the staff that will carry] the bass line Roman numerals indicating the degrees of the chords he is to connect; then he should write the bass note of the first chord and go on to complete the first chord by adding the other three voices. Whether it is to be in close or open position with the third, fifth, or octave on top – this he will decide for himself, *but before he goes on to work out the exercise. Thus, he sets up the exercise himself,* a procedure we will follow throughout this course of study. In *spacing* each chord the pupil will most easily avoid mistakes if he first answers the following questions in the order given:

First question: Which tone goes in the bass? (The root of the degree, the fundamental.)

Second question: Which tone in the soprano? (Accordingly as he has chosen to put the octave, fifth, or third on top, his choice should be indicated by placing the 8, 5, or 3 next to the Roman numeral indicating the degree.)

Third question: What is missing? (The tone or tones that are still missing will be so spaced that close or open position results, whichever the pupil has chosen.)

Proceeding now to connect the chords, the pupil will do well* to ask himself the following questions:

1. Which tone is the root? (Remember: it goes in the bass!)

* From years of experience in teaching I recommend to the pupil most emphatically that he work out the exercises by actually asking and answering these questions. It will favor greater insight and skill if he goes about it this way than if he merely follows the dictates of his ear or of a particular pattern of notes that he remembers. He will easily get accustomed to thinking through these questions quickly, so quickly in fact that he will not neglect them even when he works out the exercises at the piano (as he should also do, without fail). The advantage of this procedure is that the pupil works thoughtfully at every turn, thinking quickly, fully aware of what he is doing, thus does not depend on his memory and some ready-made devices he has stored there.

2. Which is the common tone? (Sustained!)
3. Which tones are still missing?

Again, to avoid mistakes that cannot be explained until later, we shall always double exclusively the octave [root] in the initial chord of the first exercises. As the pupil will see, the succeeding chords will thereby never appear with the fifth or third doubled. These doublings we shall use only whenever the voice leading requires them, since we are not concerned here with sound effects (*Klangliches*).

We will connect I and III, then, with the help of the questions, as follows (Example 8a):

1. bass note (IIIrd degree): *e*;
2. common tones: *e* and *g* (held over in the soprano and alto);
3. the missing tone: *b* (the tenor goes from *c* to *b*).

Please note: The pupil should always conceive the chord connections as resulting from the movement of parts. Thus he should not say: 'I'll give the *b* to the tenor', rather, 'the tenor goes from *c* to *b*'; he should not say: 'I'll give the *e* to the soprano, the *g* to the alto', rather, 'the *e* is held over in the soprano, the *g* in the alto'.

The pupil must distinguish between *root* and *bass tone*. (The former is the tone on which the triad is built, the tone that gives its name to the degree; thus, the root of the IInd degree is *d*, that of the IIIrd, *e*, etc. The bass tone, on the other hand, is that tone which is put in the bass.) In our first exercises, and until other directions are given, we shall *always put the root in the bass*. Later, however, chord components other than the root will also go in the bass; therefore, the pupil must guard against confusing these two notions.

For the present we shall work out our exercises in whole notes, without bar lines.

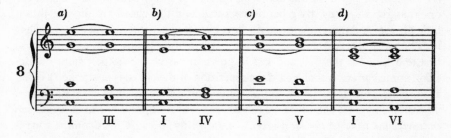

Example 8a shows the connection I–III in which two tones (*e* and *g*) are common tones; in 8b and 8c respectively (I–IV and I–V) only one tone is common, in I–VI [8d] two tones again. The pupil should indicate with ties the sustaining of common tones.

Following this model the pupil is now to practice connecting each of the other degrees with the chords available, as indicated by the table: thus, II with IV, then with V and with VI (*the VIIth degree is not to be used at all for the present, as it demands special treatment*); the IIIrd degree is to be connected with

I, V, and VI; the IVth with I, II, and VI; and so on, up through the VIth degree (*omit VII here, too*).

CONNECTION OF THE DIATONIC PRIMARY AND SECONDARY TRIADS IN SHORT PHRASES

The pupil's next task is to construct short phrases from the six chords at his disposal. These phrases should, so far as the available means allow, display some degree of variety and be just as interesting as possible. The pupil should also aim at a certain effect in these exercises, even if it now be only in an embryonic form, an effect that we shall strive for later with more adequate means and thus with greater determination: namely, to express to a certain extent the key. To compose phrases that meet these requirements we shall have to satisfy some conditions. (N.B.: Again, these conditions do not amount to eternal laws, even though such are relatively harmless; for a few exceptions will do away in a flash with 'law' and 'eternal'. They amount rather to directions, to be followed only as long as their aim seems worth the effort, and to be set aside as soon as higher aims appear.) Of course the phrases will have to be very short, since only six chords are available, whose admissible connections are restricted by yet other conditions (common tones). Repetitions can easily become monotonous, unnecessarily monotonous, if they do not acquire an altered coloring from their surroundings or do not otherwise have some purpose; or the repeated chord can take on extraordinary significance among the other chords, since repetition usually amounts to a reinforcement. Thus, repetition will generally be avoided, as long as it is not our aim to allow a chord any such extraordinary significance. At present we can have this aim with one chord only, with the Ist degree, the one that gives the key. By repetition we will lend this chord prominence in our little phrases and thereby express the key, even if at present not very convincingly. The most practical arrangement for this repetition is simply to put this chord first and last; for the first and last impressions leave the deepest imprint. Besides, some variety is achieved if the repetition of the chord is postponed as long as possible, so that in the meantime something different, some contrast occurs. Therefore, the first condition we impose reads as follows: *The phrase begins and ends with the triad on the Ist degree.* Consequently, because the common tone is required, the next to last chord must be able to connect, according to our table, with the Ist degree: thus, it will have to be III, IV, V, or VI. To guard against errors that would be unavoidable if our exercises were too extended, we shall be content in the beginning to connect four to six chords. Of these the first and last will be I; hence, between these two will come at most two to four other degrees, better fewer than more since *repetitions* should be *avoided*.

Following the table, the pupil can now set up his own exercises, beginning with the Ist degree and then putting after it one of the degrees with which it has a common tone: first, for example, III. Then he will look in the table for a degree that can follow III. These are I, V, and VI. Since I has already been used, however, and since it may be repeated only once, its repetition would bring the phrase to a premature close; therefore he will choose either V or VI. To proceed systematically we shall use V for the first example, which thus so far reads: I, III, V. After V, as the table shows, can come I, II, or III; since I and III were already used, II would be the next chord. The example would then stretch out, however, to at least six chords. So that the first examples are kept as short as possible, we shall close this one now with I. It therefore reads: I–III–V–I. These connections should now be worked out precisely in the manner suggested for connecting chords, by answering the three questions. (See Example 11a below.)

In setting up his other little phrases the pupil will best proceed systematically, that is, by beginning again with I and III and continuing differently after III: thus, for example, I, III, VI; after VI can come I in one phrase, in another phrase IV and then I. When everything has been worked out with I–III, he can then begin with I–IV, then with I–V, and finally with I–VI, continuing differently each time.

Here we should say something more about voice leading. It should be melodic. 'Melodic', however, should not be taken here to mean that the voice leading has to be, like that of a song for example, expressive or beautiful, richly inflected or ornamented, or even articulated. 'Melodic' in that sense is out of the question here, because all the prerequisites are missing. We are working here without rhythm, thus without motives, and [melodic] articulation and ornamentation are hardly conceivable without rhythm. What we have to understand as 'melodic', for the present, may perhaps be best expressed this way: the part should not be unmelodic, that is, it should avoid those intervals and successions of intervals that strike us as unpleasant. For such it is hard to find a criterion; what was formerly unmelodic is today quite often felt to be melodic. Bellermann,[1] for example, finds it necessary to point out that Handel used a leap of a minor seventh in a melody. Of course the composers of the fifteenth or sixteenth centuries would not have done that, but then sixteenth-century standards no longer applied in the seventeenth century. The same is true of most other prescriptions, such as some would make, say, for our time on the basis of Handelian melody. These would hardly agree in every respect even with the linear techniques of Haydn, Mozart, and Beethoven, let alone those of Schumann, Brahms, or Wagner.

Now it should be considered, however, that in purely harmonic operations the melodic aspect remains in the background, as previously mentioned, because the motive is missing, because not only is the necessity for richer ornamentation excluded, but also the occasion, the inducement. Our present

[1 Heinrich Bellermann, *Der Contrapunkt* (4th ed.; Berlin: Julius Springer, 1901), cf. pp. 104–5.

In a letter to Hugo Leichtentritt (1938) Schoenberg included Bellermann's work in a list of German books on music theory that had interested him. He remarked that those books 'might help to convert [the Americans] away from their fossilized aesthetics' (*Letters*, pp. 206–7). Unfortunately, there is no English translation of Bellermann's work.]

responsibility can only be to write those steps or leaps that are necessary for connecting the chords: that is, generally, as little movement as possible. For the less the voices move, the fewer the errors in voice movement, in voice leading. Yet, because the conduct of exposed voices, of the two so-called outer voices (soprano and bass), attracts some attention to itself, and because a certain monotony could impair the impression of harmonic effectiveness, it will be necessary later on to mention some remedies. For the moment we shall consider only the bass, for it alone often makes rather large leaps, whereas the other voices move mostly by step. So, it will do for now to mention such errors as can appear in the bass. Of course we are talking, in part, about progressions that today no one will find objectionable. Nevertheless, the old harmonic theory was to a certain extent right in requiring that they be avoided. The reasons for these requirements may seem to us now untenable. But since in our little phrases we are working out the simplest of musical exercises – exercises whose musical effect is so rudimentary that the ear accustomed to Wagner's harmonic freedom would be almost justifiably uncritical of them – since they are so simple, it is advisable not to rely on the ear of today but on the ear of that time. The sense of beauty of that time undoubtedly got from the material such satisfactions as were in accord with the total effect of such simple forms. If then these little phrases should, even now, have *style* – as should everything that is supposed to develop artistic sensitivity and a sense of form – that is, if they should, even now, show a certain balance between the effect and the means, then it will be useful to consider the instructions given by the old harmonic theory. We may and shall drop them without further ado whenever our means become richer, that is, whenever we have a larger stock of possibilities for wresting effects from the material. We do not take even these instructions for rules, that is, something that can be suspended only by an exception. They are just instructions and nothing more. And it is clear, is it not, that we shall consider them for one reason alone: we can get stylistically correct results only if our use of the means befits their simple ends.

One of these instructions [for handling the bass] is: *two consecutive leaps of a fourth or a fifth in the same direction are to be avoided, because the first and last tones form a dissonance.* Or, to put it somewhat more generally: two leaps in the same direction, whose intervals add up to a dissonance, sound unmelodic.

For example:

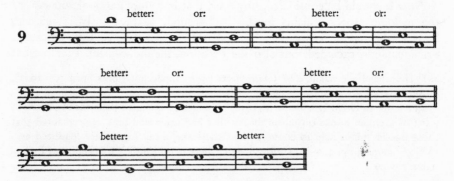

This instruction was absolutely correct from the standpoint of the older harmonic theory. Its instructions referred primarily to vocal music, which was frequently sung without accompaniment, *a cappella*. The performers, professional singers or amateurs, sang their parts mostly at sight, without much rehearsal. This practice of sight-singing in performance was the precondition to which everything else was adapted. To write well for voices meant then, above all, to avoid difficulties where possible. And since the singer, unlike the instrumentalist, does not have fixed tones nor even any fingerings that will give him such, certain intervals, even today, offer him intonation difficulties. Even if the scope of that which is singable is continually increasing, this advance is still slower than the corresponding advance in instrumental music. It is after all understandable that the ear resists dissonances (more distant overtones) not only in simultaneous sounds, in chords, but in successions of tones as well, in the melodic line; it does not grasp them as quickly; it perceives them as obstacles and longs for their removal, for their resolution. And that the ear allows them at all is possibly just because of the resolution, because of the sense of satisfaction that this effect evokes. To the listener the dissonance, its urge toward resolution and the resolution itself, may be pleasurable; to the singer, though, this obstacle can become troublesome.

The second of these two melodic instructions reads: *no voice shall make a leap larger than a fifth* (the octave leap, whose effect is almost the same as that of repeating the tone, was naturally permitted). Why the leap of a seventh should not be used is clear already from what was said above concerning dissonant leaps. It is less clear, why the leap of the sixth should not be used. Bellermann[1] reports that the effect of this leap was formerly considered delicate, weak (*weichlich*). That may very well be, but there must have been a cause. Such is to be found, I believe, in two circumstances, which, although they produce not delicacy but rather the contrary, harshness, nevertheless explain why this leap should be avoided. Whether it is right or wrong to call a seldom used, unaccustomed interval delicate or weak is of rather slight importance. The one cause may well be sought in the many kinds of difficulties in voice leading that the leap of a sixth brings with it: the leap requires room and certain forbidden parallels often appear (these will be discussed later).

Unison

10

The second cause can be that the sixth is less familiar to the ear; for, although in the overtone series this interval does appear as a relation of the fundamental (*e–c*), it appears in the opposite direction: the fundamental is above the third (*c, c, g, c, e͞, g͞, c͞*). Therefore, it sounds in fact stranger and should then have

[1 Bellermann, *ibid.*, p. 105.]

been called harsh rather than delicate. Possibly for these two reasons the leap of the sixth was seldom used, if at all. Hence, it may have seemed strange, unconventional to the ear through lack of use, and, probably just as a result of misinterpretation, it was described as delicate.

In Example 11 there now follow some complete phrases as we have assembled them according to the table.

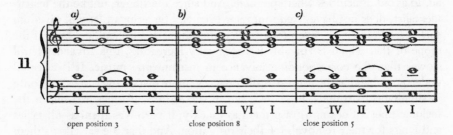

The pupil can also work out these very same examples by choosing another spacing (close position instead of open, open instead of close) or by beginning with the fifth or octave on top instead of the third. It is absolutely necessary to practice each new assignment in other keys as well, but not simply by transposing, rather by setting up the exercise anew in each key.

THE VIIth DEGREE

The triad on the VIIth degree, the diminished triad, requires special consideration. Its structure is different from that of the other triads we have seen, which all have at least one thing in common: the perfect fifth. The triad on the VIIth degree has a diminished fifth; such a fifth is not found among the closer overtones and is therefore heard as a dissonance. That the dissonance requires special treatment, and for what reasons, I stated previously when I discussed its appearance among successive tones, that is, in melodic movement (two consecutive fifths or fourths in the same direction).[1] Clearly, the dissonance is still more striking whenever its tones appear simultaneously. The listener can fail to hear dissonance produced by tones that follow one another, should he, for example, forget the pertinent preceding tone. Dissonance produced by tones sounding together he cannot fail to hear.

How dissonances ever came to be used at all is open only to conjecture. It must have happened quite gradually; and the attempt to mingle the more remote overtones, the dissonances, with the consonances must have been undertaken at first just occasionally and with great caution. I imagine that at first the dissonances were simply made to rush by, as it were, more or less this way: over a

[1 *Supra*, pp. 44–5.]

sustained triad, *c–e–g*, a melodic voice slid down, so to speak, from a long *g* through an extremely fleeting *f* to a long *e*. Something like a more or less fully executed portamento or glissando (colloquially,* 'Schmieren' [smear, glide]), whose individual tones are hardly distinguishable. Later on, one of these tones may have become fixed as a scale tone. Thus I believe that dissonance appeared first in passing from one tone to another through intervening tones and that such passing stemmed from the portamento, from the desire to soften leaps, to connect disjunct tones melodically, in this case by scale step. That this desire coincides with another, with the desire to make use also of the more distant overtones, is perhaps only a fortunate coincidence, such as historical evolution indeed often produces. Perhaps, however, it is all the same principle, the portamento being one of the forms in which it is realized. The portamento could also be, like the scale, a horizontal rearrangement of the overtone series. If the ear has stopped in midstream, if it has not chosen those dissonant overtones that actually make up a tone but stylized and tempered average tones instead, then that can be explained as a compromise between an end and its attainability, as I suggested before in discussing the origin of the scale.

The use of such ornamentation as touched upon dissonant tones was allowed in the form of the so-called 'Manieren' [ornaments],[1] was indeed almost demanded by the taste of the time. These 'ornaments' could not be notated because the notational system had no symbols to represent them; therefore, the figures involved, the appoggiaturas, trills, portamenti, etc., could only be propagated by tradition. As a result of their use, however, the feeling that the dissonances touched upon in these ornaments belonged to the fundamental tone may have gradually insinuated itself into the consciousness of the analyzing ear, producing the desire to fix in the notation at least some of the more frequently occurring tones.

The passing tone is, then, nothing else but a 'Manier' as it was fixed in the notation. As the notation always lags behind the sound (not only in melody, perhaps even much more in rhythm, where, with the compulsion of the bar line, the written symbols are often hardly even approximately correct), so the

* It should be noted here that music, too, has a colloquial form, which could serve as a source of evidence in explaining the historical development, much the same as folk speech does for the written language: namely, folk music. For it, too, contains alongside the peculiar products of its own development musical conventions of earlier times. And one should also examine and reappraise the banalities and trivialities. For the most part these will not turn out as really *vulgar*, but as worn out by use, antiquated. *Hackneyed,* as dilettantes like to say.

[1 Cf. C. P. E. Bach, *Essay on the True Art of Playing Keyboard Instruments*, trans. William J. Mitchell (New York: W. W. Norton, Inc., 1949), pp. 79–146: *Manieren* (ornaments or embellishments) 'connect and enliven tones and impart stress and accent. . . . Expression is heightened by them. . . . Without them the best melody is empty and ineffective' (p. 79).

In Schoenberg's view, *Manieren* have had a more profound function in music; he considered them a main avenue through which music has evolved, through which the implicit has become explicit. Cf. *infra*, p. 320, pp. 331–2, *et passim*.]

notation of these ornaments is of course also imperfect if judged by the sounds [composers surely] imagined. It can be understood, however, as one of those simplifications the human intellect must create if it is to deal with the material. The supposition prevails here, too, that the system that simplified the object (*Sache*) was taken to be the system inherent in that object itself; and we can safely assume that our traditional treatment of dissonance, although originally based on a correct intuition, nevertheless proceeded more to develop the system of simplification than really to reach an understanding of the nature of dissonance. Perhaps I fall into the same error if I retain here this same manner of handling dissonance; but I can cite two considerations in my favor: first, I give the instructions necessary for complying with the system, but not (as I have often emphasized) as rules, nor as aesthetics; and the second consideration is that our present-day ear has been educated not only by the conditions nature imposed on it, but also by those produced by the system, which has become a second nature. At present we can hardly, or just gradually, escape the effects of this artificial, cultural product; and *reflection on nature* may have value for the theory of knowledge without being thereby necessarily capable of bearing immediate artistic fruits. It is certain that this path, too, will be taken again sooner or later, the path that leads to new secrets of nature. It is certain that these, too, will then again be thinned out to make a system; but before anything the old system has to be got out of the way. The line of thought (*Erkenntnis*) I have presented here can perhaps serve as a means to that end.

The notation of dissonances brought about by passing tones may have led to the confirmation of the phenomenon of dissonance itself. Two impulses struggle with each other within man: the demand for repetition of pleasant stimuli, and the opposing desire for variety, for change, for a new stimulus. These two impulses often unite in one relatively common impulse characteristic of beasts of prey: the impulse to take possession. The question whether then repetition or change shall follow is for the time being cast aside. The more robust satisfaction the consciousness of possession gives, with its possibilities for deciding this way or that, is capable of suppressing the subtler considerations and of leading to that conservative repose which is always characteristic of ownership. Faced with the dilemma, whether repetition of the stimuli or innovation be preferable, the human intellect decided here, too, to take possession; it founded a system.

Thus it can also be imagined how the chance occurrence of a dissonant passing tone, once established by the notation, after its excitement had been experienced, called forth the desire for less accidental, less arbitrary repetition; how the desire to experience this excitement more often led to taking possession of the methods that brought it about. But, should the excitement of the forbidden lead to uninhibited indulgence, that essentially despicable compromise between morality and immoderate desire had to be drawn, that compromise which here consists in a looser conception of the prohibition as well as of that which is prohibited. Dissonance was accepted, but the door through which it was admitted was bolted whenever excess threatened.

The *treatment of dissonance*, in which psychological and practical considerations play similarly decisive roles, could have arisen in this manner. The caution of the listener, who wants to enjoy the excitement but does not want to be too greatly alarmed by the danger, is in accord with the caution of the singer. And the composer, who dares not spoil it for either, invents methods that pander to this goal: how do I hold the listener in suspense, how do I startle him and yet not go so far that it is no longer possible for me to say, 'It was only in fun'? Or: how do I introduce, slowly and carefully, what indeed has to come if I do not want to bore the listener; how do I persuade him to accept the sour grapes, too, so that the sweet ones, the resolution of dissonance, will stimulate him so much the more pleasantly? How do I induce the singer to sing a dissonant tone in spite of himself, in spite of possible intonation difficulties? I do not let him notice its entry and I whisper to him in the catastrophic moment: 'Easy! It's practically over.' Careful introduction and euphonious resolution: that is the system!

Preparation and resolution are thus a pair of protective wrappers in which the dissonance is carefully packed so that it neither suffers nor inflicts damage.

Now, applied to our present case, to the diminished triad, this means that the dissonant diminished fifth will be prepared and resolved. That in the diminished triad the dissonance cannot be some tone other than the fifth follows not only from comparison with the overtones, where a fundamental always has a perfect fifth, but also from comparison with the other triads, which all have perfect fifths. There are various kinds of dissonance treatment, various kinds of resolutions above all, but also various kinds of introductions. The first and simplest form of introduction we will meet is the preparation. Here the tone that is to become dissonant should already be sung by the same voice in the preceding chord, as a *consonance*. The purpose of this preparation is clearly as follows: to introduce the tone first where, as a *consonant* component of a major or minor triad, it will cause the singer no difficulty; and then to sustain it while the other voices move in such a way that it turns into a dissonance. As our first form of resolution we will use a method whose practicality is, from a psychological viewpoint, easy to see. Namely, if a barrier is set against the harmonic flow through insertion of the dissonance, somewhat comparable to a dam in a brook, then this resistance should create an accumulation of energy that takes the obstruction, so to speak, 'in full swing'. An energetic move should be used to get over the barrier. The leap from the Vth degree to the Ist can be regarded as just such an energetic move. Expressed more generally, this is the leap of the fundamental to the fourth above.* I have already pointed out, in my critique of the notion of 'dominant', how strong an attraction the tonic exerts on the dominant. I mentioned further that every fundamental tone has the tendency to be overpowered, to be overcome by a fundamental tone a fifth below. If we give in to this tendency of the fundamental, to its tendency towards resolution into a higher, stronger unit in which it becomes a subordinate component, to its tendency to serve a cause greater than its own, then we fulfil, as it were, the

---

* It would actually be better for me to say, 'leap to the fifth below'. For the reasons given in the note on p. 116, I prefer the terminology here.

most urgent yearning of the fundamental: that is, we make the strongest leap. It is thus clear that the use of this the strongest leap on such a special occasion, as is the appearance of a dissonance in our harmonic life of the moment, is required just as much as, say, putting on holiday clothes for festive occasions in civic life. Of course there are also other means by which dissonance can be resolved; and once it has lost, through frequent use, some of the uncommonness it now has for us, we shall handle it less ceremoniously and shall not always immediately seize upon the strongest means.

If in resolving the dissonant fifth of the diminished triad we make the root jump to the fourth above (or to the fifth below), then the chord that resolves the VIIth is that of the IIIrd degree.[1]

The dissonant tone itself is resolved here by moving it a step downward, from *f* to *e*. There are different ways in which the dissonance can relate to the chord of resolution. It can fall, rise, or remain stationary; but it can also move away by a leap. For our first example we choose to let it fall, that is, move by step to the next scale tone below. One reason for this procedure is that this voice, which has drawn so great attention to itself, becomes then the octave of that fundamental we have found to be eminently suitable for resolving dissonance. This voice thus confirms, so to speak, the fulfilment of the tendency of the fundamental. But there is another reason as well, which we will have opportunity to explain later [pp. 81–2].

Here we sometimes have to do without the common tone, if we are to get a complete chord. If the common tone, the *b*, is sustained (Example 12*b, c, d*), then the voice that has the *d* is compelled to leap to the *g* above or below. This leap will often create difficulty, as for example in 12*b*, where, because of the downward leap, the alto goes below the tenor, or where, if the alto proceeded to the higher *g*, it would go above the soprano. But, as I have already said (p. 40), we should avoid the *crossing of voices*. The solution 12*c* is good, and useful. Only, it will be necessary, since here the upper voice moves by leap, to devote some care to its melodic line, to what follows. On the other hand, the progression in 12*d* produces too great a separation of two neighboring voices, no matter whether the alto springs upward or downward. In the first case alto and tenor are a tenth apart, in the second, alto and soprano. We shall always avoid that sort of spacing wherever possible, for, as experience teaches, it yields a less

[1 In his efforts to be systematic and to keep the pupil under strict discipline, Schoenberg presents here an unusual resolution of the diminished triad on VII, postponing until later (Chapter VIII) the more common treatment.]

balanced sound. (Whenever something of this sort appears in the music literature, it may have been planned that way or it may have happened as a byproduct of other, more important aims.) Here, then, the solution given in 12e (without sustaining the common tone) is preferable. The pupil may use the common tone one time and do without it another, according to the requirements of the phrase. What considerations are relevant here will be analyzed later when the melodic tendencies of the parts are discussed. For the moment let me merely suggest that it will be best not to stray too far from the spacing with which the phrase began, and, whenever there has to be a departure from that spacing, to return to it upon the first opportunity.

Here we have occasion to make a rather important observation. For the first assignments we chose to write only those chord progressions that permitted the sustaining of a common tone. That seemed [then] to be a rule, but it is not. Its purpose was rather just to ensure the doubling of the octave [root], and to avoid certain other difficulties in voice leading, which will be discussed later. Now it becomes occasionally necessary to disregard the common tone. Thus, the earlier instruction is suspended by a higher necessity. We are not making an 'exception to the rule', because we had no rule; we had an instruction, which gave just as much as it took. Certain errors could be avoided; for, although the instruction did exclude some things that might be good, it also excluded others through which the errors could arise. Once the pupil has attained sufficient mastery within this restriction, and whenever higher necessity requires, he can do without this simplification. In general we shall indeed continue the practice of allowing the voices to move only as much or as little as is absolutely necessary. Nevertheless – and this should be said here – every instruction is suspended whenever a higher necessity so requires. Thus, here there are no eternal laws, only instructions, which have relevance as long as they are not suspended, wholly or in part, by others: i.e. whenever other conditions are imposed.

Concerning the question, which tone of the VIIth-degree triad is suitable for doubling, the following is to be said: we shall of course prefer the root, simply because we have been working up to now just with root doublings, but then also for the same reason that we preferred the root in the other triads. As for the third and fifth, that is another matter. The third now takes precedence over the fifth because the VIIth degree is neither major nor minor, but a diminished triad. Here the third does not determine mode and is therefore less noticeable. The fifth, on the other hand, as a dissonance, is the most noticeable tone of the VIIth degree and would not be doubled for that reason alone. Moreover, as a dissonance that we shall resolve, it is compelled to move a certain way: that is a step downward. Should we double it, then the other voice in which it appeared would also be obligated to move a step downward (12f). Thereby, a certain voice leading would result concerning which more is to be said later. For the present it is enough to say that two voices would carry out the same step. This is superfluous, because one is enough. The diminished fifth is therefore not to be doubled.

Now the preparation. The dissonant tone is to have been consonant in the preceding chord, and then is to be sustained in the same voice while becoming a dissonance. Each tone of the scale appears in three different diatonic triads: once as the root, once as the third, and once as the fifth. Our dissonant *f* is the root of IV, third of II, and fifth of VII; hence the chords on the IVth and IInd degrees are available to us [as preparatory chords]. To the three questions [p. 40f] that we set up [as guidelines] for connecting consonant chords, a new one is now added. The questions therefore now read:

1. Which tone is the bass tone?
2. Which tone is dissonant? (If there is a dissonance, then preparation or resolution, whichever is of immediate concern.)
3. Common tone? (Sustained *wherever possible,* thus, no longer invariably.)
4. Which tone is missing (or which tones)?

Example 13 shows several preparations and resolutions. In 13*a, b,* and *c* the preparation is accomplished by means of the IVth degree (since here the tone to be prepared is the octave of the preparatory chord, this is called: *preparation by means of the octave*), in 13*d* and *e* by means of the IInd degree (*preparation by means of the third*).

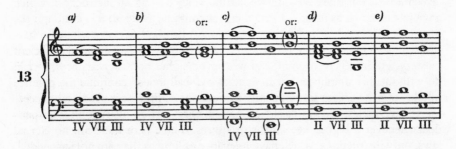

The pupil should now practice the preparation and resolution of the VIIth degree in as many examples as possible (in other keys, too!). The degree progressions will read: IV, VII, III or II, VII, III. *After VII we shall use for the moment nothing else but III, before VII only IV or II.* Once the pupil has sufficient skill in handling the VIIth degree, he should then proceed to use it in little phrases. *It goes without saying that here, too, III must always follow VII, IV or II must introduce it.* As for the rest the pupil can be completely governed by the table (p. 39), in which the restrictions pertaining to the VIIth degree are now discarded.

THE INVERSIONS OF THE TRIADS

In the assignments we have completed so far it was actually of no consequence how the components of the chord were distributed among the upper voices; and only the one condition was imposed, that the bass had always to take the root. However, various circumstances require – and permit – that chord tones other than the root appear in the bass. They require it, and they permit it: a necessity and an advantage. This remarkable coincidence will appear with almost all technical considerations in art. It is improbable that one would obey a necessity if it did not bring yet other advantages beyond those issuing merely from its minimal requirements; it is also improbable that an advantage would appear that is not attached to the fulfilment of certain necessities. This looks mysterious and is indeed so: that one does something because necessity compels it and thereby unintentionally produces beauty; or that one has the impulse to create something beautiful and thereby fulfils necessity. It is one of those mysteries that make life worth living. This reward, which surprises the fully active searcher on a plane higher than that of his expectations, always appears of its own accord in true art and in true morality. The intelligent craftsman, the intelligent craftsman of art, will, however, take it under consideration from the outset. It would seem to him ill-advised to allow himself to make an essential alteration because of a momentary advantage. Even a small alteration in the basic structure of an organism has far-reaching consequences. Even if they are not immediately evident, they will show up later without fail. He would thus allow such an alteration only if he could anticipate a certain number of likely consequences and could estimate and weigh in advance their value or lack of value. It is certain that if such an alteration is alien to the nature of this organism, then the majority of its consequences will be harmful, and the apparent necessity that induced the alteration is to be traced back to an incorrect judgment. If, however, the alteration really agrees with the nature of the organism, with its developmental tendencies, then there will result from such an objectively correct measure not only those advantages one expected but others, as well, that one had not aimed for. And, conversely, if one starts with the desire to gain new effects from an organism, effects inherent in its nature, then it will always turn out that one has at the same time been obeying a necessity of this organism, that one has been promoting its developmental tendencies.

Applying these notions to our present concern, we find the following: Any setting of a chord that has the root in the bass imitates most closely the acoustical relation of the tone to its overtones. Once we put another tone in the lowest position, we depart from the natural model. Now, is that good? It is both good and not good; one time it is better, another time less good, one time stronger, another time less strong. Undoubtedly, to give a chord a bass tone other than the root produces at least a different effect, if not a weaker one. If we assume what is least desirable, that it is a weaker effect, then the exact imitation of the natural tone, with the root in the bass, is the stronger. Thereby arises the possibility of setting a chord with now a stronger, now a weaker effect, hence giving it now more, now less significance. Yet this can be an artistic advantage! For if in the course of a longer phrase, say, one that is to be about ten chords long, it becomes necessary to repeat a chord (after all we have only seven), then this chord will stand out over the others, as I have already indicated. If it is supposed to do so, then all is well; but if it is not supposed to do so, yet there has to be a repetition anyway, then we have to consider how the effect of this repetition can be weakened to such an extent that the repeated chord does not take on undue significance. When, in accordance with this aim, we have a triad in its weaker form follow that same triad in its stronger form, then the weaker cannot easily impair the effect of the stronger; and there is still the possibility that a later, second repetition in the stronger form can be sufficiently effective. Perhaps this is just the reason why in recitatives the sixth chord, the less complete form of the triad, is so frequently used: to express transition, to postpone definite commitment to the key of the following aria. The effect of the sixth chord, however, is not just weaker, it is also different. And this circumstance naturally offers nothing but advantages. Above all: variety, shading.

If it thus proves advantageous to put a tone other than the root in the bass, still that does not mean one is free to waive these advantages at will. For not only are these advantages a necessity of all harmonic writing; not only is it necessary to differentiate the chords in their effects, to shade them according to their value, to give attention to variety: all this also coincides in two respects with the needs of the bass. On the one hand, it is often not otherwise possible, except through use of a sixth chord, to make the bass line more melodic or to give it greater melodic variety; on the other, the conditions imposed by the range of the bass voice will often lead us to choose a sixth chord.

Thus we find the following: Should we start with the aim of making the bass voice leading more melodic and use a sixth chord to that end, then we would get the additional advantage, the unexpected advantage, that the sixth chord does not impair a prior or subsequent appearance of the same triad. In fact these repetitions may become possible only through use of the sixth chord. Moreover, this chord brings variety into the environment of triads in root position. Should we start, conversely, with the aim of securing variety by means of a sixth chord, then there can be the advantage that the bass becomes more melodic and can perhaps remain in a comfortable register or leave an uncomfortable one. Or again, should we start with the aim of choosing a sixth chord because the bass would otherwise enter an uncomfortable register, then the other advantages mentioned could also accrue, even though we did not actively seek them. Of course still other advantages are created besides those discussed here. Moreover, as we shall often see later, the use of the triad inversions is sometimes almost a necessity if we are to make certain harmonic connections and get certain harmonic effects.

The historical origin of the inversions is of course not to be attributed to such reasoning. It is probably not to be attributed to reasoning at all, in spite of the attractiveness of the preceding notions and of still other notions such as these: that the same tones in different arrangements also have to produce usable sounds; and that the overtone series again provides the model for such arrangements, if one disregards enough of the lowest tones. The inversions probably did not even originate by way of harmony in the first place, but rather by way of independent voice leading – that way seems by far the most likely – whereby three or more voices, following their natural courses, came together to form these and similar chords. The ear could approve them because they reminded it of the natural model and were therefore comprehensible.

The term, inversion of a triad, is derived from the inverting of the lowest tone in the schematic form of the triad ('to invert' means: to put a low tone of a chord or interval an octave higher, [or] a high tone an octave lower, while the other chord tones remain in their places); thus the *c* (14*a*) is put an octave higher, over the *g*. The third thereby becomes the lowest tone in this schematic arrangement, and the *first inversion* results. This should actually be called a six-three chord; but, since it is the first in the series of sixth chords, it is called simply the *sixth chord*. Now if we invert in turn the lowest tone of this sixth chord, then the fifth becomes the lowest tone, and we have the *second inversion* (14*b*), *the*

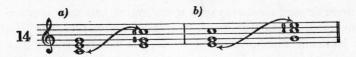

six-four chord. In other words, whenever the *third* is the bass tone, the triad is in the sixth-chord position; whenever the *fifth* is the bass tone, it is in the six-four-chord position.

As far as the harmonic evaluation is concerned, that is, in judging the mere succession of chords, it makes no difference whether we use a triad in root position or in inversion. On the other hand, the inversions lend themselves to creating rhythmic and melodic nuances. For if the root position, as the closest imitation of the natural tone, presents the strongest form of the triad, then the two dissimilar imitations, the inversions, are the weaker forms. It is then self-evident that the three forms of the triad can provide different degrees of accentuation. That one is to make use of this property is an obvious requirement of workmanlike economy. The melodic possibilities other than rhythmic that the inversions offer were already indicated.

(a) THE SIXTH CHORD

In the use of the sixth chord only this one limitation was imposed: it was not to be used at all as the closing chord and seldom as the opening chord. The desire of our forebears to express the tonality as unambiguously as possible made them avoid everything problematic and questionable, especially at the beginning and at the end. Beginning and end were to be definite, clear, unambiguous, and for this purpose the inversion, as the weaker form of the triad, is less suitable than the root position. The infrequent occurrence in the older literature of an opening intentionally vague in tonality (Beethoven's First Symphony, which begins with a seventh chord on the first degree that leads to the subdominant) has only recently found a counterpart in that composers have ventured to fashion even less definite endings. Now although the harmonic significance is not affected by the use of an inversion, as said before, we shall always choose root position for the opening and closing chords of our exercises. We shall do so simply *because* the harmonic significance is not affected: namely, the harmonic significance that was the original reason for beginning and ending with the first degree, the expression of the key. To begin and end with other than the root position may have value for melodic and rhythmic expressiveness or mood, but is of no consequence for the harmonic structure; and such would be the only consideration that could prompt us to arrange opening and closing chords differently – for these the root position was chosen for harmonic reasons.

Otherwise, however, the sixth chord is unconditionally permitted, wherever the same degree is possible in root position, so long as certain stereotyped patterns (cadences, etc.) are not involved. These will be discussed later. In fact the sixth chord offers scarcely any problems, and the only reason we are drawn into a more detailed discussion of it is that restrictions were imposed on the other inversion, the six-four chord. Because, as we shall see, these restrictions are also harmonic, that is, because they influence the harmonic progressions, it is necessary to investigate the reasons why such restrictions are not also attached to the sixth chord, which after all does not differ in its essence – in its derivation – from the six-four chord.

The older theory declares that the bass is the foundation of harmony. This is perfectly true, however, only for that musical epoch when the bass voice always carried the roots of the harmonies used. The foundation of harmony can of course only be formed by the roots of the chords. For in them alone is expressed the forward drive of musical sound (*Klang*) and its capacity for shaping progressions. The roots alone instruct us as to the character and direction of progressions. The roots alone thus provide the basis for what happens harmonically. As soon as the bass voice develops more independence, however, and becomes what I should like to call the second principal voice, the second melody, it has to make use also of tones other than the roots. Then the bass is no longer the foundation of the harmony, rather, at most, the foundation of the harmonic treatment, and this is a great distinction. For if the bass tone is *e*, for example, but *e* as the lowest tone of the sixth chord (*c* and *g*), then this *e* of the bass is completely irrelevant to the character of the connection this chord will make with the next. It is rather the *c*, the root, by which the force and significance of the harmonic progression is measured. Thus the treatment of the harmonic events is referred back to root relationships, even if in the notation it does rest on the bass voice. That the bass voice is accorded unusual significance nevertheless reflects a correct intuition. Its significance is not, to be sure, that it is the foundation of harmony, as I said before; for the bass line is indeed, in relation to the line constituted by the roots, only a sort of lowest middle voice. Its significance is rather just that it was made the foundation of the harmonic treatment. And the justification for that special role may be explained as follows:

In the first place, the bass was once in fact the foundation of harmony, that is, so long as it contained the roots. From that time forward the ear was accustomed to concentrating its attention on the bass. Then there is, in addition, its special prominence as the second outer voice, as an extremity of the body of sound. And yet another important consideration: the analogy with the phenomenon of tone, of which the chord is after all an imitation. In the tone, too, which is indeed composite, the lowest tone is recognized as the one that produces the whole complex, the one for which the total phenomenon is named. The following is to be regarded, however, as the most important reason for the special importance of the bass: Since the lowest tone of the body of sound, the bass tone, lies farthest from the [upper] limit of perception, it has overtones that are clearer and of greater intensity than those of any of the higher voices. Of course the influence of these overtones is less significant than the influence of the tones that form the harmony; the latter are actually sung and even produce overtones of their own. Yet the ear, which does indeed grasp the tone in its totality, unconsciously perceives the influence of the overtones as well. Now if the chord formed by the actual voices corresponds to the overtones of the bass, then the effect is similar to that of any single tone: the total phenomenon is named for the lowest tone, the bass, and is diagnosed as the fulfilment of the necessities of the bass tone. Thus the bass tone, by virtue of the reinforcement brought to it by the upper voices, is here predominant and conspicuous. If, however, the actual tones and the overtones of the bass do not correspond, then clashes are produced among the elements above the bass. These clashes may be felt as barriers, as resistance [to the harmonic flow], over which the will of the bass, the participant whose overtones are most numerous and most audible, prevails. Hence, here again the bass voice stands out with special prominence.

The harmonic treatment is thus justified in taking the bass as its foundation, because this voice plays the leading role in the generation of such harmonic situations. If we now compare the sixth chord and the six-four chord with the triad [in root position], the decisive question in this comparison (since the tones are the same) is the position of the bass. Whatever distinction there is can depend only on this point. And now we find that the overtones of the bass tones (*e* and *g*) are contradicted by the make-up of the chord. Consequently, neither the sixth chord nor the six-four chord are as consonant as a triad in root position. With the sixth chord musical practice takes note of this distinction in treating it as less appropriate for determining the key. Yet there must be still another distinction between the two chords, for the six-four chord is even regarded as relatively dissonant. Since the chord components are identical, the distinction cannot be sought in them, but rather, again, only in the overtones. Now if we also take the overtones of the other chord components into consideration and compare the three sets of overtones with one another, we arrive at the following results: The bass tone of the six-four chord finds earlier, therefore stronger support in the overtones of the other chord components than does the bass tone of the sixth chord. The second overtone of *c* is *g* (supports the root [that is, the root of the overtone triad on *g*]); and likewise the second overtone of *e* is *b* (supports the third). In the sixth chord, on the other hand, the *e* finds support for its fifth only with the fourth overtone of *g*, the *b*; and likewise the octave of *e* appears only as the fourth overtone of *c* [see overleaf].

In the six-four chord, therefore, the setting of the chord tones more closely resembles the overtones of the bass than does that of the sixth chord. In the six-four chord the sound of the bass tone itself finds in the chord tones *less resistance to its will*, or (one could probably also view it this way) its chord tones are better disposed towards *recognizing the predominance of the bass tone* and submitting to it. If we now assume that the bass tone aspires to get, in the actual chord tones, a sound that resembles its own as closely as possible; if, that is, we attribute to it the will that its own overtones prevail: then the bass of the six-four chord has more chances of realizing its aspiration than has the bass of the sixth chord. The six-four chord, then, as well as the sixth chord, contains problems. Both are actually dissonances. But the problem of the six-four chord has

e		e		b	e	$g\sharp$	b	
	g		g		d	g	$\boxed{b}$	d
		c		c		g		c	$\boxed{e}$

Sixth chord

g		g		d	g	b	d	
	c		c		$\boxed{g}$		c	e	g
		e		e		$\boxed{b}$		e	$g\sharp$

Six-four chord

more prospects of being solved, and is consequently *more urgent, more conspicuous*. The problem of the sixth chord is no less real, but it is farther from solution. The movement latent in it is not great enough to compel action and *may be ignored*. Nevertheless, its problem was not completely overlooked; the chord was indeed felt to be less suitable than the root position for defining the key. The problems shown here are of course quite small; they are set off, as it were, in the smallest decimal places. Yet they were apparently perceived; otherwise a distinction would never have been made between the two inversions of a triad. Since the ear has proved so subtly discriminating in the problem occasioned by the overtones of chord tones, we may well hope it will not disappoint us in the further development of music, even if this development should follow a course of which the aestheticians can already predict with certainty that it will lead to the end of art.*

* I read this little digression, which, as will be seen, plays no outstanding role in my book, to a young music historian. Once again I found out how impossible it is to think through all the objections that can be raised. But how useful it would be to an author if he could know these at the right time; for it is generally much easier to refute them than it is to raise them. And it is in fact easy enough to raise objections! Nevertheless, I was disconcerted at first when the following was held up to me: If the six-four chord is a greater dissonance than the sixth chord, because the chord tones of the former support the bass and its overtones, then this means that, generally, a chord is that much more dissonant, the greater its [the bass tone's] chance of becoming by virtue of this support a fundamental. And conversely: the smaller this chance, the less dissonant the chord. If this is true, however, a dominant seventh chord, whose bass tone can never become a fundamental, should be less dissonant than the six-four chord.

I recovered quickly and refuted the objection; but I did not present all the grounds for refutation – just one, and not the strongest one at that. They may all be included here: (1) I did not say that the *dissonance* increases or decreases. I showed, rather, why these two chords are not perfectly identical with a consonance. This had to be pointed out, since it is indeed puzzling, why three tones can in one arrangement be purely consonant, while in the others they are relatively dissonant – a situation that has no

The sixth chord has, then, as I have said, no harmonic significance, but rather melodic; it is suitable for introducing variety into the bass line and, consequently, into the other voices. It may be used freely except for one, small, relative restriction, based on the reasoning to follow. We established earlier that the third is considered for doubling only after the other two tones: because it appears after them in the overtone series, and because, since it is relatively prominent as the determiner of mode, its doubling would thus only emphasize still more an already conspicuous sound. Hence, it will be clear that, generally, if one wishes to get a well-balanced sound in which nothing is unnecessarily prominent, *doubling of the third in the sixth chord* would be superfluous, that is, *of little advantage*, since it is already especially conspicuous as the bass tone and would acquire even more prominence if doubled. Of course this restriction holds only as long as it is not necessary also to have the third in one of the upper voices, a necessity we shall soon encounter. One does what is necessary; what is superfluous should be avoided.

In Example 15 the sixth chord on the Ist degree is presented in various arrangements, in 15*a* with the octave doubled, in 15*b* with the fifth doubled. The pupil should first practice writing these chords and then those on the other degrees in the same manner.

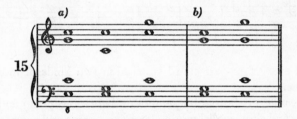

Here, for the first time, we double the fifth. Consequently, we must consider

---

parallel anywhere else in harmony. (2) I showed the *distinction* between these two chords. This distinction is not that one is more dissonant than the other, but rather that the problem of the one is *more readily solved than that of the other*. Perhaps our forebears were better able to deal with the clearer problem, simply because it is clearer, than they were with the unclear one, whose implications (*Willen*) they did not understand. (3) The bass of the dominant seventh chord has no need to find support for its urge to become a fundamental; for it *is* indeed already a fundamental. It is precisely the fundamental of the tones *actually sounding*. (4) The dominant seventh chord (this is the reason I gave the young music historian) is already dissonant just by virtue of the tones actually sung. There is, then, no need to appeal only to the overtones on defining the dominant seventh as dissonant. It is already more dissonant than the six-four chord because the tones actually sung and absolutely audible create dissonance, whereas the dissonance of the sixth and six-four chords is produced only by the scarcely audible tones, the overtones.

I relate this experience here merely because it seems to me typical of the way objections are raised.

[This footnote was deleted from the seventh edition of 1966 (see *supra*, Translator's Preface, p. xvi).]

here a problem that arises when in the connection of sixth chords the fifth is doubled.

Parallel Octaves and Fifths

Chord connection produces three kinds of relationship between two moving voices:

1. While one voice moves, the other holds (*oblique motion*), Example 16a;
2. While one voice goes down, the other goes up (*contrary motion*), Example 16b;
3. Both voices move in the same direction, both go simultaneously up or down (*parallel motion*), Example 16c.

In almost every four-part chord connection two kinds of motion appear, often all three.

Thus, Example 17 shows oblique motion between soprano and alto, tenor and alto, bass and alto; parallel motion between soprano and tenor; and contrary motion between soprano and bass, tenor and bass.

Although the older theory permitted oblique and contrary motion unconditionally, it prohibited parallel motion, in some cases conditionally, in others absolutely. The latter prohibitions are known as parallel octaves and parallel fifths.

Example 18a shows parallel octaves, 18b parallel fifths.

The pertinent laws defined what was prohibited as follows: Whenever two voices go from one octave relation by parallel motion into another octave relation, or from one fifth relation by parallel motion into another fifth relation, the result is *parallel octaves* and *parallel fifths* (open octaves and fifths, open parallels).

The more rigorous version of this rule reads: The parallel movement of two voices into a perfect consonance (octave or fifth) is forbidden.

This version forbids what is called *hidden octaves* and *hidden fifths* as well, and so could also be formulated this way: Whenever two voices moving parallel from any simultaneous relation whatsoever (thus also from the octave or the fifth) come together in an octave or fifth, open or hidden parallel octaves or fifths result.

Open octaves or fifths were absolutely forbidden, yet certain hidden ones were conditionally allowed. Chiefly those that could not be avoided. (*Not kennt kein Verbot!* – Necessity knows no law!) There are, for example, among the octaves* those that almost always appear in the connection of V with I

---

* Although the abbreviated forms 'octaves' and 'fifths' for 'parallel octaves' and 'parallel fifths' are quite incorrect, they are nevertheless so commonly used that we may tolerate them, as we tolerate everything in language that is common usage.

(Example 20a). Here the hidden octaves could only be avoided if the bass were to go down to c, which is, however, too low. Nor can one easily get around the hidden fifths between alto and tenor (Example 20b), if the soprano melody has to be g–b–c.

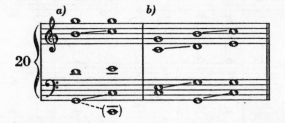

Hence, exceptions were established, declaring: Hidden octaves and fifths are permissible provided they occur between two middle voices, or at most between a middle and an outer voice, so that they attract less attention. And: hidden octaves are better when one of the two voices moves by step and the other leaps a fifth or a fourth. Or: it is 'least objectionable' when the upper voice is the one that moves by step, say, from the seventh to the octave, or from the third to the fourth. Then too: parallel fifths are 'milder' if a harsh dissonance draws attention away from them. (They are less bothersome than the harsh dissonance, nevertheless more rigorously forbidden!) And then one spoke of 'horn fifths', 'Mozart fifths', and – in contrast with such fifths, which those with good ears overlooked – 'intended' fifths, that is, fifths that those without good ears at least saw in time. Yet: when one may do something intentionally that is so fundamentally and rigorously forbidden, and why – that was shrewdly kept quiet. It would be dangerously close to asking whether an intended murder is more pardonable than an unintended!

Horn fifths

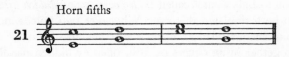

These commandments were founded upon the contention that the independence of the voices is cancelled by such parallel movement. That was the more intelligent form of justification. The other simply declared that such progressions sound bad. These two arguments were reconciled by the proposition that parallel octaves and fifths sound bad because the independence of voices is cancelled. Now it is perhaps not incorrect to say that, with parallel octaves, in the precise moment of going from the one chord to the next, the independence of the voices is apparently lost. But to declare that they sound bad, or even that they sound bad *because* the independence of voices is cancelled, is absolutely wrong; for parallel octaves are used as doubling, sometimes also for reinforcement. Naturally, because of the *good* sound; no one at all would have written parallel octaves because of the bad sound. And the mixture stops on the organ give each voice not only octaves but also fifths, all sounding simultaneously.* For the sake of the stronger sound; but, since it is a question of artistic beauty, the stronger sound is also the beautiful sound. Therefore, that parallel octaves sound bad in themselves is a completely untenable position. This leaves us with the other notion, that they cancel the independence of voices. To be sure, whenever two voices sing the same thing they are not absolutely independent. Whenever they sing approximately the same thing, namely, octaves (the two tones of an octave are not quite identical), the content of what they sing is of course the same, but the sound is different. Now if two voices sing for a long time exclusively in unison or in octaves, then we could speak of a relative lack of independence in the content. (Even here, though, with regard to the unison, we should consider the question of mixture of timbres, to which each voice contributes in a thoroughly independent manner.) If, however, each of two voices sings something completely different in content from the other, and they come together on the same track, so to speak, only in one exceptional moment or in a few such moments, then perhaps it is possible, anyway, to say that in such moments their independence is to a certain extent diminished; but to say that they actually lose their independence is surely a pedantic exaggeration, which ignores the fact that the voices were all the while independent of each other in content, save for these few moments. These moments, however, apparently do not keep us from distinguishing clearly the essential difference in content. This exaggeration also ignores the fact that the voices were at *all* times distinct from each other in *tone quality. Here again,* therefore, *one could hardly speak of cancelling absolutely the independence of voices.*

It would be more correct to speak of something different, of conditions, the fulfilment of which is *requisite to every good handicraft:* Assuming that, after mature consideration and examination, one has determined the number of voices [for one's writing], then this decision should be proved correct in every single moment of the piece, in that fewer voices would clearly not be enough to

* This chapter [i.e. this section on parallel octaves and fifths] was published in the August, 1910, issue of the magazine *Die Musik.* It became the subject of debate, and I learned of some of the 'objections' that were raised. These pertain to the mixture stops of the organ, as well as to organum at the fifth and parallel thirds (see the footnotes [*infra,* pp. 66, 67]). It is a pleasure to have the opportunity to reply to them. I said, 'the mixture stops give each voice . . .' – it could have been taken for granted that, if I know of the mixtures, I also know when they are used. Even if I do not say explicitly: in the full organ. It is of course clear that, when these stops are used, they give 'all voices . . . etc.' Now comes this objection: yes, but in the full organ, and then they [parallels] are not heard. This is a priceless objection. [The mixtures] are added because they are not heard! But why use them then? Why then are precisely fifths, etc., added to the voices, and not Bible verses or cannon shots? Answer: 'They are not heard as fifths, but only as fullness, as sharpness, as reinforcement of sound.' Yes, but they are then heard *nevertheless;* as *what* should they be heard, anyway? Wherein should one hear the effect of a change in timbre, if not in the change of timbre itself? As voice leading? Indeed, does one then hear octave doublings as voice leading?

[This essay on parallel octaves and fifths was not published in the August issue, but rather in the *2tes Oktoberheft,* 1910 (pp. 96–105). In the August issue, cited here by Schoenberg, appeared some of his 'Aphorismen'.]

present everything, while more would hardly add anything significant. Accordingly, every voice should have something to do at every moment *that it alone does*. Thus, if in a thin harmonic texture the aim is to go from *d* to *e*, and one voice is enough to accomplish it, then – *if going from d to e was in fact and exclusively the aim* – it is *superfluous, that is, bad,* if another voice also goes from *d* to *e*. If one cannot think of anything else to do with this other voice, it should rest. But that one cannot think of anything else is in general not a sign of superlative skill. One then has to make an effort to do something else with it! If, however, the step from *d* to *e*, for which one voice indeed suffices, is *not* the *chief aim*, if the chief aim is rather *to get the sound of an octave* between two voices that both go from *d* to *e*, then the question of independent voices is no longer pertinent; it is now simply a question of the sound. Therefore, since parallel octaves neither sound bad nor absolutely cancel the independence of voices, it is senseless to throw them out of the art with the vehemence (*Pathos*) that the apostle of beauty brings to this his appointed task. They have never submitted completely to this treatment anyway, for they have popped up again and again in the literature.

In our exercises, devoted exclusively to harmonic considerations, the task of doubling to create sound effects can of course never be assigned. Therefore, we shall strictly avoid parallel octaves in these exercises. There is another reason, suggested earlier, which will bring us to the same decision, to reject the use in our harmony exercises, not only of parallel octaves, but of parallel fifths as well. Up to about the middle of the nineteenth century parallel fifths and octaves were almost entirely avoided and even since then have been used relatively seldom; *school assignments* that overstepped this rule would then produce stylistically incongruous results. And the pupil does not yet know the harmonic means by which to create balance, whereas one who does know these means can ignore the prohibitions. The pupil is still not composing; he is only working out harmonic exercises whose average plausibility can be maintained only if he is always working for at least average quality. The teacher, since he cannot teach the pupil absolute perfection, must at least keep him away as long as possible from that which is questionable.

Justifying the prohibition of parallel fifths gave the theorists more trouble. Thus their justification is so much the easier to refute. It was declared that progressions in parallel fifths sound bad; or that, since the fifth is an overtone, it is as it were only a shadow of the fundamental if it moves parallel with the latter; if the fifth is to appear independent, then its movement should differ from that of the fundamental; and so on, in the same vein. Curiously, progressions in fourths were only conditionally forbidden, although the fourth and fifth are identical as far as harmonic content is concerned.

Were this content considered, then parallel fourths should also be forbidden. Strictly speaking, the connection of the degrees involved could not then be allowed in the first place; for the harshness (*Härte*) of the content, that is, the harmonic harshness, can only be attributed to that which is harmonic, to the degrees. Parallel fourths are permitted, however, if they are 'covered' by a lower third (Example 22c). Could not parallel fifths be just as freely used if they were also covered by such a lower third (Example 22*d*)? Harmonically, there is no distinction at all. Now, since this parallel movement does not sound bad and parallel thirds and sixths even sound good, since all other parallel movement sounds at least conditionally good, is it then just parallel movement in fifths that sounds absolutely bad? Parallel octaves, for example, embody one extreme: namely (in content) the complete cancellation of independence of voices, and

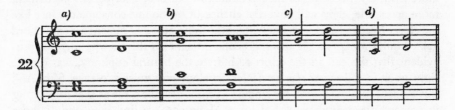

(acoustically) progression in the most perfect consonance.[1] Nevertheless, parallel octaves are at least conditionally allowed as doubling on account of the *good* sound. And parallel thirds and sixths are likewise permitted, even though they, too, take away the independence of voices with respect to content, whereas, acoustically, they are progressions in consonances less perfect than the fifth! Therefore, it is not just progression of the most perfect consonances that is allowed, for thirds are less perfect than fifths; nor is it parallel movement, say, just of imperfect consonances that is permitted, for octaves are more perfect than fifths. And all objections one raises against parallel fifths apply just as well either to parallel octaves or to parallel thirds. *Consequently, there must be other grounds* [for the exclusion of parallel fifths].

I will try to resolve this question in a simpler manner.

The evolution of polyphony can be envisioned as follows: The first push may have been given by someone's urge to participate in singing songs that were ordinarily sung by a single performer. Two or more sang the same melody. Were precisely the same type of voices to sing together, for example, just low male voices, then it is fairly obvious that only unison singing could be considered pure, that is, singing identical tones, the most perfect consonance. If women's voices were added and the melody lay neither very high nor very low, then the second possibility was manifest: singing in the second most perfect consonance, in octaves. But if the melody lay in such a range that it went too low for the high male and female voices or too high for the low voices, then there was the need to find something else for these voices. As long as actual polyphony had not been invented (if one does not wish to regard singing in octaves as already relatively polyphonic), nothing was left but to sing the same melody beginning on some other consonant tone. Since the unison and the octave had already been used, the ear had *necessarily to choose the next most perfect consonance, the fifth.* Thus began *organum at the fifth,* or what is here the

[1 *Vollkommenste Konsonanz:* most (nearly) perfect consonance, or the highest degree of agreement between two tones. In the next (long) paragraph below, we find that the unison is the 'most perfect consonance'.]

same thing, organum at the fourth.* That the third was not employed for the same purpose until much later, that indeed the third had not yet won recognition as a consonance at a yet much later time, is evidence in support of the hypothesis repeatedly mentioned in this book: namely, that the distinction between dissonances and consonances is only gradual, one of degree; that dissonances are nothing else but more remote consonances whose analysis gives the ear more trouble on account of their remoteness; but once analysis has made them more accessible, they will have the chance of becoming consonances just like the closer overtones. (Incidentally, that the unprepared dominant seventh chord gained quick acceptance is an additional argument for this viewpoint.) It is thus evident that the ear, in the effort to imitate the natural euphony, was on the right track in following *this particular* development: unison, octave, fifth. And it is evident that the reason for singing in fifths was the same as that for singing in octaves: the sound pleased the ear. Moreover, we find here one of those peculiar coincidences that so often give the secrets of acoustics a cabalistic appearance: namely, that *singing in fifths, or in fourths, was completely in accord with the limitations of the human voice.* For the tenor range lies on the average a fifth above that of the bass, the alto approximately a fourth to a fifth above the tenor, and the soprano likewise a fifth above the alto. Thus, we see that a genuinely artistic kind of solution was instinctively found here: two flies with one swat.

The subsequent evolution I envisage as follows: It was presumably soon after the third was recognized as a consonance that the possibility of contrary and oblique motion was discovered. In addition to parallel unisons, octaves, and fifths, there arose the possibility of parallel thirds and probably soon thereafter,

---

* Just now [1911] as I am preparing these pages for publication, I am delighted to find my conception of this stage of the evolution confirmed by so astute and deep a thinker as Riemann. Consulting Meyer's *Konversationslexikon* I find there nearly word for word what is written here as the result of my own reasoning: 'Actually, organum was not yet real polyphony, but rather doubling at the fifth, *the most natural step forward from the octave doubling of voices that had long been practiced.*' I find also in the *Lexikon* an explanation of the *fauxbourdon,* of which I was totally ignorant. (The reader must forgive me; I am no scholar [*Wissenschaftler*]. I am self-taught and can only think.) *Fauxbourdon* meant singing in sixth chords. That is indeed the next step in the evolution! And Riemann says also that soon afterward the true principle of polyphony was discovered, contrary motion. That is precisely what I did not know, but only guessed; for I have never yet read a history of music. – On the question of organum I would like to mention something else: I am told that 'scholarship' '[*Wissenschaft*'] doubts whether there has ever really been such a thing. That is what scholarship always does when something does not fit into its scheme of things. Organum is, however, so self-evident that, if it by chance had not actually existed, we should now invent it and insert it retroactively into the past. But I believe it must have already existed – the doubt of scholarship reassures me in my belief.

[Meyer's *Konversationslexikon* (the edition containing Riemann's article) was unavailable for collation. In Schoenberg's youth this encyclopedia seems to have been one of his chief sources of information about music. See Willi Reich, *Schoenberg – a critical biography,* trans. Leo Black (New York: Praeger, 1971), p. 3.]

as I have said, the possibility also of contrary and oblique motion, hence, an immense enrichment of means. Now it seems to me the following train of thought, only too firmly rooted in man's nature, gives psychological explanation of the question [of forbidden fifths]:

Singing in octaves and fifths no doubt satisfied in a thoroughly natural way the taste of the time; it was in accord with the nature of sound and with the nature of man, thus it was beautiful. Nevertheless, the possibility of adding thirds* to the octaves and fifths and of using contrary and oblique motion very likely produced a heady enthusiasm that came to hold everything of an earlier time to be bad, although it was merely outmoded; such enthusiasm we can indeed observe in every great advance – not only in art. [The enthusiast] so completely forgets to be grateful for the preparatory work done by the predecessors that he hates that work and does not stop to think that the present advance would be impossible without it. Yes, even if that work was full of errors. And the contempt for what is outmoded is just as great as it is unjustified. Whoever keeps a correct sense of proportion will say: I personally would not like to do what is outmoded because I know the advantages of what is new, and because it would be untimely. One should be untimely only in running on ahead of the times, but not in limping along behind. We are thus justified in making fun of someone who today writes 'gegen dem'; but we should know that, since 'gegen' was in fact formerly used with both the dative and accusative cases, 'gegen dem' is not false, only outmoded.[1] And Schaunard was right when he characterized the style of his fellow Bohemian, Barbemuche, with a single word, 'hinfüro', which allegedly often appears in Barbemuche's novel.[2] I think that such

---

* Here an objection was raised: why did not the same fate, prohibition, also overtake the parallel thirds? Elsewhere I have cited this very case, parallel thirds, as an argument for my view; I left it out here only because it did not seem essential. Since it is brought up as an objection, I will examine it. First: Parallel fifths were indeed not justifiably thrown out of music; their rejection was unjustified. Now one cannot even maintain that a correct perception applied to an analogous case must lead necessarily to another correct judgment. But to demand that an illogical judgment absolutely must repeat itself in another illogical judgment – that indeed goes too far! Secondly: It was not even necessary to prohibit fifths, for they were just too artless when used as the exclusive harmonization. Thus, thirds did not have to be forbidden either, for they are good if not used exclusively. But as proof that, where they were used exclusively, they were indeed regarded as a less significant method of voice leading, we may cite the expression, 'austerzen' [adding thirds], which is explicitly based on the idea of true, actual voices. The thirds are only filler voices, however, in the doubled counterpoints: sound effects (*Klangliches*) that were added without contributing, just by virtue of their addition, anything special to voice leading. Finally, though, parallel thirds (used exclusively) and parallel sixths are also felt to be artless, yes, even banal. Proof: folk music whose polyphony consists of scarcely more than these parallels. They are perhaps banal, but not impossible, and can on occasion (as in *Siegfried*) be artistic.

[1 The preposition *gegen* is now used only with the accusative case: *gegen den*.]

[2 The up-to-date German word is *hinfort* (henceforth). Schaunard and Barbemuche are characters in the mid-nineteenth-century play *La Vie de Bohème* and novel *Scènes de la Bohème* by Henri Mürger. The libretto of Puccini's opera is based on these works.]

observations concerning the human nature of the artist are just as important for judging the evolution of art as is physics. One must reflect that art has set its course not only by the nature of tones but by the nature of man as well, that it is a compromise between these two factors, attempts at mutual accommodation. And since the tone, the inanimate material, does no accommodating, it is up to us. But we sometimes find accommodation difficult. Hence, when we have succeeded, we often overestimate our accomplishment and underestimate the accomplishment of those who took the preparatory step, a step perhaps as great and as difficult as the one we have taken.

Such must have been the case with forbidden fifths. If the joy in the accomplishment keeps company with the demands of the guild, the child of this union can only be orthodoxy. Orthodoxy, which no longer has need to win recognition for the novel accomplishment, now assumes the task of holding fast to the accomplishment through exaggeration. It does, to be sure, think through and exploit the implications of its premises; through its exaggeration, however, it not only leads to errors, but also erects a bulwark against any other innovation. Thus one can well imagine how the following statements were interpreted: 'It is no longer necessary to compose merely in octaves and fifths'; 'thirds can be added to octaves and fifths'; 'contrary and oblique motion can be used, as well as parallel motion'. One can well imagine, I say, how these were interpreted to read thus: 'It is bad to compose in octaves and fifths'; 'the third must be added to octaves and fifths'; 'contrary and oblique motion are better than parallel motion'. Now if it be considered that such interpretations were given and accepted as rules, as rules whose violation placed one under an interdict, it can be seen how easily their origin could be forgotten: how easily it could be forgotten that *octaves and fifths were not in themselves bad,* but on the contrary *were in themselves good*; that they had merely come to be considered outmoded, primitive, relatively artless; that there was *no physical nor aesthetic reason,* however, why they should not on occasion still be used. And if one considers that these rules, in the form 'Thou shalt not . . .,' were spread abroad over centuries, then it becomes clear that the ear forgot the sound once found to be euphonious, and its use aroused antagonism because of the *oddness the new always has about it.* I am saying that, since progression in parallel octaves and fifths was not practiced for centuries, the ear was disposed to regard the occasional appearance of such connections as new,* as odd, whereas the opposite is

* This circumstance also speaks absolutely against (I can't help it: the *circumstance* speaks) those pseudo-modern methods that set entire melodies and the like in fifths to profit from this newness and oddness. To me the effect is unpleasant, not because it seems new, nor because it is actually old; nor again because the merit of such progressions is no greater than that of the sixth-chord progressions that the predecessors of such innovators wrote in similar passages. I find it unpleasant, perhaps, because of the mischievousness and ostentation apparent in such methods: that sort of thing is not noble; very probably, though, it is unpleasant to me primarily because I find, more and more, something right about the prohibition of fifths, something that was just wrongly interpreted. I mean the aversion to the consonance, which is perhaps inversely identical with the urge to introduce the more remote consonances, the dissonances, into composition. [This is a new footnote, added in the revised edition.]

actually the case: they were old, only forgotten. And so it is no evidence against the view presented here whenever a musician says: 'Yes, but I *still* notice these fifths. They call attention to themselves. And I think they sound unpleasant.' The new does indeed always attract attention, and its sound is considered unpleasant, although it is not.

And now, the hidden octaves and fifths. They are explainable quite simply on grounds of orthodoxy: just in order not to write any open fifths or octaves parallel movement into these perfect consonances was altogether avoided. Every attempt *to deal differently with hidden parallels may be disregarded.* Not merely because *even the open parallels do not sound bad,* but above all because this law *has been nothing but a phantom of the textbooks,* whereas in practice, that is in the masterworks, *it has been more often violated than observed.*

How then should the pupil approach this problem of parallels? I want to deal with this question rather thoroughly now, because I intend later simply to refer back to this general discussion without going into its details every time. The question could be raised: if parallel fifths and octaves are not bad, why then should the pupil not be permitted to write them? My answer is this: he will be permitted to write them, but not until a later stage. The course of instruction should lead through the historical evolution. Should it not do so, should it give unsupported final results in the form of rules, then the petrifaction of these results, uprooted from the evolutionary thought processes that produced them, could lead to errors similar to those I have just exposed. And as instruction can restrain further development through too strict formulation, so it would also obstruct the view back into the past and would make incomprehensible much of what was once vital.

For a similar reason I am no friend of the new orthography, although I understand very well the practical advantage of brevity, and understand very well that the effort to express in spelling only what one actually hears spoken is in part justified. Nevertheless, I find it questionable to cull out so unsparingly those symbols that often manifest rudiments of former syllables. The possibility of recalling the root word is easily lost thereby, and it is inaccessible to us whenever we want to trace the true, the original meaning of an expression. And the danger arises that our script will become too poor in such points of reference as could indicate to anyone the way back to the origin. The origin will finally be known to historians alone, and will then have disappeared from the living awareness of everyone.

Should harmony instruction proceed in a similarly thoughtless manner, then many problems of voice leading in the older masterworks would be beyond our understanding. And another thing. In the work of arranging and editing, so often necessary in those older works where the harmony is indicated only by figured basses – works which we make more accessible, the more genuinely we reproduce their style – the use of inappropriate techniques of voice leading would inevitably produce incongruence between the content and the form of realization, incongruence offensive to the sensitive listener. Such incongruence would also result, were the pupil to work out his assignments without regard for these prohibitions.

Of course if one were to write a harmony text that expressed only the harmonic taste of us ultramodernists, allowing what we do, forbidding what we avoid, then all these considerations here could be discarded. Today we have already come so far as to make no more distinction between consonances and dissonances. Or, if a distinction remains, it is at most that we like to use consonances less. This is possibly just a reaction to the preceding epochs of consonance, an exaggeration perhaps. But to draw the conclusion that consonances are forbidden because they no longer appear in the works of this or that composer would lead to errors similar to those produced by our predecessors' injunction against fifths. As far as I personally am concerned – but only because and so long as I do not know better – I could easily say to a pupil: Any simultaneous combination of sounds, any progression is possible. Nevertheless, even today, I feel that here, too, there are certain conditions on which my choice of this or that dissonance depends. Today we do not yet stand far enough away from the events of our time to be able to apprehend the laws behind them. Too much that is unessential crowds into the foreground of our awareness, covering up the essential. If I stand in the middle of a mountain pasture, I see every blade of grass. But that is worth nothing to me if perhaps I am looking for the path to the summit. If I stand at some distance the blades of grass escape me, but I shall probably see the path. I hold the opinion that the path, even this path, will somehow connect logically with the stretch already travelled. I believe that in the harmony of us ultramodernists will ultimately be found the same laws that obtained in the older harmony, only correspondingly broader, more generally conceived.

Therefore, it seems to me of great importance that we conserve the knowledge and experience of the past. Precisely this former knowledge and experience will show, I hope, how correct is the path along which we are searching. Moreover: should I allow the pupil from the outset to ignore the restriction on fifths, then I should have just as much right to disregard all those instructions that deal with the treatment of dissonance, tonality, modulation, etc. These, too, have now been superseded. Here again we may not overlook the fact that only the small group of ultramodern composers goes so far. Almost all great masters of our time – Mahler, Strauss, Reger, Pfitzner – still adhere largely, for example, to tonality. A theory, a course of instruction that advocated only the goals of a presently small group, however rigorous the logic with which it were formulated, could be not unjustly criticized for being partisan. And precisely that which I aim to give [here], although it does not serve a particular party – or, far more, for that very reason – arrives at results considered correct by the group that thinks as I do. My aim is just that: to show that one *must* arrive at these results.

Thus the pupil may as well follow the path taken by the historical evolution. If he is learning harmony only out of an interest in the music literature, if he only wishes to gain thereby a better understanding of the masterworks, then for him it does not really matter, for the short time he is himself creating musical patterns, whether he works out exercises in a modern or an unmodern style. What does matter, however, is that he be led to a correct attitude toward what is new. This purpose is accomplished by a course that, in its freedom from aesthetic preconceptions, reveals the mortality of many an eternal law, and gives thereby an unobstructed view of the evolution of the beautiful: that is, a view of how conceptions change; of how, by virtue of these changes, the new, which the ear of tradition proscribes, becomes the old, which is then pleasant to the ear; of how this new [tradition] in turn denies another, still newer innovation, which is in turn temporarily proscribed, access to the ear. If the pupil is a composer, however, he should patiently wait to see in which direction his development, his nature will take him. He should not wish to write things for which only full maturity can assume responsibility, things that artists have written almost against their will, in obeying the compulsion of their development – [in obeying this compulsion] but not out of the poorly disciplined wantonness of the one who, insecure in matters of form, writes arbitrarily.

The pupil will, therefore, avoid open octaves and fifths as long as he has need of instruction. But he may use them at such time as his inclination, taste, and artistic understanding make it possible for him to take responsibility for them. Hidden octaves he may write now as he chooses, with a few exceptions that will be discussed as the occasion warrants. Hidden fifths he may use at any time, without restriction.

Connection of the Triads with the Sixth Chords, the Sixth Chords with the Triads, and the Sixth Chords with One Another

We now turn to the task of examining and working out the chord connections indicated in the following three tables (A, B, C):

A. Triad of   I with the sixth chords of I, III, IV, V, VI
    Triad of   II with the sixth chords of II, IV, V, VI, VII
    Triad of III with the sixth chords of III, V, VI, I etc.
    Triad of VII with the sixth chord of   III;

B. Sixth chord of   I with the triads of I, III, IV, V, VI
    Sixth chord of   II with the triads of II, IV, V, VI, VII etc.
    Sixth chord of VII with the triad of III;

C. Sixth chord of   I with the sixth chords of III, IV, V, VI
    Sixth chord of   II with the sixth chords of IV, V, VI, VII etc.
    Sixth chord of VII with the sixth chord of III.

The pupil will do well to work his way through everything in these tables (in as many keys as possible). Here for the first time there are difficulties in voice leading, and the pupil will best deal with such at once. It is well that he get the necessary practice here at the outset, so that he will not fail later in more important matters – because he cannot manage voice leading.

Only the Ist degree is worked out in Example 23. The pupil should now work out the other degrees according to this model (do not forget other keys!). In some cases he will encounter parallel octaves and fifths and must discover how to evade them. In some others it will be necessary to dispense, in part, with the sustaining of common tones because otherwise the superfluous doubling of the third would result.

The connection of a triad with one of its own inversions and vice versa is called *exchange* (I–I_6 or II_6–II or IV–IV_4^6 or V_6–V_4^6). With no harmonic change

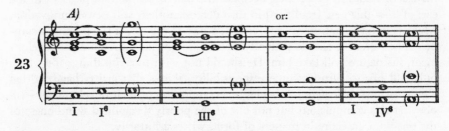

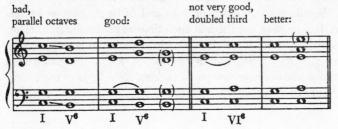

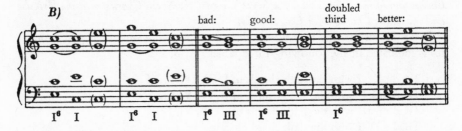

(hence, exchanges have only melodic value) two or more voices, one of which in our present examples is the bass, exchange roles.

The pupil will do well to work out every pair of chords twice (at least twice!): once by doubling the octave of the sixth chord, once by doubling the fifth. This will always bring about different solutions and often new difficulties. The pupil should search these out and as often as possible find more than two solutions; for with almost every arrangement something different appears. In addition he should try doubling the fifth of the final chord.

The VIIth degree requires special attention.

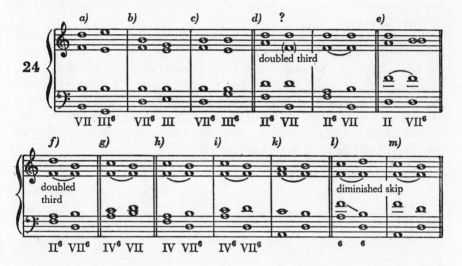

In Example 24*d* we meet a new situation. The chord of the IInd degree is here a sixth chord. Hence, the *f* necessary for preparing the diminished fifth is found only in the bass, which must move to *b* in the next chord. Thus, the diminished fifth cannot be prepared unless the *f* appears also in an upper voice. Therefore, the *f*, the third, must here be doubled. With this it is worth noting how necessity cancels an instruction. The situation is similar in Examples 24*i* and 24*l*. In 24*i* the *c* of the tenor could not go to *b* because of the parallel octaves between tenor and soprano, nor to *f* because this tone, being a dissonance, should not be doubled. The only other alternative is to take the *c* to *d*, that is to double the third in the sixth chord of VII. An alternate solution to the same problem is shown in 24*k*, where the third of the first chord is doubled. In 24*l* considerations similar to those that applied to 24*i* compel the tenor to leap a diminished fifth. Such a leap should be avoided, according to the old rules, because it is unmelodic, or perhaps more correctly, because it is difficult to sing in tune. And we shall indeed generally avoid such leaps (as I said before), so as not to disturb the stylistic balance. But when necessity compels us to make such a leap (which, after all, is unavoidable in the bass), then, wherever possible, we shall try to 'resolve' the dissonance (i.e. the intonation difficulty) contained in a diminished or an augmented interval. This is best done by taking the *b*, the 'ascending leading tone', up to *c*, and the *f*, the 'descending leading tone', down to *e*. Since that is not always possible, however, some other possibilities are also given in Example 25 (measures 5–10).

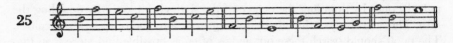

Close attention to such details as these makes it possible to achieve formal rounding and seems to me therefore quite appropriate in laying a foundation for the development of the sense of form. Naturally the exercises will still not sound especially 'gripping', but they no longer have to sound quite as stiff as the very first ones.

The pupil may now use the sixth chord in making his little phrases and may take the following as his guidelines: A sixth chord can be written wherever there can be a triad – only the opening and closing chords (always the Ist degree) have to appear in root position. If it is necessary in the course of a phrase to repeat a degree, it is a good idea sometimes to choose a sixth chord. But it is not good to use too many sixth chords. The phrases can now be eight to twelve chords long; to make them longer is superfluous since too many repetitions would then be necessary. Example 26 shows a few such phrases.

In choosing between a sixth chord and the root position one must naturally also take into consideration the melodic line of the bass. In general the bass should not be sustained, wherever it is possible to do otherwise. Sometimes that can be avoided, as in Example 26a, by introducing an octave leap to change the register, sometimes by choosing a sixth chord instead of the root position or vice versa. Moreover, repetitions of a bass tone can cripple the progression, even if one or two other tones intervene. If, for example, in 26a I had written the VIth degree as a sixth chord instead of in root position, it would have done little good even to have leaped to the lower octave. Repetitions of that sort the pupil should avoid, if at all possible, and the teacher should correct them. For wherever, as here, the repetition is not justified by a motive, it impairs the progression. The situation is different, however, in 26e, where the repetition of *c* and *e* could hardly be disturbing: not so much because one time two chords intervene, the other time three, as, far more, because the line continues after each of the repeated bass tones in another direction. In judging whether a bass line is good or not, the melodic principle one should consider first is just that of variation. Whenever repetition of tones is unavoidable, some other tones should at least intervene, or the direction of the line should change. The pupil will also do well to keep an eye out, even now, for the highest tone of a line. This tone should always be treated as the climax, that is, it should appear only once; for its repetition is, in general, more acutely disturbing than that of other, less noticeable tones.

(b) THE SIX-FOUR CHORD

That different treatment is proper for the six-four chord, and why, was mentioned earlier (see pp. 56–8). We should review here still another reason given by the older theory. The fourth was considered an imperfect consonance, indeed, even a dissonance. This view reflects a correct intuition; for the fourth does actually appear among the first overtones, but in the opposite direction [i.e. its root is on top – C-c-$\overline{g}$-$\overline{c}$] and is therefore a less simple consonance than those intervals produced by the ascending order of the overtones. In almost every consonant chord, however, we find the fourth between two of the voices and regard it as a dissonance only whenever its lower tone is in the bass. The older theory says it is permitted if a lower fifth or third 'covers it'; in all other cases it is to be prepared and resolved as a dissonance. A unique claim is thus made for the fourth: that its two tones form now a dissonance (when the lower tone is in the bass), now a consonance (when it is 'covered'); furthermore, in another position, in the inversion, the same two tones produce a perfect consonance, the fifth (concerning inversion [of intervals], the following rule holds: Inversion of every perfect consonance yields a perfect consonance, inversion of every dissonance yields a dissonance). That is too contradictory, not simple enough to be natural.

To me the following explanation seems simpler: A bass tone that is not at the same time the fundamental seems to have the urge to replace the chord tones with its own overtones, that is, to become itself the fundamental. Now, as has already been shown (see page 58), the bass tone of the six-four chord finds plentiful support for its urge in the overtones of the other chord components.

There is then in the six-four chord a conflict between its (outward) form, its sound, and its (inner) constitution. Whereas its outward form indicates, for example, the Ist degree, its constitution, its instinct demands the Vth degree. This conflict may indeed have a certain similarity to that which is thought to reside in the dissonance, since the latter also strives for a change of the fundamental. Nevertheless, whereas in the actual dissonance tones sound together that can never in any arrangement be consonant, the tones of the six-four chord are in other arrangements absolutely consonant (triad, sixth chord). The demand of the six-four chord for resolution, to be treated as a dissonance, is thus by no means as stormy as that of a real dissonance. The six-four chord and the actual dissonance have only this in common, that in both lies a conflict that attracts attention, that seems to have a right to special consideration, to special treatment. This special treatment [of the six-four chord] would not have to consist just in preparation or resolution, as with the dissonance. And what is called preparation and resolution of the six-four chord has little similarity to the preparation and resolution of the seventh chord. But this much is certain, anyway, that the six-four chord, whose problem could be felt but not understood, was always treated in a special way. This fact alone would have been enough to give it a unique position. The problems inherent in the six-four chord may be less significant or different; the method by which it was treated perhaps exaggerates these problems, perhaps without even dealing adequately with them. But, whether its unique position has its origin in convention or in nature, that position is nevertheless quite definite. And since in practice the chord was always regarded as a singular phenomenon, to be used in a special way, since particular events always preceded it and particular events always followed, it has an effect similar to that produced, say, when part of a popular quotation is cited: 'Love conquers . . .'[1] – one fills in what comes before and after. The merest hint at the well-known cause awakens the expectation of the well-known effect. With the first word we understand; we then await a particular continuation. This is how the cliché, the formula works. The six-four chord developed into just that, a permanent formula with the effect of a cliché; one cannot imagine its occurring out of the accustomed context. Accordingly, whether the mode of treatment expressed by this formula is appropriate or not matters little in establishing the significance it has had in music for more than three centuries. Even so, it may be well to consider this question.

I must recapitulate: the urge of the bass tone to become the root is supported by the overtones; the six-four chord should thus be resolved by actually letting its bass tone become the root. For example: the six-four chord of the Ist degree moves to V over a sustained *g*. That is precisely the *one* way it was handled. Yet the conflict in the six-four chord and its tendency toward resolution are not absolutely compulsory; one does not have to give in, for nothing more than overtones supports this tendency. It is perhaps possible to bypass its tendency carefully by drawing attention away from the conflict. That can happen if one of the two prominent voices shifts the responsibility for the harmonic proceed-

[1 'Wo alles liebt (kann Karl allein nicht hassen).']

ings to a melodic line. This voice draws the attention away from the vertical and towards the horizontal, away from harmony and towards melody. A good way to do that is to use a section of the scale in the bass, three or four adjoining tones, of which one, wherever possible a middle one, carries the six-four chord. If the ear catches a melodic progression of that sort, it then hears this progression as the principal concern of the moment, decides that the fleeting six-four chord is only incidental, and feels satisfied.

That could all be explained differently, as follows: In the six-four chord two tones struggle for pre-eminence, the bass tone and its fourth (the actual root). The following chord is a concession either to the bass or to the root. If the bass tone is victorious, then I goes to V. Sometimes, however, the concession does not go so far, but chooses rather a middle course. Then it can even happen that the third (*Terz*) becomes the root (*wenn Zwei sich streiten, freut sich der Dritte* – when two parties quarrel, the third rejoices*), that I goes to III. And something similar takes place if the fourth (the root) does not give in. Then after I comes IV or VI. In these three cases both of the struggling chord tones in fact succumb. In III *g* is only the third, in IV and VI *c* is the fifth and the third respectively. Each has the satisfaction, however, that the rival did not win; and the chord tones seem to become very nearly as spiteful as people the moment they come into contact with the latter. That then is the other way one can deal with the problem of the six-four chord: the method that has it occur with a passing note in the bass. These two methods bear similarity to some forms of the other dissonances and their treatment. Therefore it may be justifiable to speak here, also, of resolution, although resolution of the other dissonances has a different psychology. Yet, one should distinguish between forms that allow harmonic explanation (replacement of the chord tones by the overtones of the bass) and those that are derived from voice leading (occurrence of the six-four chord as a passing chord). Or one must do what I do: expand the idea of resolution accordingly.

The so-called preparation can be explained the same way. One of the two chord tones was there first: the root, if IV or VI preceded (possibly the seventh chord of II, whose seventh is *c*), or the bass tone, if V or III preceded. Whichever was there first would stake its claim to victory on grounds of its seniority. One could also view the matter this way: that, to prepare for this conflict, at least one of the tones is introduced beforehand; or also (to explain the stepwise introduction of the six-four chord) that a melodic bass line alleviates the harshness of the phenomenon.

The customary treatment of the six-four chord is difficult for me to explain in every respect, with nothing left over, because I find that this treatment does not completely fit the problem inherent in the chord. I admire the capacity of our forebears for fine discrimination; they rightly felt that the six-four chord is

---

* The Europeans (I and V), who have mangled one another for the benefit of the subdominant (Japan) and the upper mediant [*Obermediante*] (America) or some other mediant of culture.

[Schoenberg added this footnote in the revised edition of 1922. It was deleted from the seventh edition of 1966.]

not the same thing as a triad. But I know also too well how the intuitively discovered knowledge, subjected to the exaggerating treatment of orthodoxy, becomes far removed from the original, brilliant insight into nature. Nevertheless, we shall now work with the six-four chord according to the dictates of the old theory (for reasons I have already frequently mentioned).

According to the rules of that theory the six-four chord should be

1. prepared,
2. resolved, or should
3. appear only as a passing chord; and
4. the bass voice should neither reach nor leave its tone by leap; either it should be sustained or it should come and go in the midst of stepwise progression. (This rule corresponds to a certain extent to 3.)

The preparation of the six-four chord differs from that of the dissonance in that here two tones are to be considered. We can prepare either the fifth (the bass tone) or the root; that is: one of these two tones should have been a component of the preceding chord, and should appear in the same voice in the six-four chord. The resolution takes place as follows: either the bass tone is sustained and the other voices over it change to a new chord, or the bass tone moves a step up or down and becomes the root or third of the next chord. *A six-four chord should neither immediately precede nor follow another six-four chord.* That would mean setting directly beside one unresolved problem another problem, also for the moment unresolved. That is obviously contrary to the sense of form. This progression also reminds us of parallel fifths, which usually come about because the fifth of one degree goes to the fifth of another.

The treatment of the six-four chord as a passing chord is concerned only with the bass voice. I have already mentioned that we are not, then, dealing with a harmonic means, but rather with a melodic; for the effect of this form depends upon drawing the attention to a melodic progression. Such a melodic progression is that scale segment of three tones whose middle tone carries the six-four chord. The scale can be regarded as melody, even if only as the simplest, most primitive melody. Primitive, because it is deficient in articulation and variety: in it there is only one principle for the succession of tones (step by step) and only one direction (either up or down). A more complicated, more interesting melody is more richly, more variously articulated. The direction and the size of intervals change more frequently, indeed continuously; and the repetitions by which one can perceive the system manifest, if not several principles, at least variations. The scale is still a melody, however, for it does have system and structure. It is a primitive melody, a relatively artless pattern; but it is all the same a melody, even an art form. I have mentioned this property of the scale here because occasions will still frequently arise where certain problems, only apparently harmonic, are to be traced to melodic origins and are to be dealt with melodically. Thus, for example, the good effect of a diatonic or (completely or partially) chromatic scale in the bass is only a consequence of melodic energy, hence is almost more the effect of a kind of polyphony than of harmony.

This effect of a melodic line in writing devoted primarily to harmonic ends, although not thereby necessarily superior, is yet so striking that it yields a formal satisfaction equalling the satisfaction evoked by harmonic means. It is not necessary that a complete scale always be used for this purpose. A scale section, three or four adjoining tones, will also be heard as progression, as melody. Now such melodic progressions also appear frequently in harmonic phrases where no six-four chord is being dealt with. One could thus think this technique ought to be used more sparingly, so that when it is used it will have the needed force. That does not seem to be necessary, however, for the six-four chord in this form should not attract attention; it should only pass by un-obtrusively. Were the scale section a means used exclusively for this purpose, the six-four chord would then inevitably stand out.

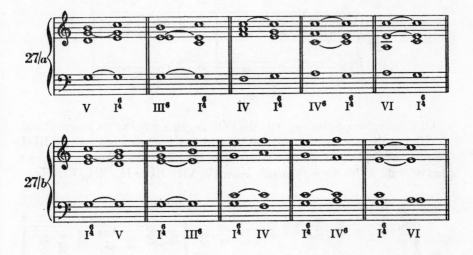

Example 27a shows a few preparations, 27b resolutions; in Example 28 preparation and resolution are joined in progressions of three chords.

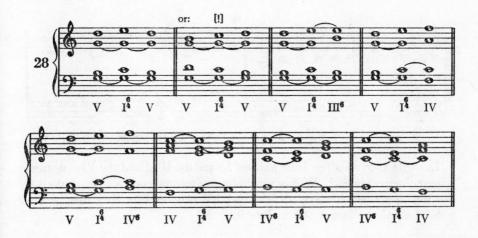

VI   I⁶₄   IV   VI   I⁶₄   V   V   I⁶₄   VI   IV   I⁶₄   VI

The pupil should also practice the preparation and resolution of the six-four chord on other degrees besides the Ist. Even if these are in general less common, certain of them do frequently appear. Special attention should be paid to the VIIth degree since, for yet another reason already cited, its fifth is a dissonance.

29

IV   VII⁶₄   III   II⁶   VII⁶₄   III

Obviously, here, as before, only the IVth degree (only in root position) and the IInd (only as a sixth chord) can be used in the preparation and the IIIrd degree exclusively (only in root position) in the resolution. Thus the progression with the VIIth degree can only read: IV, VII⁶₄, III or II₆, VII⁶₄, III.

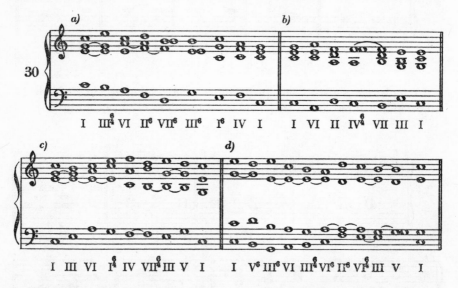

a)
I   III⁶₄   VI   II⁶   VII⁶   III⁶   I⁶   IV   I

b)
I   VI   II   IV⁶₄   VII   III   I

c)
I   III   VI   I⁶₄   IV   VII⁶₄   III   V   I

d)
I   V⁶   III⁶   VI   III⁶₄   VI⁶   II⁶   VI⁶₄   III   V   I

Example 30 gives a few little phrases. In 30*d* the IIIrd and the VIth degrees appear three times each. Without intending to recommend these repetitions, I put them here nevertheless, so that the pupil may see how they may be improved simply by means of a well-varied bass.

SEVENTH CHORDS

A seventh chord consists of three thirds built up over a fundamental; that is, of fundamental, third, fifth, and seventh. The seventh is a dissonance and thus belongs to those phenomena produced by the desire to bring into use the more remote overtones. I mentioned already, in my discussion of the VIIth degree, one way these may have come into common usage: as passing tones; a voice that would otherwise leap a third, for example, connects the two outside tones of this interval by giving the intervening, dissonant parts. It gives them fleetingly, only in passing as it were, without emphasis (on the weak beat) in order not to draw attention to them. A different use of the dissonance, probably a later form, introduces it *with emphasis* (on the strong beat). How this usage came about can be imagined as follows: Say a voice is to sing the tone progression, *f–e*. This melodic step could be accompanied by two chords: *f* perhaps by the IVth degree, *e* by the Ist. Now perhaps at a particular point in a phrase, one wishes to present this step, so as to make it more forceful, as the fulfilment of a necessity; or, inversely, one wishes to express the necessity manifest in this step, at this particular point, in the harmony as well (purposes reflecting very superior reasoning in the handicraft of art): then, one of the most appropriate means to this end would be to make the first tone a dissonance. The progression IV–I allows the melodic step, *f–e*, but the progression does not require this step. In the first place, the *f* could just as well go to *g*, and secondly, the IVth degree could just as well be followed by the IInd or the VIIth or some other degree. If one could put under the step *f–e* a harmony that could give it the force of necessity, then the effect of the step would be more organic. That is of course not easy to do, for there are no means by which the *f* could be absolutely compelled to go just to *e* and nowhere else. One can give the *f* prominence, however, by setting a chord under it with which it is dissonant. It thereby becomes an event that cannot be passed over without special consideration. I have already pointed out [see pp. 46ff.] in connection with the VIIth degree that in simple harmonic phrases a dissonance is especially striking; and I showed that in such surroundings its appearance will always necessitate the use of strong means. The same is true here. If the *f* has become a dissonance, therefore a prominent tone, then, to bring about a resolution, one must cause the harmony to move with such energy that the momentum with which it seems to follow its instincts bears the responsibility for everything, thus also for the dissonance. In that previous discussion we established that the leap of the root a fourth upward seems eminently suitable for such a purpose. This leap occurred there with the same tone, *f*, where its root, *B*, leaped up to *E*. But the *f* can become dissonant also as the seventh of the Vth degree (*G*). Then the best degree for resolution is the Ist (*C*). With this resolution an aura of necessity seems to compel *f* to go to *e*. To take *f* to *c* would be unfavorable because the unmotivated leap is not convincing. Resolution to *g* would be no more favorable because *g* already appeared in the preceding chord [i.e. in the V₇ chord], and, as the tone of resolution, would therefore not announce forcefully enough that a new consonance has come about through its influence. Consequently, the *f* goes best to *e*.

It was shown here what purpose can be served by making the *f* dissonant. It does not inevitably have to go to *e* (this inevitability does not exist); but if it does go to *e*, that will be the most satisfactory continuation, so long as other considerations do not intrude. The value of the dissonance we learn from the satisfaction obtained from the *resolution*. This satisfaction is produced by a strong root movement in conjunction with a complementary movement of the dissonance. For the time being we shall use this method in resolving seventh chords because it directly embodies the simplest implications of our basic assumptions. But there are, of course, other forms of dissonance resolution. These will be discussed later when we advance from the simpler, more natural functions of the fundamental tone to the more complex, the more artificial. For the moment we shall work with this, the simplest form of dissonance treatment and shall use in the resolution of the seventh chord the same root movement that we chose for the VIIth-degree triad: *the root will leap a fourth upward*. Here the descending dissonance becomes the third of the new chord, whereas in the chord that resolved the VIIth-degree triad it became the octave.

We *prepare* the seventh chord the same way we prepared the triad on VII. The tone to be prepared should be a consonance in the preceding chord. Thus, if we want to prepare the seventh chord on the Ist degree, the seventh of this chord, the *b*, could in the preceding chord be either the root (octave) of the triad on VII, fifth of the triad on III, or the third of that on V. There are, then, three possible kinds of preparation, which we shall examine in turn. First we choose the preparation by the third because its root makes the upward leap of a fourth. Concerning preparation and resolution there is nothing further to say here that was not already said in connection with the VIIth degree.

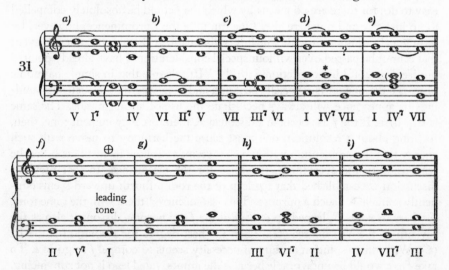

The seventh chords were prepared and resolved here, in these first examples, by means of and into triads in root position (inversions will follow later). In the resolution it is usually necessary, if a complete chord is desired, to take the third of the seventh chord (in 31*a* the *e*) down a third to the fifth of the resolving chord rather than up to the root, which would actually be the nearer. This point is obvious, however, in light of the fourth question: 'What is missing?'

Special care must always be devoted to any examples in which the VIIth degree appears, since it contains a dissonance. Thus, in 31*c* the *f* must descend to *e*, whereby it becomes impossible to get a complete seventh chord on III. The seventh and the root may of course not be left out, since they form the characteristic interval. On the other hand the third or the fifth can be omitted since here neither is particularly characteristic. Were one of the two characteristic, then the other would be more appropriately omitted. For example, if the fifth were diminished or the third major (as in *a* minor). In 31*d* the seventh chord on IV cannot be complete because the VIIth degree, the resolving chord, requires preparation of its *f*. Therefore, the *f* of IV must be doubled and the fifth or the third omitted (31*e*). In 31*i*, where the seventh chord of the VIIth degree is dealt with, both the fifth and the seventh of VII must be prepared and resolved, since both are in fact dissonances.

In Example 31*f* the *b* in the tenor should go to *g*, according to what was said above. Now that is contrary to a rule that requires the *b* to go to *c*. The *b*, the seventh tone of the scale, is called the *leading tone*, more precisely the ascending leading tone. To take it up to the eighth tone conforms to the model given by the ascending major scale. It will have to obey this melodic tendency, however, the leading-tone tendency, only when it actually participates in a melodic situation, and then only when it is the third of the Vth degree and the following chord is I. The seventh tone has the leading-tone characteristic, with respect to melody, only in the ascending major scale. In the descending scale the *b* goes easily to *a*; otherwise, resolution of the seventh chord on the Ist degree, for example, would be impossible. The melodic necessity for taking *b* to *c* can arise, at the moment, only in the top voice. But here, too, it can often be disregarded (above all and always when other requirements have priority); it is most of all in the cadence, when the *b* is in the top voice, that it should go generally to *c* rather than downwards.

The pupil should now practice preparing and resolving seventh chords on all degrees, at first in little phrases made up only of the three chords involved (in various keys). Then he should go on, as before, to the invention of little eight to twelve-chord phrases, in each of which, along with all that was practiced earlier, his task is to prepare a predetermined seventh chord. Planning the root progressions should proceed as before, always according to the table [p. 39]. He may decide, for example, to use the seventh chord of I in the first phrase. Since the Ist degree is the opening and closing chord and should appear both times in root position, it will be difficult here to avoid monotony. The seventh chord of I should not be introduced too soon after the opening chord, rather only after at least three or four chords have intervened. Thus, perhaps: I, VI, II, V, then the seventh chord of I, the resolution on IV, and finally the cadence, II, V, I [Example 32].

This example is of course rather bad because of the repetition of II–V–I.

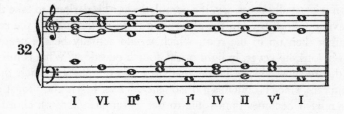

The pupil should notice how here (through the use of the sixth chord of II) the phrase goes from close position, in which it began, into open position. In this matter, also, he should aim for variety.

Example 33*a* deals with the seventh chord of II, 33*b* with that of III.

Since the pupil has already had sufficient practice in observing the instructions concerning parallels, he can now occasionally lead a voice in other than the shortest way, if his intention is to improve the upper voice melodically (as, for example, in Example 33*b* at the sign †). Of course only the top voice comes under consideration here, for the moment, and it can only be a matter of avoiding the excessive monotony that could result from too frequent repetition of a tone. But it should be noted that it is not the long sustained tone which is monotonous; for it is not being introduced anew and therefore creates no motion. Dullness results rather from the repetition of a certain progression or from the repetition of a tone after two or three other tones have intervened, if these did not sufficiently modify the line by a significant change of direction. The pupil should not worry too much about such melodic questions. At present, whatever smoothness he can achieve is quite meager. As our means increase, so we can set our aims correspondingly higher.

Preparation by means of the fifth now follows, subject to the same conditions as that by means of the third.

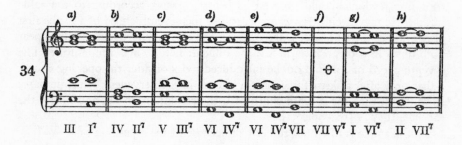

In these examples there are always three common tones that can be sustained as harmonic links. The root of the seventh chord on the IVth degree must be doubled, as before, so that the *f* of the VIIth degree is prepared. The VIIth degree is not suitable for preparing the seventh chord on V, because it does not fulfil the requirements we have set for preparatory chords. They should contain the tone to be prepared, as a consonance; the *f* in the VIIth-degree triad, however, is a diminished fifth, a dissonance. One could ignore this objection since the *f* was previously prepared for the VIIth degree and is simply held over all the way through in the same voice. But the connection has something weak about it; for the striking effect of the dissonance, *f* against *g*, is destroyed by the preceding dissonance of the same *f* against *b*. The addition of the *g* in the bass hardly heightens the effect, but gives rather the impression that the *g* had merely been omitted before. Hence this progression should be rejected.

The preparation of the seventh chord by means of the octave is omitted for the present. We will come back to it later [in Chapter VII]. Now we have only to consider the preparation and resolution of seventh chords by means of sixth and six-four chords.

In preparing the seventh chord by means of the third, whenever the preparatory chord is a sixth chord, one must double the third (Example 35—1, 3, 5, 7, 9, 11, 13). Preparation by means of the six-four chord, on the other hand, is accomplished without difficulty.

That here we *must* double the third in the sixth chord shows how bad it would be to give a rule: 'In the sixth chord the third may not be doubled.' We see now that it has to be doubled on occasion. As long as conditions so indicated, our directions read: 'Doubling of the third is superfluous.' Here, however, it is necessary, therefore no longer superfluous. Even if I had given a rule, I would not have done so without adding that every rule is annulled by a stronger necessity. I would almost say that this is the only rule one should give.

If the sixth chord of VII be used to prepare the seventh chord of III (Example 35–5), then the latter cannot appear as a complete chord. Either the fifth or the third will have to be left out, because the resolution of the diminished fifth, *f*, compels doubling of the fundamental, *e*. (Two other points should be kept in mind here: (1) Obviously, the preparatory VIIth degree must itself be prepared. (2) It is appropriate to ask, as the second question [cf. p. 52]: 'Which tones are dissonant?' For two are present: the diminished fifth of the preparatory chord, which must descend, and the seventh of III, which must be sustained.)

In preparation by means of the fifth it is advisable to double the fifth of the preparatory sixth chord in preference to the octave [root]; but of course the octave doubling can be used, too, if hidden fifths are not considered objectionable. Even the third could be doubled here, too, if it is important to sustain all the upper voices. But that is not necessary (Example 36–1, 1*a*, 1*b*).

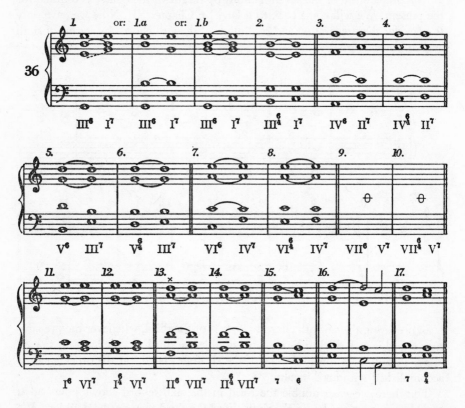

I cannot recommend resolving the seventh chord into a sixth chord. We will see later, in Example 244, that this connection, which we must do without for now, will be possible under certain conditions (Example 36–16); but at present we must be content to avoid it. Hidden octaves emerge here (36–15), because the seventh and the bass (the root) must go by parallel motion to the same tone, if the bass is to follow the shortest way; and these hidden octaves are the only ones I consider really bad in harmonic writing. My reason is as follows: The seventh is an aggressive tone, that is, a tone exhibiting drive towards resolution into another. In our present case the seventh of the first chord is followed by the third of the next. This same third, however, is now to become the bass tone as well; and if the bass goes the shortest way, as is only reasonable, then it too will descend. (The upward leap of a sixth would be of little use here; for the sixth has become for our ears – perhaps only through convention, only because it was always used that way – more a melodic than a harmonic skip.) Thus it happens that the bass goes to a tone that was expected in another voice. If the appearance of this tone in the other voice brings satisfaction, so its effect in the bass is weak, because the arbitrariness of the latter choice cannot compete successfully with the forceful necessity of the seventh. Here one could really speak of diminished independence in the bass voice.*

Resolution into the six-four chord, on the other hand, gives no difficulty (Example 36–17).

Here, as before, the pupil should practice first the individual chord connections by themselves, and then go on to construct phrases, working through the problem as systematically as possible.

Planning the bass voice is no longer as easy as before. With the possibility of choice comes also the obligation to make a good one. Such inversions should always be chosen as will allow melodic voice leading in the bass. Still other conditions present themselves, however: should one, for example, want to prepare a seventh chord by means of a six-four chord (the pupil should always set up the problem this way), then the six-four chord must itself be prepared; hence, the pupil will do best to put the problem he has set for himself in the middle, work backwards from it to determine the beginning, and then determine the continuation.

Perhaps, for example, I have set up the following problem for a phrase: the seventh chord of III, prepared by the six-four chord of V, and the seventh chord of VII, prepared by the sixth chord of IV. My next step is to write the figures indicating the degrees and the bass line, and then the bass notes themselves, in the middle (Example 37):

* The question could be raised here, whether I, too, am making an exception, even though I so strenuously condemn exceptions. In reply to this question I submit the following for consideration: As a matter of fact, this case is an exception, but – and this is important – an exception to a rule I did not make. On the contrary, it is an exception to a rule I refuted. And if I give validity here to a rule I refuted, then that is still no exception. For my refutation does not deny that for several centuries composers complied with this rule; it asserts rather that this compliance was unfounded. I did not, therefore, contest the fact that this rule was observed in practice; I merely showed that there was no justification for doing so [cf. p. 69]. If, however, this rule does have a trace of justification, then this particular progression is one of the most glaring cases. These hidden octaves are in truth very nearly as bad as open octaves. And if I advise avoiding open octaves, then I may also prohibit those hidden ones that I find almost as bad as the open. Let this be understood: '. . . that I find almost as bad as the open.' Indeed, just how bad do I find open octaves? The answer to this question had to be obvious in my refutation!

$$V^6_4 \quad III^7 \quad VI \quad IV^6 \quad VII^7 \quad III$$

Before the *d* of the six-four chord of V I could put only *d*, *e*, or *c* as the bass tone. The bass tone *e* could be: IIIrd degree, Ist degree sixth chord, or VIth degree six-four chord; *e* six-four is eliminated at once, since we would otherwise have two adjoining six-four chords; nor is *e* as the IIIrd degree advisable, since the III follows two chords later. The sixth chord of I would be possible, but it would bring about a repetition of the tone *e*, which we shall avoid if we can. Thus, only *d* or *c* can be chosen as the preceding bass tone. With *d* there could only be II or VII. The VIIth degree is eliminated because it would have to resolve into the IIIrd degree; II is left, and it would be good if it did not mean sustaining the bass – this is at least a small defect in the beauty of the line. Should *c* precede *d*, then only the Ist degree could be considered (at least for the present); for IV and VI have no common tone with V. The best solution then is to introduce the preparatory chord of this seventh chord, the six-four of V, immediately after the opening chord (I).

$$6 \quad 6\atop4 \quad III^7 \qquad I \quad IV \quad II \quad 6\atop4 \quad III^7$$

Example 38 shows how this beginning could be fashioned differently. Example 39 gives a completed version of the whole exercise.

$$I \quad V^6_4 \quad III^7 \quad VI \quad IV^6 \quad VII^7 \quad III \quad V \quad I$$

Here yet another difficulty appeared; for the resolution of the seventh chord of III ends on *a*, and the preparation of the seventh chord of VII by means of the sixth chord of IV begins with *a*. To get around this difficulty one would have to insert at least three or four chords, and it is questionable whether even then a good bass would result. Joining these two chord progressions by means of a sustained *a* is the least objectionable solution if one does not choose the most fundamental correction: to avoid juxtaposing these two chord progressions in such a short example and to substitute another progression for either the second or the first. That is not necessary, however, for it suffices to find the best solution relative to the particular circumstances; and, after all, it does not always matter as much that the pupil turns out faultless work, as that he has the opportunity to think through everything that is relevant. These mental gymnastics, even if none of their results are free of error, nevertheless often effect a greater advancement in ability than could be achieved by producing faultless examples. Such are only possible if one clears away all difficulties for the pupil, thus taking from him the trouble of choosing, but at the same time diminishing his joy in accomplishment. The solution he finds on his own, although it may be more defective, not only gives him more pleasure but also strengthens more intensively the muscles involved.

INVERSIONS OF THE SEVENTH CHORDS

Like the triads, the seventh chords can also be inverted; that is: a component other than the root can appear in the bass. When the third is the bass tone, the chord is called a six-five chord (more precisely: six-five-three chord); when the fifth is in the bass, a four-three chord (more precisely: six-four-three chord); and when the seventh is in the bass, a two chord (more precisely: six-four-two chord).

The inversions of the seventh chords can now be used for the same reasons the inversions of the triads were used: to make possible variety in the bass voice and to avoid unpleasant repetitions. No new instructions are given here.

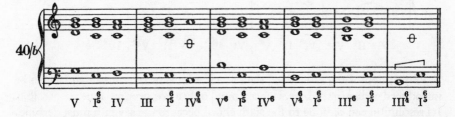

In Example 40*b* the six-five chord of I was prepared and resolved. For its preparation by means of the third (Vth degree), the root position, the sixth chord, and the six-four chord are all suitable; for preparation by means of the fifth (III) the root position and sixth chord are suitable, but not the six-four chord (because of the leap of the bass from *b* to *e*). The six-five chord can resolve to the root position (root progression always an ascending fourth) or to the sixth chord, not, however, to the six-four chord. In resolving the six-five chord into the sixth chord one could give preference, because of the hidden octaves, to contrary motion between the bass and the descending seventh. But that is not absolutely necessary. What has been said here will be found true of the six-five chords on the other degrees; only the limitations on VII will need special consideration.

The treatment of the four-three chord formerly had some restrictions attached, because, if the seventh is disregarded, it is a six-four chord (since the fifth is in the bass), a six-four chord with added seventh. The pupil can indeed treat the four-three chord that way, as if it were a six-four chord. That would mean: not entering and leaving the bass by leap (*sprungweise*), not writing two four-three chords in succession, and not connecting a four-three chord with a six-four chord. This treatment, however, is not absolutely necessary; for it is too often contradicted by the living example [of practice], where we frequently find just such a progression as that in Example 40c.

Example 40d shows preparation of the four-three chord by means of the third and fifth, and resolution to the root position and sixth chord. The six-four chord is impossible on account of the 'leap' (40d–3 and 4).

Preparation of the seventh of the two chord means of course that it must be introduced earlier in the bass. Hence, [now] only a few progressions are possible. Its resolution can only be to the sixth chord because the seventh must descend.

With the VIIth degree we find the following:

$$\text{IV VII}^{6}_{5}\text{III} \quad \text{IV}^{6}\text{VII}^{6}_{5}\text{.III}^{6} \quad \text{IV}^{6}_{4}\text{VII}^{6}_{5}\text{III}^{6}_{4} \quad \text{II VII}^{6}_{5} \quad \text{II}^{6}\text{VII}^{6}_{5} \quad \text{II}^{6}_{4}\text{VII}^{6}_{5}$$

$$\text{IV VII}^{4}_{3}\text{III} \quad \text{IV}^{6}\text{VII}^{4}_{3}\text{III}^{6} \quad \text{IV}^{6}_{4}\text{VII}^{4}_{3}\text{III}^{6}_{4} \quad \text{II VII}^{4}_{3} \quad \text{II}^{6}\text{VII}^{4}_{3} \quad \text{II}^{6}_{4}\text{VII}^{4}_{3}$$

Here it must be kept in mind that not only the seventh but also the diminished fifth must be prepared and resolved; note particularly Example 40*g*–1 where the *f* of the bass must also be prepared. Obviously, as in some earlier cases, it is necessary to double the third, for example, when the six-five chord resolves to the sixth chord (40*f*–2); or the third of the preparatory sixth chord must be doubled (40*f*–5) to prepare the diminished fifth. Preparation of the four-three chord by means of the sixth chord of IV is omitted because the diminished fifth must be prepared (40*g*–2, likewise, 40*g*–4 and 6). Furthermore, the four-three chord cannot resolve to the sixth chord, because the *f* is not to go up, but rather down. The two chord can be prepared only by means of the IVth degree, sixth chord, and the IInd, six-four chord.

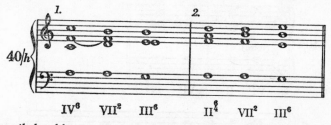

$$\text{IV}^{6} \quad \text{VII}^{2} \quad \text{III}^{6} \qquad \text{II}^{6}_{4} \quad \text{VII}^{2} \quad \text{III}^{6}$$

The pupil should now practice preparing and resolving the inversions of the seventh chords in various keys and should then go on to work out little phrases.

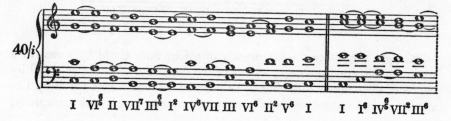

$$\text{I VI}^{6}_{5}\text{II VII}^{7}\text{III}^{6}_{4}\text{I}^{2}\text{IV}^{6}\text{VII III VI}^{6}\text{II}^{2}\text{V}^{6}\text{I} \qquad \text{I I}^{6}\text{IV}^{6}_{5}\text{VII}^{2}\text{III}^{6}$$

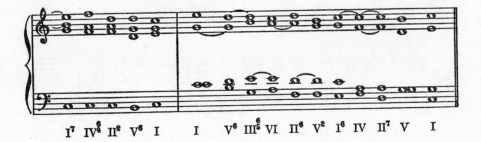

I⁷ IV⁶₄ II² V⁶ I   I   V⁶ III⁶₅ VI II⁶ V² I⁶ IV II⁷ V   I

CONNECTION OF SEVENTH CHORDS WITH ONE ANOTHER

If we retain just the most important of our instructions, namely, that the seventh be resolved by taking it down a step; if we disregard the requirement of a strong root progression; and if we are satisfied with a preparation in which the preparatory tone was a consonance in the preceding chord (is thus free; does not have, so to speak, a way prescribed for it!) — with these allowances we can join a seventh chord with another seventh chord. If only these two conditions are fulfilled: the preparatory tone should have been a consonance, and the resolution should take place through descent of the seventh. This corresponds to the procedure I announced in my discussion of the VIIth degree. There I stated that the dissonance requires this careful handling only so long as it is still a striking occurrence in our harmonic life [see page 50].

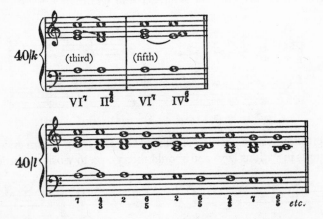

Example 40k shows the preparation of a four-three chord by means of a seventh chord (preparation by means of the third) and of a six-five chord by means of the same seventh chord [the preparatory tone is here the fifth]. Example 40l shows a progression of several such connections, in which, naturally, the position (inversion) of the seventh chord is given by the bass tone of the moment. Such a progression, particularly one so extended, actually holds no interest for us. It was shown only because in older compositions something of that sort often forms the harmonic framework for the sequential repetition of motives.

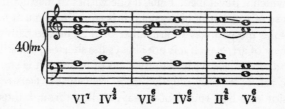

$$\text{VI}^7 \quad \text{IV}^{\frac{4}{3}} \quad \text{VI}^{\frac{6}{5}} \quad \text{IV}^{\frac{6}{5}} \quad \text{II}^{\frac{4}{3}} \quad \text{V}^{\frac{6}{4}}$$

In Example 40*m* some connections are shown in which the bass moves by leap while the seventh resolves and a consonant tone prepares another seventh chord. During the resolution two other voices exchange positions [i.e. those that contain neither seventh].

Once the pupil has some skill in handling dissonances, many of the restrictions imposed here will be removed. But not yet; for there are still things to be considered from the viewpoint of these restrictions. Now with that someone will surely ask: if it can be done more simply, why not simplify right away?

I have the following to say against that proposal: The characteristics of this harmonic system show up most distinctly in the treatment of dissonance. Indeed, since it is only a system of *viewing and handling* the things, not a system of the *things themselves*, one could disregard all of it and say to the pupil: 'Write what your ear dictates!' But it will not be easy to accept that logic. Dimly each of us feels that, should we leave the novice to the discretion of his ear, he would write things that would of course not be necessarily wrong – even if they did not fit into our notion of artistic order – but at the same time would not be necessarily right. Dimly each of us feels the contradiction in this order that claims to be natural, and is nevertheless disavowed by the good ear of one who is in the natural state, of one who is uncultivated: disavowed, because it is not natural order, but artificial; because it is a product of learning, of culture. To be sure, nature admits of such diverse interpretations that we can include in it even our artifacts, our cultural products (*unser Künstliches*); and still other systems could surely be inferred from nature just as naturally as ours. But also just as unnaturally! For it is the artificial (imperfect) representation of an apparently natural (perfect) matter whose essence the pupil should be taught. We must be clear on this point, that we are not teaching him eternal law, laws handed down by nature as the only laws, the immutable laws of art! We have rather the task, because of our inability to grasp the unordered, of presenting him the traditional handicraft of our art in the form of a closed theory, as if it were grounded in nature, *inferred from nature*. This theory *can* indeed be inferred from nature. It is possible, but nothing more! Even if our art and its theory do appeal with some justification to nature, a person untutored in the art does not have to be wrong if he produces something different.

For art reduces the perceptible to the expressible. Hence, one can perceive differently and express differently. Above all, however, art is not something Given, like nature, but something that has Become. It could then also have become other than it is. The path along which art has evolved, the historical development, perhaps often better indicates what it has become than does nature, from which it developed. Thus, if one wishes to instruct the pupil in the traditional sense of our harmonic system, it is sometimes much more pertinent to lead him along the pathway of art rather than along the pathway of nature. And the pathway of art, even if it is not always the shortest, can still be travelled. And even if it does not always lead to the facts of nature – it is enough if it leads to the facts of art. If it really only led to all conceivable facts of art, it might then on occasion also be a roundabout way, leading through those phenomena that had no influence on its direction, none, that is, that can still be clearly recognized. It is at least the pathway. A new pathway could be shorter, could avoid superfluous digressions and delays. Who knows exactly, however, so exactly that at any moment he could assume responsibility for a future development, which of these digressions and delays are actually superfluous, actually without influence on the future?

Should one really give the pupil immediate freedom in the treatment of dissonance, the question of the limits of this freedon could still not be left unanswered. And I could perhaps grant myself that luxury. I have such complete confidence in the ear of the gifted pupil that I am certain he would even then find the right way. And my experience with pupils and with my own development could reassure me in following this course. Nevertheless, I have seen in myself and in others that the need arises to know more of these things, even to assimilate them so thoroughly that they are understood as order, as being coherent. Moreover, there are also individuals whose talents are such as require instruction, a number of them, perhaps, only to save time. Such time as is spent in finding out for oneself is indeed not time lost absolutely, not even when one errs. It can be used more economically, however, if a sure and careful hand leads the way.

V THE MINOR MODE

Up to now we have worked out our exercises only in the major mode. Now we will go on to apply what we have learned to the minor as well. First, though, the nature of the minor mode must be clear to us. The minor mode and the major are both a residue of the seven church modes. Our present major is the Ionian of old, our minor the Aeolian. The other church modes began as follows: Dorian on *d*, Phrygian on *e*, Lydian on *f*, Mixolydian on *g*, and Hypophrygian on *b*.

Each of these modes consisted of the seven tones of a diatonic series: for example, in the series *c*, *d*, *e*, *f*, *g*, *a*, *b*, Dorian began on *d* and read: *d*, *e*, *f*, *g*, *a*, *b*, *c*. These scales, like our major and minor, could be transposed, so that there were actually eighty-four scales available; but, to be sure, not all transpositions were commonly used. A more detailed account of the church modes can be looked up in one of the older works.[1] I will discuss here only the characteristics relevant to our task: those which, as far as I can discover, influenced the historical evolution. They not only should, they must be considered,* if we are to give an idea of that harmonic sense of form which serves as the basis for our own. Thus, it should be pointed out that the church modes had a tendency to imitate a certain characteristic of the Ionian, whose seventh tone is an ascending leading tone, that is, a tone only a half step below the eighth. I have already said I hold this tendency to be the reason for the dissolution of the church modes. Their distinguishing characteristics were thereby cancelled out, and the individual modes became so similar to one another that in the end only two main types were left that are clearly distinguishable: *major*, which brought together the characteristics of Ionian and the other major-like modes; and *minor*, which brought together those of Aeolian and the other minor-like modes. The minor mode is thus purely synthetic, a product of art, and attempts to represent it as something given in nature are pointless; its naturalness is not direct, but, like

* The idea of considering the church modes in the discussion of the minor mode I got from a harmony text by Max Loewengaard [or Loewengard. This pedagogue wrote various theory textbooks, among them a *Lehrbuch der Harmonie* (1892) which ran through several German editions and was translated into English by Frederick L. Liebing (*A Manual of Harmony*, 1907) and by Theodore Baker (*Harmony Modernized*, 1910). Neither of these translations mentions church modes. The original and yet another translation (1905), as well as the other works by Loewengard, were unavailable for inspection.]

[1 In view of the detailed information on this topic to be found in many scholarly works, editorial comment here seems unwarranted – except to suggest comparison of Schoenberg's references to the church modes (here, in Chapter X, *et passim*) with the views of Heinrich Schenker on the same topic in his *Harmony*, ed. Oswald Jonas, trans. Elisabeth Mann Borgese (Chicago: University of Chicago Press, 1954), pp. 45–76. This suggestion assumes special relevance in view of Schoenberg's own references to Schenker's work (e.g. *infra*, p. 119, Appendix, p. 428).]

that of the church modes, indirect. Now it is true that major and minor have evolved historically, that they represent an essential simplification over what came before (for they are a sum, containing everything that appeared in the seven old modes); and it is true that the dualism presented by major and minor has the power of a symbol suggesting high forms of order: it reminds us of male and female (*Zweigeschlechtlichkeit*) and delimits the spheres of expression according to attraction (*Lust*) and repulsion (*Unlust*). These circumstances could of course be cited to support the false doctrine that these two modes are the only truly natural, the ultimate, the enduring. The will of nature is supposedly fulfilled in them. For me the implications are different: *we have come closer to the will of nature*. But we are still far enough from it; the angels, our higher nature (*Übernatur*), are asexual; and the spirit does not know repulsion (*Unlust*).

Our forebears undoubtedly considered the church modes just as perfect as we our major and minor. The number seven has just as much symbolic power as the number two; and instead of the two principal spheres of expression recognized by scholarship there were evidently seven that were sanctified by the imagination. Had they been shown the future: that five of their seven would be dropped – just as the future is being shown here: that the remaining two will eventually be one – then they would have argued against such a possibility just as our contemporaries do. They would have spoken of lawlessness, of anarchy, lack of individuality (*Charakteristik*), impoverishment of artistic means, and so on; their complaints would have sounded just as complaints today would sound, should something else now evolve, something different from what those who love the cosiness of the fireside would like – those who will not understand that with every advance something must be lost on the one side if anything is to be gained on the other.

The preliminary work is the investment; in the advance, however, which is the profit, the preliminary work is still present, if not with everything of which it formerly consisted, nevertheless with what is most important. And, viewed historically, every advance is only preliminary work. Consequently, there are no unsurpassable peaks of achievement, because the peak itself is only relative to the peaks already surpassed. And so I do not believe, either, in inescapable decadence in the life of nations. I believe that the Romans could yet have surpassed even the highest stage of their development, had an event not intervened entirely extraneous to those factors relevant to the evolution of a civilization: the great migrations.[1] True, the vigor of a nation could at that time be manifested above all in its military prowess. But, let it not be forgotten: a *Kultur* (a high civilization) was conquered by an *Unkultur* (by barbarians); it was not that a *Kultur* failed, became unproductive, was worn out and had to be disposed of. This disposal could have been accomplished within the organism by revolution, which would have culled out the dead organ while retaining the organism. The migrations would actually have to be viewed as a consequence of the decadent over-refinement (*Überkultur*) of the Romans, if one would ascribe the

[1 More literally: 'I do not believe that the Romans could not yet have surpassed even the highest stage of their development, had an event not intervened. . . .']

destruction of Rome to the waning vigor of the nation. Even pessimists will not want to go that far, those who scent decay and downfall on all sides where the courageous find traces of new vigor.[1] The decline of the church modes is that necessary process of decay from which sprouts the new life of the major and minor. And even if our tonality is dissolving, it already contains within it the germ of the next artistic phenomenon. Nothing is definitive in culture; everything is only preparation for a higher stage of development, for a future which at the moment can only be imagined, conjectured. Evolution is not finished, the peak has not been crossed. It is only beginning, and the peak will come only, or perhaps never, because it will always be surpassed. 'There goes the last wave,' Gustav Mahler said once – pointing to a river – to Brahms, as the latter in a fit of pessimism spoke of a high point of music that he held to be the last.

Our present-day minor is, then, the old Aeolian, whose scale reads: *a, b, c, d, e, f, g.* Occasionally, whenever the seventh tone was to go to the eighth, the seventh was turned into a leading tone, that is, *g♯* took the place of *g.* This change, however, created the augmented interval, *f–g♯*, which was preferably avoided in older music. Therefore *f♯* replaced *f,* also, so that where there was a leading tone the scale read: *e, f♯, g♯, a.* That the interval, *f–g♯*, is hard to sing in tune is probably still true, even today. It is certainly not easy to sing it perfectly in tune. And the use of such intervals may contribute much to the difficulty choruses have in keeping on pitch when singing *a cappella.* The objection may be raised that the older keyboard music also avoided such intervals, even though for the keyboard one interval is as easy as another; hence, the appeal to intonation difficulties fails to explain the matter. This objection is disposed of as follows: such intervals are hard to sing in tune because they are hard to imagine, and for that very reason also hard to perceive. Moreover, instrumental music and vocal music are at no time differentiated as far as stylistic essentials are concerned. That means the what and the how of expression remain the same in harmony, counterpoint, melody, and form. The use of augmented intervals at prominent melodic places in keyboard music would have to have led to the use of such intervals in vocal music as well. Since, however, musical practice was oriented to vocal music, such intervals were understandably avoided, not only in vocal but also in instrumental composition.

A raised tone was substituted for the seventh, hence, also for the sixth, only where a leading tone was desired. If such was not the aim then the unaltered scale tones were retained. It is therefore incorrect to base the treatment of these tones on the so-called harmonic minor scale. The only correct way, it seems to me, is to take the Aeolian mode as the point of departure. After all it also has the characteristics of the melodic minor scale. We must, however, keep in mind that the raised tones were used only when a leading tone was needed, that is, for a cadence on *a.* Only then was *g♯* used in place of *g,* and *f♯* was then chosen only for the sake of the *g♯.* Consequently, there are two forms of the minor

[1] Schoenberg added a footnote here in his revised edition, namely, some remarks on the aftermath of World War I (see Appendix, p. 425). This footnote was deleted from the seventh edition.]

scale, which together are known as the melodic minor scale: the *ascending* form, which substitutes the raised seventh and sixth for the natural tones; and the *descending*, which uses the plain series of unaltered tones. The two forms are not mixed. In upward progression only the raised tones may appear, in downward only the natural tones. What was said here, summed up in rules, yields the *four laws of the pivot tones* (*Wendepunktgesetze*) *of the minor scale:*[1]

First pivot tone, g♯: g♯ must go to *a;* for g♯ is used only for the sake of the leading-tone progression. Under no circumstances may g or f follow g♯, nor may g♯ go to f♯ (at least for now).

Second pivot tone, f♯: f♯ must go to g♯; for it appears only for the sake of the g♯. Under no circumstances may g follow, nor, of course, f. Nor e, d, a, etc. (for now, at least).

Third pivot tone, g: g must go to f, because it belongs to the descending form of the scale. Neither f♯ nor g♯ may follow it.

Fourth pivot tone, f: f must go to e, because it belongs to the descending form of the scale. F♯ may not follow it.

Adherence to these instructions is indispensable, since the character of the minor scale is hardly manifest without them. We must put aside chromatic steps for the time being, since we have not yet explained their conditions. And any other treatment of the raised sixth and seventh tones can easily serve to erase the feeling of tonality, which we want at first to keep absolutely pure and unequivocal. As soon as we have richer means at our disposal we can easily keep more adventurous excursions, apparent departures from the key, within bounds. But at present we are hardly able to do that. The third and fourth pivot tones can be handled somewhat more freely later by analogy with the Aeolian mode. This mode corresponds, so long as raised tones are not substituted, to the Ionian, to our relative major [i.e. the tones are the same]. The laws of the pivot tones refer more to the modern melodic minor, in which a treatment common in the Aeolian seldom appears: that is, rather long passages without raised tones, in which of course then the sixth and seventh unaltered tones freely go their way. In this sense a freer treatment could even now be permitted. Then it would be possible for an *a* to come after a *g* (say in an inconspicuous middle voice) or a *g* after an *f.* But these steps in the vicinity of raised tones can easily evoke the impression of unevenness similar to that produced by the so-called cross relation (which is to be discussed shortly [p. 102]). In such cases the g or the f should be, so to speak, resolved: the g should go to f, the f to e, before raised tones appear. Even if f and g be treated more freely now, the rules for-

[1 Robert Adams translated the term *Wendepunktgesetze* as 'turning points' (*Theory of Harmony*, p. 49). Schoenberg, in his *Structural Functions of Harmony* (New York: W. W. Norton, 1954), pp. 9–10 *et passim*, called these alternate sixth and seventh degrees 'substitute tones' because, he said, one does not 'raise' or 'lower' tones, one substitutes, let us say, g♯ for g in the ascending *a*-minor scale, g for g♯ in the descending scale. (Cf. *infra*, p. 100, Schoenberg's footnote, and p. 387.) In this translation, as in that of Adams, Schoenberg's original metaphor, *Wendepunkte*, is retained – but translated here as 'pivot tones'.]

bidding *g* and *f* to go to *f♯* and *g♯* still hold absolutely. It is more practical, however, to save this freer treatment [of *f* and *g*] for later.

The *a*-minor scale, as we are handling it, is thus a *C*-major scale that begins on *a* and in certain circumstances (leading tone) allows the seventh tone to be raised a half step; and, for melodic reasons, for the sake of the seventh, the sixth may also be raised. If these tones are not raised, then everything is the same as in the relative major. If the tones are raised, then the instructions pertaining to the pivot tones apply.

THE DIATONIC TRIADS IN MINOR

Example 41 presents the triads that are possible in minor. There are six more than in major, since the raised tones naturally participate in chord formation; and the order, species, and constitution (*Zusammensetzung*) of the triads are also essentially different. Thus the first degree is a minor chord. On the IInd we find a diminished and a minor chord, on the IIIrd a major chord and one whose form is new to us. (It is the so-called augmented triad, which will be given special attention.[1] It consists of two major thirds which add up to an augmented fifth. The augmented fifth does not appear in the first overtones and is thus a dissonance.) On the IVth degree, as well as on the Vth, appear a minor and a major chord. On the VIth degree, as well as on the VIIth, appear a major triad and a diminished. For connection of these chords the following instructions are to be observed: As before, we shall choose at first only chords that have one or more common tones (*harmonisches Band*); we can therefore continue to use the table given previously [p. 39]. The chords in which no raised tones appear give no difficulty in their connections *with one another*. The relations here are no different from those in the relative major. Of course the diminished chords that appear here will be handled just as before: that is, the triad on II, *b–d–f* (identical with the VIIth in major), is prepared by means of IV, *d–f–a*, and VI, *f–a–c*, and resolved to V, *e–g–b*. It can also be resolved to V, *e–g♯–b*, as is shown later. On the other hand, when these triads are connected with those that have raised tones, and when the latter are connected with one another, the directions for handling the pivot tones must be observed. Naturally, some difficulties arise here, and there is a whole list of connections that cannot be used at present.

The pupil will again be guided in his work by the questions [p. 52].

[1 *Infra*, pp. 106–7 and Chapter XIV.]

Consistent with the new conditions imposed by the laws of the pivot tones, the second question will now read:

Second question: Which dissonance (dissonances) or pivot tones (tones with prescribed paths) are to be dealt with?

42

                    I   III   I   IV   I   V   I   VI

Example 42 shows connections of the first degree with the pertinent unraised degrees;* all these connections are easily made. Following this model the pupil can work through the other unraised degrees. (At first only in root position, as before.)

43

        I   III   I   IV   II   V   I   V   I   VI

Example 43 is an attempt to connect chords containing the raised sixth or seventh tone. The connection of the first degree with the augmented triad (III) should be left out for the present. On the other hand the connection with raised IV works quite well, only it is bound to a certain continuation, since after IV no other degree can follow at present except the raised II. Connection with raised V goes smoothly; but that with raised VI is at present unusable, for VI is a diminished triad and would therefore have to be resolved by the root pro-

---

* The expressions 'raised' or 'unraised degrees' are incorrect in two respects: (1) The tones are raised only in our notation (by ♯ or ♮); otherwise, however, they are not raised, but are replaced by higher tones. One can speak of 'raising' tones in chromatic progressions; consequently, we should avoid this expression [here], as well as in referring to secondary dominants. (2) The degrees themselves are not raised, but simply use raised tones or have such tones substituted. Perhaps, to be correct and complete, one should say: x degree with major third, perfect or augmented fifth. But that is too long. It would also be possible to say: 'x degree upwards', or 'ascending' (if tones of the ascending scale are used), and downward. I prefer, however, 'raised' and 'unraised' because they are flexible and short and still no more wrong than the expressions, 'altered', 'altered upward and downward'. For 'altered' could likewise imply mistaking the one for the other (*verwechselt*), and not, as is assumed in the everyday language of music, changed (*verändert*). ['Altered': change of some aspects without complete loss of identity. G♯ is not an alteration of *g*, except in our notation, but a different tone. – Schoenberg added this footnote in the revised edition.]

gression of the ascending fourth – yet the *f*♯ of the bass must go to *g*♯ (second law of pivot tones), thus cannot move by leap.[1]

Example 44 [1 and 2] shows the connection of II (diminished triad) with V, prepared once by IV, once by VI. (Prepare and resolve!)

Example 44–3 shows the raised II connected with IV. This connection would of course work, but it is not practical; for, as we will see later, the only choice after IV would be II again, and only IV could precede II, as other examples show. Consequently, the progression would read: IV–II–IV–II. This would surely be needless repetition. The raised II goes to the raised V without trouble. But II–VI is excluded, because VI had to be excluded, as well as II–VII, because VII is also unusable at present, as will be shown.

The IIIrd degree unraised naturally cannot be connected with chords containing *f*♯ or *g*♯. The only degree to be considered, should we ignore the third law of pivot tones (and we may not ignore it), is VI. The degrees could then perhaps be connected by taking *g* to *c*, thus circumventing the step *g–f*♯; but then the *c* (diminished fifth) would be unprepared, and even if we were willing to accept that, there would still be the two *f*♯s, *both* of which would have to go to *g*♯. And even if we did not double the *f*♯, there would still be the *f*♯ in the bass. *The augmented triad on III we leave out for now.* It will be considered in another context [*infra*, p. 106].

The only raised triad that could follow the unraised IV would be V, since

[1 To understand why Schoenberg excluded progressions, or imposed restrictions on them, the reader should bear in mind the rules (or rather the 'directions') currently in force. Here, they are:

1. Root positions only (until *infra*, p. 105);
2. Common tone required;
3. Pivot tones;
4. Dissonances (and only those that have been allowed) to be prepared, then resolved by root progression a fourth upward.]

raised III and VII are excluded. But the V is also excluded for now since there is no common tone. That we cannot connect unraised IV with raised II or VI is quite clear, for *f* may not go to *f♯*; and that another voice should go to *f♯* is forbidden by the so-called law of cross relations.

This law is as follows: Chromatic raising or lowering of a tone should occur in the same voice in which this tone was previously unraised or unlowered. This means that, should two successive chords employ *f* and *f♯* respectively, then the same voice that had *f* must take the *f♯*. Thus, for example, if the alto just had *f*, the tenor should not have *f♯* in the next chord. I should not like to apply this law with maximum rigor, for usage too often contradicts it. Formerly the law was just the opposite, namely, that the chromatic raising of a tone would *never* occur in one voice, that another voice had to take the *f♯* whenever *f* preceded. Neither is an aesthetic law. They are rather two different attempts to overcome intonation difficulties. To sing a chromatic half step perfectly in tune is indeed not easy. I would prefer the first formulation of the law [given above], since chromatic progression generally produces a good melodic line. By virtue of our instructions concerning pivot tones, the handling of these tones regulates itself, and differently;[1] consequently chromatic progressions are temporarily excluded.

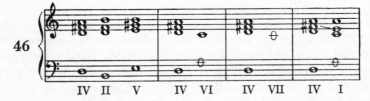

Raised IV connects smoothly with raised II, but connection with unraised II is excluded. It does not connect with raised VI (diminished triad) because the diminished fifth, *c*, of the latter must be prepared. We also omit the connection with the diminished triad on VII, *g♯–b–d*, because this triad is not presently usable. It requires special consideration, which will come later. Even the connection of raised IV with I is not possible, for *f♯* should go to *g♯*.

The unraised Vth degree cannot be connected with chords containing *f♯* or *g♯* (for the same reason the unraised IV could not be so connected). On the

[1 'And differently' (*und anders*): Presumably, Schoenberg meant that the instructions for handling pivot tones are different from either of the two rules governing cross relations. The use of the pivot tones is determined by the direction of the melodic line.]

other hand the raised Vth degree connects easily with I; but the connections with II raised and unraised and with VII must be left out. Because $g\sharp$ cannot go to $f\sharp$, raised II does not work; and II unraised is a diminished triad whose diminished fifth, f, must be prepared. Connection with the IIIrd degree is excluded for now.

The unraised VIth degree cannot be connected with chords containing $f\sharp$ or (at least temporarily) $g\sharp$. The diminished triad, $f\sharp$–a–c, of the VIth degree cannot now be used at all, because the $f\sharp$ should go to $g\sharp$, whereas the diminished triad requires the root movement of a fourth.

Now, again, little phrases are to be constructed. Generally, it will be advisable to use the degrees with raised intervals less often than those with unraised. An exercise in which several unraised and raised degrees appear will of necessity be relatively long, because a number of chords must almost always be used to get from the one region to the other. In general the obvious thing to do is to put the raised degrees in the vicinity of the cadence, because they do exist, after all, for the sake of the cadence. A progression of chords with raised tones will always have to go to the first degree. Repetition would result if they were introduced in the middle. Moreover, the introduction of raised degrees is possible at the moment only after I or II. The pupil should use the Vth degree for his penultimate chord and then always with the raised interval (as the dominant). The raised degrees are indicated in the figured bass by putting a sharp or a natural beside the numeral designating the interval raised: for example, $3\sharp$, $5\sharp$, etc. (or in c minor $3\natural$, $5\natural$).

In Example 49–1 only unraised chords were chosen, except for the cadential V. In Example 49–2 all are raised except the two chords on I. Neither example can be much longer if we do not wish to continue after I. Example 49–1 could possibly be extended after the II by means of the unraised V; then, however, we would need another series of chords to get to the cadence, say: II, V, III, VI, II, V, I. This is obviously almost identical to the preceding progression and thus would give scarcely any advantage. Of course it would be permissible to close in an entirely different way, by putting I right after VI. Under no circumstances may the pupil close right after III, since this chord contains *g*, which cannot go to *a*; and besides, for the cadence we should introduce rather the leading tone, *g♯*. The cadence IV–I would also be possible. This cadence, however, as well as the cadence VI–I, the pupil may write only whenever an example would otherwise become too long. Only then. In all other cases he should work toward the V as the penultimate chord. In general not very many examples can be devised with just these means, and in those examples not much variety is possible; therefore, the pupil should practice what little there is in as many keys as possible.

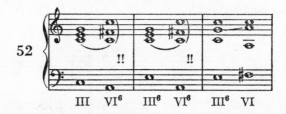

INVERSION OF THE TRIADS IN MINOR

Through the use of sixth and six-four chords some connections become possible which were unavailable above. Otherwise there is nothing new to say about the inversions. What was admitted before in the inversions in major is also admitted here: that is, the sixth chord is entirely free, and we shall neither reach nor leave the bass tone of the six-four chord by leap.

In Examples 50–55 appear some connections that were impossible [in the preceding section] prior to the use of inversions. The pupil will be able to find still more such connections. Only, he must observe strictly the directions pertaining to pivot tones, and may not forget that diminished fifths are (still, for the present) to be prepared and resolved, consequently not doubled. Thus, for example, we cannot leave the sixth chord of raised IV by leap, because *f♯* is supposed to go to *g♯*; it would be possible, perhaps, to go to raised II by putting the *f♯* of II in another voice and then letting this voice take over the progression of *f♯* to *g♯* (Example 53*a*). The harmonic requirements would thereby be satisfied, but not the melodic, from which these instructions sprang. Later the pupil will naturally be able to handle these things much more freely; and I think it is better for him to wait, to avoid such treatment until later, until he has developed a secure feeling (*Formgefühl*) for the characteristics of the minor mode. I have shown why exceptions may not appear in a theory. But I would have to make exceptions if I wanted to broaden what is too restricted here. It will soon become apparent how these restrictions are lifted of their own accord, as soon as the point of view from which I have dealt with the minor scale is fully exploited. What is superfluous will eliminate itself, whereas what is commonly used will be revealed as usable. The pupil can thus patiently await this stage of development. His freedom will be then so much the greater.

The sixth and six-four chords can now also be used in phrases.

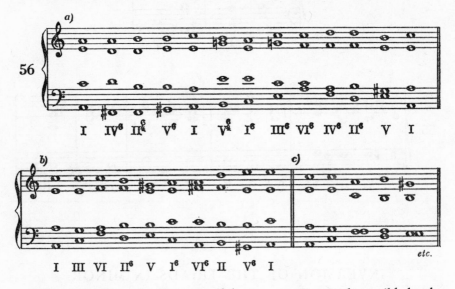

In Examples 56a and 56b certain of these connections made possible by the inversions are put to use. For example: the sixth chord of raised IV can go by way of the six-four chord of raised II to the sixth chord of V (the dominant), whereupon I follows. But the example does not therefore have to close here, for now the bass melody can keep going quite well in the direction in which it has started; and the melodic energy developed by this continuation is even quite capable of covering the ensuing repetition. Thus it does not matter if I comes here after the sixth chord of V, then the six-four chord of V, and then I again as a sixth chord. The melodic line of the bass, $g\sharp$–a–b–c, improves the effect of the whole in a thoroughly satisfactory way.

In Example 56b the sixth chord of raised VI was connected with raised II. Note [also] in this example that the tenor goes from g of the second chord to a of the third chord. Since $g\sharp$ comes soon thereafter, this arrangement will be considered uneven. Therefore it is better to lead the tenor as in 56c. Then the g has been resolved and the following $g\sharp$ does not disturb. Likewise inadmissible [now] is the movement of the alto from $f\sharp$ to the e of the penultimate chord. Later, when we are working under different rules, we can bypass this restriction, since the sixth chord of V could not otherwise be connected.

The augmented triad on the IIIrd degree in minor can now also be introduced in our exercises. We will have much to say about this chord later, for it has had great influence on the development of modern harmony.[1] As a diatonic triad in minor its treatment is fairly simple. Its augmented fifth requires dissonance treatment. Because, however, as the first pivot tone it cannot

[1 *Infra*, Chapters XIV and XX.]

descend, the resolution comes about – here for the first time – through ascent. The augmented fifth can be prepared, though, just as in our previous dissonance treatment. Actually, only the Vth degree is now available for this task, but, as we will soon see, VII can also be used. The chords of resolution are I and VI.

Let us mention at once a certain characteristic of this chord: the distance from *c* to *e* is four half steps, from *e* to *g♯* likewise four half steps, and from *g♯* to the recurrence of the root, that is to the octave, again four half steps. The tones *e* and *g♯* thus divide up the octave into three perfectly equal parts. The constitution of this triad is thus remarkable in that the distance between any two tones is always the same, so that in inversions the relation of the tones to one another does not change. Consequently, this chord is essentially different from all the chords considered up to now. This characteristic, concerning which still more is to be said later, makes it possible to permit even now something that we shall soon permit with all the other chords (in the next chapter): that is, it may be connected with those chords with which it has no common tone. Moreover, we can dispense with the preparation of the augmented fifth. With this latitude come many possibilities of great advantage for the construction of our little phrases. At the same time the laws of the pivot tones must of course be carefully observed. That even now we are handling this chord more freely, while so many restrictions still hold for the other chords, is explained this way: the formulation of these restrictions applies only in a very loose way to the augmented triad. I would have to formulate them differently, and I have no wish to do that at this stage where we are virtually at the point of loosening the other restrictions.

* The connection of adjacent degrees is discussed in the next chapter. – The use of VI in the fourth example of 57b – without resolution of the diminished fifth – is likewise premature, and appears here only for the sake of completeness.

The connections shown in Examples 57a and 57b are therefore possible: preceding III are I, II, IV, VI, and (as in Example 58) VII; following III are I, IV, VI, and V (II cannot follow because *g♯* must go to *a*).

The diminished triad on VII should (as diminished) be prepared (by means of IV or II) and resolved (to III).

Naturally, neither the diminished fifth nor the root can be doubled, for the diminished fifth should go downward, the root, as leading tone, upward. Hence, only the third can be doubled.

The discussion of these two chords had to be postponed because they become available to us only through the inversions of the triads. There was no other reason for this postponement.

SEVENTH CHORDS AND THEIR INVERSIONS IN MINOR

Through the use of raised and unraised tones we obtain two seventh chords on every degree, and on VII as many as four. Not everything that we obtain here is immediately usable, if we adhere to the directions previously given. Obviously, the connection of seventh chords without raised tones with triads without raised tones gives no trouble. Of the seventh chords that have one raised tone, some are only conditionally usable, whereas others, as well as those with two raised tones (on VII *g♯–b–d–f♯*), are at present, according to our directions, absolutely unavailable.

I IV⁷ VII VI IV⁷ VII V⁷ I II V⁷ I III VI⁷ II I VI⁷ II IV VII⁷ III II VII⁷

Example 60 shows the preparation and resolution of seventh chords without raised tones: preparation by means of the third and the fifth, resolution by means of root movement a fourth upward. This all happens as before without new directions. The connection of these seventh chords with triads that contain raised intervals is possible, according to our existing directions, only in a single instance: the seventh chord of II resolves to the Vth degree with major third. None of the others works: for example, the seventh chord of I does not work because the *g* cannot go to *f♯*, etc.

In Example 61 we shall examine the chords containing raised tones.

61

I⁷ IV II⁷ V V III⁷ VI VII III⁷ I IV⁷ VII VI IV⁷ VII

II V⁷ I VII V⁷ I III VI⁷ II I VI⁷ IV VII⁷ II VII⁷

a)

VII⁷ VII⁷ III⁷ VI⁴⁶ IV⁷ VII⁴⁶ III VI⁷ II⁴⁶ V⁶ VII⁷ III⁴⁶ VI⁶

We find, for example, that the seventh chord of I, *a–c–e–g♯*, is unavailable to us at present because the seventh, *g♯*, should as leading tone go up, but as seventh down. The *f♯* and *a* of the IInd degree (*b–d–f♯–a*) should both go to *g♯*, the one as pivot tone, the other as seventh; but the *g♯* cannot be doubled, because, if it were, both *g♯*'s would have to go to *a* (parallel unison or octaves).

The triad on VII cannot serve as preparation for III because the *g♯* should not move by leap. For the same reason the seventh chord of VI cannot resolve to II (root position), although resolution to the six-four chord of II is naturally possible. The same grounds also exclude, for the moment, the use of the seventh chord of VII, *g♯–b–d–f*. The other seventh chords of the VIIth degree, *g–b–d–f♯* and *g♯–b–d–f♯*, cannot be used because the seventh, *f♯*, would have to go to *g♯* – but also because these chords could easily lead out of the key. The seventh chord of IV cannot resolve to the unraised VIIth degree because *f♯* must go to *g♯*, nor to the raised VII on account of the doubling of the *g♯*. It is possible to avoid this doubling by using the six-four chord of VII for the resolution. Through use of inversions of the three chords involved, many things naturally become available. The pupil is by now surely able to examine these and to recognize their possibilities on his own. Consequently, I may dispense with any further examination of them.

Most of these chords that here, too, turn out to be in part unusable (temporarily!) are usually not considered at all, but are simply designated as unusable. I should not want to do that, for some can be connected, in inversions and with inversions, in spite of our extremely restrictive ground rules. However that may be, possibilities for using a number of them will arise later. It is always more to the point to admit as many chords as possible, eventually even such as in general are rather rarely used, because they enrich the harmonic possibilities of a key – it is more to the point, more consistent with our aims to admit them than it is to exclude *a priori* what is not in common usage merely because it cannot be connected according to the rules. If we resolve the seventh chords into six-four chords, then still more possibilities open up (Example 61*a*).

The pupil should now work out the preparation and resolution of seventh chords in little phrases. Example 62 gives a few models.

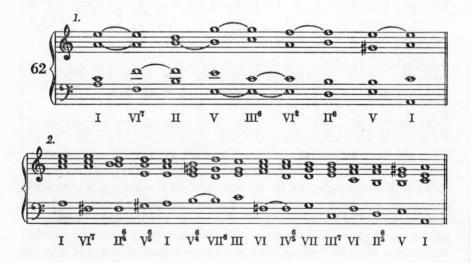

For the *inversion* of seventh chords in minor there are again no new directions to be observed; it is necessary merely to observe those previously given. Again, the use of inversions makes possible certain connections that were previously excluded, largely because the raised sixth or seventh tone, if it is in the bass and the progression allows, can first be sustained, and then move on. Obviously, seventh chords can be connected here with one another. Even if many of these connections seldom appear in music, the pupil will yet do well to practice everything. It will increase his insight and his skill, and that is something, too. Besides: Must there be an [immediate] advantage for us in everything we do?

VI CONNECTION OF CHORDS THAT HAVE NO COMMON TONE (*HARMONISCHES BAND*)[1]

The connection of chords that have no common tone was omitted at first only because difficulties in voice leading could result and the planning of the root progressions could easily turn out less well. If we now introduce such connections in our exercises, we must consider some measures for surmounting such difficulties. First, the difficulties of voice leading. The other matters we shall discuss in detail in the following chapter.

The connections involved are those of a degree with its two neighbors, with the one immediately preceding and the one immediately following: for example II with I and with III. Should we allow all voices to take the shortest way, parallel octaves and fifths would result.

Here, consequently, the shortest way is impossible. To avoid the parallels we must use contrary motion. The pupil is advised to make clear to himself in advance which voices present the danger of parallels.

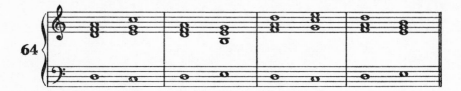

If we use sixth chords, it is still easier to avoid fifths and octaves.

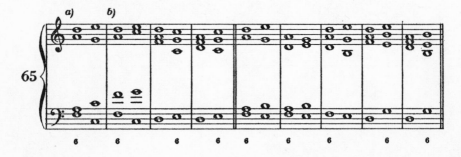

[1 *Supra*, p. 39.]

In connecting two such sixth chords it is advisable to double the third in one of them, although the connection can be made without that.

I should like to mention here an assumption of the older theory:[1] namely, that in the connection of two adjacent degrees, specifically of the lower with the higher (Example 67, II with III), the first chord is the incomplete representative of a seventh chord whose root, missing here, lies a third lower (thus, seventh chord of VII); and it was assumed that in the connection of the higher with the lower (Example 67, III–II) the first chord represents a ninth chord whose root and third are missing. The older theory had exact methods for resolving every tone in the seventh chords and ninth chords, and contrary motion resulted as a matter of course. Although this assumption is somewhat complicated, it does have something good about it: it refers these connections, too, back to the root progression of an ascending fourth, thus to the strongest progression.

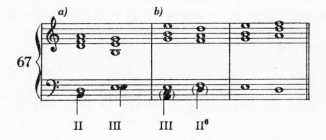

I mention this assumption here because, on another occasion [p. 117], one that seems more important to me, I will argue similarly. I am thus in favor of this interpretation, but I do not advise that the connections here be worked out from this point of view. To do so appears to me superfluous.

Before we proceed to work out these connections in little phrases we shall

[1 Cf. Simon Sechter (1788–1867), *Die Grundsätze der musikalischen Komposition, Erste Abtheilung: Die richtige Folge der Grundharmonien, oder vom Fundamentalbass und dessen Umkehrungen und Stellvertretern* (*The Principles of Musical Composition, Part I: The Correct Sequence of the Basic Harmonies, or The Fundamental Bass, its Inversions and Substitutes*) (Leipzig: Breitkopf und Härtel, 1853), pp. 32–4. For another example of Schoenberg's debt to the 'older theory', see *infra*, p. 270, where he mentioned Sechter by name.]

now add the preparation of seventh chords by means of the octave [i.e. the root of the preparatory chord].

If the pupil takes care to avoid parallel fifths and octaves these examples offer no new difficulty. Only, in connecting the root positions of both chords (as in Example 68a) it is sometimes hard to get a complete chord. That can only be done by skipping from the third of the first chord to the fifth of the second (Example 68b). If this leap is a diminished fifth (Example 68a), it should actually be avoided on account of the unmelodic interval. But if some advantage or necessity makes the complete chord worth the effort, then the pupil can henceforth use this leap without hesitation.

Example 69 incorporates the foregoing in a little phrase. Obviously these phrases can henceforth be more elaborate. (To be practiced also in minor.)

VII SOME DIRECTIONS FOR OBTAINING BETTER PROGRESSIONS; CONCERNING MELODIC CONDUCT OF THE TWO OUTER VOICES; THEN CONCERNING CLOSES, CADENCES, DECEPTIVE CADENCES, AND THE SIX-FOUR CHORD IN THE CADENCE

From now on, planning the bass voice becomes more and more difficult. If the many possibilities are to be exploited, then the management of problems even now presupposes a certain skill in the ordering of progressions, since the pupil is indeed always working on a particular problem.[1] Because the effort invested in drafting the examples demands a greater return than merely that of the schematically correct solution, they are approaching that point at which we must begin to accord the sense of form a richer satisfaction than heretofore. In a word, since the resources are now richer, the phrases should begin to be more rounded, more polished. Thus, for example, we see in Example 69 a shortcoming that the pupil cannot at present easily avoid, so long as he honors the law of the nearest way. The soprano voice, beginning as it does in the middle range, is not able to escape the persistent descent into the lower range, at least not with the necessary energy. The resultant monotony can readily undermine the effectiveness even of an example whose harmonic progression is faultless. For this reason, and only for such a reason, we shall concern ourselves with melodic questions.* But there is something else disturbing about Example 69. The connection of certain chords produces a frequent sustaining of the other principal voice, the bass. And even the root progressions are not all such as will yield a really satisfactory harmonic progression. We shall thus also have to give close attention to the bass melody and to the root progressions.

First of all, the root progressions. We have recognized previously that the

* This seems to contradict my contention that harmony instruction should talk about progressions of harmonies, not about voice leading. But the contradiction is only apparent; for my polemic was aimed at the figured-bass method, by means of which the pupil develops skill in the conduct of voices but not in the conduct of harmony. Moreover, the view that harmonic usage is often created by coincidences of voice leading is, quite to the contrary, one of the bases of my study, as is shown in my discussion of dissonance treatment, ornaments (*Manieren*) and the like [*supra*, pp. 47–8]. One must distinguish between a pedagogical method that drills voice leading (when it should be drilling the conduct of harmony) and a manner of presentation that, fully aware of the influence of voice leading on harmonic events, accords voice leading its rights where it is appropriate to explain the problems.

[1 '. . . da der Schüler ja immer auf einen bestimmten Fall hinarbeitet.' As the number of possibilities has greatly increased, so has the complexity of any particular instance; therefore, the rules can no longer direct the pupil's every step. His skill, his 'sense of form' must now begin to guide him where the rules cannot.]

strongest movement of the root is the leap of a fourth upward, because this movement seems to correspond to a tendency of the tone. With this progression the following change takes place in the harmony (Example 70):

The tone that was previously the principal tone, the root, becomes in the second chord a dependent tone, the fifth. More generally, the bass tone of the second chord is a higher category, a higher power, for it contains the first, the tone that itself was previously the root. In the triad on *G* the *g* is sovereign, but in the triad on *C* the *g* is subordinate and the *c* is sovereign.* A progression that evokes this situation, which, so to speak, sets a king over a prince, can only be a strong progression. But the *c* not only subjugates the root, it forces the other chord components as well to conform to its requirements; and the new chord contains, apart from the vanquished former root, nothing that recalls the former government. It contains, apart from that one, nothing but new tones. One can justifiably assume that progressions which produce similar situations are equally strong, or nearly so.

The next such progression is the root progression of a third downward (Example 71).

* This tendency of a tone to lose itself in a lower tone obviously contradicts the tendency to become and remain the root, which it exhibited in another, an earlier stage. This contradiction is its problem; from this problem it evolves. [That is, tonality evolves, a theory of tonality generated by this conflict.] So long as a bass tone is not the root, its sole drive is to become just that. Once it is the root, then it has a different goal: to lose itself in, to become part of a higher entity. – It would actually be better for me to say the leap of a *fifth* downward, for the tone has the tendency to become part of a tone a fifth *below* it. Merely in order to retain the metaphor of rising and falling intervals I speak of the *ascending* interval as a fourth *upward* and of the *descending* as a fourth *downward*. (This is only a metaphor, as is our designation of pitches as high and low. Since the tones are literally neither high nor low, we could just as well express this distinction by means of other antitheses: for example, sharp and blunt, short and long, etc.) This nomenclature is at least not entirely unjustified; although the intervals do 'rise' in that direction we call low, the intensity nevertheless rises. And it is the direction of *increasing* heaviness and length of strings.

This happens as follows: The former root is overcome and becomes a mere third. But the earlier third becomes the fifth, thus advances; and the new chord is differentiated from the former by only one new tone. Although it is the root, the progression, measured by the degree to which the root is victorious, cannot be considered as strong as the progression a fourth upward. It still recalls too much the former government; it contains too many of the former tones. It is nevertheless one of the strongest progressions, as can be inferred from the fact that two such progressions one after the other yield the same result as that a fourth upward (Example 72).

It is somewhat more complicated to judge the two root progressions a second upward (II–III) and a second downward (II–I). There are many reasons for designating them as the strongest root progressions, but their use in music does not support this view. If we look at the outcome of these progressions, at the composition of the chords, we find that all tones of the first chord are overcome, since in both cases all tones of the second chord are new. In this respect they go further than the progressions examined so far. They connect a degree with precisely those two degrees that have nothing in common with it, to which it is least related. These progressions force the connection; and it may be for this reason that the older theory[1] explains them in a unique way: each as the sum of two progressions, of which one, the more important, is a root progression a fourth upward. These sums read: V–VI = V–III–VI (Example 73*a*) and V–IV = V–I–IV (Example 73*b*).

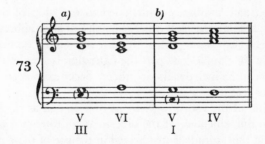

In the connection (Example 73*a*) of V (*G*) with VI (*A*) it would actually be the IIIrd degree (*E*) that is connected, only the root of the latter is missing; in that of V (*G*) with IV (*F*) the (tacit) I (*C*) would play the same role.

[[1] *Supra*, p. 113.]

This conception has much to recommend it and fits perfectly into the system of presentation, which accomplishes its purpose when it accommodates the events with such logical uniformity that broad perspectives are opened up and exceptions are superfluous. This explanation is indeed persuasive; it also suggests something quite different. It would almost lead us to believe that our forebears, who sat at the source when harmony gushed forth, who were there as it grew, could have known precisely that such a progression amounts to a sum; and that they may have used this summarizing, this abbreviation, as one uses a character in shorthand, for clearly recognized ends: for example, the deceptive cadence. *Then this explanation would be more than a theory; it would be a report.*

Such procedure – where in place of a connection otherwise made by means of three chords only two appear, best explained as an abbreviation – is indeed often found in other circumstances as well. For example, as we shall see later, the same thing happens with the dominant of the dominant (Example 74) where the I (six-four chord) and V, ordinarily coming between this dominant and the closing chord (74*a*), are often left out (74*b*).

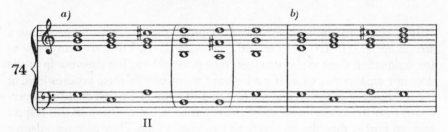

74

II

Moreover, [such abbreviation] operates in the manner of the cliché, which was already mentioned but in a different sense: a stereotyped usage does not have to be written out in full. Everyone knows that *i.e.* means 'that is'. Everyone knows that the IInd degree as dominant of the dominant will at some place or other, with some means or other, produce I. Consequently, we can omit the intervening chords and put the effect immediately after the cause. And that is presumably what happened here: the progression was ultimately assumed to be a kind of cliché, and familiarity with it led to omission of the superfluous. Moreover, there are in music still other examples of such abbreviations. Whoever understands transposition will see that it is a similar occurrence when, as often happens, in the double-bass part the figuration is simpler than that of the cello. Merely the principal details are there. Secondary details are left out. Even if for other reasons.

The conception of the root progressions of a second as sums, as abbreviations, testifies to the reluctance of the older masters to regard them as normal progressions; and this attitude is manifested in the use of these progressions in the masterworks. Were one of them the strongest progression (which one?), then it would have to play a different role in the articulation of the key: that is, in the cadence. This leading role is played, however, by the root progression of a fourth. The cadential progression, IV–V, is by no means insignificant, but II–V can replace it unobtrusively; and the same cannot be said of V–I. The conquest of the subdominant region (IV) by the dominant region (V) does appear, however, as an auxiliary progression alongside the final, decisive progression, which does then indeed have an easy time of it. Likewise, the deceptive cadence is a strong means by which to introduce a secondary matter: it leads to a digression. Its work is always done either at secondary places or for secondary matters, but it is mostly hard work (*grobe Arbeit*) that is expected of it. It is strong, no doubt, even excessively strong, since it adds together two strong progressions. But probably too strong for everyday use: *Allzu scharf macht schartig* (Too much sharpening makes jagged edges).

I should therefore like to call this root progression the 'superstrong' (*überstark*) progression. Or, since I call the strong progressions '*ascending*',* one could possibly also describe it as '*overskipping*' (*überspringend*), whereby the abbreviation would be expressed. It is clear that strong or ascending progressions together with weak or descending, as means of normal strength, will always as a rule be permissible, whereas there must be a special occasion for using the *superstrong*, those that '*overskip*'. It is likewise clear that here, as elsewhere, the use of brute force does not guarantee the strongest effect.[1]

Now the two remaining root progressions, a fifth upward and a third upward, I call *descending* progressions. What happens here is as follows: the progression of a fifth upward (Example 75*a*) turns a tone that was before relatively subordinate into the principal tone. The fifth, a *parvenu*, is promoted, becomes the root. That is decadence. One could counter with the assertion that this advancement testifies to the power of the one promoted and that here the root was overcome. But the power of the promoted one consists only in the former root's yielding, deliberately yielding, its power to the new; it gave in voluntarily to the new, for the latter, the fifth, is after all contained within it; it gave in only, so to speak, out of its good nature, as when the lion enters into friendship with the rabbit. The same happens, yet more noticeably, in the progression a third upward. Here the former third, the weakest interval, becomes the root, and the new chord distinguishes itself from the preceding only by a single tone: the fifth alone is new (Example 75*b*). This progression thus seems to be the weakest of all. This apparent weakness perhaps follows also from the fact that

---

* Dr. Heinrich Schenker (in his book *Neue musikalische Theorien und Phantasien* [Vol. I: *Harmonielehre* (Vienna: Universal Edition, 1906); Abridged English translation: *Harmony*, pp. 232–40]) also uses this designation for the root progressions. Only, he calls (inversely) the fourth progression upward 'descending'. When I obtained the book recently I thought at first I had got from it the idea for this nomenclature. This would not have been impossible, since I had read some of it four years ago. Then, however, I remembered, and was able to confirm by asking around among my pupils, that I had already used these expressions in teaching long before (at least seven years ago). Thus, the two of us, independently of each other, have arrived at something similar. But to me this is easily explainable: anyone who knows Brahms's harmony will, assuming correct observation, reach the same conclusions.

[1 In his *Structural Functions of Harmony* (pp. 6–18), Schoenberg used the English terms 'strong' or 'ascending', 'descending', and 'superstrong'. No translation of 'überspringend' appears in that work.]

the juxtaposition of two such progressions yields the same result as the progression of a fifth upward (Example 75*c*).

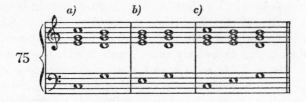

75

Since here such a gross distinction was constructed between strong and weak progressions, we must now say emphatically that it does not mean we should always use strong progressions exclusively. The use of weak progressions would then be excluded entirely, for weak ones would be bad ones. Therefore, I prefer to classify the progressions, as I have said, with the terms *ascending* and *descending*. The progressions of the fourth upward, the second upward and downward, and the third downward I call ascending progressions, the fifth upward and third upward, descending. These terms are intended to indicate which ends are served by the one and which by the other. That there are such ends is obvious; for the articulation of a phrase, in music as in language, demands the rise and fall of tone, of emphasis. The use of descending progressions is therefore just as much an artistic means as the use of ascending progressions. Here, to be sure, where we cannot be concerned with articulating phrases, *in planning our root progressions we shall give absolute preference to the ascending progressions and shall use the descending ones primarily in those chord connections where the total effect is still that of ascent.* For example, if the progression a fifth upward is followed by that of a second upward, the result is a progression a third downward, thus, an ascent of the harmony (Example 76*a*). The same result is obtained, if a third upward is followed by a fourth upward (76*b*) or even by a second upward (76*c*).

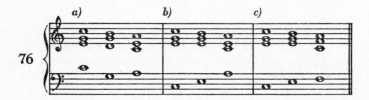

76

The impression is then more or less as if the intervening chord had been inserted merely for melodic reasons. Anyway, the descending progressions should be used in our exercises only in this sense.

Now to review briefly: These are the root progressions the pupil should use, so long as he is concerned only with harmonic means and so long as it is not possible for him to aspire, say by means of melody, rhythm, or dynamics, to some other effect or style (*Charakteristik*): progressions a fourth upward, a second upward and downward, and a third downward – the ascending progressions.

The descending progressions, fifth and third upward, he should use only in connections like those shown in Example 76.

Of course these instructions do not unconditionally guarantee good harmonic progressions (Example 77*a*), nor do they by any means exhaust the possibilities of good progression. Most important, however, they are not meant to be an evaluation, rather only a characterization of effects. For, as said, good progressions are also possible in which descending progressions are connected with ascending. And a series of descending progressions is no less musical (Example 77*b*). Nevertheless, until the pupil's ear becomes a dependable guide, making it possible for him to judge new things independently, he will do well to abide by these instructions. For the possibilities they present will almost always turn out well; only in exceptional cases will they turn out badly, whereas through unfortunate choice of descending progressions weaknesses often emerge. And I think this should indeed be the objective of a course: to show the learner that which is without doubt good, that which has something at least moderately good about it; and at the same time to open up for him a view of that which, once he has attained maturity (*Kultur*), he can create through his own inventiveness (*Kombination*).

Example 77*a* presents a series of exclusively ascending progressions and yet the phrase is not very good (if viewed, naturally, only from the standpoint of harmony; there could be a magnificent melody above it which would erase all my present objections). For the juxtaposition of so many stepwise progressions sounds unquestionably monotonous and cold. Here, too, the pupil will find it necessary to introduce variety. This means avoiding progressions that are too uniform; it means mixing, often and well, root movement by step with movement by leap. For a series of nothing but leaps would have little value in itself, merely as harmony; it is too mechanical (Examples 78*a*, 78*b*, and 78*c*).

With this we have come to a second requirement to be considered in the planning of good phrases: the demand for variety. This requirement is difficult to handle without speaking also of its complement, repetition. For as the former produces diversity, so the latter gives the former coherence, sense, system. And system can be founded only on repetition. Yet repetition will be of little use to us here. One of the few instances to be considered for harmonic construction, which, although it touches on the motivic, does not absolutely require a theme, is the sequence. Other repetitions we should actually avoid, or, if they cannot be circumvented, we should hide them. We must forego for the present the advantage of using repetition to attain effects; but on the other hand we must guard against the disadvantages it brings with it. Our bass voice has within a key a range of between twelve and fourteen tones. Should the phrase use more than fourteen chords, then even the possibility of putting tones that have appeared before into another octave no longer suffices to avoid repetition. It is not so much the repetition of a tone that is irksome as, far more, the repetition of tone progressions. Even this does not necessarily disturb if at least different chords are set above the repeated tones. And if only enough different material intervenes between such repeated chords [tones?], then the repetition should inflict no damage at all. The worst form of repetition will be that which brings back the highest or the lowest tone of a line a second time. Particular attention should be devoted to these two points: the high point and (if one may say it this way) the low point. Almost every melody will have such tones, and the high point in particular will hardly be repeated. Obviously, this applies only to our simple structures here, in which it is impossible to correct with other means what is objectionable in a line. And if, for example, in a Schubert *Lied* it should be shown that the highest tone appears several times in a melody (for example, 'Mit dem grünen Lautenbande'), then that is naturally a different case; for there other means are used to provide the necessary variety. Moreover, it is not to be concluded from all this that disregarding a high point must under all circumstances yield bad results. Above all, however, let us emphasize that here, as before, we are not proposing a standard for judging works of art, but only, at most, a standard for judging the work of pupils. We are again merely pointing out something that, if it is observed, can at least do no harm and can sometimes produce significant improvement. The pupil will do well, then, to restrain himself from violating this limitation until his sense of form has been sufficiently trained.

The repetition of a series of tones creates an unfavorable impression not only in the upper voice but also in the bass, and sometimes even a different harmonization cannot correct this shortcoming.

To get round it (79*a* in the bass, 79*b* in the soprano) is generally rather easy; all that is needed is a well-timed change of register in the soprano by means of a skip or the choice of a different inversion in the bass. The repetition of tones in a voice, however, makes us suspect that repetitions also take place in the root progression. Then the defect must be sought in the original sketch and there corrected.

In general the pupil must not go too far in the effort to introduce great

variety; for it is not his task to write melodiously, to produce effects – he could not succeed at such. The aim here is more to avoid what is unmelodious than to write compelling melody.

Now, in the following, the

GUIDELINES

for using the means so far introduced are to be reviewed and completed. By observing them the pupil will be able to raise his exercises to a somewhat higher level. Much is excluded, for the most part only what is not accepted usage; in that which is permitted will be found, for the most part, only what is accepted usage.

I. *Concerning Root Progressions*[1]

1. The *ascending* root progressions, fourth upward and third downward, can appear at any time, although here, too, mechanical repetition is to be avoided.
2. The *descending* progressions, fourth downward and third upward [should be used] only in such connections which, as was shown (p. 120), yield overall ascent.
3. The 'overskipping' progressions [should be used] sparingly, so long as no more explicit instructions are given; these progressions are not excluded.

II. *Use of the Chords*

A. *In Major and Minor*
1. (a) *Triads* in root position can appear anywhere.
   (b) *Sixth chords* serve for attaining richer variety in the voice leading, especially in that of the outer voices (bass and soprano), and in addition, for making possible the preparation of dissonances.
   (c) *Six-four chords* are, in general, to be used most sparingly. The best use of all is in cadences (to be shown in the next division of this chapter, pp. 143–5). The forms appearing as passing harmony, sparingly used, are to be recommended because the bass moves. Those, however, in which the bass must be

[1 Schoenberg's outline form is largely retained here and in the subsequent 'Guidelines'.]

sustained are to be used with care. Sometimes they are necessary for preparing dissonances.

2. (a) *Seventh chords* can be used wherever triads can be used, if preparation and resolution are provided. They will be used preferably, however, where the seventh can give the chord a tendency requiring resolution or some other treatment. Thereby, the progression needed (V–I and, as will be shown in the following division of this chapter, V–VI and V–IV) is, so to speak, obliged to follow.

(b) *Inversions of the seventh chords* [are to be used] under the same conditions as their root positions for improving the voice leading. Here the two chord is especially well-suited for introducing a sixth chord.

3. *Diminished triads* (at first only in the progressions already practiced: II–VII–III and IV–VII–III), as dissonances, are likewise suited for lending an impression of necessity to the introduction of a chord (III). The seventh chord on the VIIth degree intensifies this impression. Inversions [are used] for the same purposes as the inversions of the other chords.

B. *In Minor*

The requirements of the pivot tones must be added, as well as attention to the two regions: the ascending scale (with raised tones) and the descending (with natural tones).

1. (a) *The pivot tones* must be considered from the outset, as the root progressions are being sketched out, to make sure the tones involved will be able to follow the prescribed route.

(b) Triads must often be put into inversions if there is a dissonance to be prepared or resolved, especially when a pivot tone lies in the bass.

(c) What applies to triads applies also to seventh chords.

(d) After the diminished triad and the seventh chord of II (unraised) it will be better in general to write V with the major third rather than with the minor, because this degree has a conventional meaning in the cadence, as will become clear later.

(e) All diminished triads (II, VI, and VII), along with their seventh chords, are suitable for the same purposes as are served by the diminished in major: through the dissonance they acquire an explicit tendency.

(f) The augmented triad can just as well follow as precede the regions of the ascending and descending minor scale, a versatility further enhanced by its being a dissonance. It is therefore eminently suitable for going from one region to the other.

2. One may not stay exclusively in either of the two regions for too long a time without jeopardizing the character of the minor mode. This [character] is best expressed by suitable exchange and connection of the two regions. Crossing over from one region to the other can happen only after all the obligations of the pivot tones are met. This crossover occurs

(a) *directly*

(1) from the *ascending to the descending region,* when the raised III, V, and (as will be shown later) VII are followed by I or unraised IV or VI (no unraised chord can follow chords containing the raised sixth tone);

(2) *from the descending to the ascending* when the unraised II, IV, and VI are followed by the raised III, V, or (as will be shown later) VII. All raised chords can connect with I; however, raised chords cannot follow chords containing the unraised seventh tone.

(b) *indirectly*

(1) from the *ascending to the descending* when chords containing the raised sixth tone (II, IV, VI) lead first to such as allow progression to the raised seventh;

(2) from the *descending to the ascending* when chords containing the unraised seventh tone (III, V, VII) lead first to such as admit the unraised sixth.

III. *Voice Leading*

1. Unmelodic (dissonant or dissonance-producing) steps or skips are to be avoided. Avoiding such intervals is advisable so long as we are not using altered chords. Those intervals would not be suitable for the chords we use prior to that time;
2. Disturbing repetitions of tone progressions are to be avoided, especially whenever the repeated tones also have the same harmony as before;
3. Wherever possible, a high point is to be respected, and perhaps a low point as well;
4. Greatest possible variety [should occur] in the use of steps and leaps in the succession of intervals. Here care should be taken to maintain a certain middle range;
5. Should the voice leave this middle range by leap, then, wherever possible, a progression or a leap should soon lead back to it; and vice versa; thus, compensation for change of register;
6. If the middle register was left by stepwise motion, balance could be restored, perhaps, by means of an octave leap or the like;
7. If repetition of a tone or a tone progression is unavoidable, then an immediate change of direction could help.

So far as these directions apply, they apply equally to soprano and bass. Indeed, if the pupil could observe them even in the middle voices, the smoothness of the total effect would be absolutely enhanced. But it is not necessary for the pupil to go that far at present; it is enough if he works out the two outer voices with the greatest possible care.

CLOSES AND CADENCES[1]

To a vessel of porcelain or bronze, for example a vase, one cannot attach yet

[1 'Schlüsse und Kadenzen'. Cadences in general Schoenberg called 'Schlüsse' (closes). He reserved the word 'Kadenz' for the authentic perfect cadence. – Cf. pp. 305–8, where he pursued the topic introduced here and attempted to classify cadences.]

another piece of porcelain or bronze without going through a complicated procedure. At least it is questionable whether it would still be a vase and whether the attached piece would even stay attached. Having seen, however, that a piece of music has arrived at a certain point where a close would be conceivable (for example, at the repeat sign in a sonata; or, better still, just before the trio of a scherzo); having seen how at these and similar places the music does nevertheless continue – so, even at the point where a piece does indeed end, we can easily doubt whether this absolutely has to be the end with no possibility of continuation. And as a matter of fact (if we ignore the sense of form) it would be conceivable, after the final tonic, to go on once again to just such chords as have already often appeared at analogous places.

Thus, we may well ask: Why, in what manner, and when does a piece of music close? The answer can only be a general one: As soon as the goal is reached. What this goal is, however, we can scarcely even hint at here: when the sense of form is satisfied, when enough has happened to fulfil the urge for expression, when the idea involved has been clearly presented, and so on. For our pedagogical ends only this is relevant: the attainment of the goal. To the extent that our exercises are inferior to the work of art, to this extent it is easier to say what their goal or purpose is. Our exercises always have some specific purpose or other, the work of art never; the artist perhaps sometimes has one, or at least thinks he has, while in reality he is not carrying out a purpose but rather obeying his instincts. Because of this distinction it is possible for anyone to put together harmony exercises, whereas to almost everyone is denied the ability to create, or even only to comprehend, a work of art. Even if the higher sphere transcending ordinary purposes (*Zwecklosigkeit*) is the region in which the artist orients himself, still, attention to purposes (*Zweckmässigkeit*) forms the only dependable basis for teaching the handicraft of art. This pedagogy thrives on and exists by virtue of its efforts to establish as obligatory what with the artist was utmost freedom. And the power of this utmost freedom, viewed from the proximity of the handicraft of art, is inconceivable without laws or purposes. Here, only one who is far enough removed from such an expanse can see the true picture. Here, proximity makes petty, whereas only respectful distance reveals the true greatness.

Our purpose could be, for example, to prepare and resolve a seventh chord, to connect a sixth chord with a six-four chord, and so on. At the same time the pupil could always set for himself the secondary purpose of reviewing what was learned earlier. According to what was said before, we should stop the moment such a purpose is accomplished; for only such modesty can excuse our attempts. The moment at which we are to stop is thus easy to determine. However: to stop is not to close. Stopping is simple; it means not continuing. Closing, though, is different. To close, one must use special means.

Now I must say at once I do not believe it possible to fashion a close, an ending, in such a way as to rule out every possibility of continuation. Just as the *Magic Flute* and *Faust* can admit of a second part, so can every drama, every novel 'Twenty years later'. And if death does mark the end of the tragedy, it is still not the end of everything. Hence, in music as well one could go on and on attaching new chords, as is indeed demonstrated by the many cadences and frequent repetitions of the concluding chord found, especially, in the older masterworks. Yet, even here, there could undoubtedly be a continuation, the idea could be spun out still further or new ones attached. To do so might impair the balance (*Ebenmass*), but for this we have no formula. And it has happened often enough that what was at first considered immoderate, distorted (*Übermass*), turned out later to be well-proportioned (*Ebenmass*). In this respect music is comparable to a gas, which is in itself without form but of unlimited extension. If, however, one introduces it into a form, then it fills this form with no change in its own mass and content. Entertaining such thoughts, I have to conclude that it is difficult, yes, almost impossible to fashion an absolutely compelling and final close. It is indeed not improbable (perhaps it is even certain) that inherent in every idea and in the way it is elaborated there is something that indicates boundaries to be reached but not overstepped. It is not improbable, though not absolutely certain either, that every idea has some such proportion within it; however, it is also possible that this proportion is not in the idea, or at least not in it alone, but in ourselves as well. Only, it does not therefore have to be in us as something immutable, as something given in our nature, hence incapable of change or development; rather as something that is modified according to changing tastes, perhaps even according to fashions, keeping up with the spirit of the times (*Zeitgeist*). I do not believe in the Golden Section.[1] At least I do not believe it is the sole formal law governing our perception and sensations of beauty, rather, at most, one among many, one among countless such laws. I do not believe then that a composition must run to just such and such a length, no longer, no shorter; nor that a motive, regarded as the germ from which the composition grew, would have admitted none other than this one, single form of elaboration. Otherwise it would hardly be possible to write two or more different fugues on the same subject, as Bach and others did repeatedly. If there are such laws, we have not yet recognized them. But I do believe in something else: namely, that every era has a particular sense of form, a norm which tells the composer of that era how far he must go in working out an idea and how far he may not go. Hence, [to close a piece of music] I believe we simply fulfil the requirements recognized by the conventions and the sense of form of the era, requirements which, in defining the possibilities, evoke expectation and thereby guarantee a satisfying close.

Up to now music had the possibility of drawing such boundaries through adherence to the laws of tonality. I have said earlier that I do not hold tonality to be a natural law nor a necessary prerequisite of artistic effectiveness. The laws by which tonality itself comes about are then still less necessary, far less; they are merely the simple exploitation of the most evident natural characteristics;

[1 A Euclidean formula – 'to cut a finite line so that the shorter part is to the longer part as the longer part is to the whole' – long regarded by aestheticians as a definition of ideal proportions in art. 'From about the middle of the last century it begins to be treated with great seriousness. . . . [Since the 1870s], practically every work on aesthetics includes some consideration of the problem' (Herbert Read, *The Meaning of Art* [Penguin Books, 1949], p. 22).]

they do not teach the essence of the matter but merely aim at the orderly and mechanical elaboration of a device that makes it possible to lend musical thoughts the aura of completeness (*Geschlossenheit*). I will return to this topic, tonality, repeatedly and in detail, and shall say again here only what is necessary at the moment. Of course the idea of closing with the same tone one began with has something decidedly right about it and also gives a certain impression of being natural. Since indeed all the simple relationships derive from the simplest natural aspects of the tone (from its first overtones), the fundamental tone then has a certain sovereignty over the structures emanating from it just because the most important components of these structures are, so to speak, its satraps, its advocates, since they derive from its splendor: Napoleon, who installs his relatives and friends on the European thrones. I think that would indeed be enough to explain why one is justified in obeying the will of the fundamental tone: gratefulness to the progenitor and dependence on him. He is Alpha and Omega. That is morally right, so long as no other moral code obtains. Yet, another can indeed prevail! If, for example, the supreme lord becomes weak and his subjects strong, a situation that arises only too often in harmony. Just as it is hardly inevitable that a conqueror will endure as dictator, so it is no more inevitable that tonality must take its direction from the fundamental tone, even if it is derived from that tone. Quite the contrary. The struggle between two such fundamentals for sovereignty has something indeed very attractive about it, as numerous examples of modern harmony show. And even if here the struggle does end with the victory of the one fundamental, that victory is still not inevitable. This one question [which fundamental shall reign] could just as well remain unanswered, seeing that so many others are still unanswered. We bestow no less interest on the problem itself, than on the alleged solution. It is superfluous to hark back every time to the ancestors, to show every time with utmost thoroughness the derivation of chords from the fundamental; it is superfluous to prove their lineage every time when it is familiar to everyone and lives in everyone's memory and sense of form – not only to prove it every time with absolute thoroughness, but also to set everything up in such a way that these relationships jump right out at us. The ceremonious way in which the close of a composition used to be tied up, bolted, nailed down, and sealed would be too ponderous for the present-day sense of form to use it. This precondition, that everything emanates from the [fundamental] tone, can just as well be suspended, since one is constantly reminded of it anyway by every tone. And whenever we let our imagination roam, we certainly do not keep ourselves strictly within boundaries, even though our bodies do have them.

The sense of form of the present does not demand this exaggerated intelligibility produced by working out the tonality. A piece can also be intelligible to us when the relationship to the fundamental is not treated as basic; it can be intelligible even when the tonality is kept, so to speak, flexible, fluctuating (*schwebend*). Many examples give evidence that nothing is lost from the impression of completeness if the tonality is merely hinted at, yes, even if it is erased. And – without saying that the ultramodern music is really atonal: for it may be perhaps that we simply do not yet know how to explain the tonality, or something corresponding to tonality, in modern music[1] – the analogy with infinity could hardly be made more vivid than through a fluctuating, so to speak, unending harmony, through a harmony that does not always carry with it certificate of domicile and passport carefully indicating country of origin and destination. It is indeed charming of the people that they would like to know where infinity begins and where it will stop. And one can forgive them if they have little confidence in an infinity which they have not themselves measured. But art, if it should have something or other in common with the eternal, is not entitled to shy away from the vacuum.

The sense of form of our forebears required it to be otherwise. For them the comedy concluded with marriage, the tragedy with expiation or retribution, and the musical work 'in the same key'. Hence, for them the choice of scale brought the obligation to treat the first tone of that scale as the fundamental, and to present it as Alpha and Omega of all that took place in the work, as the patriarchal ruler over the domain defined by its might and its will: its coat of arms was displayed at the most conspicuous points, especially at the beginning and ending. And thus they had a possibility for closing that in effect resembled a necessity.

We shall have to address ourselves to the task of learning the techniques by which tonality is expressed. First, let us consider that with which we have started: the close, the cadence. Once the pupil is more advanced he will see, in the study of form, that to bring about a close he will need still other means besides those merely of harmony. To explain those other means and their functions, however, that is, to give the pupil the direction he needs, is there, in the study of form, much more difficult. So difficult that it is advisable to familiarize him even now with those things on which a convincing close depends.

Melodically the key is represented by the scale, harmonically by the diatonic chords. Yet, unaccentuated use of these components alone is not enough to establish the key. For certain keys are so similar to one another, so closely related, that it is not always easy to determine which is really the key unless special, limiting means are brought to bear. It is clear which keys are most closely related: those which most closely resemble one another. First of all, the relative major and minor (*C* major and *a* minor); then keys with the same name (*a* minor and *A* major); but then, and these are here the most dangerous relations, those keys which are distinguished from one another by only one sign in the key signature (♮, ♭ or ♯: *C* major and *G* major, *C* major and *F* major). Whereas the difference between, say, *a* minor and *A* major makes itself felt at almost every moment, disappearing only at the Vth degree (as the dominant), with the last-named kind of relationship the situation is well-nigh reversed. Almost all the tones and a great number of the chords are common to both keys. *C* major differentiates itself from *G* major only by virtue of the *f* in *C* major and the *f*♯ in *G*, and from *F* major only by virtue of the *b*, as opposed to

[1] In his 'Handexemplar . . .' of March, 1922, Schoenberg underlined this parenthetical remark (which he had added in the revised edition), 'particularly the word "atonal", and wrote this word again in the margin' (see *supra*, Translator's Preface, p. xvi).]

the $b\flat$ of F major. Thus in C major it is easy to make progressions that can be heard as G major or F major.

Is this C or G?

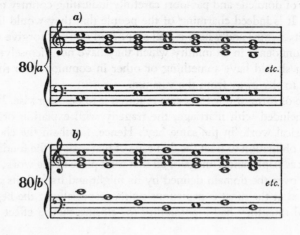

Is that C or F?

If we avoid the tone f, then the resultant progressions can just as well point to G major as to C. If we avoid the b, then we can hear the passage just as well in F major and can proceed to that key.

Should we want to establish C major in such a way that there is no doubt about it, that is, so that we can think of neither F nor G major, then we must introduce b and f. The most important means for expressing the key will thus be those that distinguish it from the keys it most resembles, that separate it clearly from its nearest neighbors. Once we have succeeded in excluding confusion even with those keys with which it could most easily be confused, then we have defined the key unambiguously.

The oft-mentioned tendency of a tone to lose itself in one a fifth lower, which is its root, to become the fifth of the lower tone, is found of course in the first degree also. For that reason F major poses the greatest threat to C. Our efforts will consequently have to be directed first towards preventing the drift to the subdominant, to the feeling of F major. We can do that melodically by means of the tone b. Now three chords contain b: III, V, and VII; hence, they are the ones to be considered for the harmonic expression of this purpose. We could use all three, but there is greater justification for giving preference to V; for its root finds in I that fundamental tone a fifth below whose fifth this root of V seeks to become [V (G) seeks to become the fifth of I (C)].

It is clear that a key could be defined by its Ist degree alone, especially if this degree is not challenged. Naturally, every chord that appears after the first degree must, as deviation from the principal tone, lead away from the key. Only by means of a certain grouping is it possible to regain control over this departure and lead back to the principal tone. Thus there is a problem in every harmonic phrase no matter how short that phrase: straying from and then recovering the path to the principal tone. Were the principal tone to stand by itself, without being challenged, then the tonality, although quite primitive, would still at least be unambiguously expressed. The more frequently the principal tone is challenged and the stronger the elements that challenge it, the stronger are the means needed to restore the key. But the more sparse the harmonic events were, the simpler the restoration will be. And so there are instances in which simply the progression I–V–I can establish the tonality clearly enough. Of course the melody can also help out, since it does itself come into being, on another level, through the functions of the fundamental tone. It can even express the key by itself, without help from the harmony, as in the familiar post-horn melody (Example 81*a*), which consists just of the first overtones, or as in primitive dances or folksongs (Example 81*b*).

Here the key is unambiguously defined, even though in the one instance only components of I were used without any harmonic accompaniment, in the other only components of I and V in the accompaniment; for these degrees are never challenged. The two simplest ways of expressing the key and forming a close are to use only the first degree (impossible for us here) or only I and V (likewise improbable here). We have arrived, even so, at the first, the simplest cadence.

In a longer piece [besides the tendency toward the subdominant] there will of course also be progressions that point toward the dominant as the key. Hence, it is necessary to eliminate this tendency as well. The melodic requirement for this purpose is *f*; harmonically the IVth, IInd, and VIIth degrees come under consideration. That VII seems as suitable here for subduing *G* major as it did before for subduing *F* could give us the idea that this degree should be given exclusive preference as the most practical means to both ends. And that did in fact happen in earlier times. But it apparently does not have the same strength for this purpose as do the other degrees mentioned. It may be, however, that the attractiveness of the key is also enhanced if a *G* chord momentarily suggests that *G* major is really the key, or if an *F* chord suggests that it is really *F* major. Perhaps it is the subduing of just such complete triads, each of which could really claim to be a key itself, the subduing of such triads to the will of the keynote, that lends such progressions their vigor and allows the tonic to assert its power ('Like servant, like master'). The obvious thing to do, then, is to choose a chord or root progression for subduing the *G*-major feeling similar

in strength to that used against F major. The one that can spring a fourth upward to V is II. It does contain f, but IV is more complete. The latter moves up
to V by the interval of a second. Such a progression we have conceived as the
sum of two progressions. Here this sum would be: IV–V = IV–(II)–V. The
IInd degree would, accordingly, be contained in the progression IV–V. Moreover, IV has yet something else about it that, in the sense previously indicated,
has a special attraction: it is the sharpest antithesis to G major (in this context),
and its relation to the tonic C is the inverse of that of the Vth degree. The way
these two degrees, V and IV, relate to I – the one, as it were, the fully illuminated past of I, the other its still shadowy future – this relation, $G : C = C : F$, is
indeed the 'Golden Section'. The smaller section, the past (G), is to the larger
section, the present (C), as the larger, the present (C), is to the whole, the future
(F). One could conclude that that activity, that movement which produces
music, is the activity implicit in the tonic alone, the activity created by the relation of its two satellites to it and to each other. This relation, being so completely
consistent, so clearly definable, seems so remarkable that it could give one the
notion that this or something similar must be found in all music if it is really to
be music. But that just does not have to be so; besides, perhaps the search has
just not been carried far enough, and for that reason, perhaps, other discoveries
have not been made. For it is quite probable that the higher, the more complicated numbers, the more complex harmonic relations conceal in themselves a
still richer *Mystik* than that of the prime numbers, of the irreducible, simpler
harmonic relations; and on this probability is based the hope for a future development still richer in interesting secrets. Consequently, I think it is important to stress all these remarkable things so frequently that they can never be
forgotten; for I am certain they also hold the key to the phenomena that at
present are still obscure to us.

The suitability of IV, together with V and I, for bringing about key definition requiring a close, is thus greater than that of II. And now we must yet ask,
whether the order of these degrees should be that presented to us by the path
along which we found them, that is, IV(II)–V–I; or whether it should be
V–IV(II)–I. Clearly, the arrangement V–IV–I accomplishes the purpose, since
it presents the same arguments for the key. Nevertheless, the sequence IV(II)–
V–I better serves the purpose, as becomes apparent in the reasoning that
follows. The root progression, V–IV, has of course fully the same value as
IV–V, and also subdues the dominant region quite vigorously by setting the
subdominant against it. But the subdominant, which in turn also feels the pull
to its subdominant, does not follow its own tendency if it be taken to the tonic;
and the appearance of the tonic is then correspondingly less positive. With the
other progression [IV–V], however, all drift toward the subdominant has found
realization in the third chord from the end, the IV. This general tendency downward is now overcome by the dominant, which then in turn follows its natural
tendency downward a fifth; and I is introduced as the self-evident satisfaction
of this tendency. We arrive at the same result if we conceive V–IV as the sum
of the progressions V–I–IV (of two progressions by the interval of a fourth)
and IV–V analogously as IV–II–V (progressions by third and fourth). Then the

one arrangement reads: V–(I)–IV–I, whereby the repetition of I, even though tacit, is somewhat weak; while the other arrangement reads: IV–(II)–V–I, whereby the tacit II proves to be the familiar rival of IV. The last three chords of our closes will then best read: IV–V–I or II–V–I.

If a composition follows a course such that one of these two progressions can be used as its close, then the possibility of articulation by harmonic means has been made actual, that boundary has been set which is also suitable for closing the piece. Obviously, there are other means for effecting a close, and, obviously, they were and are used together with the harmonic means. Rhythm and melody, quite unaided, can also bring about a cadence. Otherwise a one-line, unharmonized melody would have to run on through all eternity, and a drummer could never stop. Quite certainly there are harmonic means, which at present have just not been theoretically determined, whose capacity for forming cadences, or, far more, for admitting them, is just as great as that of IV, II, V and I. It is, however, certainly possible to bring about a close without having to use all these means simultaneously. Sometimes one is enough, sometimes several are necessary. Yet harmony is least capable of doing it alone, without help of the others, by all means not contrary to them, whereas melody will do it all by itself. That can be proved merely with simple phenomena and unsophisticated hearing. For example, if we give a familiar melody, which clearly cadences in the key, a harmony different from that appropriate for it (by means of deceptive cadences, etc.), then if we play it for someone without musical training, a child, for example, that person will know – assuming he is familiar with the melody – that it ends at the last bar here [Example 82], even though the harmony does not end. This [harmonic alteration] may perhaps be disturbing, but it changes nothing as far as the feeling of close is concerned.

82

wünscht Pa - pa - ge - no sich.

Please forgive the barbarism!

And that is understandable. To grasp what happens in a piece of music means nothing else but to analyse quickly, to determine components and their coherence. Now, obviously, in the successive aspect, melody, one has more time to interpret the impression (unconsciously) than one has in the simultaneous, harmonic aspect. Hence, it is clear why the ear is better equipped for melody than for harmony. And that is also consistent with practice. One who can grasp harmonic proceedings and remember them has reached an unquestionably higher plane than one who can only grasp melody. The efficacy (*Wirkung*) of the horizontal is thus greater than that of the vertical. A cadence made in the horizontal [melodically] will be stronger than one made in the vertical [harmonically].

Is it still necessary, then, in the music of our time, to reinforce endings by means of harmonic cadences? To this question we may answer: no. Above all because such cadences create, at most, a possibility for closing without thereby making the close more compelling. They form the characteristic of a particular musical style, in which only certain chords are used and these only in a certain way. In that style the diatonic chords are in the majority; for this reason the stylistic need for balance and habit perhaps require key definition, cadence. If, however, as in the more modern music, nondiatonic chords are preponderant, or (as I call them) vagrant chords, then the necessity for fortifying the key may be questioned.

The cadences can be still further elaborated, and we will keep an eye out at all times for new means we can use to this end. Among the chords we have learned so far, the progression IV–(II)–V–I turns out to be the strongest cadence. But even that which is weaker is attractive under certain circumstances; hence the adaptability of other degrees should also be discussed here. First of all, looking for a substitute for V, we shall consider the suitability of III. This degree has two chord tones in common with I, and that is a shortcoming here. But it has the leading tone, thus excluding *F* major, and its root progression is relatively strong (third downwards). It ought then to be suitable, anyway. Yet, it is not commonly used; hence, we shall not use it much either, but shall remember why we do not: chiefly because it is not commonly used. That means, it could be used. Its effect would very likely be weaker; above all, though, it would be unfamiliar. To what extent VII was formerly used I have already indicated. It does indeed determine the key, it does lead to the closing chord; but it, too, is not in common practice today, and so we shall disregard it. Nor can it be considered as a substitute for IV or II; for it is gossipy, it just has to tell the most important secret of V, which would follow it: the leading tone. Furthermore, the diminished fifth of VII is identical with the seventh of V (in *C* major, *f*); consequently, VII also takes away from V the possibility of leading, as a seventh chord, with still greater effectiveness to I. On the other hand it is possible, in place of IV or II, to let VI precede V. Perhaps the basis for this connection, too, is the assumption of the older theory regarding progressions of a second: that actually a tacit root a third or a fifth below (IV or II) is being connected. This progression, VI–V–I, is not uncommon, hence, is available to us.

The pupil should first practice cadences in exercises dealing just with cadences. From now on every one of our little phrases is to close with a cadence, and for that purpose there are a few more directions to be given. The inversions are not commonly used in the penultimate chord of the cadence, in the V. Quite understandably the strongest form is preferred at this point. But V does often appear as a seventh chord, again only in root position. The IInd degree, however, can be used in inversions as well as in root position, and as a seventh chord, likewise with the appropriate inversions (thus, not as a two chord). Its six-four chord is little used, but the four-three chord is quite good. The seventh chord of IV seldom appears but is certainly not impossible. Of the inversions of the triad on IV only the sixth chord is to be considered, not the six-four chord. The inversions of its seventh chord are almost entirely unused. The VIth degree as a seventh chord is unsuitable because its seventh would have to be dealt with. The inversions of VI are likewise hardly usable: the six-four chord not at all, the sixth chord little on account of the weak progression from *c* to *g* and the immediate repetition of *c*. But the latter could still be used in an emergency.

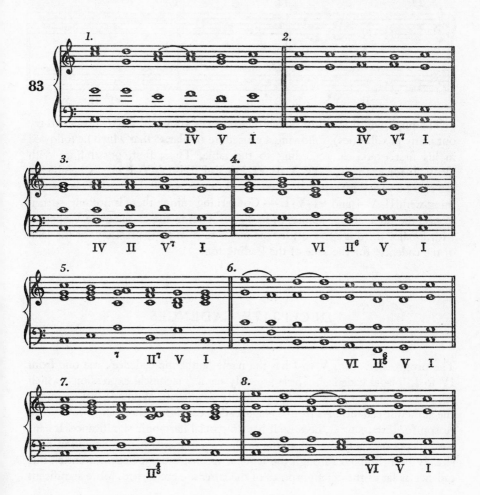

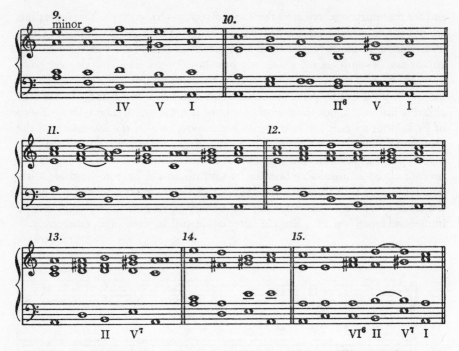

The pupil will do well to sketch the cadences systematically (in order to try out many possibilities), following a procedure similar to that which he followed in his first exercises, according to the table. Thus, first, possibilities with IV–V–I: for example, I–IV–V–I, VI–IV–V–I, III–IV–V–I, etc., whereby IV can also be varied by setting it in root position or as a sixth chord. Then everything with II–V–I and VI–V–I. — Concerning minor there is nothing special to say; the same advice applies as in major. That in the cadence the V appears with a major third is obvious; for the major third is there precisely for the sake of the cadence, for the sake of the leading tone.

DECEPTIVE CADENCES

The progression from V to I has the name 'authentic cadence', the one from IV to I, 'plagal cadence'. These are only names, technical expressions, which tell us nothing that would be harmonically significant. We have just examined the authentic cadence. As for the plagal cadence, on the other hand, we have no reason for discussing it, because it has no special harmonic significance. It can* hardly appear at any time except after the requirements of key definition have already been fulfilled through the familiar means; thus, it does not enrich our cadence as far as the chief purposes of the latter are concerned. More significant

* If it is not used merely to sound antique, to give a flavor of the church modes.

for the harmonic structure are the so-called deceptive cadences. This term is understood to mean the substitution for the expected progression, V–I, of the progressions V–VI or V–IV. This is the original form: I is expected after V, but it does not come; VI or IV come instead. But I is expected after V only at the close, in the authentic cadence; since I does not come, it is then not yet the close, rather only a deceptive cadence. A possibility of closing is set up, but not used. The effect is naturally quite strong; for the deceptive cadence creates the possibility of preparing the actual close again and, through the repetition, of ending with increased power.

First we shall introduce the deceptive cadence into the authentic cadence and exploit it for the purpose mentioned above, to lengthen the cadence. But there are some precautions to be observed. First of all, since the deceptive cadence originates with the *cadential Vth degree* (i.e. not with just any V), then this V will appear in the root position. The inversions of V are rarely used to effect a deceptive cadence. The chord on V can appear in inversion, however, in the progressions V–VI or V–IV at some other point that is not the cadence. The seventh chord of V, on the other hand, is commonly used in the deceptive cadence. Now this point requires some comment; for, although we have indeed already had seventh chords resolving other than by the root progression a fourth upward, it happened up to now only in connecting seventh chords with one another, and in a different way.

In connecting V with VI (Example 84) we can again imagine that we are connecting the ninth chord of a root a third lower, III, with VI. It follows obviously, then, that the seventh, regarded as a ninth, and the fifth, regarded as a seventh, descend.

84

V   VI

It is a more complicated undertaking to base the connection V–IV on the same assumption; for the seventh does not fall and could not possibly go to *e* because there is no *e* in IV (Example 85*a*).

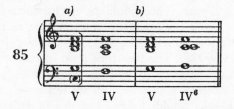

85

V   IV   V   IV⁶

Hence, we shall do better to construe this progression differently. I have already said there are different ways of resolving dissonance. To take the dissonant tone downward is one of the means. The other three possibilities are:

to take it upward, sustain it, or move away by skip. If we see that the dissonances hardly came about as our pedagogical method, for the sake of clear organization, presents them – namely, that yet another third was added above a triad – rather that they are probably notated contingencies of the melodic line, ornaments, then we shall understand that the other forms of resolution can also take place. As a voice can sing *g–f–e* against an *e* sustained above or below, so it can also go the other way, *e–f–g* (Example 86). That is the prototype for the resolution of dissonance upward, and also includes by implication the sustaining of the dissonant tone: that is, if we regard the *e* as the dissonance, then, after *e* and *f* sound together, *e* is sustained while *f* goes on.

Such a dissonance was called 'passing', and the old counterpoint had a number of rules and conditions that restricted its usage. Now if we imagine the seventh chord of V as originating through such passing tones, then the seventh chord is a phenomenon that appears 'in passing', and its rules are derived from

the form in which it appears. These could then be formulated as follows (so far as they are relevant here): The interval of a seventh can be resolved by taking the seventh downward (Examples 88*a*, 88*b*), by sustaining it (88*c*, 88*d*), or by taking it upward (88*e*, 88*f*). The bass tone must in these three instances, respectively, be sustained or go up, go up or go down, be sustained or leap away. The handling of dissonance is then after all not really such a dangerous affair. Indeed, the masterworks would almost allow this formulation of a law: The dissonance must be resolved; that is, a chord with a dissonance must be followed by some other chord (a statement which says nothing at all, but which is the most pertinent in this case). Once one has got used to this idea, then the conception of a root progression a fourth upward, I–IV, as the basis for the resolution V₇–IV (Example 85) is no longer so odd: The eleventh chord, *c–e–g–b–d–f*, resolves to *f–a–c–f* with the seventh sustained.

The treatment shown in Examples 88*e* and 88*f* is usually not regarded as harmonic. The seventh chord involved, on account of its rising seventh, is regarded as a passing chord. Nevertheless, it was common practice. But the laws of harmonic theory read as follows: A seventh must descend, or if it be sustained, then the root is to move upward. Later, an exception was made (naturally an exception, instead of conceiving the rule broadly enough to accommodate the phenomena), and it was said: if thus-and-so . . ., then one may . . ., etc., and the exceptional ascent of the seventh was admitted in order to get a complete chord. But, consequently [since that was an exception], the rule of the so-called '*böse Sieben*' [bad seventh] still held (that is a seventh whose lower tone descends [a step] while the seventh is sustained, or vice versa, the seventh ascends [a step] while the lower tone is sustained – a seventh, in short, that resolves into the octave). And the resolving of a seventh into the octave through descent of the lower tone or through ascent of the seventh continued to be forbidden, even though such resolution occurs often enough with independent voice leading in the masterworks. The progression in Example 88*d* is also forbidden for the same reason. However, since this progression apparently could not be given up entirely, the theory admitted the resolution to the sixth chord (Example 89*a*), whereby it did, to be sure, get around the difficulties of voice leading (avoiding fifths and obtaining a complete chord, Examples 89*b*, 89*c*, 89*d*). But the resolution in Example 89*d* would all the same be possible. Today,

however, we should not hesitate to resolve it as in Example 89*e*: simply by leaping away from the dissonance, a procedure that is familiar, after all, from the very commonly used forms in Examples 89*f*, 89*g*, and 89*h*.

Even the connection in Example 90*a*, which appeared often enough in the masterworks, could be admitted only through an exception to the rule, whereas, if it were not admitted, Example 90*b* would have to do as a substitute.

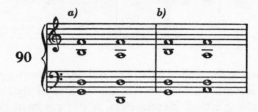

My first inclination would be to formulate the rules in a way that would embrace all these facts. There would be the danger, however, that I, too, might exclude many a good thing (what appears in the masterworks is good, but also much that has not yet appeared), or that I should have to construct exceptions. Anyway, it is clear that, with more advanced ability on the part of the pupil, at least those rules will be rescinded that I have shown to be too narrow or simply false, and in the sense that I have shown them to be so. Hence, I find it superfluous to go to any special trouble to set up new rules. And, as so often before, I shall take the following way out: After showing the pupil to just what extent these rules are not absolutely binding, I bolt the door against the bravado which would like to burst out in absolute disregard for the rules. I bolt the door by developing his sense of form, according to the rigorous old rules, to the point that of its own accord it will tell him at the right time how far he may go, and how he must proceed when he would go beyond the rules.

Therefore, for the present, we shall handle the seventh only as shown in Example 91*a*; we shall use only the forms in Example 91*b* (*x* and *y* are actually not to be regarded as deceptive cadences) and Example 91*c* (the same as 91*b*, but going from the seventh chord); and we shall exclude everything that produces a *böse Sieben* (resolution into the octave: Example 92).

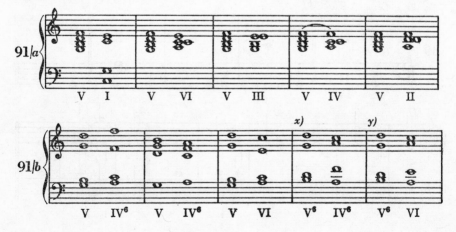

As long as the deceptive cadence is not involved, that deceptive cadence which we have recognized as a specific cadential technique, these connections can also proceed from inversions of the seventh chord (Example 93);

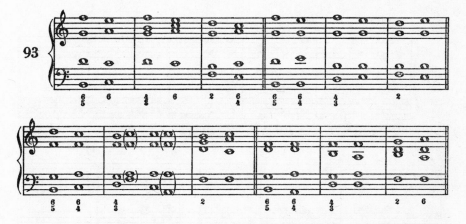

only, those progressions that go to a six-four chord will perhaps have to be treated with some care. For, as has already been discussed, the six-four chord has a very important function in a certain context, and in this particular usage amounts to a cliché. Because of that usage it happens that every six-four chord, even if it appears in only an incidentally similar context, draws attention to itself and arouses the expectation of a certain sequel.

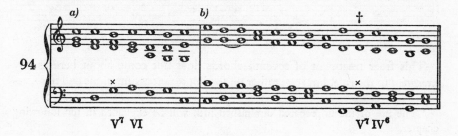

$$V^7 \quad VI$$

In Example 94 at ✕ deceptive cadences of the dominant seventh chord were used. At ⊗ and † the dominant seventh chord was introduced without preparation. I announced earlier that we should later treat the seventh chords freely.* For now we may allow use of the dominant seventh chord without preparation. The preparation can be disregarded, in particular, when the seventh appears as a passing tone, as in Example 94c (melodic justification). Example 95 shows some other instances of such a passing seventh, where other seventh chords are also created by passing tones.

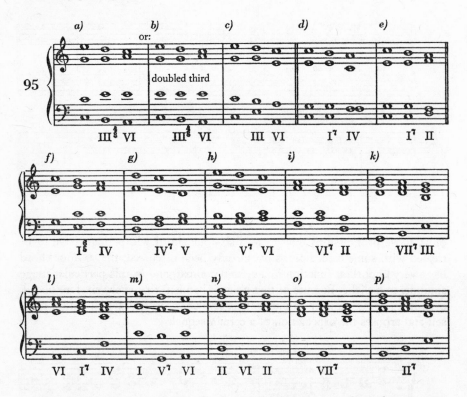

This freer treatment of seventh chords does not come about here as any *exception* to the rule, but rests rather on the important assumptions and observa-

---

* The use of the unprepared diminished fifth will be explained in the following chapter.

tions, repeatedly brought forward here, concerning the manifold origin of dissonance and its graduated differentiation from consonance. By virtue of these two presuppositions we were able to break down the law of dissonance resolution into a small number of directions for dissonance treatment which take into account the facts of art.

THE SIX-FOUR CHORD IN THE CADENCE[1]

The cadences can be expanded still more by inserting I before the V (that is, after the IV or II). The prototype for this might have been the cadence, I—V—I, which we designated (p. 131) as the first, the simplest cadence.

But this is also explained another way, namely, as IV–V–I.

When IV is to move to V, the *c* remains suspended (ornamentally) and the *f* goes (likewise ornamentally) through *e* to *d*. The *a*, on the other hand, gets directly to its place by going to the *g* of the next chord. The *e* is then a passing tone; the form in which the *c* delays its step to *b*, becoming a dissonance which must be resolved, is called *suspension*. More of that later. This interpretation has much in its favor. It seems to me probable, however, that, although either of the two interpretations could alone produce the six-four chord, it was the union of the two ideas that led to this cadential form. In the first instance (Example 96) it is enough to recognize that the twice-heard *c* of the bass is an unpleasant repetition which one can avoid by using an inversion. The sixth chord could be used just as well, as in fact sometimes happens. But the six-four chord, which

[1 Cf. *supra*, pp. 57–8, 75–80 and *infra*, pp. 382–3.]

was indeed conceived as a kind of dissonance to be resolved, and which readily resolves to V, is more suitable because it virtually compels what the sixth chord merely allows. Yet the other way of viewing this progression is also convincing. The suspension evokes suspense, which is relieved by the resolution. The resolution follows on the desired chord, whose appearance after such meticulous preparation acquires the illusion of necessity, consequently arouses an enhanced feeling of satisfaction.

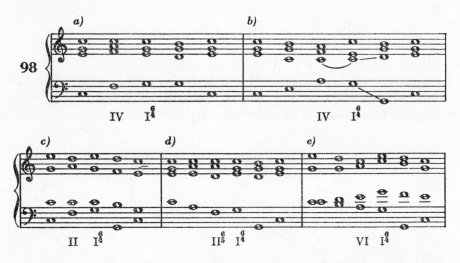

Here, some ways of using the six-four chord are set forth, which also show that the one derivation alone, according to which the six-four chord was created by passing tone and suspension, is not enough to explain it (Examples 98*b*, 98*c*, 98*d*). In Example 98*b* we cannot speak of a suspended *c* because the resolution required by this explanation is missing (in the tenor), nor of a passing *e* because the *e* goes upward to *g*. In Example 98*c* the suspension appears, but not the passing tone, as is also the case in Example 98*d*. If we think of the other explanation, then the six-four chord is readily understandable. As for the judgment of root progressions the question of origin does not matter. Viewing the six-four chord as suspension and passing tone, we figure the degrees as follows (since the six-four chord is not counted here as an independent phenomenon): IV (I$_4^6$)–V–I or II (I$_4^6$)–V–I or VI (I$_4^6$)–V–I – hence, nothing but strong progressions. If we view the six-four chord as I, then we get: IV–I–V–I, II–I–V–I, VI–I–V–I, with many descending progressions. These are compensated for, however, by the quasi-dissonant character of the six-four chord. We may assume that the familiarity of this form of the six-four chord makes it possible to disregard its origin and use it as a cliché, even if what precedes it is not exactly what it should be according to the origin, but just similar. With that assumption we can explain the freedom shown in Example 99, where II in root position simply leaps to the six-four chord, a much-used cadential form.

To avoid the monotony of the sustained *g* (not really very dangerous), the bass readily changes its position by leaping an octave.

I have repeatedly mentioned that the six-four chord holds a unique position and have shown that the problem, whether it owes this position to its own constitution or to convention, must be left unresolved. This position, of which we have spoken so often, is precisely the one just shown, its position in the cadence, used as a retardation, as a buffer, so to speak, before the appearance of the dominant (seventh) chord. Since this form has become a cliché, the quotation of which arouses expectation of a certain sequel, it is obvious why such a chord must be handled carefully in those instances where it does not have this sequel: because it is precisely the appearance of the expected sequel that must be avoided, and the resulting disappointment could easily lead to unevenness. To be sure, such unevenness can have its charm; but at present the pupil cannot strive for effects of that kind.

As the simplest way of handling dissonance we learned, in connection with the VIIth degree in major [p. 49], preparation and resolution. Now with the seventh chords [p. 138] we have seen how the dissonance can appear without preparation, whenever it comes about in passing, and how the resolution also can ensue in a different way, that is, other than through the root progression a fourth upward. What we learned with the seventh chords can be applied to the diminished triad; and thereby those forms become available that appear more frequently in practice than the ones we first dealt with.

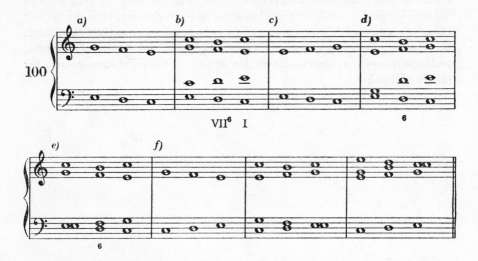

If we imagine two voices moving as in Examples 100*a*, 100*c*, and 100*f*, then we see that a sixth chord of VII appearing on *d* can be *justified* just as well by the *melodic lines* of these voices as it was previously by the preparation. Now, Example 100*e* presents a pattern that conforms to the rigorous rules of counterpoint and to usage in the older music but contrasts sharply with what we have done up to now. The diminished fifth is not only neither prepared nor resolved, it is even doubled!

I shall quote a few of the most common connections with the triad of VII and say that, generally, the root position and the six-four chord are not used; the sixth chord is the only form that is often used.

In the progression VII–I the function of VII is such that we must regard it as a substitute for V, wherein we can see the main difference from our previous progression, VII—III. That leads us to the notion of trying the VII, the substitute for V, in the other common progressions from V: VII–VI, VII–IV, and VII—II.

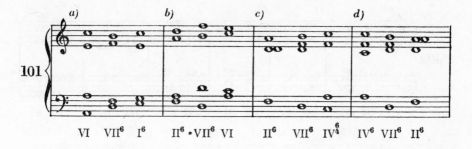

VI VII⁶ I⁶   II⁶ •VII⁶ VI   II⁶ VII⁶ IV⁴⁶   IV⁶ VII⁶ II⁶

The diminished triads in minor, those on II, VI, and VII, naturally permit this same treatment.

I VII⁶ I⁶ VI VII⁶ IV⁴⁶   IV VII⁶ VI⁶   II V⁷ I   VII⁶ VI⁶ V² I⁶

VI^[6] VII⁶ I⁶   II^[6] VII⁶ VI⁶ II V⁷ I   II⁶ III   II⁶ I

II⁶ I⁴⁶ V I   II⁶ VI⁶   VI⁶ VII⁶ I   VI⁶ V   VI⁶ III⁶

Nevertheless, the laws of the pivot tones must be strictly observed.

Particularly frequent and varied use is made of the seventh chord of VII in major and that of II in minor, as we shall see later in modulations. Concerning the seventh chord of VII in minor, the so-called *diminished seventh chord*, the following remarks may do for now: According to our former procedure, we could connect it only with III (root a fourth upward), as in Examples 103*a, b, c,* and *d.* But now we can already see some of the possibilities this extremely ambiguous chord affords.

With some of the connections of the diminished seventh chord hidden fifths appear, as in Examples 103*f* and *g.* Consequently many a connection (103*f*) ought to be completely omitted, or in others (103*g*) the third ought to be doubled, as in 103*h.* These hidden fifths, however, occur so often in the literature and are so seldom avoided that I consider it superfluous to demand that they be avoided. On the other hand I do suggest that the pupil omits those connections of VII that resolve to the six-four chord of I (103*l* and 103*m*), for reasons to be explained later.[1] In connecting diminished seventh chords it will again very likely be best that the voices go the nearest way; but in Example 104 some commonly used connections are given in which voices move by leap.

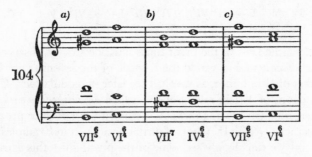

[[1] *Infra*, p. 200, and pp. 240–1.]

Many reasons will appear later to explain why with the diminished seventh chord more than with other chords it is possible to use disjunct motion in place of the simplest voice leading. For now the oft-cited reason will do: the connection is familiar. The voices do not then have to serve slavishly the realization of the chords but can be free to obey whatever melodic requirements arise.

IX MODULATION

We can assume that tonality is a function of the fundamental tone [tonic]: that is, everything that makes up tonality emanates from that tone and refers back to it. But, even though it does refer back, that which emanates from the tone has a life of its own – within certain limits; it is dependent, but to a certain degree also independent. What is closest to the fundamental has the most affinity with it, what is more remote, less affinity. If, roaming over the domain of the fundamental, we follow the traces of its influence, we soon reach those boundaries where the attraction of the tonal center is weaker, where the power of the ruler gives way and the right of self-determination of the half-free can under certain circumstances provoke upheavals and changes in the constitution of the entire structure. Of such regions, whose behavior is now neutral, now revolutionary, two are to be distinguished: the dominant region and the sub-dominant region.[1] It is not possible to define these precisely; for their ever-strong reference to the fundamental and the force of their own instincts, which creates cross references between the two regions as well, manifests relation-ships whose graphic representation in two dimensions would not be possible.[2] Such a representation would at least produce a line doubling back on itself, which would branch off, however, forming traffic arteries from every point in all directions. Nevertheless, the definition [of the two regions] may be approxi-mated as follows: to the subdominant region belong IV and its alternate, II; to the dominant region, V, and the degree resembling it, III. Relatively neutral in their behavior are VI and VII, which can alternately belong to either region or can lead from one to the other. Thus, for example, the progression III–VI creates the possibility of crossing over to IV or II, II–VII of crossing over to III. And II, the alternate of IV, leads into the dominant region, if V follows it. But V leans more towards III or I than towards II or IV, and IV more towards II or VII than towards V. Of all these, IV and V, the two chief representatives

[1] Here, and elsewhere, Schoenberg used the word 'Oberdominante', upper domin-ant, which delineates more sharply than the word 'Dominante' the complementarity of that region and that of the 'Subdominante', the lower dominant. (Cf. his graph and characterization of the relation of the upper and lower fifths to the tonic, *supra*, p. 23f., as well as his theory and chart of the 'regions' in *Structural Functions of Harmony*, pp. 19–34.)]

[2] 'Schafft' (creates), 'zeigt' (manifests). The relative pronoun, 'which', appears to have two antecedents, 'reference . . .' and 'force . . .', which are also the subjects of the verb 'manifests'. Schoenberg apparently considered 'reference to the fundamental and the force of their own instincts' (*Beziehung zum Grundton und die Wirkung ihrer eigenen Triebe*) one indivisible subject. On the other hand, we could assume error. That assumption is questionable, however; for the verbs are singular in the first edition, and in revising his work, Schoenberg did pay enough attention to this passage to substi-tute the word 'zeigt' for the word 'ergibt' (produces) of the first edition.]

of their respective regions, have the strongest mutual aversion and, relatively speaking, next to I the strongest wills in the whole district.

To establish boundaries in a district where there are so many interchanges may be a futile undertaking. For the distinctions in the tendencies and effects are perhaps too subtle. But in spite of all interchanges, [the boundaries, the distinctions] do exist, even if finely drawn. And recognizing them is useful, as will be shown later. What is important for us at the moment is to recognize how, when the affinity of the secondary triads with the fundamental diminishes, certain harmonic progressions are made possible whose reference back to the fundamental has to be established by special means. It is important for us to recognize that in tonality there are regions that will remain neutral, so long as they are forced to do so, but that, as soon as the rule of the fundamental is even momentarily relaxed, are ready to submit to the enticements of a neighboring tonality. We may not wish to regard every chord that follows I as an incipient departure from the tonality (even assuming reference back to it). We must acknowledge nevertheless that the strong will of the respective masters of the dominant and subdominant regions, together with the tendency of the neutral chords to conform to this will as well as eventually to the will of another, neighboring tonality, invites the danger of loosening the bonds. From this situation, and from the tendency of every degree either to become a fundamental or at least to gain a more significant position in another district, a competition emerges, which constitutes the excitement of the harmonic events within tonality. The appetite for independence shown by the two strongest subordinates in the district, the mutiny of the more loosely connected elements, the occasional small victories and gains of the competing parties, their final subjection to the sovereign will and their meeting together for a common function – this activity, a reflection of our own human enterprise, is what causes us to perceive as life what we create as art.

Every chord, then, that is set beside the principal tone has at least as much tendency to lead away from it as to return to it. And if life, if a work of art is to emerge, then we must engage in this movement-generating conflict. The tonality must be placed in danger of losing its sovereignty; the appetites for independence and the tendencies toward mutiny must be given opportunity to activate themselves; one must grant them their victories, not begrudging them an occasional expansion of territory. For a ruler can only take pleasure in ruling live subjects; and live subjects will attack and plunder.

Perhaps, then, the rebellious ambitions of the subjects spring as much from the tyrant's urge to dominate as from their own tendencies. The tyrant's urge is not satisfied without the ambitions of the subjects. Thus, the departure from the fundamental tone is explained as a need of the fundamental itself, in which, in whose very overtones, the same conflict is contained as a model, so to speak, on another plane. Even the apparently complete departure from the tonality turns out to be a means for making the victory of the fundamental so much the more dazzling. And if we recognize how any other chord placed beside the fundamental, even if it does not actually bring about a modulation, leans nevertheless in that direction, then it becomes clear that even excursions into more remote regions may be organic to the fundamental – more remotely organic. To relate such excursions to the fundamental is more difficult, but not impossible. The means that the principal tone has to employ to assert its sovereignty over them must be still stronger, more aggressive, commensurate with the more aggressive nature of those that seek emancipation. And the greater the lead the fundamental grants those that are breaking away from it, so much the more impetuous must be the seven-league strides with which it overtakes and captures them. The greater this exertion, the more overwhelming the effect of victory.

If we then justifiably follow the tendencies of the satraps [the subordinate chords], we see the necessity and the possibility of the digressions (*Ausweichungen*), of modulation. These are unlimited so far as the power of tonality is unlimited. If this power had limits, then suppressing the tendencies of the secondary chords would avail nothing. They would still rupture the ties, for they have no limits. Thus we may ask: is tonality strong enough to rule over all, or not?

Both. It can be strong enough; it can also be too weak. If it believes in itself, then it is strong enough. If it doubts its divine right to rule, then it is too weak. If from the outset it goes forth autocratically, believing in its mission, then it will conquer. But it can just as well be skeptical; it may have seen that everything designated as good for its subjects serves only its own interests. It may have seen how its sovereignty is not absolutely necessary for the prosperity and growth of the whole. That its sovereignty is admissible, but not indispensable.[1] That its autocracy can be, in truth, a unifying bond, but that the discarding of this bond could favor the self-directed functioning of other bonds; that, if the laws issuing from tonality, the laws of the autocrat, were rescinded, its erstwhile domain would not thereby necessarily sink into chaos but would automatically, following its own dictates, make for itself laws consistent with its nature;[2] that anarchy would not ensue, but rather a new form of order. It may add, however, that this new order will soon begin to resemble the old, until it becomes completely equivalent to the old; for order is as much God's will as change, which persistently leads back to order.

Therefore, from the nature of chords and from their relation to the tonic (*Grundton*) we can derive insights which lead us to establish the following functions:

1. The digressions from the tonic and the assertion of the tonic are such that in spite of all new elaborations of the secondary tones, however remote, the tonality[3] is finally victorious. That [function] would then really be an extended cadence, essentially the harmonic plan of every musical composition, however large.
2. The digressions arrive at a new tonality. This happens continually in the course of

[1 As indicated in the Translator's Preface (p. xix), Schoenberg's penchant for incomplete sentences is reflected in the translation, wherever the device seemed effective in English, or at least not intrusive.]

[2 The remainder of this paragraph did not appear in the edition of 1911.]

[3 In his 'Handexemplar . . .', Schoenberg underlined the word 'Tonalität', here and in '2' below, and wrote 'Tonart?' (key) in the margin (see *supra*, Translator's Preface, p. xvi).]

a piece, but only apparently; for this new tonality does not have independent meaning within a piece, but only expresses more elaborately the tendencies of the secondary chords. These remain all the while secondary chords within the piece that is circumscribed by a key.

3. From the outset the tonic does not appear unequivocally, it is not definitive; rather it admits the rivalry of other tonics alongside it. The tonality is kept, so to speak, suspended, and the victory can then go to one of the rivals, although not necessarily.

4. The harmony is nowhere disposed to allow a tonic to assert its authority. Structures are created whose laws do not seem to issue from a central source (*Zentrum*); at least this central source is not *a single* fundamental tone.

The first two functions we shall consider now; the third and fourth, so far as directions can be given for them, much later.[1] We shall work out the first, as extension of the cadence, as soon as we have richer harmonic resources at our disposal. The second, which is called modulation, is our immediate task.

The cadence, as we have seen, is the means for establishing the key. The aim of modulation is to leave the key. Whereas with the cadence it was necessary to arrange in a definite sequence certain chords that narrowly define the limits of the key, so, in order to modulate, we have to do the contrary: we have to avoid these chords. We have to construct chord progressions that not only will not confine us to the initial key, but will even define another key. If the bond of the tonality be loosened through omission of those elements that express the old key, then the new key can be reached by the same means with which the old was expressed. They just have to be transposed for the sake of the new key. These means of modulation will lead either directly or by way of large and small detours to that point where a cadence will establish the new key. The phrases in which we present modulations will thus fall into three parts:

1. expression of the key and introduction of such (neutral) chords as will permit the turn to the new key (not many chords are necessary; sometimes the I chord of the initial key is enough, for it is often at once a neutral chord as well as one that expresses the key);

2. the actual modulatory part, that is, the modulatory chord and whatever chords are needed to introduce it;

3. the confirmation, the cadence establishing the new key.

Which chords will, without themselves leaving the key, turn the phrase in such a way that the modulatory chord can render the decision? We can elicit them from the same considerations through which we previously found chords suitable for the cadence. There it was our purpose to secure the key against those related keys into which the tendencies of the scale degrees would too easily cause it to slip. Here, on the other hand, we shall want to give in to these tendencies. The simplest modulations that we shall then encounter are the one into the *relative minor* key and those into the keys of the *upper and lower fifths* together with *their relative minor keys*.

[[1] *Infra*, Chapter XIV and Chapters XIX (Sections 7 and 8) through XXII.]

Thus, from C major: the relative, a minor; the fifth above, G major (with e minor); the fifth below, F major (with d minor). These major keys are distinguished from C major by only one sharp or flat in the key signature (the relative minor keys are, as we have seen, only special forms within the major keys). Major keys so related to an initial key (tonic a fifth lower or a fifth higher) are called *keys of the first circle of fifths*.[1] (The minor keys are referred back to their relative majors, and the degree of their relationship is given in terms of the relationship of their relative majors.)

The expression, circle of fifths, comes from the fact that the names of the keys were written down on a circle in such a way that the distance between equidistant, adjacent points on the circumference corresponded to the distance of such closely related keys from one another, i.e. those whose keynotes are a fifth apart. The keys follow one another then at the interval of a fifth: C, G, D, A, etc., until they come back again to the point of departure. This return resembles the circumference of a circle (which also returns to its starting point). If we go around the circle in the one direction (C, G, D, A, etc.), we have the circle of fifths, or, as I prefer to say, the circle of fifths upward, because it consists of a succession of fifths built over the point of departure. If we go in the opposite direction around the circle, we get C, F, $B\flat$, $E\flat$, etc. Some call this the circle of fourths, but it makes little sense; for C to G is a fifth upward or a fourth downward, and C to F is a fifth downward or a fourth upward. Therefore I prefer to call this opposite direction the circle of fifths downward.[2]

The circle of fifths expresses to a certain extent the relationship of two keys. But not completely. Clearly, two keys that differ from one another by only one sharp or flat in the key signature can easily be more closely related than such as differ by five sharps or flats. Thus, $B\flat$ major and $E\flat$ major are more closely related than $B\flat$ major and $A\flat$ major. C major and D major should accordingly be more closely related than C major and A major or E major. That is not perfectly true, however. For the key signature is not the only circumstance that has bearing on the relationship; there are yet other considerations, which will receive closer examination later. For example, C major is related to A major through a minor, and this relationship is stronger than that between C major and D major, as will be seen. Hence, we shall not use the circle of fifths exclusively for determining the degree of relationship – to do so would amount to a value judgment – rather, we shall use it far more for measuring the distance, as a device to help us remember better the means that were found appropriate for a particular case.

We should observe, for example, in our circle of fifths that B major and $A\flat$ major are nine fifths apart, that is, if we reckon from $A\flat$ major (or from B major in the opposite direction, circle of fifths downward); but they are only three fifths apart if we go clockwise from B major, or from $A\flat$ major by the circle of fifths downward. In general we shall favor the shorter distance in

[1] 'des ersten Quintenzirkels'. For clarification of this abbreviated expression, see *infra*, p. 350, author's footnote.]

[2] Long footnote by the author: Appendix, p. 426.]

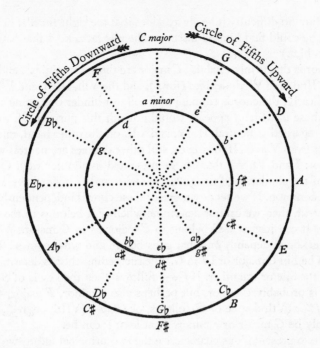

105

choosing means for modulation; yet often enough we shall choose the seemingly longer way, which, as will be seen, is often the shorter. This point is more easily discernible if we remember that, as I mentioned, the keys of the third circle are more closely related than those of the second. It can be found in the circle of fifths that *f* minor and *F* major are three fifths apart, that *f* minor and *d* minor are also only three fifths apart, but that *f* minor and *D* major are six fifths apart.

106   *Table of the Circle of Fifths for C Major (a minor)*

First Circle	(*a* minor)	*G* major	*e* minor	*F* major	*d* minor
Second Circle		*D* major	*b* minor	*B♭* major	*g* minor
Third Circle		*A* major	*f♯* minor	*E♭* major	*c* minor
Fourth Circle		*E* major	*c♯* minor	*A♭* major	*f* minor
Fifth Circle		*B* major	*g♯* minor	*D♭* major	*b♭* minor
Sixth Circle		*F♯* major	*d♯* minor	*G♭* major	*e♭* minor
Seventh Circle		*C♯* major	*a♯* minor	*C♭* major	*a♭* minor

In Example 106 a table of the circle of fifths is given for *C* major and *a* minor. The pupil should transpose these relationships to the other keys.

Since the keys of the first circle are in fact, as we have seen, the very next of kin, we shall start with them, choosing as our first example the modulation from *C* major to *G* major. (As before, I shall always give the examples with *C* major as the original key to facilitate review of what has been learned. The pupil must of course also work in all the other keys as well. This work in the other keys will give him no difficulty if he always does it at the right time. If he neglects it, however, he could find himself insecure when he faces keys that have remained strange to him.)

The chords that firmly establish *C* major are those containing *f* and *b*, namely: the IVth, IInd, and VIIth degrees (for *f*), and the Vth, IIIrd, and VIIth degrees (for *b*). Clearly, the chords containing *b* will not hinder our going to *G* major, whereas those in which *f* appears would not suit this purpose. If, then, III and V can be regarded as neutral, II, IV, and VII, on the other hand, must be omitted. Apart from V and III, however, still other degrees are neutral with respect to *G* major: I and VI. All that can be presented in another way. One can say: because of the similarity of the scales, *C* major and *G* major have a number of chords in common. If we set down one of these chords independently, taken out of its context, then we cannot determine whether it belongs to the one key or the other. It can just as well belong to *C* major as to *G* major. Which way it is to be reckoned depends on what goes before and what comes after. A triad *c–e–g* can be I in *C* major or IV in *G*. The succeeding chords determine whether it will be the one or the other. If *f–a–c* follows, then the key is of course not *G* major; it is probably *C* major, but perhaps also *a* minor, *F* major, or *d* minor. But if *d–f♯–a* (Vth degree of *G*) follows, or *f♯–a–c* (VIIth degree), then it will presumably be *G* major or *e* minor, or at least it can be.

These two presentations characterize the two principal means we shall use in our first modulations. The one is: use of such *neutral chords* as will mediate between the original key and the new key; the other: *reinterpretation of chords* common to both keys. Both means usually work simultaneously. Thus the possibility of reinterpretation is created by introducing neutral chords or at least by avoiding those others that decide in favor of the original key. And, conversely, the neutral chords are driven in the direction of the new key by the reinterpretation. Now, whether we reinterpret or use neutral chords [i.e. however we view this stage of the modulation], sooner or later we shall always reach the point at which we must decisively turn to the new key by some energetic means. What this means can be is immediately clear if we think about the cadence: first and foremost, the Vth degree; then, to put it more generally: all those chords that have the leading tone of the new key, thus frequently III and VII, as well as V. Obviously, V will be most often preferred. But the two others are also effective in bringing about a modulation, especially VII. In order to make the arrival of the new key clear and definitive we shall bring the whole procedure to a close with a cadence. The length of the cadence will naturally depend on the length and difficulty of the modulation. If the modulation was simple, then a short cadence is enough. If the modulation required richer means, then the cadence cannot easily be short. Sometimes, however, it can happen that a long modulation was so convincing because of its thoroughness, that a short cadence is enough; conversely, sometimes a modulation is so abrupt as to demand greater reinforcement of the new key by means of a longer cadence.

In surveying the means of modulation we shall do well to proceed systematically, beginning with the shortest and simplest forms and then going on to the more complicated.

From *C* major to *G* major.

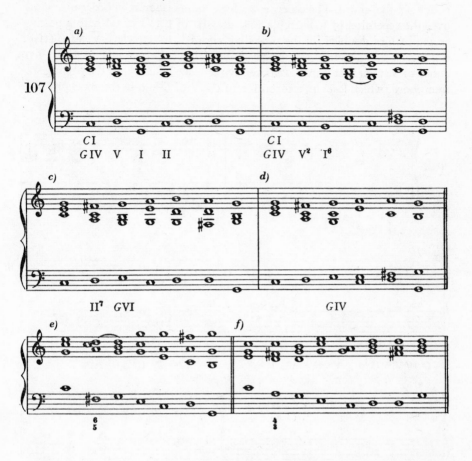

It is assumed that the key of *C* was already established. The Ist degree of *C* major is (neutral chord) IV of *G* major. The reinterpretation can begin right here. Chords from *G* major can follow, inconclusive as well as decisive ones. To be brief at first, we shall use the decisive chord immediately, V of *G* major, the modulatory chord. Then, most simply, I of the new key will follow, whereupon the modulation is complete except for the cadence (Example 107a). This cadence can be short because the modulation was short and clear. If we want to avoid the weakness produced by the two repetitions of I of *G* major, then after V of *G* we shall use either the sixth chord of that I or a deceptive cadence (107b, 107c, 107d) or we can use an inversion of the V ($\frac{6}{5}$, $\frac{4}{3}$, or 2), which is enough to distinguish it from the cadential V.

Between the initial chord and the chord of modulation there can be intermediate chords: the neutral ones, III, V, VI of *C* major (i.e. VI, I, II of *G* major).

Example 108a uses I of *G* major as a neutral chord. For the sake of the bass melody, and to avoid repetition, it is a sixth chord, and the chord of modulation

(V) is a four-three chord.* Example 108*b* uses, after VI of *C* (II of *G*), the V of *G* as a six-five chord. The cadence is a little more elaborate in order to smooth over the repetition of I. Example 108*c* uses III of *C* (VI of *G*) with a passing seventh (third doubled [in the preceding chord]!) to introduce VI of *C* (II of *G*); then it goes, again through a passing seventh (a two chord), to the six-five chord of V; after that it makes a deceptive cadence by means of the passing six-four chord, which leads to a repetition of the V of *G* and to the six chord of I.

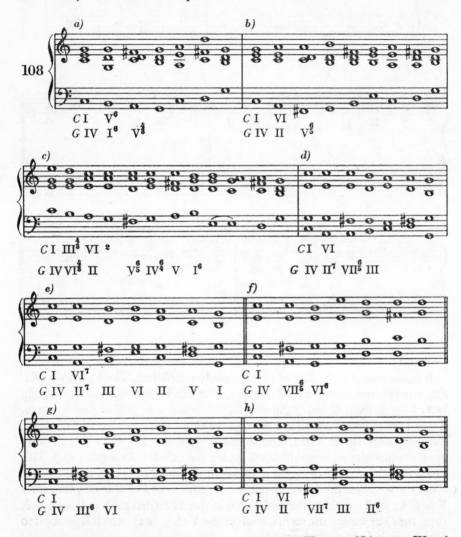

* *G* IV–I–V: those are descending root progressions. The use of I between IV and V, however, resembles that of the six-four chord of I previously noted [p. 144]. One feels immediately the transitory quality of this chord, and that it is used only for the purpose of leading to V. Thus interpreted, the I being discounted as merely a passing chord, i.e. as melodic, the progression reads: IV–(I)–V–I, nothing but ascending progressions.

Such a repetition of the modulatory chord often works very well (I call that: going through the chord again). Actually we have little need for this device here, but we shall use it later to give extra help where the modulation is not sufficiently forceful and clear (since repetition brings reinforcement). In Example 108*d* the seventh chord of VI of *C*, or II of *G*, leads to the six-five chord of VII of *G*. The latter serves here as the means of modulation; and the following III of *G*, since *g* [the I chord] does not appear until the close of the example, can be regarded as a substitute for I, with which the cadence begins. This example is noteworthy because it shows us that the modulation does not absolutely have to go to I, but that the cadence can begin with a degree that is characteristic in the same sense, say, with III, VI, perhaps even with IV or II. In principle, this example is not much different from Example 107*c*, where a deceptive cadence followed the chord of modulation. Only, in 107*c* the chord of modulation was V, here it is VII. In Example 108*e* the III of *G* is used as the modulatory chord. Here, too, I is left out and VI takes its place. Likewise, in 108*f*, 108*g*, and 108*h*, VII and III are the decisive chords. Again the deceptive cadence is to be highly recommended, since it veils the goal without obscuring it. Of course still other neutral chords can be inserted, and in different (but good) progressions. The pupil has here plenty of opportunity for practice in inventing combinations (*Kombinieren*).

One might actually give preference to modulations that, like these, are able to avoid repetitions of I and V. But since there are numerous ways to eliminate what is disturbing about such repetitions, and since the repetitions are not very bad in themselves, anyway, there is no reason here for making distinctions in value. What if the Ist degree does appear twice? It is supposed to be prominent.

Modulation to *a* minor and to *e* minor is carried out just as simply with these same means.

To *a* minor (Example 109). The means of modulation here is, primarily, the Vth degree. But II and VII can also serve. The simplest way will be to regard the first chord (I of *C*) as III of *a* minor. Here it is advisable, if the modulation is to be done smoothly, to bear in mind the rules of pivot tones applying to the natural sixth and seventh.* Thus, *g* and *f* must be treated as the third and fourth

---

* At this point I must take precautions against a misunderstanding: Here the chord of modulation should never come about chromatically, for example by movement from the *g* in I of *C* to *g*♯. That is actually self-evident. First of all, we have not yet spoken of chromatic alterations; secondly, we have made it explicit that neutral chords should precede the chord of modulation. Now, chords in *a* minor that contain *g* are of course not neutral chords. One must remember that the minor key consists of two scales, the ascending and the descending. Here, naturally, the ascending is to be used, since we want to effect a cadence, a close. And the descending scale does not contain neutral chords, or at most they are those of more remote neutrality: those in which the seventh (and sixth) tone must be first neutralized, according to the laws of the pivot tones, in order to admit the raised tones. These chords are, to be sure, relatively neutral in this sense, yet less so than those that do not offer this obstacle. And only in this sense is to be understood, farther on, the introduction of V of *C* as relatively neutral for *e* minor.

pivot tones; they must be neutralized by resolution downward before tones of the ascending scale can appear. Later we shall be less sensitive in this regard and shall not hesitate to write an $f\sharp$ after g (once the means have been made accessible, in the chapter 'Secondary Dominants etc.').

The II of minor provides a good means for modulating to the minor keys, especially as a seventh (six-five, four-three, or two) chord. For it gives opportunity to lead the sixth tone (diminished fifth of II) to the fifth tone [of the key]. Moreover, the Vth degree readily follows (II–V); but even if II makes a deceptive cadence (II–I or II to the augmented III), the result is still quite characteristic.

[NOTE The last three of these examples, 109*l*, 109*m*, and 109*n*, were added in the revised edition, as well as Examples 110*k* and 110*l* below.]

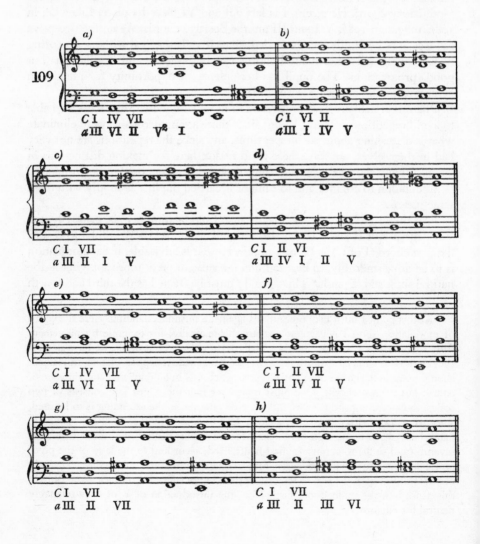

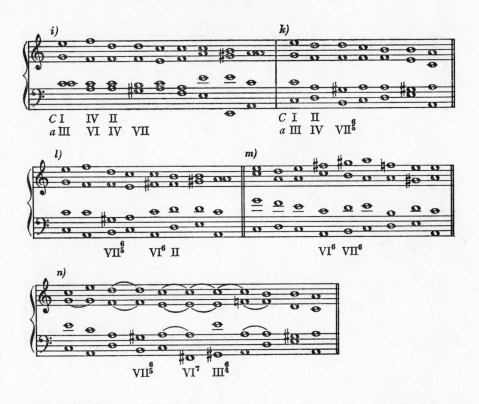

Many possibilities for variety are provided by the use of the raised III (augmented triad), VI ([diminished] triad and seventh chord), and VII (diminished triad and diminished seventh chord). But the neutralization of the seventh tone (and the sixth) still requires great care.

To *e* minor (Example 110). Neutral chords are I, III, VI, on occasion also V, of *C*. Means of modulation are again V, II, and VII [of *e*]. As in *a* minor, so, here, II of *e* minor is especially effective. It can come immediately after I of *C* (Example 110*d*). This II does not absolutely have to go to V; I or III can also follow it, whereby repetition is avoided. The forms of the raised II, III, VI, and VII already used in going to *a* minor have here, in part, better connections. Even the raised IV is also usable.

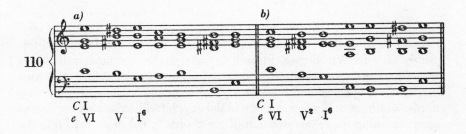

Again, as in all these modulations, a deceptive cadence should be used frequently after the Vth degree. In outlining the phrases the pupil will always write first the figures indicating the root progressions, as before, and then determine the spacings and inversions. Under the figures indicating the first chords, which are still referred to the initial key, he will write a second line of figures denoting the reinterpretation of the chords in the new key. From the chord of modulation on, the figures will refer only to the new key, the goal.[1] The pupil should, however, account most exactingly for the root progressions and not stray from the directions we have given for that purpose; otherwise he could write much that is not common usage and could overlook much that he should practice and become familiar with. He can of course allow his sense of form and his taste to come into play, in the preliminary outlining as well as in many a [subsequent] decision. But only to control and correct – not to indulge his whims (*phantasieren*).

I am treating the topic of modulation, as is evident, in great detail. Most harmony texts do not, or at least not in the way they should. Nothing is accomplished if we just show the pupil how to avoid fifths, octaves, and false relations, or how to realize figured basses. But no more is accomplished if we show him the number of keys into which the diminished seventh chord can be resolved. And not much more if we discuss in the same way still other, altered chords, however much raising or lowering the alteration involves. Nor is anything accomplished with those harmonic analyses in which numbers and letters are written under an example from the literature, numbers and letters whose significance is entirely superficial. This superficiality is precisely the reason they produce so much confusion. Never before was ignorance (*Kulturlosigkeit*) in modulation greater than it is today, since these analyses began 'enlightening' the pupil, showing him how, *without further ado*, someone juxtaposed C♭ B V – IV! a: V – C: V – (IV!) b♭: V – a: IV V – I b♭: V – a: IV V – A: I. We can only hope the pupil does not understand this secret code. I do not understand it either. But, too bad: this nonsense is just what they [the analysts] understand. It is just from this that they learn. Just this 'without further ado' is what suits them. And nobody tells them that there is no such thing as this 'without further ado' – that in art everything is 'with further ado'.

Whenever a piece of music begins to modulate, it is the result not only of a series of harmonic events, but also of a series of melodic and rhythmic events. Consideration of the latter has no place in harmony instruction. Good! But what about the former, the harmonic? It is ridiculous merely to point out that 'something else we can do with the diminished seventh chord is . . .'; or that 'the augmented six-five chord is derived thus and so'; or that 'these eight measures modulate from C♭ through a and C to b♭ . . .'; etc. Analysis would far better show *why* (yes, *why*!) a passage turns in a certain direction. And, since the method of harmony instruction is synthetic, the directions for the use of modulatory means must proceed from the '*because*'!

A modulation emerges as follows: First the tonic is given. Then come its nearest relatives, its most direct consequences. These lead away from the tonic yet are bound to it through relationship, through natural and artificial relationship. If the piece now goes on, then come the more remote progressions. The

[1 In the original edition (p. 185), the remainder of this paragraph released the pupil, 'once he has gained some facility (in modulating)', from the obligation of preliminary sketching. Schoenberg had felt that the pupil could now begin to rely on his *Formgefühl*, his sense of form. – Cf. *supra*, Schoenberg's Preface to the Revised Edition.]

bond loosens. If the whole piece is to be unified, however, then the bond must finally be tightened again; and that happens only if the progressions may actually be perceived as consequences of the initial events. It would indeed be a fine relationship if the grandchild had no features of the grandfather! Naturally, such a changeling (*Wechselbalg*)[1] as the diminished seventh chord appears 'without further ado'. But it has nothing to do with the grandfather.

It will be found curious, in a text whose purpose is presumably to explain the most up-to-date harmonies, to hear these 'old-fashioned views'. But these views are not a matter of fashion; they are just old. And therein lies their value. They contain something that will perhaps be eternal or at least of such long duration that we may just as well say eternal. It will not, however, be the laws that are eternal: Not that one must modulate gradually because it is thus better understood. Nor that one must bind successive events to the initial ones by means of the relationships. Nor that our understanding requires logical presentation. Perhaps [the eternal is] not even that which is general in these laws. Yet it is at least the circumstance that the work of art will always mirror our modes of thought, our perceptual and conceptual powers, and our feelings – that these are what we always have to look for when we analyze and not, say, that 'the diminished seventh chord may yet even . . .'

An example: when Brahms introduces the second theme of his Third Symphony (*F* major [first movement]) in the key of *A* major, it is not because one 'can introduce' the second theme just as well in the key of the mediant. It is rather the consequence of a principal motive, of the bass melody (harmonic connection!) *f–a♭* (third and fourth measures), whose many repetitions, derivations, and variations finally make it necessary, as a temporary high point, for the progression *f–a♭* to expand to the progression *f–a* (*F*, the initial key, *A*, the key of the second theme). Thus, the basic motive is given by the initial key and the key of the second theme. That is a psychological explanation. But a psychological explanation is in fact here a musical one. And every musical explanation must be at the same time psychological. It is obviously in this sense also a natural explanation. Natural according to human nature. Our way of thinking is there, our logic, which, together with regularity, not only admits but even insists on variety. [Our logic] cannot imagine that there are causes without effects. Consequently, it wants to see effects from every cause, and in its works of art it arranges the causes in such a way that the effects visibly proceed from them.

Unfortunately, I cannot of course go into everything that happens in every modulation with such thoroughness. I believe, nevertheless, since I try not merely to describe but also to weigh the individual means, that I am achieving something different in this respect from what is usually considered sufficient. Moreover, in bringing together for a particular cause as many different forms of its effects as possible, I am making rich resources available for consideration. Synthesis, even if only by way of inventing combinations (*Kombination*), must thereby produce an unquestionably better result than that obtained by those

[1 Cf. Appendix, author's footnote to Chapter X, p. 180.]

methods which, without attention to essential characteristics, mention isolated features in an unsystematic manner or according to a false system.

There is, for example, a highly esteemed harmony text[1] in which modulations are made almost exclusively with the dominant seventh chord or the diminished seventh chord. And the author shows only that one of these chords can be introduced directly or indirectly after every major or minor triad and that every key can be reached that way. If I wanted, I could dispose of this matter even more quickly; for I am prepared to show (with examples 'made to order' from the literature!) that any triad can follow any other triad. If that actually means any key and if we could really modulate that way, then these proceedings would be still simpler. But if someone takes a trip he wants to tell about, he does not go as the crow flies! Here the shortest way is the worst. The bird's-eye view from which the events are seen is a bird-brained view. If everything fuses together, anything can be everything. The distinctions are gone. And then it matters not at all whether I have made a bad modulation with the dominant seventh or the diminished seventh chord. For the essence of a modulation is not the goal but the way.

Ways that we must travel daily should be well-kept roads, which, in all that is relevant, fulfil their purpose: to connect different places, one with another, and to do so as comfortably as available means allow. The uncomfortable way is taken only if one cannot take the comfortable, or if, stimulated by a feeling of power, one finds pleasure in attaining mastery over the uncomfortable. But that is pleasure in the mastery and not pleasure in discomfort. A way by which one must leap over ditches, scale walls, and walk the edge of rugged abysses, also leads to a goal – that is, it leads the expert, the seasoned hiker, one who is sufficiently equipped. But it is not for the inexperienced, the novice.

And of course one can reach the street faster by leaping from the fifth floor than by going down the stairs – but in what condition! Thus it is not a matter of the shortest way but of the practical, the appropriate way. And only that way can be practical and appropriate which weighs the possible connections between point of departure and destination and then chooses intelligently. These modulations by a universal means, as is the diminished seventh chord, are the leap out the window. Naturally, both ways are possible. And why shouldn't one leap anyway? Particularly when one can. Yes; but anyone can leap! And so, it is not important to me that the pupil can leap. To me it is not important to hand him a universal means for composing, a 'key' to composing without original ideas, without a vocation. But it is important to me that he perceive the essence of art, even if he is learning 'only' for pleasure. Anyway, why shouldn't one find pleasure once in a while even in the good and true?

These means of modulation, as they are given and organized in most textbooks, do not aim at the right solution of a harmonic problem. They aim rather at equipping the pupil with that meager knowledge which will enable him to squeeze through an examination. But that is not enough for me. I would like to set my goal somewhat higher! It is for this reason that I consider the *way* of

[1 Ernst Friedrich Richter's *Lehrbuch der Harmonie*? – Cf. *supra*, p. 15.]

such great importance; it is also for this reason that I have so much time to be unhurried and to look around on the way.

The modulation to the first circle of fifths downward (from *C* major or *a* minor to *F* major or *d* minor) is, as remarkable as it may sound, somewhat more difficult. The reason may be that the attraction toward the subdominant, which, as I have frequently mentioned, every tone, every chord, seems to have, is almost stronger than the means we would use to get there artificially – the chord, the tone goes there naturally. I mean, it is more difficult to do something here to achieve that end because it practically happens by itself, without our doing anything. The tonic itself, its tendency to lose itself in the subdominant, is at once a means for modulating to the subdominant. Indeed, this Ist degree (of *C* major) is itself V (of *F*), with which we want to modulate. If, then, this

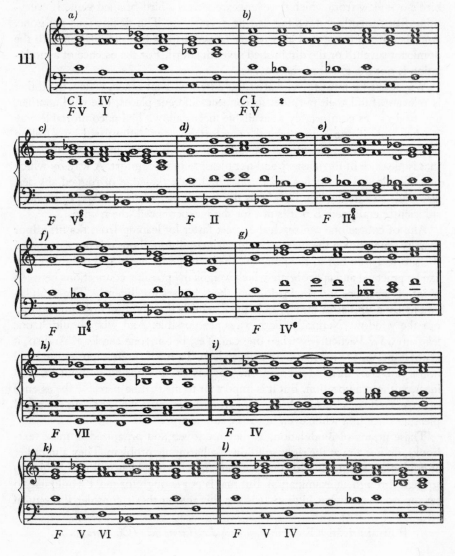

passage to the subdominant happens virtually by itself, so the feeling of having actually done something is diminished for one who would like to bring about the modulation himself. Consequently, it will be necessary later to shape this modulation more artfully, since we indeed want to feel that we have done something ourselves, since we want, not to fall downward, rather to climb downward. These modulations consequently look rather simple at present, but of course they are not therefore bad.

After I of *C* (V of *F*) I of *F* can be used immediately. Since that is hardly compelling, it is advisable to insert the seventh chord of V of *F* (Example 111*b*) in root position or in an inversion. Should we wish to use a chord other than the dominant seventh chord (which does of course introduce the *b♭*), then we can consider II, IV, and VII of *F* major. These degrees help to diversify this modulation, if for no other reason, because I and V can often be skirted and other chords can take their place. Here, too, deceptive cadences should not be forgotten.

[NOTE Example 112*k* was added in the revised edition of 1922, together with the penultimate sentence of the next paragraph.]

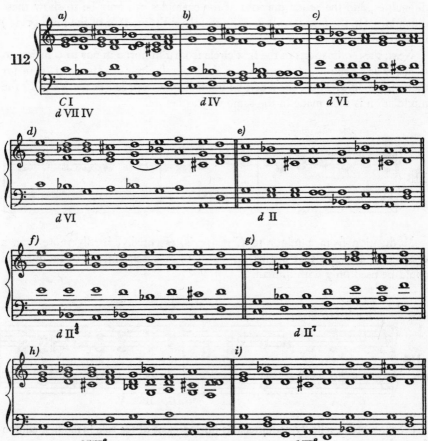

d II⁶   VII⁶   VI⁶ II

In modulating from *C* major to *d* minor it will be necessary first to neutralize the *c*, the pivot tone, before chords with the *c*♯ can be introduced. IV, II, and VI of *d* minor are suitable for this task. These are indeed already modulatory chords as well, and the cadence should begin immediately after them. But if we wish to insert V, III, or VII, then, when one or several such chords [IV, II, VI] have prepared the setting of these, the procedure is otherwise exactly the same as that we followed in the earlier modulations. Since the *c* of the bass, as the third pivot tone, must be disposed of, several of the examples are not permissible (thus, 112*b*, 112*e*, 112*h*), whereas others, where the *c*♯ comes only at the conclusion, can at least be tolerated.[1] Use of the raised degrees also creates difficulties, and the actual purpose of the examples can only be to show these difficulties. [In the first chord] doubling of the fifth (112*a*) or of the third (112*f*) in place of the octave is recommended.

Next, the modulations of the first circle from *a* minor: *a* minor to *C* major, to *G* major and *e* minor, to *F* major and *d* minor. *A* minor is a [form of] *C* major that begins on *a*. Thus, the *a* can be immediately regarded as the VI of *C*; the modulation is then made in the same way as before.

a minor to *C major*

113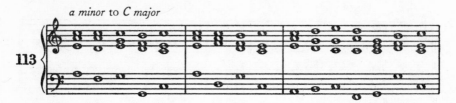

Modulation from *a* minor to *C* major is, essentially, hardly more than a cadence in *C* major that begins on VI of *C*. A special means of modulation could be used only with difficulty.

a)
a minor–G major   *b)*

114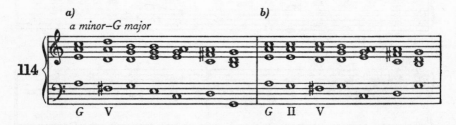

G   V   G   II   V

[1 Schoenberg explicitly permitted this infringement of the rule in the first edition (p. 191).]

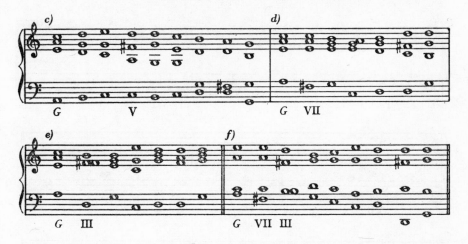

The modulation from *a* minor to *G* major, like the one from *C* major to *F* major, will easily be very short, because one of the neutral chords is omitted (III of *a* minor); and I of *a* minor will best go directly to V of *G*. VII or III [of *G*] can, however, also be used.

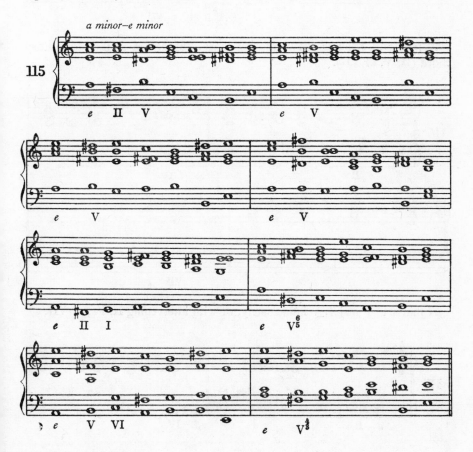

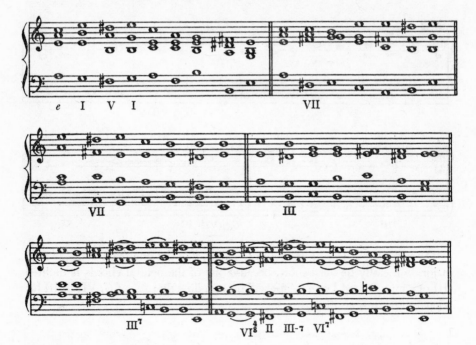

A minor to *e* minor allows the immediate appearance of the modulatory chord (II, V, or VII).

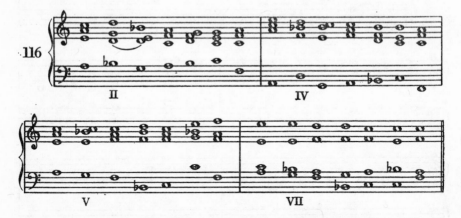

A minor to *F* major. V immediately, or with intervening II, IV, or VII.

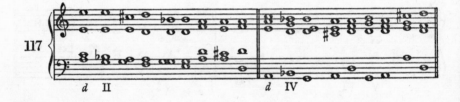

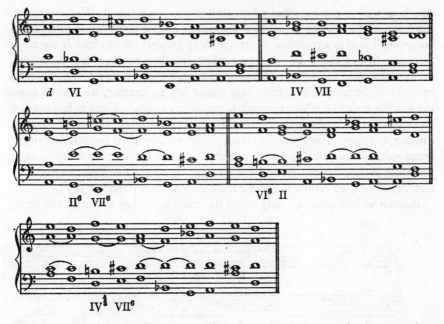

A minor to *d* minor. First, neutralize the *c* (pivot tone), that is, introduce chords with *b*♭ or *b*,[1] which at the same time happen to be modulating chords (IV, VI, II of *d* minor); then either begin the cadence, or go first to V and then to the cadence.

We have regarded the minor key as a special form of the major key, as coinciding to a certain extent with the major key. This circumstance, too, can be exploited in modulating. If we say that *a* minor, in those parts where no raised tones are used, has so little to distinguish it from *C* major that we can mistake the one for the other, then we can use this possibility of mistaking the one for the other and mistake the one for the other. Hence, if we are to go to *a* minor, we can go to *C* major, then call this *C* major *a* minor (reinterpretation) and make the cadence in *a* minor. Or if we are to go from *C* major to *e* minor, we can go first to *G* major and express *e* minor only in the cadence. Likewise, to *d* minor: first to *F* major, then the cadence in *d* minor. The same means can be used just as well in the opposite sense. Namely, if we are going to a major key, we can set up the modulation to aim, apparently, at the relative minor, define the tonic triad of this minor key as VI of the relative major, and then go to the major in the cadence. Thus, say, from *C* major to *G* major: modulation from *C* to *e* minor; *e* minor = VI of *G* major; cadence to *G*. *C* major to *F* major, by way of *d* minor with *F* major expressed only by the cadence.

Here, then, is a possibility for shaping the modulations more variously. Yet, just because these modulations employ richer means does not imply that the others are therefore inferior. In one situation these may be more fitting (or at least sufficient), in another situation, the others. In composing we must have the

[1 '. . . or *b*' ! – added in the revised edition, together with the last three modulations of Example 117.]

simple as well as the complicated possibilities at our disposal. Whether we use
the latter or the former is perhaps sometimes only a question of taste; often,
however, it is also a question of structure. In general we can say: If we are to
modulate from a major key to a major key, it is best to introduce the relative
minor as the intervening key (*C* major through *e* minor to *G* major), or, on the
other hand, in modulating from one minor key to another, we should insert
the relative major (*a* minor through *G* major to *e* minor). There is less need, in
modulating from *a* minor to *G* major, for inserting *e* minor, or from *C* major to
e minor, *G* major. These will, of course, also work. What is essential about this
enrichment is twofold: (1) the intervening key, and (2) the possibility of using
yet other chords besides merely the diatonic chords of the initial key and the
new key. We shall return to these considerations later [Chapter XV].

Balance will be achieved only when the intervening key is not all too firmly

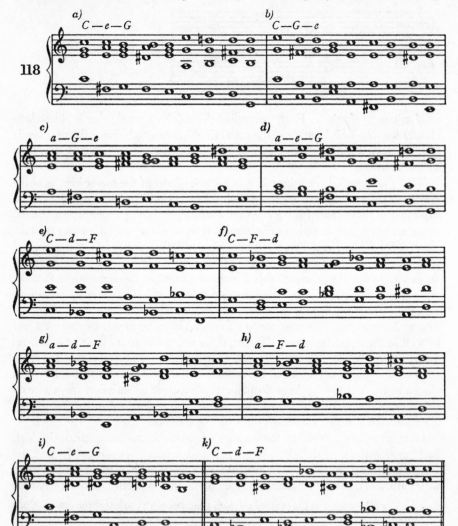

established. Otherwise, the cadence would have to be correspondingly longer. In 118*a*, for example, I of *e* minor appears twice, in 118*c* the dominant of *G* twice. Both could easily require a longer cadence. In 118*a*, however, the dominant of *e* minor shows up only once, in 118*c* the tonic of *G* not at all. If there was actually a danger here [of establishing the intervening key too firmly], it was thereby obviated.

The idea of the intervening key can also be extended to the relative major or minor of the initial key. Examples: *C* major to *G* major or *e* minor, by way of *a* minor; or, *C* major to *F* major or *d* minor, by way of *a* minor; or, *a* minor to *G* major or *e* minor, by way of *C* major; and, *a* minor to *F* or *d*, by way of *C*.

These modulations (especially Examples 119*a* and 119*b*) are indeed very short; moreover, there is scarcely any hint of the goal [before the cadence]. Nevertheless, they are not at all bad. For, in place of the effort to reach a *definite* goal, there is in these phrases the effort just to reach some goal or other – perhaps one not yet determined, or, although a definite one, by a roundabout way. Such phrases therefore have something that is surely worth as much as the confident directness of shorter modulations where the goal is clear: they are, so to speak, *underway*. That means, they give evidence of a forward drive, an impetus that will surely find a goal, even if at the beginning this goal should not be immediately and unambiguously noticeable. I must say that I regard this 'being underway' as one of the most important features of vital composition, and that on occasion it appears to me even more important than clarity of goal. We ourselves are indeed on the way without knowing the goal!

A further elaboration would use two intervening keys, say, *C* major – *a* minor – *e* minor – *G* major; or, *a* minor – *C* major – *d* minor – *F* major, etc.

Finally, the idea of the intervening key can be carried over also to the cadence. For example: *C* major to *G* major, actually reach *G* major; then, however, cadence at first as if to *e* minor or to *a* minor and from one of these points return to *G*.

X SECONDARY DOMINANTS AND OTHER NONDIATONIC CHORDS DERIVED FROM THE CHURCH MODES

I have already mentioned that peculiarity of the church modes wherein variety was produced in the harmony through accidentals (sharps, flats, naturals, which momentarily and incidentally alter diatonic tones of a scale).[1] Most textbooks commonly try to replace this richness with a few instructions pertaining to chromaticism.[2] That is not in itself the same thing, however, nor does it have the same value for the pupil since it is not sufficiently systematic. What took place in the church modes happened without chromaticism, so to speak, diatonically, as we can still see in our minor mode where the sixth and seventh raised tones ascending are as diatonic as the lowered, descending tones. Now if we apply that to Dorian (the church mode that begins on the second tone of a major scale, thus, in C major on *d*), we get the ascending tones *a, b, c♯, d*, descending, *d, c, b♭, a*. Phrygian (starting on the third tone, *e*) gives *b, c♯, d♯* (it was not commonly used in this form) and *e, d, c, b*. In Lydian (from the fourth tone, *f*) the perfect fourth (*b♭*) could be used as well as the augmented (*b*), and in Mixolydian (from the fifth tone, *g*) the seventh tone (*f*) could be raised(*f♯*). Aeolian, our present-day minor, produced *e, f♯, g♯, a, g, f*. The characteristics of the seldom used Hypophrygian are without significance for us at present. Now, should our major and minor actually contain the entire harmonic wealth of the church modes, then we must include these characteristics in a manner consistent with their sense. It becomes possible thereby to use in a major key all the nondiatonic tones and chords that appeared in the seven church modes, which were constructed on the seven diatonic tones of our major scale. Those nondiatonic tones and chords most important for us now are indicated below for the C major scale. They are:

From Dorian:

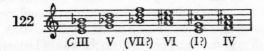

From Phrygian:

which seldom appeared.

[1 Cf. *supra*, Chapter IV, pp. 25, 28, and Chapter V.]
[2 Here, in a long footnote, Schoenberg compared his views with those of Riemann and Schenker. See Appendix, pp. 427–9.]

From Lydian:

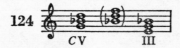

C V   III

which are also contained in Dorian.

Mixolydian:

C II   VII   (IV?)

From Aeolian, those already familiar from minor.

Naturally, the seventh chords as well.

By proceeding this way we follow the historical evolution, which made a detour when it reached the church modes. This recalls my hypothesis [p. 25] that designated as the reason for this detour the difficulty in fixing the fundamental tone of these scales. We can reach by a direct route that point to which the historical route will lead us, if we take as our starting point the tendency of a bass tone to impose its own overtones, to become the root of a major chord. In this way alone the nondiatonic major triads on the secondary degrees would be well enough established. Moreover, the other, oft-mentioned psychological explanation would also be enough in itself to establish them: that is, the principle of analogy, of imitation, which tentatively transfers the characteristics of one object to a different object, producing, for example, the raised seventh tone in minor. We shall also adhere to this principle when in the course of our study we repeatedly transfer to other degrees that which is possible, for example, on the IInd degree. The minor and diminished triads, introduced by recollection of the church modes, could be derived the same way. In all this it must not be overlooked that these chords, apparently artificial, may nevertheless be considered relatively natural in so far as they have prototypes in the overtone series. Thus there are among the overtones of *C* a chord *e–g–b*, which is to be sure remote, and a chord *e–g–bb*, which is not in tune; yet, though remote or not in tune, both are susceptible of explanation as natural. If, however, in spite of the possibility of such explanations, I prefer to go the way of history, I do so above all because the analogy with the minor, a mode that is still alive, is quite suitable for guiding us in the treatment of these chords.

Obviously, we can accomplish all this through chromaticism (and we shall do so later), that is, through going by half step from a diatonic to a nondiatonic tone. As far as the skill of the pupil is concerned, the effect could be the same; but, aside from the fact that these connections do also appear in the form shown here, the chromatic procedure would be less comprehensive and would afford less insight into the historical development and the coherence (*Zusammenhänge*) of harmonic events. We shall first go the way of the church modes and temporarily exclude chromaticism. We shall thus handle these nondiatonic tones and chords more or less as we should handle them if they belonged to a minor key; accordingly, we shall observe, so to speak, the laws of the pivot tones and apply them to those scale segments that we raise or lower. It is then self-evident that, say, the triad *a–c♯–e* will not follow a triad *c–e–g*, nor will *e–g♯–b*. [We shall work this way] only temporarily, of course – in the first exercises.

Through the use of these accidentals we obtain the following chords (the two augmented chords in Example 123 that are derived from Phrygian are omitted for the moment):

1. Triads with major third (equivalent to the leading tone of a church mode) on degrees that diatonically have a minor third: namely, II, III, and VI (less often VII; for in the scale it is diminished and would have to have two tones raised).

These are the dominants of the old church modes. They contain the raised (altered) seventh tone, the leading tone, which goes to the eighth (the fundamental tone [*finalis*]). More precisely, the IInd degree contains the leading tone of Mixolydian, the IIIrd that of Aeolian, the VIth that of Dorian, and the VIIth that of Phrygian (the last-named form was seldom used, since it is quite capable of cancelling out the relation to the tonic). These chords appeared in the church modes as dominants on Vth degrees, whereas in our keys they are built on secondary degrees; hence, we call them *secondary dominants*.* They can of course also be used as seventh chords, whereby we can also get by extension the dominant seventh chord of Lydian as a secondary dominant for our IVth degree (Example 127).

2. A major triad, *b♭–d–f* (from Dorian or Lydian), which, however, does not have the character of a dominant. Perhaps the Neapolitan sixth (to be discussed later) stems from this chord;

3. a minor triad, *g–b♭–d* (from Dorian or Lydian);

4. a series of diminished triads;

* The expression, *Nebendominanten* (secondary dominants), may not be original with me, but (I cannot recall precisely) probably arose in a conversation with a musician to whom I presented the idea of constructing dominants on the secondary triads. Which of us first uttered the expression I do not know, and for that reason I assume *it was not I*.

5. finally, also augmented triads.

The handling of all these chords is quite simple, if at first the pupil observes the rules for pivot tones. This means that every nondiatonic tone will be regarded either as the sixth or the seventh tone of an ascending or a descending minor scale. Raised tones belong to the ascending, lowered to the descending. Now depending on whether the tone be sixth or seventh, it will be followed by a whole or half step. Consequently, for example, an *f♯* could be considered the seventh tone of a *g* scale and should then go to *g* (possibly *e*; anyway, *f* should not precede it); or it could be considered the sixth tone of an *a* scale, whereupon *g♯* should follow. It is also possible, however, to have such a tone originate as a sixth tone and then to treat it (through reinterpretation) as a seventh. The *f♯* could be introduced as the sixth tone of an *a* scale but then resolved into a *g–b–d* triad, in keeping with its derivation from Mixolydian.

In order not to disturb the balance the pupil should not use too many such nondiatonic chords, especially in his first exercises. Should many such chords appear, they would at least have to be followed by a correspondingly rich and elaborate cadence. The pupil does not yet command means adequate for that purpose. And still another thing: if the pupil wants to use these altered chords in modulations, he can put them only where they will not obstruct progress toward the goal, in the sense of the chords to be excluded. Thus, for example, the introduction of a chord *f–a–c* by means of a secondary dominant *c–e–g–b♭* could be disturbing, if the modulation is to go from *C* major to *G* major. One could of course regain mastery over this disturbance, say, by taking this *f–a–c* to *e–g♯–b*, which then leads to *a–c–e* (II of *G* major). Nevertheless, until the pupil has a precise feeling for these matters of balance he will do well to use only those chords that, even if they do not help to reach the goal, at least do not stand in the way. He can best use the secondary dominants, however, in the cadence, when the key has already been well defined.

In Example 130*a* there is decidedly a trace of imbalance. The *b* is startling.

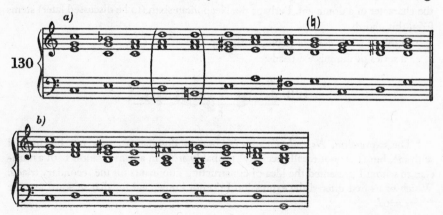

One would more likely expect *b♭*; and we did after all set out to make our modulations glide unobtrusively and clearly from one key to the other.

The solution in Example 130*b* is better. If we look closely at it, however, we find that we could actually have written this progression before, according to a previous suggestion: namely, that intervening keys be used (here it would be *a* minor). I gave this explanation involving the term 'intervening keys' only with reluctance, for it is incorrect to differentiate keys within so short a passage. Thus, as we do not call a secondary triad *e* minor, for example, but rather the IIIrd degree, so here too we prefer not to speak of keys but rather of degrees elaborated by means of secondary dominants. A degree can on occasion be treated just as if it were a key. But it is confusing, it obstructs the view of the whole and its internal relations, if we give every degree that is preceded by a dominant the name of a key. In Example 131 some modulations are given to demonstrate the use of such altered chords (that is, chords that include non-diatonic tones).

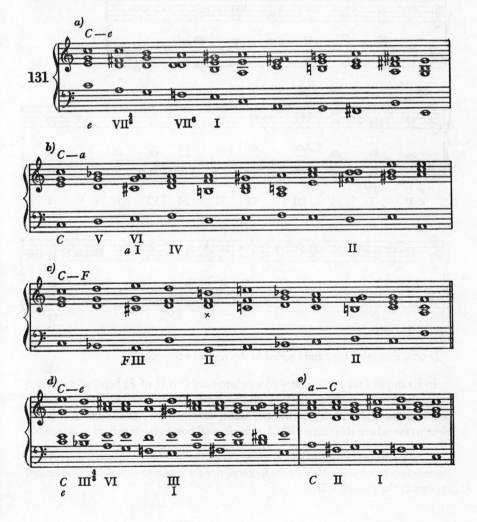

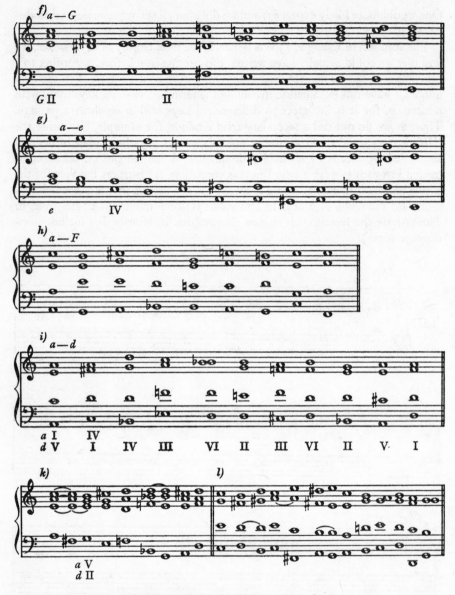

[NOTE Examples 131*k* and *l* added in the revised edition.]

In Example 131*c* at ✕ a secondary dominant (on II of *F*; here, of course, *F* major is already in effect) is resolved like a deceptive cadence. This secondary dominant on the IInd degree has the name, dominant of the dominant. It is not clear to me where this name [*Wechseldominante*] comes from and what it means.[1]

[[1] Here Schoenberg added a footnote in the revised edition (Appendix, p. 429) — a venture into etymology. Neither the footnote nor the sentence to which it is appended appears in the seventh edition.]

But the chord functions as a substitute for the diatonic IInd degree in the cadence, generally with the root progressions II–I$_4^6$–V–I; yet, often enough the dominant of the dominant is followed directly by V–I.

It is most frequently used in the six-five or four-three positions. The root position does, however, often occur. What is new for us in this case is only that here a progression like a deceptive cadence (II–I) is made from a *secondary dominant*. Such connections are of course also possible from other secondary dominants. But the pupil will do well to make sparing use of them; for he could otherwise easily write much that, though not unusable, is unusual and inconsistent with the style of the whole. True, it only applies as a norm, yet is hardly very far off the track, if we say that deceptive cadences after secondary dominants will seem mild, if the modulation is not accomplished by means of the deceptive cadence. They will seem harsher if the modulation produced by them was not prepared. Now mildness is certainly not what we principally strive for, and harshness is not what we principally avoid. These qualities merely indicate the way we recognize what is usual and what is unusual. Whatever is usual sounds mild, because it is usual; and what is unusual, in most cases only because it is unusual, sounds harsh. Now it cannot be our aim of course to write unusual progressions. That would serve little purpose in a harmony course, in harmony exercises, since we could not thereby make the unusual progressions usual. The period in which they could have made their way into common usage is already past. Should they nevertheless now become customary, it could only happen if composers adopted them for use. That is improbable, however, for we have other, stronger means. Then too: the secondary dominant was introduced to obtain for every degree a dominant chord to precede it (root progression a fourth upward). But the deceptive progression moves by step, a second, thus leads in a direction not in keeping with the purpose for which the secondary dominant was introduced. Of course it is a correct analogy (*Kombination*) if this function of a dominant (i.e. to make a deceptive progression) is also applied to the secondary dominant. Yet, that is somewhat far-fetched and perhaps just for this reason less usual. These deceptive progressions do occur, but caution is necessary. Since they are too far-fetched, they can also easily lead too far astray. Example 133 shows what must be done, when such connections are made, to preserve the key.

In Example 131a the second chord (four-three chord on *a*) can be regarded

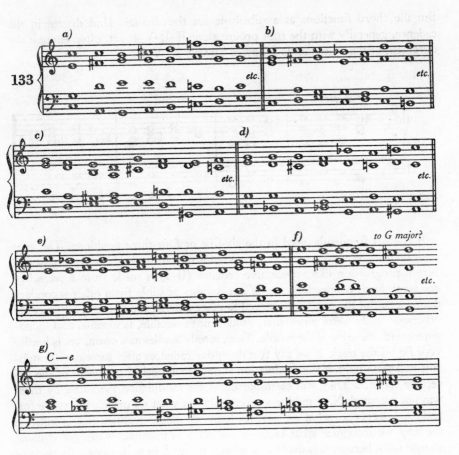

as the dominant of the dominant (II of *C*). Then the following chord on *g* is V of *C*. But the latter could also be I (of *G*); then a modulation would have already occurred here and the preceding chord would be the V of *G*, thus, the dominant rather than the dominant of the dominant. Accordingly, the fourth chord would have to be construed as V with a lowered third, the fifth chord as VI with a raised third. Hence, *G* would be here an intermediate key, an assumption that proves to be impractical. We should be equally justified in taking the sixth chord (six chord on *c*) to be *a* minor. That would then be the second intermediate key. Therefore, it is better to drop the explanation by means of intermediate keys and to relate the secondary dominants to the initial key so long as there has not been a series of chords deciding for the new key. In 131*d*, for example, it would be still more difficult to determine such intermediate keys. The second chord, a four-three chord on *bb*, could only be related to *d* minor and to be sure, the fifth chord, the six-three chord *f–a–d*, is consistent with this interpretation. But the latter could just as well be *f♯–a–d* (133*g*), and then the determination of intermediate keys would be possible only through very complicated reinterpretation.

The secondary dominants are particularly suitable for extending the cadence.

Here it is better that the modulation be short, accomplished with concise means. It is clear that the secondary dominants are likewise to be used in minor and that no new laws are thereby involved. Only, there is a matter that should be stated here in a more precise form, something that also applies to major and explains why a secondary dominant is not to be built on the IVth degree in major. The secondary dominant exists primarily for the sake of the root movement a fourth upward, as imitation of the progression V–I. But from the IVth degree (*F* in *C* major) this progression would involve an augmented fourth (*f–b*), or else would end on a tone foreign to the scale (*b♭*). At present we should not know what to do with the chord on *b♭*, and the connection with *b* would not be in keeping with the sense of this device. For the same reason we shall not at present construct any secondary dominant on the unraised VIth degree in minor (*F* in *a* minor), for it would likewise go to *b♭*. Moreover, the secondary dominants on the raised VI and VII will not be usable either. For a chord *f♯–a♯–c♯–e* (to say nothing of *g♯–b♯–d♯–f♯*) leads too far away from the key for us to venture it at the moment.

I must not neglect to caution the pupil once more against excessive use of the secondary dominants. The means at his disposal are still not rich enough, his writing could easily turn out uneven; and it would hardly be advantageous to sacrifice the smoothness of the exercises merely to include a lot of altered secondary chords. In general I recommend using scarcely more than three or four secondary dominants (etc.) in an example containing ten to fifteen chords.

We can also connect several secondary dominants with one another and with other nondiatonic chords. Only, we must take care in doing so that we do not stray too far away from the key. Just how bad the results of excessive use can be is shown in Example 135d.

C I	VI	II	V	III	VI	II
G		V	I	VI	II	V
D			IV	II	V	I

All seven chords of this example can in themselves be degrees of *C* major. But from the third chord on (if not from the very beginning) they can easily be referred to *G* major, and from the fourth one on they are diatonic chords in *D* major. Here three mistakes have occurred: (1) Both of the secondary dominants used here lead (as the figures show) into Vth degrees (*C* major and *G* major). (2) Both, the third as well as the sixth chord, are at the same time themselves so introduced as if they were Vth degrees. The third is preceded by a chord that can be considered II of *G*, the sixth by one that can be considered II of *D*: that is the way one modulates or establishes a key. (3) Connection of two secondary dominants with one another is dangerous because both are major triads; consequently, the second chord can easily sound like a tonic. A major chord, as the more nearly perfect imitation of what is given by nature, has more tendency to assert its position as tonic than does a minor chord, which, because of its imperfection, naturally has the character of something temporary. We shall be able to deal with this shortcoming only through the chromatic introduction of secondary dominants, to be discussed below. The following remarks will do as a guideline for avoiding such shortcomings: If, through use of secondary dominants, we have come too close to the region of the dominant, then, since elaboration by means of secondary dominants can easily suggest key changes, it will be well to seek out the subdominant region without delay. For example, if we have brought V or III too much to the fore, then we shall cross over through VI to II or IV. Conversely, if we have come too close to the subdominant region (II, IV), then we must try to return to the region of the dominant.

After the pupil has first used secondary dominants without chromatic movement, keeping as it were to the diatonic patterns of minor, he can then go on to produce them through chromatic progression. Then the possibilities for using them are greatly increased. Here the following is to be observed: the reason for raising [or lowering] a tone chromatically is to get a leading tone, upward or downward. Consequently, the raised tone should always go up, the lowered should always go down. Only if bad voice leading can thereby be avoided or if a complete chord cannot otherwise be obtained, and if the tone in question is in a middle voice, only then would I permit, for the present, leaping away from this leading tone. Otherwise, for now, the aim of such an alteration should be observable in the voice leading. For the same reason the raising or the lowering of a tone should be recognizable as such: the raised or lowered tone should connect directly with the preceding, unaltered tone, that is, the raising or lowering should follow in the same voice. If two voices in the preceding chord have the tone in question, then alteration in one of the voices is of course sufficient. The other can move away by leap. Now, to a certain extent, it is possible for us to get around the rules of the pivot tones in minor. The variety of means provided us by the secondary dominants and the like allows us to restore the balance in the cadence.

Example 136a shows the chromatic introduction of the nondiatonic chords. It does not offer any special difficulties. For a while we shall still omit such connections as those at + and ++. The following guidelines are recommended: I. Melodically clear presentation of the chromatic progressions as ascending or descending leading tones in the form of chromatic scale segments. II. Since they have melodic energy, it will be advisable to give them to an outer voice, soprano or bass. The bass in particular can profit thereby, since it would otherwise often be motionless. Such a static bass can also be avoided through exchanges (other inversions) and through change in spacing. III. The aim of this chromatic introduction of secondary dominants is the same as that given above where the treatment observed the principle of the pivot tones. The chromatic introduction offers the advantage, however, that there is less danger to the key; for tones reached in this way can hardly affect us as diatonic, as we have already considered when we affirmed that a dominant should never come about chromatically. Thus, the *c♯* in a VIth degree chord in *C* major, by virtue of its coming from *c*, will keep us from interpreting the following II as tonic (modulation to *d* minor). Yes, even if this II has then a major third, it could only be, at worst, a dominant. A danger such as that shown in Example 135*d* is thus easily put aside.

I. Secondary dominants

II. Augmented triads

III. The artificial minor triad on the Vth degree

IV. Artificially diminished triads

V. Seventh chords with artificially diminished fifth

The pupil will do well here, too, not to overtax himself by trying too much. Sparingly* used, these means are very effective; but extravagance with them would be a shortcoming, since even they cannot yet offer enough diversity.

Of the other chords carried over from the church modes the diminished are particularly effective. For example, *e–g–b♭* (or still better, the seventh chord *e–g–b♭–d*) as the IIIrd degree in *C* major recalls the IInd of *d* minor. Hence, *a–c♯–e* (V of *d* minor), which is VI of *C* major, follows naturally. One of the minor chords can have the same effect. For example, *g–b♭–d*: it recalls IV in *d* minor; V of *d* minor follows, or VII, both of which can go to I [of *d* minor]; this chord is, in turn, II of *C* major. The pupil should not construe these progressions, however, as if other keys were actually present. I wanted only to show how suitable these chords are for introducing secondary dominants (here, *a–c♯–e*).

For the use of the new means that are now available, a summary of instructions follows to supplement the guidelines given on pages 123–5.

GUIDELINES

I. A *secondary dominant* can be used wherever the diatonic degree of the scale can be used, provided the root progressions allow it. In keeping with the sense of secondary dominants they will of course best appear where there is a *root progression resembling the dominant function, that is, according to the models V–I, V–IV, and V–VI*. For their purpose is, above all, *to reinforce this tendency toward a dominant-like progression by means of the artificial leading tone*. The root progression a third downward is also often perfectly feasible, but it does not provide any significant enrichment. The root progression a fourth downward likewise produces chord connections that exercise hardly any other function than that of passing chords (i.e. melodic, in the sense of a change in spacing or an exchange of inversions). The progression a third upward is virtually pointless and in most cases cannot even be admitted because it often leads to chords as yet unexplained. The same reason also excludes some of the previously mentioned progressions, as is shown by the examples illustrating the seventh chords (see 137A).

---

* The illustrative musical examples are not, in this sense, to be interpreted as models, since they were conceived with the desire to show as much as possible in the least possible space. The pupil can use the guidelines given him to assess their resultant shortcomings.

II. *Secondary dominant seventh chords* can appear wherever secondary dominants are admissible and the dissonance can be successfully handled. In general they accomplish the purpose of the secondary dominant triads even better than these because as a rule the seventh enhances the dominant-like progression by giving it direction.

III. *Artificially augmented triads* are to be used according to the model given by the naturally augmented triad (III in minor). This chord can of course precede and follow all degrees, but its most important functions are III–VI, III–I, III–IV, and III–II, the last of which is, however, seldom usable because of the complicated voice leading. Obviously, the same chords that can follow the naturally augmented triad can also follow the artificial ones: secondary dominants, artificial minor triads, artificially diminished triads, seventh chords with artificially diminished fifth, and artificially diminished seventh chords. *The primary purpose of the augmented triads, however, is to give direction to a progression by virtue of the artificial leading tone* (see Example 137B).

IV. *The artificial minor triad* on V is, as the examples show, especially suitable for getting to the subdominant region (IV and II). That it is also good for introducing more neutral degrees, unraised VI and raised III, is shown in Example 137C (among others) under *a*) by the progressions beginning V–II and V–III, under *c*) by that beginning V–VII. We shall obtain the most usual forms, however, if in its V–I and V–IV progressions we interpret it as if it were II of the subdominant key (*F* major), and in its V–VI progression as if it were IV of a minor key (*d* minor). (See Example 137C under *a*) and analogous places in the following examples.)

V. *Artificially diminished triads* can be treated like the VII in major or, what is generally better, like the II in minor (almost exclusively as sixth chords [Example 137D]). Yet for almost all purposes, the chords obtained by addition of a seventh are preferable to these triads, namely:

VI. *The seventh chords with diminished fifth.* These seventh chords are preferable because, to the modern ear, the seventh defines the tendency, the direction of the chord better than the diminished fifth. Easiest to use is the one on III, which is close to the subdominant region; it is inserted in the cadence (Example 137E–1). Its most usual forms are those in which it introduces II (III–II, III–VI–II), where it is handled like II in a minor key (*d* minor). It is less convincing if used to introduce IV, because it is then used like VII in major (VII–I!!). Those chords on I and V with minor seventh are for us at present unusable, whereas the other two (Example 137E–2*b* and 4*b*) are diminished seventh chords, which will be examined in detail in the following section. The one on IV recalls II or VI in minor (*e* or *a* minor) and VII in major (*G* major). It fits into the cadence best when it is handled according to the model of a VI from (*a*) minor, whereas if treated like a II in (*e*) minor it gives too much emphasis to the dominant and, if like a VII in major, is less convincing for reasons already mentioned (VII–I!).

The new means introduced in this chapter suggest two additional observations concerning chords used earlier.

I. *As the dominant in the cadence* (hence, as the penultimate chord) we shall use only a major triad (not augmented, that is) on the Vth degree whose major third is *not* obtained by raising a tone chromatically. A preceding, lowered seventh tone (e.g. *C* major, *b*♭) should, as a subdominant characteristic, first be resolved downward in the manner of a sixth tone in minor. To be sure, different treatment can sometimes be found in the literature, but we have no occasion to make use of it [here].

II. We have good reason now to impose some restrictions on the use of certain diatonic secondary seventh chords. In the course of what follows the student will realize more and more that any given chord can have diverse functions, corresponding to its various tendencies, hence, that it is not unequivocal, and that its meaning is established only by its environment. If I then set some limits to the use of these secondary seventh chords, I do so in the effort to use them according to their most important tendencies. We can set down the following principle for this purpose: *Every chord will* (if not hindered by its environment) *require a continuation like that of* [*some prototype*] *chord* (consisting of entirely different tones) *which has identical intervals*. Thus, the constitution of the seventh chords on II, III, and VI in major is precisely the same. Now, since the one on II has a definite, familiar function (II–V–I, II–I$^6_4$–V), the ear consequently expects the same continuation from III and VI, whose structure is the same (Example 137F–*a* and *b*). With these two it is at once apparent that the progressions cannot be easily kept in the key. We should not at all conclude that only this continuation is possible; and as proof I give a few examples which make it clear that the fate of the tonality is by no means sealed at the appearance of one of these chords. Nevertheless, the usage in these examples is less characteristic than that which follows the cliché of II. Hence, we see that in Example 137F–*c* the secondary dominant on VI would work better than the III; in 137F–*d* the secondary dominant on I or III, and in 137F–*e* the one on II would work better; in 137F–*f*, moreover, there is the danger of a modulation to *G* major, but of course it can be easily controlled. Since these chords are thus questionable in their most characteristic progressions and are indecisive in others, I recommend utmost frugality in their use – and this recommendation is consistent with their use in the literature. At most they will still have a certain (melodic) value as passing phenomena (passing seventh). Otherwise, they are best replaced, according to the direction involved, with the artificial chords on the same degrees, which we have just learned: secondary dominant seventh chords, artificially diminished, etc. (compare examples 137F–*c* and *g*, *d* and *h*). Of the remaining secondary seventh chords, those on I and IV have the same structure. They, too, are most often to be used in passing. But almost always the secondary dominant seventh chord of I is clearly more telling than the diatonic seventh chord (compare 137F–*i* with *k*). The secondary seventh chord on the VIIth degree recalls too much the one on II in minor for us to use it readily in any other way (137F–*m* and *n*). The pupil can easily apply the very same principles to the diatonic secondary seventh chords in minor and will again restrict himself accordingly in the use of these chords to what is characteristic, substituting appropriately for uncharacteristic usage.

CONCERNING THE DIMINISHED SEVENTH CHORD

The systematic introduction of nondiatonic chords into the key can be continued, following the earlier procedure, by trying to transplant the diminished seventh chord as well to places where it does not naturally occur. First of all we shall put it on those degrees that call to mind a VII of minor, whose roots, that is, (like the seventh tone of the minor scale) go up a minor second to the root of the next diatonic degree of the scale. In major these degrees are III (in *C* major, *e*) and VII (*b*); in minor, II (*a* minor, *b*), V (*e*), and VII (*g♯*). Thus we obtain two chords (besides the one on VII in minor, already familiar to us): *e–g–b♭–d♭* and *b–d–f–a♭*. Then we could surely include also the alterations of root tones, since they do appear in the secondary dominants where they are in fact seventh tones. These altered tones could be used, for example, by building a diminished seventh chord, *c♯–e–g–b♭*, on *c♯* (third of the secondary dominant on *a*), or on *d♯* (third of the secondary dominant on *b*) the diminished seventh chord *d♯–f♯–a–c*, and so on. But to assume the raising (or lowering) of roots or the replacement of roots with such raised or lowered tones is questionable, because the assumption is too remote from the prototype, the triad of overtones over a fundamental. This objection also applies to the derivation of some of the diminished triads shown previously. It explains why these do not have the significance of complete chords, and it favors the idea of a missing root. In my view, this idea is here again more to the point and richer in implications. The most important and simplest function of the diminished seventh chord is, namely, not its resolution by means of root movement a fourth upward (VII to III), but rather its resolution in the manner of a deceptive cadence: the root goes up a step (VII to I).[1] It is most frequently found in this function. Theory, however, which has recognized the root progression a fourth upward to be the simplest and most natural, cannot admit here the progression a second upward as the most natural. Hence, it will do better to trace the resolution of this chord, too, back to the root progression a fourth upward by assuming that the diminished seventh chord is a ninth chord with the root omitted. That means, for example: on the tone *d* (as root) a (secondary) dominant is constructed, *d–f♯–a–c* and a minor ninth, *e♭*, is added; or on *g* the chord, *g–b–d–f–a♭*, on *e*, *e–g♯–b–d–f*, etc.

138							
	C II	*C* V	*C* III	*C* VI	*C* I	*C* VII	*C* IV
	a IV	*a* VII	*a* V	*a* I	*a* III	*a* II	*a* VI

The root (*d*) of the ninth chord thus obtained is deleted and a diminished seventh chord, *f♯–a–c–e♭*, remains. Now if this chord goes (as quasi VII) to *g–b♭–d* (to quasi VIII), or, if it comes from a secondary dominant, to *g–b–d*, then the omitted root, *d*, does in fact give us the root progression to the fourth above. This explanation corresponds to our interpretation of the deceptive cadence and is the logical extension of the conceptual system that builds chords on the principle of superimposed thirds: it arrives at the ninth chord by the addition of yet another third to the seventh chord.

[1 Cf. *supra*, p. 113, and pp. 136ff., 'Deceptive Cadences'.]

In this manner we can obtain nondiatonic diminished seventh chords on all degrees in major and minor. Only those degrees are to be *temporarily* excluded where the progression of the (omitted) root a fourth upward does not arrive at a diatonic tone: for example, IV in major, in *C* major, *f*, which would have to go to *b♭*; or in *a* minor, the IV, *d*, where *g♯*, as VII, should follow. Later, once we have spoken about the Neapolitan sixth and are more advanced in the use of the diminished seventh chord, these progressions, too, will work.

The diminished seventh chord can be used with no preparation at all. To be sure, it will be good to introduce it through stepwise or chromatic voice leading, but such is not absolutely necessary. For the chord has the following properties:

139

$$\text{VII} g♭ \quad (f♯) \quad \text{VII} a \quad \text{VII} c \quad \text{VII} e♭$$

It consists of three intervals of the same size, which divide up the octave into four equal parts, minor thirds. If we put still another minor third above its highest tone or under its lowest, no new sound enters the chord; the added tone is the repetition of one already present at the higher or lower octave. This division of the octave can be made from any tone of the chromatic scale. But the first three, chromatically adjacent bass tones produce all possible diminished-seventh-chord sonorities. For example: *f*, *a♭*, *c♭*, *d*, then *f♯*, *a*, *c*, *e♭*, and *g*, *b♭*, *c♯*, *e*; the next division, from *g♯* (*a♭*), produces the same tones as that from *f*, namely, *a♭*, *c♭*, *d*, *f*, and the division from *a* gives *a*, *c*, *e♭*, *f♯*, and so on. There are, then, as far as the sonority and the components are concerned, only three diminished seventh chords. Since, however, there are twelve minor keys, every diminished seventh chord must belong, as VII, to at least four minor keys. Accordingly, the sonority *f–a♭–c♭–d* can signify (Example 139*b*): VII in *g♭* (*f♯*) minor, if *f* (*e♯*) is considered the root; VII in *a* minor, if *g♯* be the root; VII in *c* minor, if *b*; VII in *e♭* minor, if *d*. Or if it be interpreted as a ninth chord with omitted root, it is V in these keys. (It is obvious that the manner of notation must change according to the interpretation of the chord, with *b* written as *c♭*, *g♯* as *a♭*.) Each of its tones can thus be the root, consequently each can be the third, diminished fifth, and diminished seventh. If we invert the chord, no new structural pattern emerges, unlike the inversion of a major or minor chord; we shall still always have minor thirds (augmented seconds). It will thus be unclear to which key it belongs whenever the diminished seventh chord appears out of context or in an ambiguous one. Its *g♯* can be *a♭*, its *b*, *c♭*, etc., and only from the sequel can one find out whether a tone was a leading tone and whether it was ascending or descending. That the ear cannot decide any earlier and readily adapts itself to every resolution makes it possible for something to follow the diminished seventh chord other than the continuation implied by its introduction. A diminished seventh chord containing a *g♯*, for example, can follow a triad containing *g*. But the *g* does not have to go to *g♯*, for the ear is ready to interpret it as *a♭*; yet, in spite of this interpretation, the ear allows the same tone to be treated after all as *g♯* and to continue to *a*. Hence, the rule concerning false relations can be suspended, to a certain extent, for the diminished seventh chord. Nevertheless, we shall not make needless leaps here, either, but rather present melodically (that is by approximating a scale) whatever offers any possibility for doing so.

The sonority *b–d–f–a♭* can be the ninth chord with omitted root on:

I	II	III	V	VI	VII	of
		III	V			*C* major
I				VI		*C♯ (D♭)* major
	II				VII	*D* major
		III	V			*E♭* major
I				VI		*E* major
	II				VII	*F* major
		III	V			*F♯ (G♭)* major
I				VI		*G* major
	II				VII	*A♭* major
		III	V			*A* major
I				VI		*B♭* major
	II				VII	*B* major

I	II	III	V	VI	VII	
			V		VII[1]	*c* minor
I		III				*c♯ (d♭)* minor
	II			(VI)		*d* minor
			V		VII	*e♭* minor
I		III				*e* minor
	II			(VI)		*f* minor
			V		VII	*f♯ (g♭)* minor
I		III				*g* minor
	II			(VI)		*a♭* minor
			V		VII	*a* minor
I		III				*b♭* minor
	II			(VI)		*b* minor

Later, it can also be [unraised] VI in *d, f, a♭,* and *b* minor (in parentheses) as well as IV in *D, F, A♭,* and *B* major and minor. But even now we already have available forty-four interpretations. And it will be seen later [Chapter XIV] that the relations this chord has to the keys are much richer still; that it is actually at home in no single key, is not the exclusive property of any; it is entitled, so to speak, to reside anywhere, yet is nowhere a permanent resident – it is a cosmopolitan or a tramp! I call such chords, *vagrant chords*, as I have already mentioned. Such a chord belongs to no key exclusively; rather, it can belong to many, to practically all keys without changing its shape (not even inversion is necessary; it is enough just to assume relation to a root).

[1 Natural, not raised, VII in minor; hence, in *c* minor, *b♭*, in *e♭* minor, *d♭*, etc.]

Moreover, we shall learn later that almost all chords can be treated, to a certain extent, as vagrant. But there is an essential distinction between those that are truly vagrant and those that we only make so by artificial means. The former are so already, by nature. Their inner structure makes it clear from the outset that they are different from the latter. This point is already clearly confirmed here by the diminished seventh chord, which consists of nothing but minor thirds, and will later be confirmed by the augmented triad as well. The most characteristic feature of the vagrant chords is the one great dissimilarity between these chords and those chords that represent the simplest imitations of the over- tone series – the absence of the perfect fifth. It is remarkable: the vagrant chords do not appear directly by way of nature, yet they accomplish her will. Actually, they arise only out of the logical development of our tonal system, of its impli- cations. They are the issue of inbreeding, inbreeding among the laws of that system. And that precisely these logical consequences of the system are the very undoing of the system itself, that the end of the system is brought about with such inescapable cruelty by its own functions, brings to mind the thought that death is the consequence of life. That the juices that serve life, serve also death. And that it was precisely these vagrant chords that led inexorably to the dissolution of tonality will become abundantly clear in the course of what follows here.

We shall not use the diminished seventh chord to carry out modulations to more remote regions but only to make the way easier and to promote the smoothness of connections that otherwise sound harsh. We must in every way pay close attention: the diminished seventh chord can be quite influential and is capable of making a passage sound bland, even feeble. For its decisive influence as *Modulationsmotor* comes, not so much from its own power to turn away from the key, as, far more, from its indefinite, hermaphroditic, immature character. In itself it is indecisive, it has many tendencies, and anything can overpower it. Thereupon rests its particular influence: whoever wants to be a mediator may not himself personally be all too definite. Sparingly used, however, the dimi- nished seventh chord still gives an excellent account of itself.

One rule we shall most strictly observe: we shall not use the diminished seventh chord as it is commonly used, as a panacea out of the medicine cabinet, for example aspirin, which cures all ills. For us it is rather, as a ninth chord with omitted root, never anything else but the special form of a degree. Only wherever this degree can also be used otherwise, according to the standards we have for its use – unaltered, as a secondary dominant, or with other modifica- tions – only in such places shall we write a diminished seventh chord, if it is appropriate. The decisive consideration remains, first and last, the root pro- gression. The pupil is to sketch out his exercises accordingly; and the decision whether a progression is better in this or that form, whether it is better executed by means of a secondary dominant or a diminished seventh chord or something else, belongs to a second stage in his thought.

In Example 140A the diminished seventh chords were connected with all the degrees. Many aspects of these connections are worthless, others superfluous The pupil's attention will be drawn to many a leap of augmented or diminished

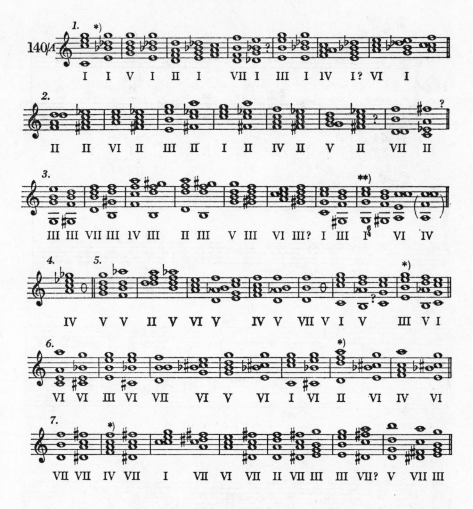

intervals (Example 140A at *). These lose here something of their dubious character; for they are often virtually unavoidable, and the enharmonic possibilities of the diminished seventh chord mollify their harshness.

In Example 140B the chord *f♯–a–c–e♭* (or *d♯*) was used in four different ways by taking it each time to a different chord. In *a*) it is VI and is connected with II; in *b*) it is V and goes to I; in *c*) III to VI; and in *d*) VII to III. In *a*) the diminished seventh chord, *b–d–f–a♭*, on the IInd degree of *F* is connected (at †) with I of *F*. This diminished seventh chord is of course designated here as the IInd degree (assumed root: *g*), which introduces the six-four chord of I. The *a♭*, however, goes to *a*, a path that according to our previous conception only a *g♯* could take; an *a♭* had to go to *g*. But if we wrote *g♯* instead of *a♭*, ignoring the derivation of the chord, and assumed that we have the ninth chord on VII of *F* major (with omitted root), then the progression would be VII–I⁶₄. That is an unlikely assumption, for the VII proves to be unsuited (as shown on pp. 240f.) for introducing that particular, cadential six-four chord. Moreover, it

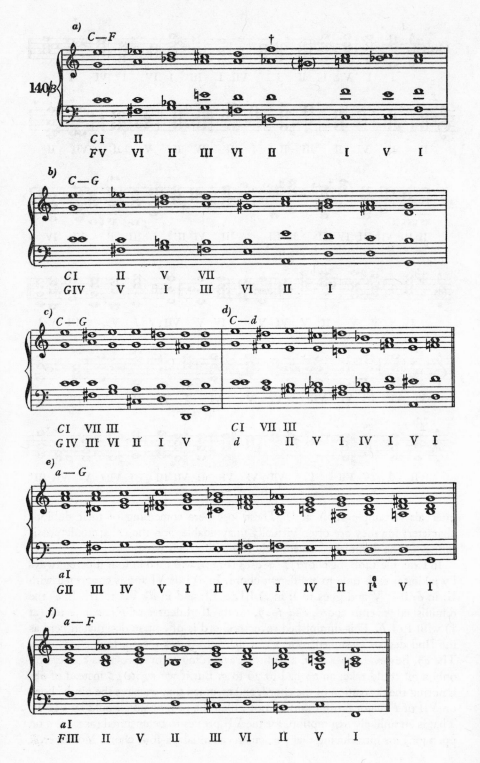

is obviously not VII but II, and the problem can be explained as follows: Were the V chord to follow here right after the diminished seventh with the six-four of I omitted, all doubt whether it is II would be removed, as is still more evident if the minor key of the same name, *f* minor, is treated under the same conditions. In minor its designation as the IInd degree is indisputable even if the six-four chord of I follows the diminished seventh. Supported by these three analogous cases, we must assume here, too, none other [than the] root progression [a fourth upward]. The treatment as *g*♯ of the tone that enters as *a*♭ can be explained on grounds of the spontaneous ambiguity of all tones of the diminished seventh chord and their consequent disposition to enharmonic change. The *a*♭, which arose as the ninth of II, is for the ear the same as *g*♯ and behaves as if it came from VII of *F* major. Hence, from the derivation it gets the right to be a part of the root progression (II–I⁶₄), from the ambiguity of the actual sound, on the other hand, the permission to take the melodic step.

Example 141*a* illustrates the three most usual progressions of the tacit root: fourth upward, second upward, second downward. We can distinguish one from another by the movement of the voices. With the leap a fourth upward all four voices move (the chord of resolution consists entirely of new tones); with

the deceptive cadence progression a second upward one tone is common to both chords while the others move; with the progression a second downward two tones are sustained and only one is new. Thus, it is not difficult to distinguish these progressions one from the other. The pupil should know which degrees he is connecting. It was possible to give directions for determining the structural value of degree progressions, judgments concerning function and effect of progressions. If we disregard the references to degrees, then we have nothing but individual cases, and we would have to make a special judgment in each case. What value there is, all theory aside, in keeping degrees in mind, the pupil will grasp only when he becomes able to accept responsibility himself for the construction of a pattern that is to be made the basis of harmonic variation.

In Example 141*a* those resolutions that do not lead to diatonic chords were omitted. They are for the moment still not usable.

Example 141*b* shows connections, including deceptive cadences, that use inversions of one or both chords. They all work very well and will later become still more free. There are only two of these connections that the pupil should not use: those at ⊗ and †. Why these are excluded will be explained later (pp. 240f.). At ∮ the six-four chord was reached by leap. That [apparent exception to the rule] is justified by the oft-mentioned cliché-like usage and will apply in particular to the cadential six-four chord of I.

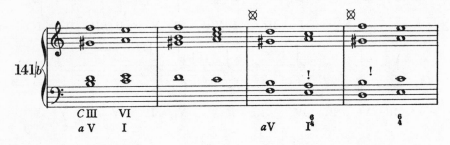

GUIDELINES

for the Use of the Diminished Seventh Chord

I. The diminished seventh chord, as the ninth chord with omitted root on a certain degree, can appear only where that degree is also appropriate in other forms and where the nondiatonic tones of the chord can move in the direction required of them as leading tones. (That seems to contradict the freedom of movement previously granted this chord. Such is not the case. It is merely to make the pupil aware that he is dealing with a progression of degrees other than the one he assumes whenever the direction of the leading tone cannot be observed. For we allow enharmonic change at present only in the case just discussed: diminished seventh chord on II [ninth chord] with the six-four chord of I in major.)

II. It can substitute for the dominant or secondary dominant seventh chords in all their functions, so long as the chords following lie within the key as we know it now (see Example 141*a*). Moreover, this is at present its most important function. In this function it is of great value in that it mitigates many a harsh progression, particularly where there is danger of false relations and where there are unexpected problems with pivot tones. Two connections should be given special mention: the one in Example 140A under 3 at **, where the diminished seventh chord brings about a deceptive cadence on VI or IV after the cadential six-four chord of I; and the one in Example 141*c*, where the chord exercises its function as II to introduce the same six-four chord. Both of these are quite common usages.

XI RHYTHM (*TAKT*) AND HARMONY

We have worked out the exercises up to now without considering meter (*Takteinteilung*). Actually, I should prefer to continue working the same way; for we have very few directions, even in the older harmonic theory, that pertain to rhythm, and even these no longer have much application in the music of Johann Sebastian Bach – they were, at least for the most part, already outdated. But in the music of Beethoven, not to mention that of Schumann or Brahms, we find just the contrary of what these rules require. Obviously, it cannot at all be the task of a present-day harmony course to lay down new laws. One could at most only attempt to organize according to general features the numerous, the countless ways in which harmony and rhythm relate to each other. I doubt whether any unifying principle could result from such an attempt. I believe this attempt would be just as difficult as it would be to try to find a key to all relations of light and shadow possible for a particular object, at all hours of the day, in all seasons, with consideration of all conceivable cloud formations, etc. And just as superfluous! Most of the rhythmic laws of the old theory are restrictions; they are never incentives. They never show how one should put things together (*kombinieren*), only how one should not. And these restrictions serve almost exclusively the purpose of avoiding or covering up some certain harmonic harshness (which to us, however, is no longer harsh). Sometimes the purpose is just the contrary: to place a harsh sound where it will create an accent. I have no doubt been somewhat pedantic in conserving any old laws that have had even the slightest influence on our present-day music. But these [the old laws of rhythm] have largely disappeared from actual use or have been transformed into their opposites. So, away with them.

Harmony texts apparently avail themselves of metrical subdivision [of exercises] so that they can give those particular assignments in which a harmonic skeleton is dressed up with passing tones, changing tones (*Wechselnoten*)[1] and other such ornaments. This method calls to mind a certain *Maurermeister* (master-mason) architecture that sticks cheap stucco over every smooth, straight surface, merely because its practitioners cannot bear smooth surfaces and straight lines. This is imitation devoid of sense; for the imitators are without the technical foundations and the imagination of the masters, whose works are the models that are aped. Naturally, I will not recommend this method to the pupil. Whenever I speak here of non-harmon ticones, *Manieren* [ornamentation], etc., it will be in an entirely different sense.[2] The notion that animated part writing can be achieved in such a manner has, for one accustomed to thinking in [composing] independent voices, something so laughable about it that I could not bring myself to use this exercise even if it offered some advantage. But, someone may say, neither do we compose by sketching root progressions

[1 *Infra*, pp. 340–1.]
[2 *Infra*, Chapter XVII. 'Manieren': pp. 320, 331–2, and 340 in that chapter.]

and then setting harmonies above them. This objection is disposed of by the clear unpretentiousness of our exercises, which invite absolutely no comparison with actual composition. Their similarity to composition indeed consists in nothing more than that in both cases chords are arranged one after the other. And these exercises are distinguished from creative activity as calculation is from invention – in this sense they are not different from the ornamentation of voice leading. Nevertheless, our exercises are morally superior. For, to come back to our analogy, the value of our exercises is similar to that of the architect's exercises in which he sketches ground plans, schooling himself in an appropriate manner for his principal task. In doing that other kind of harmony exercise, however, the pupil resembles an architect who fills any empty space at all, wherever he finds the slightest opportunity, with any ornament whatsoever that he remembers without questioning whether it has any sense or justification. The only justification, the only *Motor* for the independent movement of voices is the driving power of the motive, not however the cheap delight in cheap ornaments, in that cheap embellishment [with non-harmonic tones]. Knowing that, I am compelled to proscribe any exercise whose solution attains at most to that trashy fake art which anyone who is striving for truthfulness must hate. The art of those who always find out so quickly 'how *it* is done', but never 'what *it* is'. Aside from all that, however, such embellishment does not belong in the harmony course, but rather in counterpoint, if it belongs at all in art and the pedagogy of art. Yet, significantly, it is not taught there. It looks as if someone who teaches counterpoint cannot be so frivolous as one who merely writes a harmony text; and the very involvement with that much more serious material implies an attitude that at once suppresses any idea of faking active voices in such a manner, of faking anything at all. For that reason, apparently, and because they want to help the pupil get his *certificate*, the writers of *all* harmony texts do [include that kind of exercise]. Almost all counterpoint books, though not all, leave it out; but some authors – I will not name them, for if I do not it may be possible for us to forget them quickly – some authors [of counterpoint books] are bewildered by the success in teaching and other successes enjoyed by their pedagogical colleagues on the lower level, and they cannot see why counterpoint should not be taught just as badly as harmony; hence they show how one writes fake parts over fake harmonies to produce a fake vitality – that is how far things can go when all sense vanishes.[1]

From the preceding considerations I can elicit no incentive to examine more thoroughly the relation between harmony and rhythm (*Takt*). Moreover, music is pursuing the same course in rhythm as in harmony. It has not been content in the last 150 years to find wisdom in caution, but has chosen rather to expand its knowledge through bold discoveries. Consequently, the disparity between harmonic and rhythmic insight, already ample, has changed drastically, has become uncommonly great: if the theory of harmony, in its far higher state of development, could not keep up with the headlong advance [of practice], that of rhythm fell behind, of course, to a significantly greater extent.

[1 Author's footnote, Appendix, p. 430, added in the revised edition.]

What the tasks of the theoretical investigation of rhythm can be, and what we may expect from such investigation, may be illuminated by the following observations:

The rhythmic organization of music corresponds to natural rhythms that are artificially elaborated. It is most natural in so far as it imitates the rhythm of speech or other natural sounds. It becomes artificial (hence unnatural) where the laws of the system, through inbreeding, spawn new, derivative laws – where pure mathematics begins. Obviously, works of art can come about that way. But as soon as the system professes also to be a yardstick by which to judge some artistic innovation emerging from the rhythm of nature, we are justified in extinguishing the feeble spark that gives an aura of vitality to this phantom [i.e. to this artificial, quasi-mathematical, inbred system, with only a spark of life]. And this spark is indeed feeble. For if we ask ourselves, why we measure time in music in the first place, we can only answer: because we could not otherwise bring it into being. We measure time to make it conform to ourselves, to give it boundaries. We can transmit or portray only that which has boundaries. The creative imagination, however, can envision the unbounded, or at least the apparently unbounded. Thus in art we always represent something unbounded by means of something with boundaries. Moreover, the musical method of measuring time is exceedingly inadequate; it operates, so to speak, by rule of thumb. This inadequacy is indeed a shortcoming that is almost capable of correcting the first [i.e. the need for boundaries]. The fluctuation of our metrical units, which are intuitively determined, approaches, even if in a clumsy way, the freedom of the unmeasurable – perhaps because we determine them intuitively. And we correct the same way, by means of accents, accelerations, retardations, displacements, etc. But even so, we believe too firmly in the rigid line of the arbitrarily chosen yardstick; thus, we cannot deal adequately with the irregularity of the free, natural rhythm or its probably more much complex regularity, which likely corresponds to higher laws of number. We can concede that our system (*Kombination*) has mastered the simple numerical relations. It is probable that this system has thereby even drawn nearer to that free rhythm. But let it beware of considering its paltry principles comprehensive and of proclaiming that all music must be built on them. The musical subdivision of time would still be primitive relative to its [natural] models, even if it were built on more complicated arithmetical principles – as is just now beginning to happen, since until recently multiples of 2 and 3 were still sufficient for the system. For it was only recently that 5 and 7 began to appear, and 11 and 13 have not yet appeared.[1] Nevertheless – and this cannot be emphasized strongly enough – even though the use of unusual meters may be eminently suitable for producing the halo of originality, something truly new is scarcely attainable by this means alone. One eighth note more or less does not revitalize a worn-out idea. On the other hand, rhythmic originality can appear in ordinary four-quarter time.

[1 Cf. the edition of 1911 (p. 226): 'Only recently, 5 was adopted, and 7 is still completely strange to us.' The following three sentences were added in the revised edition.]

We can surely expect that music will not be confined to the numbers, 2, 3, 5, and 7. Particularly since the last twenty years have shown how adaptable is our feeling for time measurement, how quickly almost every musician learns the most complicated metrical divisions, and how listeners and performers of today accept such as a matter of course. The productive mind carries the search also into the province of rhythm and labors to portray what nature, his nature, reveals to him as prototypes. Hence, our metrical subdivisions, with their primitive imitation of nature, with their simple methods of counting, have long been incapable of satisfying our rhythmic needs. Our imagination disregards the bar line, by displacing accents, by juxtaposing different meters, and the like. Yet, a composer can still not give a performable picture of the rhythms he actually has in mind. Here, too, the future will bring something different. We continue to be bound by the old system, it is true, but today it no longer simplifies the [written] representation, but rather makes it more complicated. Of that fact anyone can be convinced who takes a look at the rhythmic notation of a modern composition.

It is surely obvious that there is not much to say about laws referring to the rhythmic aspect of our work here. It is enough to observe two regulations which were still half alive in the nineteenth century and consequently can promote the formal effectiveness of our examples. The one law pertains to the pedal point and will be discussed in the next chapter. The other has to do with the six-four chord that appears in the *cadence* to delay the dominant seventh chord. This six-four chord should come only on the strong (accented) beat.* The

142

a)

b) Brahms, Op. 8.

* In every meter the first beat of the measure is accented (*gut*, strong, heavy). In two-beat measures the second is unaccented (*schlecht*, weak, light), in three-beat, the second and third. In compound meters ($\frac{4}{4}$, $\frac{8}{8}$, $\frac{6}{4}$, $\frac{8}{8}$, etc.), and in subdividing the larger note values, the relation of accents depends, in the same way, on whether every two or every three [notes] form a unit, that is, whether the division is by two or by three.

dominant seventh chord comes then on two, the final chord on one. Of course, the final chord does appear often enough on a weak beat as well.

In such instances of rhythmic displacement and changes in accentuation, where the meter is often nothing more than a method of counting, it sometimes happens that the six-four chord comes on the weak part of the measure. Thus our law does not hold in every case. But in so far as the six-four chord is used at all in modern music, this law holds in almost every case. As I have said, we are concerned here with the six-four chord in the cadence. The other six-four chord, the passing six-four, is naturally free; it can come on two as well as on one. Yet the pupil is advised not to use the passing six-four chord on one, to avoid ambiguities which he cannot yet turn to any artistic advantage. Aside from these I can abstain from giving any other laws pertaining to rhythm, and the pupil may now use metrical subdivision in his exercises. It is best – since we are not concerned with rhythmic effects, but only with harmonic – that he notate every chord in half notes and put two such half-note chords in a $\frac{4}{4}$ measure.

Since modulation to the second circle of fifths [*D*, *b*, *B*♭, *g*] is founded on a more remote relationship than are those to the third and fourth, it is more complicated. Therefore, we shall deal first with the latter, postponing the former for a while.

From *C* major and *a* minor, the keys of the third circle upward are *A* major and *f*♯ minor, and of the fourth, *E* major and *c*♯ minor; of the third downward, *E*♭ major and *c* minor, and of the fourth, *A*♭ major and *f* minor.*

TO THE THIRD AND FOURTH CIRCLES UPWARD

The simplest modulations to the third and fourth circles upward are based upon the *relationship of keys with the same name* (*a* minor – *A* major, *e* – *E*, etc.).** This relationship is founded on the fact that the key note and the

* By 'upward' we mean: in the sense of increasing sharps or decreasing flats; 'downward' means: in the sense of decreasing sharps or increasing flats. Then of course we are sometimes to think of *G*♭ major as *F*♯ major, of *C*♭ as *B*, of *D*♭ as *C*♯. Thus, *D*♭ major is four steps away from *A* major around the circle upward, eight steps away downward. [*Supra*, p. 155.]

** This method is found so frequently in the classical literature, especially where a major key is the goal, that we have to regard it as the most important. There it serves mostly to lead to the new key by circuitous routes, as for example in transitional passages and the so-called 'return'. The advantage of this method is that through the visit to the minor key of the same name the ear is prepared for the tonic of the major key to be introduced, yet when the major key finally appears we are still assured of as much surprise as the change of mode can offer. Prepared, yet surprising, expected, and nevertheless new; that is what the listener's faculties of perception and taste require, and no artist can completely escape this [requirement]. Yet there lurks a piece of self-deception here: the listener wants only what he expects to happen, what he can thus guess and predict; but then he wishes to be surprised. Is it pride in the successful prediction, pride that is enhanced by the justified doubt of an ever wavering self-confidence, is this pride the reason why the appearance of the expected will be found so surprising? However that may be, it is to be kept in mind that the listener expects the fulfilment of these two requirements even in that which is new. He wants new works of art, but only such as he expects to hear; and what he expects is, fundamentally, a new arrangement of old components. But not a completely new arrangement; and the components may not be all too old. 'Modern, but not *hypermodern*' – artists who know how to work this hocus-pocus satisfy the public for a short while and save it from the dilemma of its opposing wishes; but after a short while the public has enough of these artists and thereby proves, if indirectly, that it has some instinct for the good, even if it does turn this instinct almost exclusively against the good.

dominant chord are the same for both major and minor; this dominant, under certain conditions, allows the reinterpretation. *E–g♯–b*, for example, is the dominant of *a* minor and *A* major. If this chord be sounded by itself, then either minor or major can follow, the one as well as the other; if it comes from minor (as V of *a* minor), then the task will be to suppress, to liquidate the characteristics of minor and set up this dominant so that it is free to turn either to minor or major. The possibility of going to major is further supported by the tendency inherent in every triad – particularly those with dominant character – to resolve into a major triad by means of the root progression a fourth upward. It looks then, to repeat what was said earlier, as if the triad were disregarding the boundaries of the scale and recalling its natural euphony.

It is, then, evident that this procedure of transforming a minor key (*a* minor) into the (*A*) major key of the same name can also be used for modulating *from the key relative* to this minor (*C* major), or for modulating *to the key relative* to this major (*f♯* minor). The relation of relative major and minor keys has already been frequently discussed. *C* major can be regarded as the region of the unraised tones of *a* minor. It is only a short way to the characteristic raised sixth and seventh tones of *a* minor if the five and four of *C*, the cross relations, are treated as the pivotal, natural seven and six of the minor. And, after the turn to major, *A* major can be transformed by the same procedure into *f♯* minor. Of course such a procedure of modulating from *C* major to *A* major or *f♯* minor, or from *a* minor to *f♯* minor, can also be described as from *C* major through *a* minor to *A* major, through *a* minor and *A* major to *f♯* minor, or from *a* minor through *A* major to *f♯* minor. But it is by no means necessary here to assume intermediate keys; and I recommend, as I previously explained, interpreting the *C* major that precedes *a* minor as uncharacteristic *a* minor, the *A* major before *f♯* minor as uncharacteristic *f♯* minor. Attention should be paid to neutralizing the pivot tones, and the crossover from the region of the unraised to that of the raised tones should always be brought about as before, when we modulated from *C* major to *a* minor.

The modulation to the fourth circle upward, from *C* or *a* to *E* or *c♯*, rests on the same principle: namely, on the transformation of *e* minor into *E* major. Here there is more justification for assuming an intermediate key, *e* minor. It is then a modulation in the first circle upward with which one to the third circle above that is joined (1 plus 3 equals 4). Since, however, the modulatory dominant triad of *e* minor can be a secondary dominant on VII of *C* or on II of *a*, and since, moreover, the reinterpretation can begin right from the opening chord, as we already know from the modulations *C–e* and *a–e* (I of *C* = VI of *e*; I of *a* = IV of *e*), this auxiliary notion of an intermediate key is not absolutely necessary here, either.

Our task falls into three parts:

1. Introduction of V of the new key, first as V of the minor key of the same name. Whatever neutralization of unraised tones is necessary also belongs here.

2. Transformation of this dominant of a minor key into the dominant of a major key, that is, preparation for reinterpreting it.

3. Resolution to the major key and, if desired, the further crossover into its relative minor.

Thereupon follows the cadence, as usual.

We shall take up first the *transformation of the dominant*. The simplest way would be to sustain it long enough for its derivation from minor to be forgotten, for example, by means of a fermata. As a matter of fact that means is used quite frequently in classical works for cancelling previously established obligations. Likewise, the effect of the long pause resides in the suspense created by the question: What will happen now that is different from before? For something different can happen. This method is not usable here, however, because we could only exaggerate its relative artlessness by the meagerness of the surprise that we can attain with our present means (it is now artless because it is worn out). We shall not use it for the additional reason that we have no wish here to produce effects through nuances in performance, but merely through harmonic means. We shall make use here, rather, of two forms of a similar device: namely, (1) the *sustained voice* and particularly its special instance, the *pedal point*. Thereby, as an alternative to sustaining the whole chord, to represent the whole sustained chord, only one tone – the most important – the *root*, remains stationary, while the other voices proceed with appropriate chords. And (2) we shall make use of repeated *passage through the dominant*.

The *sustained voice* here is different from the sustaining of one or more voices for a longer or shorter time that quite commonly occurs in the simplest chord progressions; for here the other voices can also form chords of which the sustained tone can hardly be considered a component. Hence, these chords can also be dissonant with the sustained tone. Usually the fundamental or the fifth of the tonic or of a dominant (including secondary dominants) is sustained, but it can also be the third under certain circumstances. The sustained voice is called a *pedal point* whenever the bass tone is the one sustained (generally – and in our work here, always – it is then the root). The pedal point serves primarily to retard or compress the movement. Wherever it is desirable to hold back a section of a composition before leaving it harmonically, e.g. in expositions, or to be explicit before a decisive turning point, e.g. before a reprise, as is demonstrated in the 'reinforcement of the dominant' – at such times the pedal point is a justified, effective, and much-used device. On the other hand, the drone-like use of the pedal point, when it is not introduced to suggest folk music, as a quasi quotation from folk music, is artistically superficial and springs mostly from lazy harmonic thinking and the inability to write a well-ordered bass line. The laws for the sustained voice and pedal point that are important here pertain to its entry and to the departure from it. (1) The *entry*, the beginning of the sustained tone should take place on the strong beat, on one. (2) The sustained voice should be consonant at the *point of entry* and before the *departure*. (3) The departure should take place on the weak beat. (4) The intervening chords will of course form reasonable progressions in themselves and should be the most closely related.

The pupil should adhere strictly to the rhythmic stipulations given here. For since we are not concerned with rhythmic effects, there can also be little value for us in rhythmic deviations, even though these rules are clearly so confining that composers have frequently disregarded them. Within the simple scheme we have chosen for it there is still enough possibility for variety in the execution of this form for us to exploit fully the means presently at our disposal. We shall write no long, extended pedal point but shall be satisfied with just suggesting its function. Most important for our purpose is that the dominant, which is to be reinterpreted, appear twice, at the beginning and at the end of the pedal. By putting it at these two points we best fulfil the condition that the sustained voice must be consonant in those places. This repetition is a reinforcement which makes us forget the derivation from minor; for the repetition increases the weight, so to speak, of the dominant itself, and this increase favors its ability to turn toward major. In the process the ear at no time forgets what is happening – the sustained voice takes care of that. In general we shall put only one connecting chord between the beginning and the end of the pedal point, so that the whole will consist of three half notes. Hence, on one (see Example 144) the V,

on two the connecting chord, on the following one the V again, but wherever possible in a different arrangement (variation). In considering which degrees are to be chosen for the connecting chord, we should at first exclude those that make the reinterpretation difficult. They are those that are more similar to *a* minor than to *A* major, that is, such as contain the minor third of the tonic, the *c*: I, III, and VI of *a* minor; and such as still belong to the *C* major region to the extent that chromatic steps would be necessary (144*d* and 144*e*), for a dominant should not arise chromatically.

As is shown in the following chapter, however, the relation to the minor subdominant is such that it allows the tonic to retain control; and since the tendency of the dominant to turn toward major is great enough, even I and VI will not do much harm. But it is far more advantageous to select chords such as secondary dominants, artificially diminished triads, and seventh chords that are equally at home in *A* major and *a* minor. Such chords are the IInd degree as dominant of the dominant (*b*–*d*♯–*f*♯–*a*) and as diminished seventh chord (*d*♯–*f*♯–*a*–*c*). Here of course the minor third *c* gives no trouble. Moreover, the chords on II, IV, and VI of *a* minor, with the raised sixth tone, are suitable, even when they contain the *c*. This *c* is a dissonance and must fall to *b* anyway (144*k*). That Example 144*b* is to be excluded is evident from the root progression (III–V), and in 144*c* (VII–V) VII is a diminished triad, which requires a different treatment.

We have now to examine the root progressions. The degrees that produce nothing but strong progressions are just IV and VI (145*e–h*: V–IV–V and V–VI–V), whereas with I and II (VII and III are to be omitted) a descending progression appears every time (145*b*, *c*, and *i*). There is obviously nothing bad about that, although I is of little use since it will appear at the departure from the pedal point as major. In 145*e*, *f*, etc., difficulties in voice leading arise, which make a diminished or augmented interval unavoidable. The downward progression of the seventh and sixth tones of *a* minor (145*g* and *h*) is easily

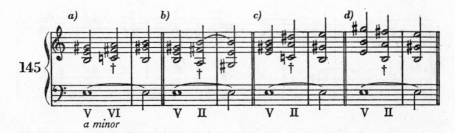

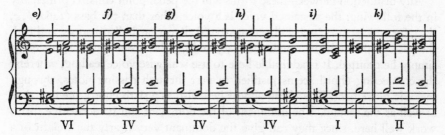

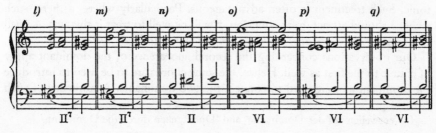

explainable if these chords are considered already to be in *A* major, an interpretation that is particularly justified if [the dominant, the pedal point] was introduced by means of the dominant of the dominant or the like. Most appropriate will be those forms in which the chord tones of V emerge from progressions produced by dissonance treatment. The connecting chord cannot be complete if it is a seventh chord. One should make sure to express the dissonance by means of the characteristic tones: root, seventh, and, where applicable, the diminished fifth.

In 'lingering on the dominant',[1] as it is called – that is, reinterpretation by means of a *sustained voice* in the upper parts – and in the so-called 'passage through the dominant',[1] the same considerations will apply as in carrying out the pedal point.

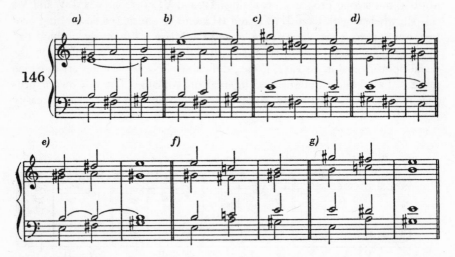

Any distinction between these forms and the pedal point consists principally in the following: the sustained voice is a voice other than the bass (146*a, b, c, d, e*), for which reason one will perhaps avoid all too harsh dissonances; and with the passage through the dominant (146*f* and *g*), the sustaining of a voice can simply be omitted. It is advisable here to use scalewise voice leading, whereby the connecting chord seems justified in part through passing notes, through melodic movement. The V can appear here also as a sixth chord, the first time as well as the second. The dominant of the dominant and its derivative forms work well here, since they can give the dominant very nearly the weight of a tonic. Such treatment is often advantageous. Particularly where, as here, such a chord should attract great attention, it will be well to treat it this way – I call this *treating the chord as if it were a tonic (tonartmässig ausführen).*

Our observations concerning the second appearance of the dominant apply of course to the first as well. Hence, the same chords are to be used to introduce the dominant as were used to connect the two dominants. A summary of such

[1 'Verweilen auf der Dominante' and 'Durchgehen durch die Dominante'.]

possibilities follows in Example 147A. (The unusable chords were already indicated in Examples 144*f–i*, where it was explained why they are not suitable for this 'lingering on the dominant'.)

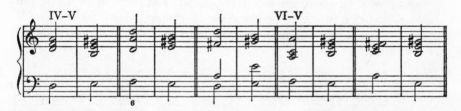

Here it is important to attend to the pivot tones – frequent reminders regarding these are quite in order; it makes no difference, whether *C* major or *a* minor is the key of departure. Obviously, we can reach all these degrees and forms just as well by using secondary dominants and other artificial chords.

We have now to discuss the departure from the pedal point. We are working toward I, but we can postpone it in diverse ways (Example 147B). The ascending root progressions are to be considered before all else for the departure (V–I, the two deceptive cadences V–VI and V–IV, and V–III, the last of which is better written as the secondary dominant on III). But the progression V–II is also conceivable, if what follows it is good. Changes of position [inversions, spacing] should be made here wherever possible. The chord of departure can follow directly, on two. One can, however, first insert the seventh chord of V or the diminished, whereby the first chord decisively in major comes on one of the next measure.

So that the exercises do not become all too long, it is advisable not to use more than four to six chords, at most, before the appearance of the dominant.

Example 149 shows modulations to *f♯* minor. In these, as in those to *A* major, we go first to the dominant in the manner described and then, after lingering on the dominant, to *f♯* simply by means of the cadence. The secondary dominant and the diminished seventh chord on III of the relative major (*A*) are quite appropriate here for the departure from the dominant.

As an additional exercise the pupil can turn each of the modulations shown here in the other direction merely by means of the cadence: those in Example 148 to f♯ minor, those in 149 to A major.

Modulation from a minor follows the same procedures.

A major   V   III   VI

In this modulation the pupil can now use more secondary dominants, diminished seventh chords, and the like, since they greatly enhance the possibility of reinterpretation. It will be to his advantage, however, if he again works out the first exercises without altered chords, or with very few, so that he may always readily see the sense of the degree progressions. He should never neglect to pay critical attention to these, even when he has greater skill in handling the individual chords, even when he believes he no longer needs the control exercised by the root progressions.

Since here he is including rhythm in his exercises for the first time, the pupil will tend to think of every two measures as belonging together in a phrase. Such phrasing is not to be recommended, especially if he wants to give the upper voice more life. Through sequence-like repetitions there often arise motivic obligations from which it is exceedingly difficult to escape. Consequently, an example too 'melodiously' devised will generally not be very good.

The modulation to the *fourth circle upward* rests, as said, on the same principle. Instead of going to the dominant of *a* minor, we simply go to that of *e* minor. The relationships of *C* major (*a* minor) to *e* minor are so close that this dominant is no more difficult to reach than that of *a* minor. Instead of viewing the initial chord as III of *a* minor we take it to be VI of *e* minor. Everything else stays the same: reach the dominant, linger on the dominant or repeat it, leave it, and cadence. The pupil can even make modulations to the fourth circle upward by transposing (with little alterations) those to the third circle, and vice versa:

those to the fourth can be transposed to make modulations to the third. I recommend that he try this method as a supplementary exercise. In general, however, he should think through and work out every exercise independently

TO THE THIRD AND FOURTH CIRCLES DOWNWARD

(from *C* major and *a* minor to *E♭* major and *c* minor,
to *A♭* major and *f* minor)

For this modulation we use a means similar to that used for the preceding, but not as complicated. We saw there how a major tonic can come after a dominant, even though this dominant originated in minor, even though a minor tonic would thus be expected to follow it. Here the procedure is reversed: the I of a major key is viewed as a dominant (or secondary dominant, as the case may be) after which comes a minor triad. Analogously, keys with the same name (*C* major and *c* minor) have the same dominant (*g–b–d*); hence, the very same *g–b–d* is followed now by a major chord, now by a minor. Thus, if we regard the Ist degree of the initial key, *C* major, as such a dominant (if *a* minor is the initial key, this major chord, as III, must first be reached), then a minor chord on *F* can follow immediately, perhaps with the help of a seventh (*bb*) to give direction to the progression. Since this *C* is now a dominant (V in *f* minor), now a secondary dominant (I in *c* minor, VI in *Eb* major, III in *Ab* major), the following minor triad, *f–ab–c*, can be interpreted as I (in *f* minor), and also as II in *Eb* major, as IV in *c* minor, or as VI in *Ab* major. Thereby we arrive in a region that we could not reach with the means previously available. This modulation is extraordinarily simple because, as often mentioned, the Ist degree has the tendency to become a part of the tone a fifth below, to become the fifth, i.e. the dominant of that tone. To be sure, this tendency is toward a major chord. But in minor, convention nevertheless permits a minor chord, even if the natural tendency of the dominant is toward major.

Here monotony easily results, as in Example 153a, if after the II (of E♭) the new key is reached by the shortest way (V–I); then there is nothing but root progressions of fourths upward. Such is not to be recommended, even though it is quite natural, not only because it is monotonous but for another reason as well: perhaps it is too natural, too obvious, for us to find any trace of accomplishment in it. And if we proscribe such progressions, we are perhaps justified, because whoever uses so obvious, so cheap a device shows too little imagination. In themselves these progressions are of course good. Just too good. So much goodness does not agree with us. Hence, the pupil should strive to avoid such frequently repeated progressions. The use of inversions, seventh chords, even diminished seventh chords, does not help much. One must take care to introduce more diversity through deceptive cadences or insertion of other degrees (Example 153f).

In the *modulation to the fourth circle* downward a deceptive cadence will be of advantage in reaching the key (153d).

The modulation from *a* minor is somewhat more difficult: the *a* stands in the way of the *a♭* soon to follow (one could call it a cross relation). To cancel out the *a* smoothly it is advisable to handle it, in a voice in which it is most noticeable (in soprano or bass), as if it were the sixth tone in *c* minor, i.e. to take it through *b* to *c* (Example 154a). The diminished seventh chord (*b–d–f–a♭*) is quite appropriate because it makes possible the passage of *a* through *a♭* to *g*, as in 154b. The solution in 154e is still better. There this movement takes place in the soprano, in the most noticeable voice, and the continuation also introduces the *d♭*, preparing thereby the most important elements of *f* minor.

In Example 154c the seventh chord on I of *C* sets the course after the diminished seventh chord. The tones of this diminished seventh chord do not absolutely have to emerge chromatically (154d). Here, and from now on, we can

also permit movement by augmented or diminished intervals (*at first only with the diminished seventh chord*).

XIII RELATIONSHIP TO THE MINOR SUBDOMINANT

With the modulation to the third and fourth circles downward we have got acquainted with the relationship of a major tonic to the minor subdominant, namely: the ability of that tonic to be the dominant of a minor triad. Obviously, this circumstance is used, not only for modulation, but also for extending the cadence, for enriching the events within a key. The new relationships created by this connection of the principal chord [the tonic] with the subdominant permit us to introduce into the key – in addition to the diatonic chords and those that we obtained by reproducing the characteristics of the church modes – the secondary triads of the keys in whose domain this minor subdominant chord belongs, the chords of the third and fourth circles of fifths. With the introduction of these chords the tonality is significantly extended. They are, in *C* major:

Before we go on to investigate the uses of the new chords, we should account for the points of view that will guide us here. We ask first: Is the use of these chords within a key admissible and necessary? The answer must be: it is natural and agrees with the evolution of harmony. In the sense being considered here it can only be the tendency of this evolution, after it has used all the three to four-voice combinations of a seven-tone scale and then admitted by way of accidentals the remaining five tones (even if in part only with one meaning: in *C* major of course an *f♯* but no *g♭*, a *b♭* but no *a♯*), to go on to exploit all combinations of the available twelve semi-tones – at first still with reference to a fundamental, that is, within a key. Now whenever a modulation merely forms a bridge between two separate and independent pieces, as in opera, then its degree of remoteness is essentially of no consequence, since each of the two pieces is bounded formally by its own tonal frame. But a departure from the key within a closed composition can be justified, in so far as the sense of tonality is harmonic unity, only if that departure can be related to the principal key. That such can in fact be the case, even in the most far-reaching departures, is shown, for example, in the music of Beethoven, who introduces into *c*-minor compositions sections in *b* minor, into *E♭*-major compositions groups in *e* minor – something that Bach and Mozart did not yet do. Now within the tonality the fundamental chords of such sections and groups, if one is to be able to grasp the unity of the latter, must relate to one another, set side by side, as do the successive chords within a section: i.e. they must be comprehensible as a unit, they must have coherence. Even in the older music the question of justifying such modulations is not a question of relationship, but rather only a question of how to present this relationship through appropriate separation in time and space and through gradual connection. But time, space, and speed are not absolutes. Hence, today we can reduce them to a minimum and can set directly together what formerly had to be kept far apart and carefully connected. The interconnections are familiar to us; they were demonstrated in former epochs, hence do not need to be spelled out anew in every composition but are accepted as given.

By virtue of the answer to the first question the answer to the second is merely of subordinate, practical significance: What value does this enrichment of tonality have, what advantages can be drawn from it? Here we shall speak only of structural values, ignoring expressive values, such as mood, character, suspense, etc. As a point of structure we already know the capacity of harmony to form a close, the cadence, the end of a whole. To be sure one can set off the parts of this whole from one another with the seven diatonic chords. Since, however, these same seven chords also appear within the parts, there is need in larger forms for more sharply contrasting means. But the further harmony evolves, the more impetuous, the more concentrated becomes the utterance, the more rapidly the harmonies are presented. For, more and more, not just simple ideas but whole complexes are juxtaposed; and this more concentrated delivery requires, for clear articulation of the whole and for keeping principal and secondary matters distinct, richer punctuation, sharper distinction of phrases, a harmony more dynamic with a greater wealth of chords, of degree relationships. The closer relationships no longer keep parts distinct, they merely connect and merge with one another. Sharper highlights, darker shadows – such is the service these more remote chords can render.

Our judgments concerning the use of these chords will be limited on the one hand by pedagogical considerations, on the other by the conviction that it cannot be our job to procure for unused or little used items an importance denied them by practice, an importance theory cannot now create. And, finally, our judgments will be limited by the question, to what extent these chords have a place in the system of presentation (*Darstellungssystem*), hence, whether they are to be used right away or later.

Above all, the source of these chords should be kept in mind: the region of the minor subdominant. They are therefore strongly antithetical to the secondary dominants, which belong essentially to the region of the dominant (only the secondary dominant on I leads to the subdominant, whereas that on VI leads to the dominant of the dominant as well). And it is evidently for that reason that many a progression is considered too abrupt and therefore not commonly used. Consequently, the minor subdominant relationships will serve in general for enriching, for giving stronger emphasis to the subdominant region and cannot always be connected easily and directly with the region of the dominant. For the relationship of the two regions is not direct – this should not be forgotten – rather, it is indirect. The VI of *C* major and the I of *f* minor are related to each other only through the relation of both to the I of *C* major: they are, so to speak, only 'related by marriage'. But just as with the humbler, simpler relationships we assume that the IV and the V of a key are related (through the reference of both to I – in another sense they are antithetical), with the more sophisticated, more complicated ones, we may also regard the relationship of VI of *C* major with the I of *f* minor as being explained by the I of *C* major. The ability to acknowledge relationship between elements more distant from one another depends principally on the understanding and the insight of the observer. The individual with the most primitive conceptual and perceptual powers regards only the members of his body and his senses as belonging to him. The more

cultivated includes his family. At the next stages of cultivation the sense of community is exalted to the belief in nation and race; but at the highest stage the love for one's neighbor is extended across the species, across humanity, to the whole world. Even if the individual at this highest stage becomes a mere speck in the infinite, he nevertheless finds a sympathetic response, knows his related-ness [*findet er . . . zu sich*] (remarkably) oftener and more fully than those whose love is more exclusive.

Thus, although within the more rudimentary relationships of tonality the mutual relationships of a number of chords are apparently not direct, they nevertheless have the capacity for creating unity – a capacity that the ear must grasp, because in the prototype, in the tone given by nature, sounds even more remotely related unite to form one composite euphonious sound. Moreover, all these components of the tone sound simultaneously, and the ear has less time to distinguish them than when they sound successively. To be sure, the indi-vidual sounds are graded in strength according to the degree of relationship, but they do sound. And this imitation [in our chord relationships] does not yet, will not yet for a long time, go as far as the prototype.

Example 156 shows connections of all seven degrees of *C* major with the new chords. Before all else, let it be said that none of these connections, how-ever uncommon, is bad or unusable. Each of them can even be, in some con-text, the only one that fits – entirely apart from their potential expressive value.

Bearing this premise in mind, let us now proceed to give

GUIDELINES

and to impose restrictions.

I. In the first place, connections that cause difficulties in voice leading are not commonly used. Our harmony is in great part derived from the events that were created in polyphonic music by the movement of voices. Hence, whatever made for difficulties in voice leading did not occur there and is not commonly used. Examples of such connections are: II [of *C*] with VI [of *f*], III with VII, VI with III (at †), avoided because of the danger of parallel fifths, and for yet another reason, which is explained later; and: III with IV, V with VI, VI with IV, and VII with VI (at ⊕), avoided because of the augmented and diminished intervals. At present the pupil will best avoid these progressions entirely. Whether he will ever use them is not a question to be taken up in the harmony course, does not depend on harmonic theory; it will be decided rather by an artist, by the dictates of his sure sense of form. What *he* does is well done. [The harmony course] recommends only what is commonly used and says what place it has in the traditional system (*Darstellungssystem*).

II. Diminished triads that are poorly introduced we omit as a matter of course (I with II, III with II, IV with VI [of *c* minor], V with VI [at ▽]).

III. The IV of *C* major with the IV of *f* minor ($\flat$). The IV of *f* minor is the subdominant of the subdominant; and in view of the natural power that the subdominant has over the tonic, it is clear that the key could easily get lost. Of course we already have plenty of means by which to recover it. But here the means for its recovery would be more interesting than those by which it was lost. It is boring if the cops are more interesting than the robbers. If we want to depart that far from the key, if we want to be so revolutionary, we shall discover later more diverting means.

IV. III with I can arouse justifiable misgivings, particularly noticeable if we reverse the order of the chords and connect I of *f* minor with III of *C* major (Examples 157*a* and 157*b*). In this unfamiliar progression the ear will tend to interpret the chord *e–g–b*, not as III of *C* major, but as a variant of 157*d*, which does indeed sound similar to 157*c*. We will tend so to interpret it partly because these two chords do not appear next to each other in any key, but far more because this similarity reminds the ear too much of the more comfortable interpretation for it to accept the other (157*c*) as correct. Nevertheless, Examples 157*e* and *f* show that this sixth chord can well be III if what follows confirms this interpretation.

V. Connections that have an analogy in some not too distant key, in a key, that is, where the chords involved appear diatonically, or where only one of the two is an artificial dominant, will give no difficulty so long as cross relations are dealt with melodically (i.e. as pivot tones or chromatic alterations). Here it will often be possible to reinterpret.

VI. The same is true of connections in which chromatic voice leading is possible, so long as augmented or diminished intervals do not become necessary in other voices.

VII. As always, the basis for decision is the root progression.

Examples 158*a–g* show those forms that connect easily with dominants, secondary dominants, and the like. And so, in 158*a* and *b*, I serves to introduce [the forms from the subdominant region], in 158*c* and 158*d* V, in 158*e* the secondary dominant on II, in 158*f* the secondary dominant on VI, and in 158*g* the diminished seventh chords on I, II, V, and VI. There is nothing new about these connections. Analogies can be found for each of them (in *c* minor, *f* minor, *g* minor, and *d* minor). The only difficulty is, at times, the neutralization of cross relations, as shown in Example 158*h*.

This difficulty is, however, easily disposed of by means of pivot-tone treatment, chromaticism, and diminished seventh chords, all techniques the pupil should know by now.

Those connections that turn a major chord into a minor chord over the same root (Example 156 at ▣) are obvious and easy to deal with. How he is to proceed here, and that the chromatic introduction of such minor chords has more melodic than harmonic significance, the pupil knows already from the chapter on secondary dominants [p. 188] where we spoke of the minor V (in *C* major), *g–bb–d*, derived from the Dorian mode. In Example 159*a* the minor chord (sixth chord on *eb*) has no influence on what follows. But in 159*b* the minor chord on V of *c* (over *bb*) does prepare for the subdominant region. And in

159c the chromatically introduced *a♭* in the bass certainly effects the unobtrusive entry of the following sixth chord, *f–a♭–d♭*.

With these connections where a major triad changes to minor it is advisable to put the chromatic progression of the third in the bass so that this voice does not stall. Even so, however, no great advantage can be drawn from this progression because too little change occurs in the total sound. That is probably the reason why such a movement of voices usually takes place in note values smaller than those of the other harmonies, why they would best appear in our work here as quarter notes, since we are writing half notes.

Of far-reaching significance are connections like that of I of *C* major with III or VII of *f* minor (I or V of *A♭* major) and similar connections of the other degrees (Example 156 ⊗). There are only two such connections with the IInd degree, whereas with the other minor chords there are three (Example 160 ♭). The relationship existing here could of course be admitted by analogy, but not by appeal to the degree of relationship with which we are presently concerned. As with this minor chord, there are two such progressions with the major chords.

The standard for the harmonic evaluation of these connections is merely the root progression. The strong leap of a third downward needs no impetus, whereas the weaker leap of a third upward is to be judged essentially as before [p. 119]. I can ignore a currently popular explanation that calls such progressions 'third relationships', 'fifth relationships', etc.; for I consider them adequately motivated just because they are related. In one way or another all chords are naturally related to one another, as are all men. Whether they make up a family, a nation, or a race is certainly not without interest; but it is not an essential question if we place it beside the idea of species, which gives perspectives other than those admitted by the special relationships.

There is a means that is always appropriate for making such chord connections smoothly and convincingly: chromaticism. Formerly, when we were dealing with simpler connections, with the most immediate relationships, a diatonic scale segment from the fundamental key or a related key assumed the responsibility for what happened harmonically. Here, more and more, a single scale assumes all such functions: the chromatic scale. It is easy to see why. Since we acknowledged that the [diatonic] scale is a simple melody, a musical form based on a law rudimentary and easily comprehensible, so we cannot now deny that the chromatic scale also has this property. Its melodic power helps to connect what is more distantly related: such is the sense of chromaticism.

The connections in Example 160 at ⊕ are somewhat difficult to handle (because of the voice leading). Here an uncommon leap of a voice will not always be easy to avoid. The pupil will do well at the beginning to arrange the chords so that such an interval is not necessary (Example 161). Once he has mastered such arrangements he can then of course risk augmented or diminished intervals as well, especially in the middle voices. These intervals are much less disturbing now, for the melodic and harmonic events refer less and less often solely to the model of the major or minor scale. And here it is no longer out of place to presuppose the reinterpretation of a tone (enharmonic change), which then generally brings about melodic balance. Naturally, the closer the voice leading resembles the major or minor scale, the more easily the voices can be understood. The pupil should still strive for such voice leading, even here. For augmented seconds I recommend following the model of the so-called 'harmonic minor scale' (in which I see the real *melodic* minor scale).

Some examples now follow to show the potential uses of these chord connections.

For these examples I chose [to show how these chords can be used in] the cadence, since everyone will prefer to think these progressions modulate rather

than cadence. And the theorists will probably maintain that those are modulations from *C* to . . . 'and back'. That can happen, too; but here one could speak of modulations only in that previously mentioned sense in which most strictly speaking any other chord following the tonic chord already represents a departure, a modulation. This view, that here modulations in the more limited sense do not occur, has above all the advantage of teaching the pupil to perceive the whole as a unit. This view is certainly more consistent with musical thought, as exhibited, for example, in the harmonic variation. Often the theme clearly does not leave the key; but in the variations key relations are used that one likes to consider modulations because it is so much more convenient to do so. They are, however, no more modulations than were the corresponding places in the theme.

Of the connections given in Example 156, those at ○ have not yet been discussed. It is only a matter of appropriate introduction and continuation. Here, too, melodic voice leading serves best.

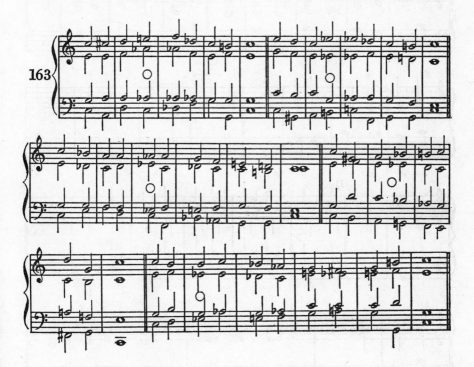

Examples 164 [and 165 further] illustrate the use of chords related through the minor subdominant. In minor I recommend using at first merely the relationships through the parallel major key: thus, in *c* minor, the chords related to *C* major through its minor subdominant. Later the pupil can make use of the more extensive relationship (through the relative major, i.e. in *c* minor that of *E♭* major). At the beginning it will often get him into difficult situations.

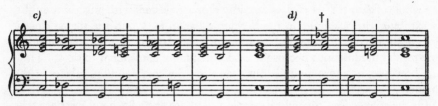

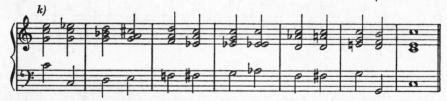

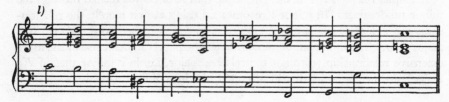

In Example 164*g* it would be better to take the *b♭* of the bass to *a♭*; nevertheless, the continuation shows – as in Example 164*k*, where *c* goes to *d* but would better go to *b♭* – that strong chords afterwards help to overcome such misgivings.

In Example 165, first from *c* minor, the minor subdominant relationships of the parallel major (*C*) are used, then, from *a* minor, the more extensive relationships of the relative major.

The pupil will even now have to show taste and sense of form. We can no longer manage the abundance of possibilities (*Ereignisse*) through instructions alone. I think it is better that he worry than that he be bold, better that he hesitate to make harsh (*hart*) connections than that he decide for them all too lightly. He should discriminate! And even if one goes far beyond what can appear here, even if nothing be bad in itself, nor perhaps good in itself either, nevertheless, that faculty (*Organ*) that is to be developed – the sense of form – is sooner activated through careful choosing than it is when there are no restrictions.

In Example 164*d* at † the so-called 'Neapolitan sixth' was used. It is a sixth chord obtained through the minor subdominant relation, which in *C* major and *c* minor reads *f–ab–db*, and in this context refers back to its appearance as a diatonic chord in *f* minor, as VI (or in *Ab* major, as IV). In *f* minor its connection with V of that key is nothing new (VI – V, Example 166*a*). But the typical use of the Neapolitan sixth is patterned after that of the IInd degree in the cadence (166*b* and 166*c*). Hence, it was assumed to be a chromatic alteration of II. To be correct, however, we must call it a substitute for II.

That is to say, if we assume it is a chromatically derived modification of II, then that means the root and fifth are lowered. But the assumption that the root is lowered is to be definitely rejected. Aside from the fact that the assumption of the lowered root is used only in one other case (in the augmented six-five chord, soon to be discussed) and therefore constitutes one of those noted exceptions, it is the most preposterous thing one can do. The roots are, in our conception, fixed points from which relationships are measured. The unity of all the measurements we have found is guaranteed by the immobility of these points. But then one may not move them!! It is something quite different to assume that at the second place of the scale there are two roots: *d* and *db* (as in minor at the sixth and seventh places and at many places in the church modes). That is an assumption that can easily be extended to all parts of the scale, whereby we obtain the chromatic scale as the basis for considering harmonic events. Hence, in *C* major there can be two chords of the second degree. Perhaps a new theory will be founded upon the chromatic scale; but then the degrees will probably be differently named.

The manner in which the Neapolitan sixth appears also speaks against the assumption of the lowered root. It is commonly used as follows (167*a*, *b*, *c*, *d*, *e*): coming directly after I (but also after many other chords appropriate for introducing it), it resolves generally to the six-four chord of I or to V.

If the root were in fact lowered, then the chord ought to appear just as often in the manner shown in Examples 167*f* and *g*. These instances are naturally not exceptions, but they are rare. And that they do occur does not prove the derivation by lowered root but merely that everything can be good in the right place.

The Neapolitan sixth is thus best regarded as a substitute for II in the cadence. In this sense it is sometimes also used as a six-four chord (168*a*), and even as the chord made up of the same tones in root position (cliché effect, 168*b*). Whether this chord still deserves the name, Neapolitan sixth, in cases (168*c*) where it does not have the typical function of that chord (as a substitute degree in the cadence) is doubtful, but unimportant.

In Example 167*g* a way of leading to the Neapolitan sixth was shown in which root and fifth are simultaneously lowered. This introduction is possible (provided we want to avoid parallel fifths) only if the voices involved are fourths, or through especially artful voice leading (168*d*). Obviously: this introduction is neither bad nor forbidden. But in spite of the mediation of the minor subdominant relation: these two chords are about as remotely related as chords can be. And if we connect them so directly we are right on that boundary where we can say: all chords can be connected with one another. Since such progressions are uncommon anyhow, the pupil will continue to avoid them for the time being. For the same reason (as was already said) he will omit the analogous connections from the other minor chords (III and VI, Example 156 at †).

Every sixth chord of a major triad can imitate the function of the Neapolitan sixth, including the sixth chord of I and that of V. Of course these two do not lead to diatonic chords and are therefore not now usable (169g and h). If we go

about it the other way around, i.e. if we seek out for the diatonic chords those sixth chords, sometimes nondiatonic, that relate to the diatonic chords as the Neapolitan sixth relates to the six-four chord of I or to V, then we get the forms used in Example 169.

Here one should give heed; the connection with the six-four chord, because of the six-four chord cliché, can easily lead astray, beyond the harmonic meaning this quasi-Neapolitan progression has for the key. One can of course easily control such an ambiguity, but one must give heed to it. Therefore, it is to be recommended that these chords be used rather in their other function, according to the model II–V.

Only a few connections within the sphere of minor subdominant relationships remain unexamined. Assuming the principle that any connection can be good at the right place, we may say that hardly anything of real value has been left out.

XIV AT THE FRONTIERS OF TONALITY

More about the *diminished seventh chord*; then about the *augmented triad*; further: The *augmented six-five, four-three, and two chords* and the *augmented sixth chord* (of the IInd degree and on other degrees). – Some *other alterations of the IInd degree*; the same alterations on other degrees. *Connections* of altered and vagrant chords.

The chords discussed in the previous chapter can be introduced much more mildly, less abruptly, by means of vagrant chords. At present we know two such chords: the diminished seventh chord and the augmented triad. We have seen (p. 193) how the diminished seventh chord can appear in major and minor, if we regard it as a ninth chord with root omitted and construct it not only on V but on other degrees as well (by analogy with the secondary dominants). Then, when (in Example 141a) the two most common deceptive cadences were examined, the way was opened to a large number of heterogeneous chords, and we saw the superb ability of the diminished seventh chord to bring distantly related chords closer to each other and to mitigate seemingly forced connections. It is because of these abilities that the chord played such a great role in the older music. Wherever something difficult had to be done, one enlisted the services of this miracle worker, equal to every task. And whenever a piece is called 'chromatic fantasy and fugue', we can be sure the chord plays a leading role in creating this chromaticism. But another meaning was also found for it: it was the 'expressive' chord of that time. Wherever one wanted to express pain, excitement, anger, or some other strong feeling – there we find, almost exclusively, the diminished seventh chord. So it is in the music of Bach, Haydn, Mozart, Beethoven, Weber, etc. Even in Wagner's early works it plays the same role. But soon the role was played out. This uncommon, restless, undependable guest, here today, gone tomorrow, settled down, became a citizen, was retired a philistine. The chord had lost the appeal of novelty, hence, it had lost its sharpness, but also its luster. It had nothing more to say to a new era. Thus, it fell from the higher sphere of art music to the lower of music for entertainment. There it remains, as a sentimental expression of sentimental concerns. It became banal and effeminate. *Became* banal! It was not so originally. It was sharp and dazzling. Today, though, it is scarcely used any more except in that mawkish stuff (*Schmachtliteratur*) which sometime later always apes what was formerly, in great art, an important event. Other chords took its place, chords that were to replace its expressiveness and chords that were to replace its pivotal facility. These were the augmented triad, certain altered chords, and some sonorities that, having already been introduced in the music of Mozart or Beethoven by virtue of suspensions or passing tones, appeared in that of Wagner as independent chords. None of these chords, however, was quite the equal of the diminished seventh – an advantage for them, actually; for they were thus better protected against banality, since they were not open to such excessive use. Yet, these too were soon worn out, soon lost their charm; and that explains why so quickly after Wagner, whose harmonies seemed unbelievably bold to his contemporaries, new paths were sought: The diminished seventh chord provoked this movement, which cannot stop before it has fulfilled the will of nature, and not before we have reached the greatest possible maturity in the imitation of nature: so that we can then turn away from the external model and more and more toward the internal, toward the one within us.

I will find an opportunity later to take up the question, what it is about such chords that seems to us so expressive. Here, then, I will say only this: I value originality, but I do not overrate it – as do most who do not have it. It is a symptom that, although hardly ever missing from something good, does nevertheless appear in inferior things as well; it is consequently in itself no criterion. Yet, I do believe in the new; I believe it is that *Good* and that *Beauty* toward which we strive with our innermost being, just as involuntarily and persistently as we strive toward the *future*. There must be, somewhere in our future, a *magnificent fulfilment* as yet hidden from us, since all our striving forever pins its hopes on it. Perhaps that future is an advanced stage in the development of our species, at which that yearning will be fulfilled which today gives us no peace. Perhaps it is just death; but perhaps it is also the certainty of a higher life after death. The future brings the new, and that is perhaps why we so often and so justifiably identify the new with the beautiful and the good.

Since he should know [them] firsthand, the pupil must try to use as many of the properties of the diminished seventh chord as he can for the benefit of modulations and cadences. But he should not overrate the value of the chord and should not use it excessively; otherwise (and this would be just too horrible) his exercises might turn out as badly as the first act of *Tristan* (according to the saying of an old composition professor, a very old one, in fact he is already dead). We young people went to every Wagner performance just for that purpose – though we were perhaps not aware of why we went – just to find out why the professor had said what he did; and we could not explain it. Finally it came to us. The old gentleman had said: 'The first act of *Tristan* is so boring because there are so many diminished seventh chords in it.' Now, at last, we knew.

In general the pupil will do well not to go too far, temporarily, in using the

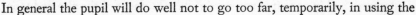

171

IV

chords from the minor subdominant region. For it is not always easy to restore balance, even with this universal means, 'the diminished seventh chord'. Besides, the use of a universal means is quite inartistic. Unimaginative and convenient, inept! Hence, I find the progressions in Example 171 really bad.

I have already explained in the chapters on modulation why a gradually unfolding modulation is more appropriate for exercises. For the reasons given there I cannot consider extensions of the cadence good, either, if done by such [universal] means. At the same time it should be said that the situation is already different here. The inclusion of so many relationships in itself has already turned tonality into a phenomenon of greater activity. It now contains more unrest, in light of which a more vigorous action is no longer so inappropriate. All the same, whereas the diminished seventh chord can do many things, it cannot do everything. Therefore, the pupil should not use the diminished seventh chord, for example, every time he wants to go from a diatonic to a nondiatonic chord. The connection is often harsh, and, although harshness is no calamity in itself, it does not conform to our present aims.

These progressions (Example 172) are of course not absolutely bad. There can be a good melody over them; indeed, just better voice leading in the soprano will perhaps make them milder. But in themselves they are more abrupt, harsher than anything we have permitted up to now. Much will depend here on the voice leading. It will be best to shape each voice so that it resembles a neighboring minor or major key. In 172a the trouble is perhaps in the tenor, which gets to the tone d♭ in a way that would hardly be used, say, in f minor or A♭ major. Perhaps the trouble is also with the 'open' a of the bass, which is not neutralized; and in 172b it is perhaps in the movement of the alto and tenor.

On an earlier occasion (p. 148) I excluded a particular use of the diminished seventh that often appears in masterworks. It is that form in which the diminished seventh (ninth chord with omitted root) of V precedes the six-four chord of I.

The old rule seems to have been: the diminished seventh chord can be connected with any chord, hence, also with the six-four chord of I. But, whether it be interpreted as VII (of c minor) or as V – it weakens the succeeding dominant, for it contains the most important elements of the latter: the ascending and descending leading tones. Moreover, the VII is generally only a substitute for V anyway, so that the root progression would then read VII (= V), I, V, I, not a very favorable progression. Although such does appear in the works of masters (Mozart, Beethoven, Weber, Wagner, etc.) – for it is perhaps wrong only in relation to the other rules that the harmonic theory of that time gave – the pupil should not use it: Harmony exercises are not masterworks. The ear of these masters was of course right when it told them that the diminished

seventh chord can be connected with any chord; it is not for the reason they assumed, however, that this particular connection is also good, rather, because every chord can be connected with every other. Under certain conditions and with certain reservations, naturally, which one must first know, which must first be part of one's sense of form, and for which one must be able to take responsibility. Therefore, such things are not for the pupil in his harmony exercises, but for the artist in his creative freedom.

THE AUGMENTED TRIAD[1]

The constitution of the augmented triad is similar to that of the diminished seventh chord. Its form, too, has something circular about it, something that doubles back on itself. If we transpose its lowest tone an octave higher the interval between the previous high tone and the present one is the same as it was between the other tones [before transposition], between the first and second, and second and third: a major third (Example 174a). The minor third divides the chromatic scale into four equal parts, the major third into three. As there are only three different diminished seventh chords, so here there are only four different augmented triads (174b). Therefore, apart from any other reason, by analogy with the diminished seventh, every augmented triad belongs to at least three minor keys (174c).

[1 Cf. *infra*, Chapter XX.]

If in all three minor keys to which it belongs we regard as its two most important tonal resolutions those to I and to VI, then we find that the same sonority, now called *e–g♯–c*, now *e–g♯–b♯* or *e–a♭–c*, connects with three

different roots, twice with each one. Each of these is, in the one case, root of a major chord, in the other, root of a minor. These connections are as follows:

in *a* minor with *a–c–e* (I) and *f–a–c* (VI)
in *c♯* minor with *a–c♯–e* (VI) and *c♯–e–g♯* (I)
in *f* minor with *f–a♭–c* (I) and *d♭–f–a* (VI).

Since in the resolutions to the major chords (III–VI of minor) the roots make the leap of a fourth, it is evident that the augmented triads may be used to produce a tonic, and that, to this end, they may be introduced artificially on the V of the major key in question, following the idea of the secondary dominants. They are most simply introduced through chromatic alteration upward of the fifth.

This chromatic introduction can also be used on the secondary degrees, in which case the third will sometimes also be raised (Example 177). But the aug-

mented triads can also be introduced chromatically by the other degrees [that is, by altering other than the fifth of a chord] (178a), and also without chromaticism (178b). Finally every degree can also be connected with the other augmented triads (as in 178c). For the augmented triad is by virtue of its constitution, as indicated by its belonging to three keys, a vagrant chord like the diminished seventh. Although it does not have as many resolutions as the diminished seventh chord, it is nevertheless like that chord in that it can be introduced, because of its ambiguity, after almost any chord. And it, too, permits augmented and diminished steps since the meaning of a tone introduced nondiatonically is by no means clearly settled at the moment of its entry.

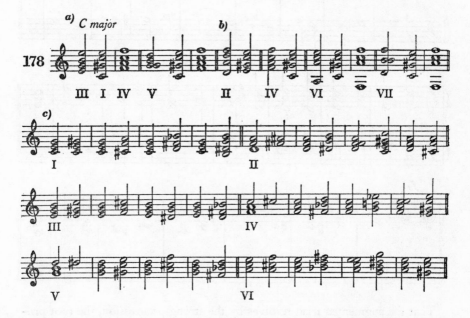

Some examples follow. The pupil can add to these at will by trying out everything that has been suggested in the foregoing discussion. With the augmented triad it is not necessary to make a distinction between root position and inversions. It is indeed almost always reinterpreted, and, that being the case, the feeling of a six-four chord can hardly ever arise. To avoid complicated notation one will often use enharmonic change. Thus, for example, in 179d *a♯* should be written instead of *b♭*; but we prefer to avoid the note *a♯* in *C* major.

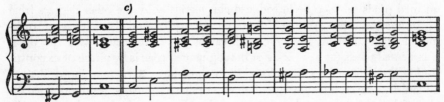

That the augmented triad resolves by the strong progression, the root progression a fourth upward, to a major key, even when it was derived from the minor key of the same name, favors its use for connection of major and minor. The pupil will be able to take advantage of this feature in modulations, but (as with the diminished seventh chord) I do not advocate basing a modulation solely on this chord. From first to last the pupil will do well to set up and make use of a plan for [each] modulation, a well-thought-out plan which will prepare for reaching the goal.

There are still two other treatments of the augmented triad to be mentioned. They are not important harmonically, yet they should not be excluded. By lowering each of the tones, one at a time, we get three new major triads (Example 180*a*); by lowering every pair of tones, three minor triads on these same three roots (180*b*).

These resolutions are more likely to be heard as resolutions of suspensions, since they are built on a descending root progression (third upward). But they can be used as preparation for a strong progression immediately to follow.

AUGMENTED SIX-FIVE, FOUR-THREE, TWO, AND SIXTH CHORDS, AND SOME OTHER VAGRANT CHORDS

The derivation of the augmented six-five chord is usually explained in the following manner: in major, we can raise the root and third of the six-five chord on II and lower its fifth; in minor, we can raise the root of the seventh chord on IV. We obtain thereby two chords whose sound is identical and whose respective functions are similar.*

Both can resolve to the six-four chord of I (Examples 182*a*, *b*); both can also resolve to the triad on V (182*c*) since, although the notation is different, the

---

* The derivation of these chords that I have cited here is by no means the only one. I know the others and the many different names that exist for them only by hearsay. But I must mention that, apparently, the chord commonly designated 'augmented four-three chord' is completely different from the one to which the term properly belongs. If the tones of the augmented six-five chord are arranged differently, so that other tones of the chord appear alternately in the bass, then we can interpret chords so related only as inversions of a single chord. Particularly when the functions are identical! Then why all the names?

sound is identical. In the latter resolution parallel fifths appear, because of which the spacing in Example 182d is often chosen. Or on the other hand one says, 'Mozart fifths', meaning that such are allowed, not because they sound good, but because Mozart wrote them. I am all in favor of this respect for the works of the masters. Hence, I think that theory should permit at least everything written by the masters, who did not worry about permission. But theory is then being rather more practical than theoretical: it is making the necessary effort to accommodate what actually occurs and thereby loses the right to give aesthetic-theoretic evaluation. Nevertheless, if carried out thoroughly and uniformly, such [practicality] is the right basis for instruction in the handicraft, whereas in the aesthetic-theoretic system it is nonsense to introduce a unique case for the sake of its practicality. We shall regard these fifths no differently from the others: we think they sound good, but wherever possible we shall not yet write them. Not yet: the pupil can write them later. Wherever possible: if he cannot get around them, he can write them now, immediately.

In the derivation of the augmented six-five chord mentioned above, we find again the assumption of a raised root. I regard this assumption as incorrect in a system that considers roots (that can only be unraised ones) its unit of measure. Moreover, to derive the chord from two degrees is impractical; for not only does such derivation cloud the function, it also fails to reserve the enharmonic reinterpretation of the ambiguous tone ($d\sharp - e\flat$) which could perhaps resolve [the conflict between use and derivation]. If, for example, 182d appears in C major, the tone should be $d\sharp$ according to this derivation. Therefore, I find it more appropriate to derive the augmented six-five chord from the ninth chord on II in major or minor, by way of the secondary dominants, that is, from the diminished seventh chord. Then it agrees with both major and minor; thus: IInd degree in (C) major or minor, secondary dominant, secondary dominant seventh, secondary dominant nine-seven chord; root omitted, diminished seventh chord, fifth lowered.

In the diminished seventh chord the reinterpretation of the *e♮* as *d♯* was already assumed, anyhow; thus, this chord derived from the diminished seventh can also be used with both meanings. The question, how it is to be derived, seems to me less important than the question, what harmonic necessities or possibilities brought it into being. Answering this question shows us how to handle the chord, how to introduce it and how to progress from it. It is most frequently found where there would otherwise be II or IV: namely, in the cadence, before the six-four chord of I or before the dominant seventh chord (V) (Example 182). It can thus be regarded as substituting for one of these degrees, either II or IV. It is most advantageous to assume it to be a substitute for II, as I just pointed out. We have already seen similar occurrences on II; moreover, II–V is [part of] the authentic cadence, and II–I is like a deceptive cadence. So viewed, the use of the augmented six-five chord turns out to be quite simple: in major it is introduced in the same manner as were the chords of the minor-subdominant region; in minor its introduction is similar to that of a secondary dominant or a diminished seventh chord. If it comes in the cadence its progression to V or I is obvious, or if it goes perhaps to III (182*e*, *f*, *g*) the progression is still easily understood: II–V, II–I, II–III, the authentic progression (fourth upward) and the two most common deceptive progressions (second upward and downward): the three important ascending progressions.

What necessities and possibilities find expression in the augmented six-five chord? In fact, we can ask the same question of other vagrant chords. Above all, such chords will be good wherever they fit into the environment, that is, where they are not isolated occurrences of that sort of thing, thus do not fall outside the style of the whole. Wherever they appear, vagrant chords usually join forces, so to speak, and give the harmony of a piece a distinctive coloring ('Chromatic' Fantasy and Fugue of Bach). Of course, since nothing is bad in itself, we cannot say that the isolated occurrence must be in every case bad. But it is evident that chords remote from the key, appearing in large numbers, will favor the establishment of a new *conceptual unit* (*Auffassungseinheit*): the chromatic scale. It is not to be ignored that through accumulation of such phenomena the solid structure of tonality could be demolished. This danger is of course easily repulsed, and the tonality can always be reinforced. If a rupture does nevertheless occur, the consequence is not necessarily disintegration and formlessness. For the chromatic scale is a form, too. It, too, has a formal principle, a different one from that of the major or minor scale, a simpler and more uniform principle. Perhaps it is an unconscious striving for simplicity that leads musicians here; for the replacement of major and minor with a chromatic scale is no doubt the same sort of step as the replacement of the seven church modes with merely two scales, major and minor: greater uniformity of relationship within an unchanged number of possible relationships. However that may be, the vagrant chords demonstrate the effort to make use of the chromatic scale and the advantages of its complete set of leading tones, to obtain more convincing, more compelling, and more supple chord connections. The fortunate coincidence of so many favorable circumstances may well be called the reward for handling the material in a manner consistent with nature. One may hope, in this little matter, to have guessed the will of nature; and by following these enticements, one is yielding to her power. Sometimes that is indeed nature's way. She has us desire and enjoy that which fulfils her purposes.[1] Perhaps through the very yearning [for fulfilment].

The augmented four-three chord and the augmented two chord are to be regarded as further inversions of the same parent chord: that is, the four-three chord as the second, the two chord as the third inversion (Example 184a); or simply as inversions of the augmented six-five chord.[2] Obviously then there is nothing further to say about their treatment. They appear wherever the augmented six-five chord can appear and the melodic line requires a different bass tone. Only, the augmented two chord will sometimes create difficulty because (Example 185d) the repetition of the c in the bass is not very apt. Since this chord consists of four tones, there has to be yet a fourth position (Example 184e). According to my derivation from the ninth chord, that is simply the fourth inversion of a ninth chord. According to the first-mentioned derivation, it would actually have to be the root position; and again we see how unnatural this conception is. There is nothing special to be said concerning the treatment

[1] Insert here: '[Her purposes are fulfilled] for example, through love and through hunger.' This remark from the first edition (p. 273) was apparently omitted by oversight in the revision. However that may be, it provides transition to the concluding remark and makes the latter less cryptic.]

[2] Here Schoenberg considered d the tacit root of the chord; therefore, the first chord in Example 184a (f♯–a♭–c–e♭) would be, strictly speaking, the first inversion, the augmented six-five chord. It is of course more customary to designate the inversion a♭–c–e♭–f♯ as the augmented six-five chord, c–e♭–f♯–a♭ as the augmented four-three chord, and so on.]

of this position, either. At most, one will perhaps have to be careful in resolving it to the six-four chord of V (Example 184*f*). But that is nothing new, either, since it recalls the similar case of the diminished seventh.[1] The resolution to the sixth chord of I is very common (184*g* and *k*).

The so-called augmented sixth chord (184*b*) is nothing else but an augmented six-five chord without the ninth (or the seventh, whichever it is called) and thus relates to the latter more or less as the diminished triad on VII relates to the seventh chord of V or also to the seventh chord of its own root (VII). This augmented sixth chord needs no further explanation. It goes wherever the augmented six-five chord (or four-three, or two) can go – presumably wherever one does not dare write parallel fifths (184*d*). Of course its tones can also be arranged differently (i.e. in inversions). It is not necessary to prepare the augmented six-five, four-three, two, and sixth chords after the fashion of the other seventh chords. For the tone that is the seventh, according to the derivation, is actually only a diminished fifth, since the assumed root does not sound, and the ninth is only a diminished seventh. Both of these we have already been using freely. On the other hand, the third of the assumed root sounds like a minor seventh, as even becomes visible with the enharmonic change (184*c*); but here, as the third, it certainly does not have to be prepared. The sound of these chords is identical with that of a dominant seventh chord (on a♭: a♭–c–e♭–g♭); only the notation is altered. This double identity can be put to use, as will be shown later [p. 254].

a) Major

185

I   I⁶₄   II

III   IV

V   VI

[1 Cf. *supra*, p. 240.]

b)

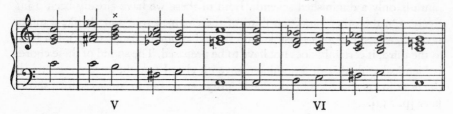

c) $\frac{4}{3}$- chord

As we extended the idea of the dominant by analogy to create the idea of the secondary dominant, as we created artificial diminished triads, seventh chords, and the like – so here, as well, we make appropriately similar alterations of other degrees according to the model of the IInd degree. With this operation we obtain the following chords (the other inversions, four-three, and two, as well as the augmented sixth chord, the pupil can work out himself):

Progression to these chords will be accomplished either through use of the minor-subdominant relation in major or chromatically. There are not very many examples in the literature to illustrate the use of these six-five, four-three, and two chords derived from other degrees. All the same, I have seen them in the music of Brahms and Schumann. The examples given here show that they are usable, though, even if vigorous means are sometimes needed to restore the key.

The fact that the sound of an augmented six-five (four-three, two, or sixth) chord is identical with the sound of a dominant seventh chord can now be easily exploited by treating (introducing and continuing) the one as if it were the other. For example, an augmented six-five chord on some degree is taken to be the seventh chord with the identical sound and is resolved according to the patterns V–I, V–VI, or V–IV (Example 188a). Or a dominant (or secondary) dominant) seventh chord is interpreted as an augmented six-five, four-three, or

two chord and resolved accordingly (188*b*). This technique, together with the idea of the Neapolitan sixth on secondary degrees, produces great enrichment of the tonality.

Obviously, there are chords here that can be interpreted differently. But, since we are not occupied with analysis, it does not matter to us. We are only concerned with a system that stimulates interest and excites the imagination by organizing and unifying the greatest possible variety of events. It goes without saying, there is not much point in cracking one's skull over the question whether, because of the harmonic meaning, we should write *c♯* or *d♭*, *g♯* or *a♭*. We write what is most simple. The shortcoming lies in our imperfect system of notation. In nothing else.

Before I go on to make suggestions concerning the connection of these different vagrant chords with one another (suggestions: for to illustrate everything that can be done here is in fact hardly possible), I want to discuss two other chords that also belong with the vagrant chords.

The one (Example 189*a*) is best derived from the IInd degree in major or minor, by raising the third and lowering the fifth. By raising the third we create an ascending leading tone, by lowering the fifth, a descending. The resulting chord combines dominant (and secondary dominant) possibilities with the minor-subdominant relationships. The second chord (189*b* †) is familiar to us from the minor-subdominant region. Thus considered, it is, as it were, II of *c* minor or VII of *E*♭ major. But the context in which it appears here is new to us. One would be inclined here to think of its *d* as *e*♭♭. That would be particularly necessary if, for example (189*c*), one conceived it as emerging from an inversion of the augmented six-five chord. Of course the same resolution can occur with the first chord as well (189*d*). One might thus conclude that the root of these two chords is not *D*, but *A*♭(189*e* and *f*). This interpretation apparently finds support in the fact that the second chord can also resolve to a minor chord on *D*♭ (189*g*), as can of course the first, as well (189*h* – *f*♯ always equals *g*♭ here). In this case the *d* would then be a lowered fifth, the *f* (as *g*♭♭) a lowered seventh. On the other hand, however, the most common resolutions of these chords are, because they are the most direct, those in Example 189*i*. Here we can regard them as IInd degree chords, with the root progressions II–V, II–III, and II–I; if we consider *A*♭ their root (VI of *c* minor), we do of course get VI–II (fourth upward) for the connection with *D*♭, but for the connection with *c* we get VI–I (third upward). That interpretation is of course possible but not convincing. In the first place, our presentation is more uniform if we refer these chords, also, to the IInd degree, as we have done with so many others; to derive it from the VIth would be a novelty (*Novum*). The introduction of such a novelty would be impractical for the technical system, for actual application, even if it would be less harmful to the conceptual system. Secondly, the following is to be said against [the assumption that *A*♭ is the root]: if the chord in Example 189*i* be on the IInd degree, *d* is the root; but if the chord be on the VIth degree, the *d* would be an imprecise notation of an *e*♭♭, that is, of a nondiatonic tone, of the lowered fifth of *a*♭ (the diatonic fifth would be *e*♭). This same nondiatonic tone is now, in the chord of resolution (V), suddenly supposed to be a *diatonic tone*! That is of course not impossible, either; but it is complicated. And with the other interpretation such complexity is not necessary. The only connection that could be somewhat difficult to explain is that with the $D\flat$ (or $d\flat$) chord. For this connection would have to be designated as II with II. There would then be no root progression. But that is nothing new to us. In the first place, we have already had instances where in a progression of two chords no root progression is to be imagined: for example, where a triad is followed by the seventh chord on the same degree, or by the secondary dominant, the secondary dominant seventh, the diminished seventh (ninth) chord, etc. Secondly, however, we saw an instance quite similar to the very one we are now discussing when we connected the augmented six-five chord (IInd degree) with the Neapolitan sixth (IInd degree) [Example 188*a*]. Thus, it is quite systematic to assume the same thing here as well.

We obtain thereby the same advantage we found elsewhere when we made our root references uniform: we can undertake the same alterations on other degrees. Then we get the chords in Example 189*k*, of which those marked are already familiar to us, as is one of those on the VIIth degree. Some of the others are perhaps somewhat difficult to introduce, but, with the means now available to us, no longer very difficult. Above all, this transfer by analogy to other degrees will make clear to what great extent these chords are vagrant and with what little justification analysis refers them to this or that key.

In themselves these chords do not require such lengthy discussion, for they are indeed not particularly complicated. But since they play a great role in Wagner's harmony and since so much has been written about them, I, too, am compelled to take a position with regard to them. (I do not know those writings but have only heard of them.) The chord in Example 189*b*, transposed a minor third higher and enharmonically altered (189*l*), is known to everyone as the so-called 'Tristan Chord'.[1] To be sure, this chord does resolve to *E*, thus is analogous to Example 189*b*. The continuation should then be that in Example 189*l*, that is, should indicate *e♭* minor [or *d♯*]; but Wagner treats the *E* as the dominant of *a* minor (189*m*). There has been much dispute over the question to which degree that chord belongs. I hope to contribute to the disentanglement of this question, but I think I can best do so if I give no new derivation. Now, we may regard the *g♯* as a suspension going up to *a*, in which case the chord has the form shown in Example 189*a*; or it would also work to call the *a* a passing tone going (through *a♯*) to *b*; or we may yet assume the very worst: namely, that the 'Tristan Chord' is actually derived from *e♭* minor (189*n*) (if it absolutely must be derived from something) and, being a vagrant chord, is reinterpreted and taken to *a* minor. (The latter seems to be the most extravagant interpretation. But it is not, for *a* minor and *e♭* minor actually have in common not only this chord, but simpler ones as well. For example, the VI of *e♭* minor is identical with the dominant of the dominant of *a* minor, the secondary dominant on II; and the Neapolitan sixth in *a* minor is V in *e♭* minor; moreover, the Neapolitan

[1 Cf. Schoenberg's analysis of the opening of the 'Prelude' to *Tristan* in *Structural Functions of Harmony*, p. 77, Example 85*a*.]

sixth of *e♭* minor and the V of *a* minor are the same chord.) Which of these interpretations [of the 'Tristan Chord'] we adopt seems an indifferent matter once we have seen how rich the relationships among keys become, however remote these keys, once vagrant chords create new routes and new modes of travel. Of course I do not actually wish to say that this chord has something to do with *e♭* minor. I wanted only to show that even this assumption is defensible and that little is actually said whenever one shows where the chord comes from. Because it can come from everywhere. What is essential for us is its function, and that is revealed when we know the possibilities the chord affords. Why single out these vagrant chords and insist that they be traced back at all cost to a key, when no one bothers to do so with the diminished seventh chord? True, I did relate the diminished seventh to the key. That relation is not supposed to restrict its circle of influence, however, but should rather show the pupil systematically its range of practical possibilities, so that he can find out through inference (*Kombination*) what his ear has recognized long ago through intuition. Later, the pupil will best take all these vagrant chords for what they are, without tracing them back to a key or a degree: homeless phenomena, unbelievably adaptable and unbelievably lacking in independence; spies, who ferret out weaknesses and use them to cause confusion; turncoats, to whom abandonment of their individuality is an end in itself; agitators in every respect, but above all: most amusing fellows.

Once we abandon the desire to explain the derivation of these chords, their effect becomes much clearer. We understand then that it is not absolutely necessary for such chords to appear just in the function their derivation calls for, since the climate of their homeland has no influence on their character. (Moreover, as will be shown later, this same characteristic can be proved true of many other chords, where one would not suspect it at first.) They flourish in every climate; and it is now understandable how another form of this chord in *Götterdämmerung* is resolved the same way (Example 189*o*) and leads to *b* minor. My first derivation (189*b*) is then confirmed after all by another example from Wagner; for Example 189*p*, the schematic reduction of the quotation in 189*o*, is without doubt a form of the function shown in 189*b*, transposed a half step down. I am not saying, however, that that is the derivation; for this chord appears in the music of Wagner with a great variety of other resolutions:

etc., and it is easy to add yet many others. But as these examples show, the chords of resolution are principally those whose tones may be reached by chromatic steps; or they are other vagrant chords, whose origin and relation do not require elaborate demonstration in the voice leading.

The following observations should guide the pupil in his own efforts to find resolutions for such vagrant chords: since here close attention to the sequence of degrees, the root progressions, often does not assure control over the quality

(*Wert*) of a progression, control through the melodic lines [voice leading] could be substituted, as has indeed been frequently reiterated. Thus, in general, the best connections of simple chords with vagrants or of vagrants with one another will be those in which the second chord contains, as far as possible, only tones that appeared in the first or are recognizable as chromatic raising or lowering of tones of the first. In his first attempts the pupil should make this origin explicit in the voice leading. An *eb* in the second chord should actually appear in the same voice that in the first chord had the *e*, from which the *eb* came. But such is only necessary at the beginning. Later, when he is familiar with the function of these phenomena, the pupil may also abandon this deliberate expression of the derivation in the voice leading.

Nevertheless, in the following connections of vagrant chords with one another, let us keep in mind the key and plan the progressions in such a way that the key is expressed and we remain aware of the degree relationships.

We shall connect:

1. diminished seventh chords with one another (Example 191); then with: augmented triads (192), augmented six-five, four-three, and two chords (193), Neapolitan sixths (194); and finally (195 and 196) also with the vagrant chords of which we last spoke (p. 256);
2. augmented triads with one another (197); then with: augmented six-five, four-three, and two chords (198), Neapolitan sixths (199), and the other vagrant chords (200);
3. augmented six-five, four-three, and two chords with Neapolitan sixths (201) and with the other vagrant chords (202);
4. Neapolitan sixths with these last-named vagrant chords (203);
5. these vagrant chords with one another (204).

The connection of diminished seventh chords with one another is quite simple, and of course the voices can all move by chromatic half steps or by skips (191*b*). Difficulties are at most notational. That is, it could sometimes be hard to decide whether to write *eb* or *d#*, *g#* or *ab*. Let us review the advice

given before: One should be guided by the key which the passage that is momentarily in question most resembles rather than by that indicated in the key signature of the piece, and should try to relate the connections for the moment, through the notation, to that assumed key. But one must not be all too pedantic; I prefer that manner of writing that avoids such complicated visual images as double sharps and double flats. To me, the right notation is that which needs the fewest accidentals. It will be good to express every chord through a notation that recalls another, a familiar notation. Moreover, with regard to the melodic lines, all progressions should be written in such a way that at least segments of three or four successive tones in a voice refer to a major or minor scale or to the chromatic scale; and the transitions from one scale to another should be written in such a way that they could appear in some model scale. This orthography has the advantage that it is easy to read, whereas the other does not even do what it is supposed to do, namely: express the derivation. The use of a great many diminished seventh chords in a progression is objectionable; their effect is intense, but there is little merit in this intensity. It is too easy to attain for one to feel particularly proud of attaining it.

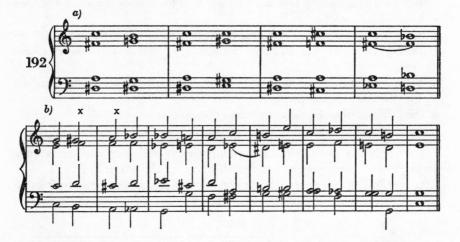

The connection of diminished seventh chords with the augmented triads is shown in Example 192*a*, using one of the diminished sevenths. A phrase in *C* major shows an application (192*b*).

Augmented six-five, four-three, and two chords with diminished sevenths. Here only the ones derived from II are presented. The others the pupil can easily try out on his own (following the model Example 193*b*).

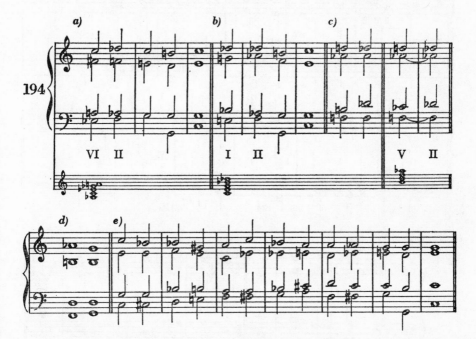

The connection of the Neapolitan sixth chord (IInd degree) with two of the diminished seventh chords goes splendidly (194*a* and *b*). The one at 194*a* is to be construed as derived from VI, that at 194*b* from I of *c* minor (minor-subdominant region) or *C* major, interpretations that yield good root progressions. The third one, however, can only be interpreted as V. To connect it with II is, in itself, hardly worthwhile because the root progression is a descending one. This connection is relatively weak also by virtue of the fact that two tones are common, only one proceeds chromatically, and the third one [the fourth, i.e. the other tone], if written as it actually should be (*b*), would have to make an improbable step to *d*♭. If this connection is thus seen as worthless in the harmonic sense, it can nevertheless be quite useful as a means of expression. That the Rhinegold motive (194*d*) is based on the same root progression[1] testifies to [this distinction between harmonic and expressive significance] (see also Example 173).

Example 194*e* gives examples of Neapolitan sixths on other degrees.

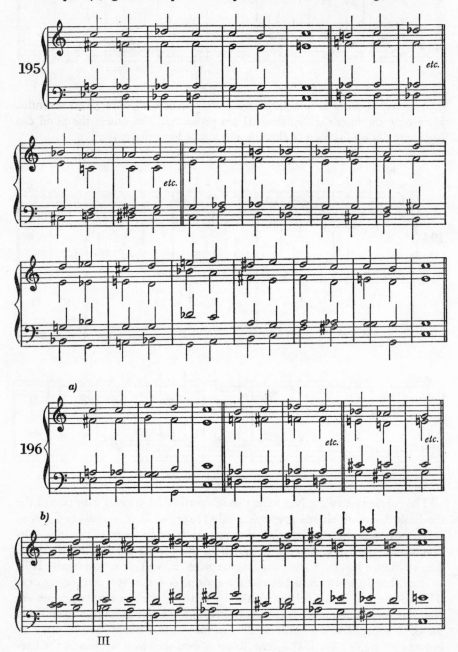

[1 There is no *root* progression; both chords have the same root.]

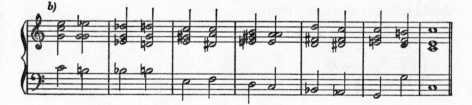

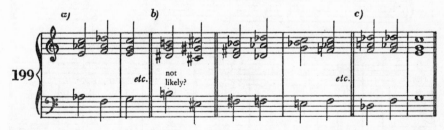

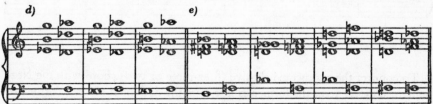

The two augmented triads in Example 199*b* pose significant difficulties. Hardly a position is to be found in which one may get by without reinterpretation (enharmonic change), augmented, or diminished intervals. The pupil should still omit such connections.

To connect the augmented six-five (four-three or two) chord with the Neapolitan sixth, we treat the former as if it were the dominant seventh (or one of its inversions) of the Neapolitan sixth; for, as previously noted, the sound of the augmented six-five chord is identical with that of the dominant seventh. In such cases this six-five chord is generally so written: that is, as in our example, with *g♭* instead of *f♯*. An excellent progression results (201*a*) if the six-five reappears after the Neapolitan sixth and then goes on to the six-four chord. Such a repetition is well suited for re-establishing a key that has begun to falter.

These augmented chords are also frequently connected with the other vagrants on II, although the chord in Example 202*a*, since *f♯* goes to *f*, does little to promote the setting of V in root position (because *g* is in the bass). But since the six-four chord [or the chord on V] does not have to be the goal, the continuation 202*c* is also possible. The bass interval here (†) and that in 201*b* (†), *d♭ – f♯*, is of course only practicable if one thinks *g♭* and makes the enharmonic change. But one can of course do just that!

In all these examples the voice leading was such as our first instructions required, wherever possible. That is, we avoided augmented and diminished intervals, parallel fifths, etc. Where problems arose with a connection, augmented intervals could of course not be avoided. And then they are even good. For necessity is the strongest commandment. But whenever, as here, the relation of such chords to one another refers back to keys far removed from one another, then it would be pedantry to try to keep the voice leading within a key, within a major or minor key. The singer who has to sing such intervals will just have to make enharmonic changes if he wants to simplify an augmented interval. True, the tone got by enharmonic change does not agree with that of the tempered system, and that problem creates great difficulties in today's choral music. But of course it cannot hold back the development of our music; for it is obvious that we want to use the same harmonic resources in choral composition that we use in composing for instruments. It may be that little choral music will be written until a means is found to get around that problem. However, since this means must be found, it will be found. To instrumentalists the intonation of such intervals, and of other, far more complicated progressions, no longer presents any great difficulties. The range of what one may easily require of them is becoming more and more inclusive. But of course the pupil should by no means try to use all these possibilities at present. He should continue to express melodically the chromaticism in his voice leading; he should continue his efforts to relate what happens in a voice as long as possible to one key, and to make the change to another key with utmost care. As I have mentioned repeatedly: since his voices are nothing more than the necessary connectives in a harmonic structure, since their development is neither generated nor justified by a motive, he should never stray from the simplest presentation, unless there are compelling reasons for doing so.

In conclusion, yet other possibilities for resolving the diminished seventh chord should be added here.

Example 205*a* shows how a diminished seventh chord can be changed into four different dominant seventh chords: each time a different tone of the diminished seventh falls a *half step* and becomes the root. (Our assumed root [of the diminished seventh as ninth with tacit root]!) If (205*b*) we sustain one tone each time as the root and take the other three up a half step, then we get four other dominant seventh chords. By the same method, but with appropriate adjustments in resolving, we get major or minor chords [triads] on the same degrees (205*c*). If we sustain two nonadjacent tones (diminished fifth or augmented fourth) and take the other two nonadjacent tones up a half step, then we obtain two forms of the altered chord presented on page 255 (205*d*). If (205*e*) we sustain three tones and let one ascend, then we get secondary seventh chords with the same form as those on VII in major or II in minor. If we sustain two adjacent tones and let the other two adjacent tones ascend, then we get secondary seventh chords like those on III in major (205*f*). When three tones fall and one is sustained the resultant chords are the same as when three are sustained and one rises, but in other keys (205*g*) (VII of major, II of minor) [cf. Example 205*e*].

I have mentioned such connections as an addendum because: (1) their root progressions are not always good; (2) this method, making alterations in a chord, does not agree with the method of presentation otherwise practiced in this book; (3) these connections generally have only pseudoharmonic significance: they are found mostly as melodic conduct of the harmony, so to speak, whereby they conform rhythmically to the movement of a principal voice. Such connections are of course much used in modulations, but usually without awareness of the root progressions; and that makes little sense.

XV MODULATION TO THE IInd, Vth, AND VIth CIRCLES OF FIFTHS, TO THE VIIth AND VIIIth, AND ALSO TO MORE CLOSELY RELATED CIRCLES BY SEGMENTS AND THROUGH INTERMEDIATE KEYS

For his very first exercises in these modulations the pupil will best do without the enrichments of harmony he has just learned. Again, he should first make these modulations with the simplest means and should use the simplest and closest relationships. They could of course be effected more speedily through use of the harmonic resources that became available in the preceding chapter. But it is important that the pupil knows the simple, the basic means as well and learns to reach the goal smoothly and appropriately through these alone, so that he acquires a sense of form. He should thus master the simpler means before he ventures on to use the more complicated. With the latter, because of the immense number of possibilities, instructions cannot be as precise as those given for the simpler means. Hence, in using the more complicated the pupil has to depend increasingly on correction through his own sense of form.

The modulation to the second circle of fifths is most simply done by breaking it up into two segments. The original key and the new key have very few common chords. These are, from major upward, the chords of the dominant region, III and V, of which the III is closer to the second circle of fifths; from major downward the common chords are those of the subdominant region, II and IV, of which IV is closer to the second circle. Of course, a modulation merely through use of these common chords is not impossible. And in most textbooks this is the way it is shown. Upward, the sequence I–III–V produces nothing but descending root progressions, whereas I–V–III is quite good (Example 206).

Downward, the order I–IV–II provides a usable and fairly rapid modulation.

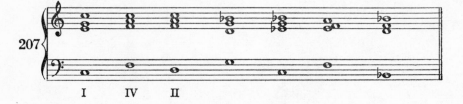

But, unless one is actually in the examination room, where haste is necessary, one can take time to modulate, can plan the modulation. One can make the modulation so that it really goes by way of intrinsic relationships and not by way of coincidences. One can make it so that, for obtaining a characteristic effect, characteristic means are used. Modulation to distant keys by means of a simple series of triads, the way recommended in most textbooks, is absolutely bad. That does not follow the trail of art but serves merely the purposes of the many examinations, to which those with no calling are subjected to protect those who are called against those who are chosen.[1] And this is the purpose they [these modulations] accomplish: to give the pupil a handy scheme, easily understood and remembered, that will seldom fail him – even if, and this is the most outstanding result of the examinations, even if he is apprehensive. One very seldom has occasion to make a fast modulation, certainly not where only simple harmonic means are being used. Modulations to distant keys appear in the literature only where rich means for modulating are available. If anyone doubts that statement, let him take a look at Bach's modulations. What he will find is this: whenever there is a modulation to a distant key, it happens gradually, by segments, or if suddenly, then through use of the very strongest means. Generally, through the diminished seventh chord, for Bach did not know other strong means of modulation. But Bach's modulations happen also, and this is very important, through preparatory passing and changing tones that suggest the key relationships. The essential point is that an apparently sudden modulation, almost without exception, has already been announced beforehand: either through a certain restlessness or looseness in the harmony or through alteration, generally enlargement, of intervals in the melody; in the counterpoint through characteristic increase or decrease [of parts?]; in the dynamics; that is, in everything that is pertinent. Moreover, in the harmony quite often the modulatory potential of the pivot chord has been suggested beforehand. This chord has already been shown in an ambiguous light, so that its reinterpretation then has the effect of fulfilling a necessity. Now, the pupil can supposedly accomplish all that through harmony alone, using no other means but triads and dominant seventh chords (dominant! seventh chords!); and, as the plan underlying the whole thing, he need use nothing else but the coincidental possibilities of a cool relationship. 'Because you are my father's brother-in-law's nephew, I am your friend.' I am not advocating an aesthetic; I am not saying, this is not beautiful; I do not condemn as ugly something I do not

[1 Schoenberg added this remark – paraphrasing the biblical assertion that many are called, but few are chosen – in the revised edition. It is not immediately apparent how those with a calling (the 'Berufene') are protected against the chosen (the 'Auserwählte') if only the 'Unberufene' are subjected to the examinations. Perhaps he meant that the examinations are weapons to protect those of average talents against both the untalented and those rare creative talents who, in obedience to the laws of their own genius, scorn the laws they have been taught. These geniuses would have a natural calling, would be the Chosen People, but would perhaps be neither called nor chosen by the examiners.]

understand; but if there is anything that has no poise, no elegance (*Ebenmass*), it is this manner of modulating.

Breaking up far-reaching modulations into segments, like so much of what is noteworthy in this book, is not my invention. It is found in the teachings of good, older theorists (S. Sechter,[1] for example). But those shallow simplifiers, so quick to take shortcuts only because they find *sense* solely in the result, not in the *way* it is obtained, help to corrupt the old theory while they obstruct the development of a new. For them formulas are the important thing; consequently they give as the final product something that is only a device, a trick. And since to these paralyzed brains art must be 'Ideal', they hand down the formula as a law of aesthetics. The Why, When, and How of such laws they either never knew or long ago forgot; hence they hold the laws to be eternal. A good handicraft, however, can easily attend to its practical necessities without having to appeal to aesthetics. This they will never understand. One must not be ashamed of satisfying the practical requirements of the material, and may confess it openly, without adorning it, without glorifying it. But then one will not always do the opposite of what is right. Those who on the one hand simplify (by suppressing sense and preserving only its shell, the formula) complicate on the other hand (by 'artistically' embellishing the shell). Thus they fail in everything that matters: because instead of sense they always give the form, the formula. Their simplicity and their complexity are incorrectly related to the content.[2] They are simple when one must be complex; they are intricate when one may be straightforward. I have known this for a long time in my own rather narrow field, but in another I had to learn it from a rough slap in the face, which I deserved. That slap made clear to me how much our taste in almost all fields is corrupted by the 'decorators' (*Ornamentierer*) (as Adolf Loos[3] calls them) disguised as simplifiers. I once sketched out a plan for a music stand and showed it to a carpenter. It was to have two columns, held together by heavy wooden braces. I had imagined the heavy wooden braces would be beautiful (beautiful!). The carpenter, a Czech, who could not even speak good German, said: 'No good carpenter will make that for you. We learned that a connecting piece must be lighter than a column.' I was thoroughly shamed. I had considered beautiful what was simply impractical, and a carpenter who understood his craft could of course throw out this beauty without hesitation. Of course: material sparingly used! That is, indeed, artistic economy; only such means are to be used as are absolutely necessary for producing a certain effect. Everything else is beside the point, hence crude, can never be beautiful because it is not organic. Whoever thinks otherwise is a ridiculous dilettante, an aesthete (*Schönheitssucher*) without reason, without insight into the nature of things. The carpenter understood his craft; he knew that one must use material sparingly. I would have gladly paid the slight additional cost of the material; but it seemed to him so ridiculous that, being an honorable and skilled carpenter, he could

[1 *Die Grundsätze der musikalischen Komposition* . . ., pp. 32–4. Cf. *supra*, p. 113.]

[2 That is, their simplicity or complexity is external, *a priori*, not inherent.]

[3 The architect and friend of Schoenberg. Cf. Schoenberg's *Letters*, pp. 144–6, 197, and 259.]

not be a party to such nonsense. All the same our aestheticians seek beauty. They see discovered forms as given, casual formal possibilities as formal necessities; and in these they claim to see eternal laws, even though they themselves know forms to which these laws do not apply. Such forms are then the exceptions. The aestheticians seldom think about finding the origins and the deeper significance of these forms in the purely practical, in what is appropriate and sensible to the craftsman. They prefer to seek 'their way in the fog'. In that chaotic, primeval fog of irrationality, from which even so a rational world could by some accident emerge. But to take then this rationality to be the rationality of the world and the world to be this rationality is questionable.

So it is of course possible to modulate in the way these textbooks recommend. I prefer the older method, however, especially when dealing with simpler harmony. There a modulation was not shoved directly down a track to its destination. Instead, breaches were made at several points in the tonality, and at least two or three principal currents, coming from different points, were then united at some point for concerted action.

The keys of the second circle of fifths are less closely related to one another than are those of the first, third, or fourth circles. In the first circle of fifths there was a direct relation between I of the one key and V of the other: I of C major was IV of G or V of F. And in the third and fourth circles the use of V of a minor key to obtain a major triad looks like the realization of a tendency of this Vth degree, like a necessity. True, here in the second circle, G is also IV of D major and F is V of $B\flat$; but C is not a degree of D major nor of $B\flat$ major. The reinterpretation can be done only as follows: I (V) of C is IV (I) of G, I (V) of G is IV (I) of D; and: I (IV) of C is V (I) of F, I (IV) of F is V (I) of $B\flat$. Here we see at once the necessity for key combination and the kind of combination involved. Most simply, one will choose as the 'intermediate key'* the key of the first circle of fifths that is right on the way, thus, in effect, adding together two first-circle modulations: 1 plus 1 equals 2. Later the pupil can choose other intermediate keys as well (eventually several). We go, then, from:

* I have postponed this assumption of an intermediate key as long as possible, and even here I can accept it only as an aid to learning. Above all, because it seems to me superfluous; for we can present what the intermediate keys accomplish much more generally by means of the secondary dominants. But then, in addition, because it is possible, and better, to view all that happens within a piece as emanating from a tonal center. Otherwise, the form in which almost all modulations appear in works of art has no real sense. Otherwise, there is no real sense in returning to the principal key, if the straying from it and return to it are not conditioned by a single source of energy: the basic key. I assume intermediate keys here, again, only in the sense in which I admitted them previously: as an aid in learning, as a means by which the pupil simplifies what is complex, by breaking it down into parts. Only because that way it is easier to grasp. Once the chromatic scale is established as the basis for harmonic thought, then we shall be able to interpret even such modulations as these as functions of the key, and to assume, here also, that we do not leave the key. This is similar to what we are doing, even now, in our cadences, which will soon contain everything formerly regarded as modulatory, now serving just to express the key.

C major through *G* major or *e* minor to *D* major
C major through *G* major or *e* minor to *b* minor
a minor through *G* major or *e* minor to *D* major
a minor through *G* major or *e* minor to *b* minor
C major through *F* major or *d* minor to *B♭* major
C major through *F* major or *d* minor to *g* minor
a minor through *F* major or *d* minor to *B♭* major
a minor through *F* major or *d* minor to *g* minor

The intermediate key is of course not so firmly established as the key that
is the goal of the modulation; it would otherwise also require a cadence. It is
kept loose enough to permit easy movement away from it, yet is stated clearly
enough to set aside the original key. As long as the stronger means of modulation discussed in the previous chapter are not used, the pupil will do well to
treat sensitive tones like the sixth or the seventh tone of a minor scale. Obviously we can also use two intermediate keys, for example, *C* through *G* and *e*
minor to *D*. Only a few examples follow. The pupil is now able to carry out
modulations in the first circle of fifths in many ways. He may thus obtain a
large number of beginnings and just as large a number of continuations.

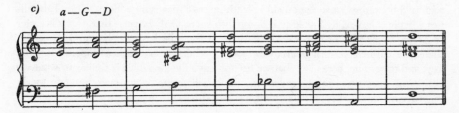

In the cadence the pupil can use some of the secondary dominants and other nondiatonic chords. Generally, however, it will be advisable to use such sparingly here, since the first half of the modulation is quite simple. In Example 208*b* secondary seventh chords were introduced without preparing them. That the pupil may later write them as he writes a triad, unprepared, even without the appeal to the 'passing seventh' that is used here, needs no further explanation. Naturally the deceptive cadence plays a big role in these modulations. We can use it to get around the danger that the two halves of the modulation may resemble each other too closely. It is also recommended that one of the keys be expressed by means of chords other than the dominant and the tonic (208*d*). Where several intermediate keys are used there should not be a succession of all minor or all major keys. In Example 208*f* the *c♯* of *b* minor is prepared by the movement of the bass melody from *b* through the sixth and seventh tones of *e* minor. The modulation is thereby quite smooth.

Particularly in the modulation to the second circle of fifths downward, it will be necessary to make a good distinction between the means used in the first half and those in the second. Perhaps here the pupil can even now make frugal use of secondary dominants and diminished seventh chords. Obviously the cadence must then be more elaborate. In Example 209*a* at † a secondary seventh chord was again used, unprepared, as a passing chord. In 209*c* the diminished seventh chord at † is in light of what follows still to be ascribed to *d* minor, in spite of the following six-four chord on *f*. The chord at ⸕ enters as a Neapolitan sixth, but is then treated as IV of $B\flat$. Obviously one can make all these modulations shorter. But one should not do so; the pupil, in particular, should not. He should learn, rather, to make full use of the means he has been given. And

here he has an abundance of opportunities for doing so. I have worked out this modulation in such long phrases deliberately; to include here as much as possible is actually an end in itself. His sense of form will soon lead the pupil to observe that, whenever he has worked out one part more extensively, certain obligations are imposed on what follows. What follows cannot be as long or short as he likes, but will have some inescapable requirement: the use of a particular means in the harmony or perhaps also in the melodic line; anyway, the continuation is not free, it is bound. It is not bound by laws, however, but by the sense of form. The pupil will do well to pay strict attention to this point and not to pass over it lightly by suppressing his formal conscience.

Once he has had enough practice with these simple means, he may then go on to the more complicated. I recommend that his assignments take up the various types of chords more or less in the sequence in which they were introduced in the preceding chapters. That way, what has been learned will be reviewed, and the number of possibilities [for using each kind of chord] will be increased.

In Example 210a two quarter notes were used in the alto to include the seventh of the dominant seventh chord. Occasionally, the pupil may do likewise; but he may also use the seventh freely, regardless of a cross relation, especially with the dominant seventh chord.

In 210a at ⊕ the degrees are designated as II–I–II, although the chords have little similarity to the diatonic chords on these degrees. But we know of course what this II is: an inversion (root position) of the tones of the Neapolitan sixth chord. Here, and in similar cases, to orient ourselves more easily to the root progressions, we may imagine the Neapolitan sixth to be a tonic and temporarily call it I. Then the following diminished triad is VII of this imaginary I, and the progression is I–VII–I, which is quite familiar. Since the Neapolitan sixth here is on II, however, the succession of degrees that looks like I–VII–I of $C\flat$ major is a form of II–I–II of $B\flat$ major, and the Neapolitan sixth is treated here as a *quasi* tonic, *as if it were $C\flat$ major*. The pupil should not speak here of

C♭ major, though, but should rather keep in mind that he is merely imagining it this way as an aid to learning.

FIFTH AND SIXTH CIRCLES OF FIFTHS

The simplest modulations to these circles will also be those that are sub-divided. They will best be composites of two, possibly three, simple modulations (such as those to the first, third, and fourth circles). The modulation to the fifth circle can thus be a combination, 4 plus 1 or 1 plus 4: that is, first to the fourth circle and from that key to its first, or the other way around, first to the first circle and then to the fourth of that key. Modulation to the sixth circle of fifths can be made up of 3 plus 3. Since the latter leads to the same key, whether it goes upward or downward (*C* major to *F♯* major or *G♭* major), we can carry out 3 plus 3 in two ways, upward or downward. But the way to 6 could also be put together so: 3 plus 4 minus 1, or 4 plus 3 minus 1, or minus 1 plus 3 plus 4, or minus 1 plus 4 plus 3, or yet 4 minus 1 plus 3 and 3 minus 1 plus 4, etc.* One can also put together the modulation to 5 in manifold ways: 3 plus 3 minus 1, or 3 minus 1 plus 3, or 4 plus 4 minus 3, etc. One will sometimes even use the composite, 3 plus 2 or 2 plus 3, although 2 itself is already a composite, 1 plus 1. As for the extent to which the intermediate keys are established, what was said for the modulations of the second circle holds here as well. Secondary dominants, diminished sevenths, and other vagrant chords will be useful here. But here, again, the pupil is advised first to try exercises with simple means. The following modulations are to be practiced: from *C* major and *a* minor to *D*♭ major, *b*♭ minor, *B* major, *g*♯ minor, *G*♭ major, *e*♭ minor, *F*♯ major, and *d*♯ minor.

* Plus and minus are to be understood here in relation to the direction involved at the moment. Hence, with the circle of fifths downward a minus (−) indicates the opposite direction, upward. We can then express these modulations mathematically: to the ± 5th circle of fifths: $\pm(4+1)$; or to the ± 6th: $\pm(3+4-1), \pm(-1+3+4)$ etc.

c) C—B (1+4)

d) C—g# (3—1+3)

e) C—Gb (3+3)

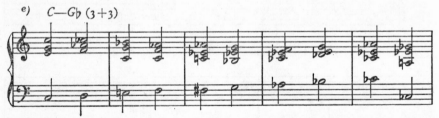

f) C—eb (3+3)

g) C—F# (3+3)

h) C—d# (4—1+3)

i) a—Db (4+1)

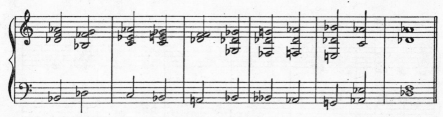

In these examples I made extensive use of the modulatory means last studied. For example, in 211c the modulation C–G is introduced by the Neapolitan sixth, and in 211f the Neapolitan sixth of f minor is itself introduced by the appropriate augmented four-three chord. These means permit us to omit the 'lingering on the dominant' in the third and fourth-circle modulations. I should like here to point out a distinction between my modulations and those 'quick' modulations that I censure. It could be said: I set such remotely related chords next to one another that there is, after all, no difference between mine and those other, 'quick' modulations. But there is a distinction: in the others these chords are supposed to effect the modulation, whereas in mine they only introduce it, they prepare the way for it; they bring that uncertainty that will admit a modulation. Here, the eye is kept on the goal, and the arrival at that goal is prepared. I find in a very well-known harmony text[1] similarly distant modulations carried out with the means censured here. Nevertheless, the examples in that book work well, and one could conclude that it is superfluous to deal so ceremoniously with this point as I am doing here. But if one takes a close look one will note that the author of these examples – who was a composer quite skilled in matters of form – follows his sense of form and achieves his smooth modulation by doing essentially the same thing as I do, but unconsciously: he prepares the new key, the goal. It is far more by this means that he achieves his purpose, unconsciously, as I said, than by the modulatory means he actually recommends. But then why does he not recommend the former means instead of the latter? Because he is not aware of the discrepancy, and neither is his collaborator, his writer, whose eloquence is linguistic [rather than musical].

A satisfying modulation indeed depends on this preparation of the new key! For example: in 211a the second chord, the augmented six-five chord over the bass tone, e, already hints at the g♭ of D♭ major, and the resolution to the six-four chord is another such hint. Neither is yet D♭ major, but only a step in that direction. Something similar happens in 211b. In 211c the third measure, which could be called b minor, points toward the B major of the cadence; in 211k the Neapolitan sixth over b♭ (third measure) points toward b♭ minor, etc. The pupil will find a lot more of that sort of thing in the examples. He himself should of course strive for something similar. And even if it does not turn out well, no harm is done. (My own examples are certainly not outstanding 'artistic accomplishments' and are supposed only to suggest, to stimulate; they are by no means to be considered exemplary.) What is important is: that one strives for something. Whether one reaches it is only of secondary importance.

A device that is recommended in most textbooks and that also appears occasionally in Example 211 is the *sequence*. The sequence is a kind of repetition well suited for creating coherence. Repetition can be monotonous; rightly used, it strengthens and intensifies. There are many kinds of repetition that in one sense or another help create form. To expound them, however, belongs to the study of form, since they bring up right away the subject of themes and motives. Therefore, only the following general observations pertain here. The sequence

[1 This text is not identified in any of the editions of Schoenberg's work.]

is an exact repetition of some segment of the music. The harmonic sequence is as follows: some harmonic progression (of at least two chords) recurs immediately after its first appearance; but the second time (and this is the distinction between a sequence and a simple repetition) it starts from a different degree, a major or minor second or third, a perfect or augmented fourth, higher or lower. The harmonic sequence is a highly favored and quite effective means of creating musical form; for it insures continuity and coherence, and by virtue of clear, broad exposition it is a boon to the perception of the listener (since it does repeat what he might have missed the first time). And all that is accomplished without the composer having to invent a differently-shaped continuation; thus he does not have to tax his spirit any more than is necessary to join well the two equal forms of his thought with each other, to connect them without leaving gaps. Because it is good in itself, the sequence has been much used. Because, however, little merit is to be detected in such comfortable 'acquisition of territory', immoderate use of it must be condemned. I have nothing against the pupil using it occasionally. Indeed, he is to be commended for his accomplishment, if he has arranged his material so that a sequential repetition is possible. Nor have I anything against his using it as recommended, for example, to make a modulation so to speak in two starts. But I must warn against too frequent use; because of the schematic character of such work, it offers little reward.

To a certain extent the transposed repetition of a segment of melody is also to be regarded as a sequence when the harmony that goes with it is not sequential. To me this kind of sequence always has more merit, since it is not so mechanical. Examples are to be found in the soprano voice of 211*m* and 211*p*.

The pupil can select the other compound modulations himself. If he has chosen, say, 4 plus 3 minus 2 for the fifth circle, then the modulation could be as follows, for example: from *C* major through *E* major to *C*♯ major and back (through *F*♯ major) to *g*♯ minor (212*a*).

But such a plan would probably be too complicated. If one wished to carry out quite extensively every single part of this modulation, then the whole thing would become very long. If one makes it brief, however, then it comes right back to that all-too-quick modulating, which I could consider good only

if very strong means are used. The pupil will have to decide. If he chooses such a manifold, composite route, then he has to consider that the example will be very long and that he will have to erase the seams between the individual stages, as much as possible, with strong modulating devices. Example 212*b* shows another solution to this problem, based on a plan that is less complex.

Generally speaking, modulations to keys as distant as those of the fifth or sixth circle of fifths will not appear very frequently in pieces with simple harmony; for a composition that modulates so intensively needs correspondingly stronger means of modulation. Hence, such exercises done with simple means can never turn out to be as smooth as those that modulate to closer keys, nor can those that modulate by simple means to the seventh, eighth, ninth circles, and so on. The latter are compounds that would be more easily reached as the fifth, fourth, third circles, etc., of the opposite direction. Thus, for example, modulations from *C* major to *C♭*, *F♭*, and *B♭♭* major would, in the opposite direction, be modulations to *B*, *E*, and *A* major. Nevertheless, one must often take the more complex way; the pupil should therefore practice it. But I give no examples for it. In a simple example it would look incongruous; but in a complicated one, since we have here no reason for being complex, it would look overblown and pompous. To make such examples is easier for one who can do nothing than for one with great ability. The older masters generally limited their modulations, even in development sections, to closely related keys. Nevertheless, one does often find a distant modulation inserted suddenly, with coarse means, as a surprise without harmonic preparation (Beethoven, *c*-minor Trio).[1]

Such frequent change of key in such a small space as shown in Example 213 occurs only in the literature from the post-Wagnerian era. There, the aim is of course not to reach a new key, but to leave an old one without ever having settled in it in the first place. The harmony is then led as it were by the melody. The richness of the harmony, its restlessness, its rapid twisting and turning correspond to these same characteristics in the principal melody, on which the harmony depends as a sort of contrapuntal accompanying voice. That sort of thing, in the form of exercises, can hardly turn out well, as is shown by my Example 213 – shown, if not proven: for I could certainly produce something better. All the same, the pupil should attempt such, because otherwise he will not get to know his resources for modulating.

[1 First Movement, beginning of the development, and near the end of the last movement (*e♭* minor to *B* major, *c* minor to *b* minor).]

I am incorporating these exercises in my book, even though I have some objections to them, because I take a different view of their purpose. First of all: one does not harmonize, one invents with harmony. One then perhaps makes corrections. Theory, however, does not bring the defective spots to one's attention; these are discovered by the sense of form. Moreover, the correction itself is not found through theory. Sometimes, perhaps, it is found through much trial and error; generally, though, it comes through a flash of insight, that is, intuitively, through the sense of form, through the imagination. At least that is what my experience tells me; and the contrary can only be advocated by one who himself 'harmonizes', who is thus not capable of *inventing a melody with harmony*. We cannot deny that there are themes whose harmony should be other than that with which they were originally conceived. And we must admit that sometimes, in an otherwise usable idea of a beginner, a harmonic weakness appears at some point whose correction requires a different harmonization of the whole idea. But neither of these possibilities corresponds to what we actually understand as 'harmonizing'. In neither case is a harmony added to a melody that was given without harmony. In both cases we have a harmonically articulated melody, whose harmony and articulation its author knows and merely undertakes to alter. On the one hand, when he alters it for the sake of variation, his task is just that: to make use of other harmonic possibilities inherent in the idea, to exploit its individualities. And on the other hand, when he corrects, it is only a matter of isolated spots that are bad; but the whole thing is harmonized and he knows this harmony. He probably just wrote it down incorrectly, or in continuing the theme did not hear out well the tendencies of the harmony. This 'not hearing out well' I have often observed in pupils. It even happens with gifted ones, but it is easy to overcome.

But even in making corrections, as well as in harmonic variation, the new form should not be calculated, but invented. It is a mistake to think that art may be calculated; and the notion the aestheticians have of the 'tasks' of the 'thinking' artist is entirely false. They would have us believe that this artist's whole achievement consists in choosing, with good taste and close calculation, the most effective of the available possibilities. Yet artistic creativity operates on a somewhat higher plane. In my own composing I have all too often seen how what was not good in the first draft never became good, not even if I made a hundred corrections. Usually, though, the forms that emerged in the first draft are of a smoothness such as no correction would ever produce. I should like to say, therefore: if a defect is found in an idea, a defect that cannot be corrected while the original inspiration is still working, then it is perhaps better to drop the idea, or to keep it along with its inborn defect. This defect will always be slighter than those that would be introduced by correction. This is not to say that a pupil should not make corrections, for, if he did not, the teacher could not improve him either. On the contrary, the pupil should exercise fully his intellect and taste. He is still a pupil, still studying; he is simply practicing. He wants simply to advance far enough that he can say something, should he have anything to say. The pupil should think; but the artist, the master, composes by feeling (*Gefühl*). He no longer has to think, for he has reached a higher kind of response to his need for self-expression. The pupil should correct (*verbessern*), but he should not get the idea that by virtue of corrections a work becomes better (*besser*). The benefit he can derive from correcting can only be this: it can make him aware of how the work might have been better if it had not been saddled with this defect from the outset. And it can help him know what to do the next time. Then he can take greater care right away, in the act of invention; and whatever he corrects 'in statu nascendi', while the first heat of inspiration is still present, will hardly do any harm. But later correction seldom does any good.

An objection could be raised here: If I condemn exercises in harmonizing because the artist does not harmonize, but invents the harmony with the melody, why then do I have the pupil produce phrases by writing down the roots (figures) and constructing the phrases from them? Harmonization is, after all, only an exercise, as is the sketching of roots, and what matters is the benefit the exercise offers the pupil. My reply to this objection is as follows: First, sketching root progressions has at least one similarity to reality, that in so far as the roots represent harmonies the pupil is actually thinking harmonies, even if it is by the roundabout way of numbers. At first he is thinking numbers, later, however, chords (*Klänge*)! Harmonization, on the other hand, has almost no similarity to reality. Secondly, even though the pupil must indeed do, as exercise, much that the master does not do, as I have shown above, it does not follow that the pupil *should* also do what the master *must not do*! Thirdly, we have advanced, I hope, through all the previous exercises to a degree of skill such that we should no longer want to do such an exercise, even if it were better than sketching out roots. But it is not better.

If I then give exercises in harmonizing, my purpose is not to teach the pupil how I do what I should not do; it is rather to strengthen his sense of form by a sort of example in which his imagination (*Phantasie*) does not yet have to take part. He is given a melody. It is not his own; thus his harmonization of it can never be as good as that with which it was invented. Since he is then not to blame for the partial failure of the example, it matters little that what he produces is imperfect; and no damage is done to the melody that he is mistreating, for it is of course not tied permanently to the bad harmony. On the contrary. This work is like the exercises in dissection performed by young doctors on cadavers: if they cut too deeply, nobody's hurt. What does it matter, if the chorale harmonization does turn out badly? It is not to be published anyway. But by such a simple example the pupil can learn to concentrate his sense of form on what happens in a melody and can practice thinking a melody as a whole, preparing for the time when he himself will have to invent a melody whole, with harmony.

I shall thus use the exercises in harmonizing as prevention, to guard somewhat more thoroughly than usual against those mistakes that occur because the sense of form is untrained. But I shall not give modern melodies for these exercises. The form of the chorale melody is so simple and lies so far behind us that we can perhaps see through it; we can perhaps really perceive its relationships with the precision necessary for close imitation. Moreover, it is then not absolutely necessary to give instructions properly belonging to the study of form. But more modern melodies, even if I included under this heading only such as those by Mozart or Beethoven, show such complicated diversity of form that the pupil could not approach them without special preparation.

Of course a pupil with a gifted ear might even then reach a good solution. I have no objection if the pupil makes such attempts on his own. He would best copy a theme from Beethoven, Mozart, or Brahms, or from the works of another master (but a master it must be; any other is not good enough!), try to harmonize it, and then compare it with the original. Most important, it should be clear to him that his harmonization is inferior to that of the model, and he should now try to discover why that is so. In fact, the pupil could just as well harmonize a theme he has heard and remembers and then compare it with the model. The purpose of this exercise will be accomplished even if the pupil remembers the harmonization of the original and merely writes it down from memory. For the purpose of all these exercises is indeed not so much actually to construct a harmony (to construct!) as it is, if the solution is not to turn out leathery, to use skilfully and monitor by means of theoretical awareness what the ear *remembers* from similar cases.

But to invent melodies myself with whose harmonization the pupil is to be afflicted – I refuse to do it, even though I am sure I could invent something better than that miserable stuff certain authors of harmony texts have the nerve to write. Such nerve betrays their inability to discriminate in matters of form. If I allow the pupil the freedom to do what occurs to him, it matters little if the product is not especially smooth. For the chief aim is that he should practice independently the arranging of harmonies. The mistakes that occur lie in his thought and can be dealt with there. If I subject him, however, to the requirements of a given melody, then it should be as good as only a master can produce when he is inspired. Otherwise the mistakes will lie not merely in the pupil's thought but also in the defective thought of the one who invented a defective melody. Correction will then be difficult, because it is not easy to find out whether the mistake is in the harmony or in the melody; and it will also be unfair to the pupil, who can hardly defend himself against a mistake of his teacher. For my part, I have no inspiration to invent melodies for harmonic exercises. If I had, I should not then have any for my compositions, not because the purpose is too slight, but just because it is a purpose. And if the others, those who do impose their own melodies on the pupil, should claim to have been inspired in the invention of them, I cannot think very highly of this inspiration, considering the leathery, clumsy results. If a pupil's work is clumsy and full of errors, that is indeed no calamity, if only the clumsiness is his and the errors are his. He can cross them out again and again. But if the teacher fails in the one way in which he must never fail: as the *model* (so Gustav Mahler characterized, in a single word, the essence of the teacher), then that is a crime. A teacher who requires pupils to harmonize melodies that he himself has put together, but melodies that are not good, that cannot be good – this teacher is not fit to be a model. The pupil who desires practice in harmonizing more modern melodies should take these also from the works of pertinent composers. As I said, I do not consider this practice particularly necessary. But whoever believes in it may do it; and if he does it in the manner recommended, it will at least do no harm.

Now to the chorale.

Like every art form, the chorale is clearly articulated. Articulation (*Gliederung*) is necessary for every idea, the moment it is expressed; for, although we think an idea at once, as a whole, we cannot say it all at once, only little by little: we arrange the different components in succession, components into which we divide up the idea differently from the way we put it together,[1] and thereby reproduce more or less precisely its content.[2] In music we regard melodic or harmonic progressions as the components of an idea. That notion is correct, however, only as it applies to what is visible or audible, to those aspects of music that can be directly perceived by the senses; it applies only by analogy to that which makes up the actual content of a musical idea. But we may still assume that the notation successfully symbolizes the musical idea, and that the form and articulation manifested by the notes corresponds to the inner nature of the idea and its movement, as the ridges and hollows of our bodies are determined by the position of internal organs – as indeed the external appearance of every well-constructed organism corresponds to its internal organization, hence the native external appearance is not to be regarded as accidental.

One may therefore draw conclusions from the external form concerning the inner nature.

The chorale is articulated by a pause at the end of each musical phrase coinciding with the end of each line of the text; these pauses divide the thought up into parts. The individual parts in such simple art forms relate to one another by the simplest forms of contrast or complement. Such mosaic-like assemblage of parts permits no very complicated relationships and favors, as its unifying element, the principle of more or less simple repetition. What draws out the movement latent in an idea, through which alone an idea acquires life, are especially the contrasts produced by the simple digressions from the key. These contrasts are only moderate; they are not so great as to make connection difficult. What binds them together is the uniformity of the rhythmic movement, the straightforwardness, the simplicity, and above all the key; what separates them, what makes the subdivisions, is actually something negative: the virtually complete lack of motivic activity in development and connection. Thanks to this absence of motivic obligations, which keeps the parts from being more closely connected, the unconnected parts have no particular duty toward one another; perhaps they are on the whole just next to one another

[1 '. . . Bestandteile, in die wir ihn anders auflösen als zusammenfügen . . .']
[2 Cf. the edition of 1911, p. 322: '. . . we have to divide up the idea into its components, and these, put together again, reproduce more or less precisely its content.']

more than in relation to one another. Naturally, tendencies toward motivic activity are not entirely missing; for the simple rhythmic principle of the almost unbroken, uniform movement in half notes (or quarters) is itself to a certain extent a motive, or at least a formal principle approaching the motivic, even though very primitive. Naturally, one can discover still other types of connection; but the modesty of the whole leaves the motive (rhythmic and melodic, wherein for the most part the rhythmic, almost never the melodic, is the connecting element) in such an ambiguous state that relations, coherence in the melodic line can be recognized almost solely by the contrasts. Nevertheless, contrasts are relations, too. And if with one line of the chorale text the melody rises, but with the next it falls, then this is a contrast that connects. The descent relaxes the tension created by the ascent; 'question and answer' is an apt metaphor for such occurrences. Since in the simple art forms the main direction of the movement is always quite clear, it is obvious that the harmony will keep to the same path as the melody; it is obvious that the harmony must seek to follow precisely the implications, the tendencies of the melody, to support them, to plan ahead for their greatest advantage. A counteraction, blocking, turning about, like all psychologically more sophisticated techniques of art, we should more or less exclude from the straightforward, primitive, folklike forms. Since we find ourselves in the unnatural position of constructing the harmony for a melody already given, whereas the harmony ought to be conceived along with the melody, close observation of the peculiarities of the melody is indispensable. Here, too, one is ultimately guided by feeling; and these exercises will best succeed whenever the pupil, once he has learned many chorales as harmonized by masters and has worked out many himself, no longer works them out by calculation, but can dash them off by ear. Even then, however, it will sometimes be advantageous to acquire foresight, through calculation, concerning what is to follow.

Characteristic of chorales, as I said, is the cadence at the end of each line of text.* The relation by contrast is clearly expressed in these cadences: contrast which is at the same time cohesive, those contrasts that are necessary in a tonality, that express the tonality. To exaggerate a little – I will say in a moment how far the exaggeration goes – we can consider the chorale, as well as every larger composition, a more or less big and elaborate cadence. We would thus consider as the smallest components of this big cadence, not all chords that

---

* Let the pupil take the melodies from a collection containing chorales harmonized by masters. Many of the melodies he will have to exclude; they are modal, hence he does not know how to deal with them. The closing chord can serve as a characteristic, by no means always reliable, for distinguishing keys from modes. If this chord agrees with the key signature, being the pertinent major or minor tonic, then the chorale can generally be treated as major or minor. But to be sure, many a chorale that could otherwise pass for major or minor begins and ends in a way contradicting that major or minor. In such chorales this is generally because the treatment suppresses the characteristics of the mode, although such treatment does not necessarily mean stylistic ignorance or lack of skill. This kind of chorale, should the pupil choose it, will give him plenty of difficulty.

appear, rather, the chords that close the lines of text. Put side by side, these make up a cadence. And herein lies the exaggeration; for, to make an effective cadence, these chords would first have to be *put in order*. Such a cadence then looks perhaps less rich than the events that, in the piece, produced the degrees constituting this cadence. Even so, we need not be astonished if the plan is simple, its implementation more complex. Once we have adjusted to the simplicity of such a plan, then it is evident that we may consider here even the very simplest of cadences, i.e. those with a minimum of different degrees, so that conceivably a cadence consisting of just the Ist degree alone could be enough. That is improbable, however, as I have already explained in the chapter on cadences; for the key can hardly be expressed with any persuasiveness unless we use its contrasts to arouse that activity, that competition for supremacy in which the tonic is victorious. Thus it is clear, and such is the aim of this analogy, that in putting together this extract from the whole, this hypothetical cadence, we use the same degrees as before, even if perhaps in some other sequence. Primarily, of course, I, then V and IV: that is, the tonic and the regions of the dominant and subdominant. The regions, hence also the other chords belonging to them: III, VI, and II.

There is another little inaccuracy in the analogy: whereas in the cadence, especially when it is short and simple, hardly any degree besides the first would be repeated, in this hypothetical cadence the repetition even of V or VI (or others still), though not inevitable, is by no means excluded.

What is essential and new for the pupil here is that he work out individual degrees of the key, by means of cadences, as if they were themselves tonics. This procedure will give no difficulty for it is similar to the use of intermediate and transitional keys in the composite modulations, where, likewise, episodes occur in a foreign key, the characteristics of the original key are absolutely suppressed, and in their place the characteristics of the episodic key are brought out with the familiar techniques. The close on the degree in question can ensue – and will, for the most part – as if this degree were the tonic of a key. For example, if one is to make such a close on III of *C* major, then the cadence should proceed as if it were establishing a modulation to *e* minor; and this modulation should have been prepared beforehand.

Now if the pupil has a chorale melody before him, let him inspect the phrase endings, designated by fermatas (⌢), to find to which degrees the closing tone can belong. (We shall assume that in general a new harmony appears with each half note. Obviously two or even more chords could be set to one half note. But we shall ordinarily avoid such a setting and use it only when it has a particular purpose.)

The $b\flat$ of the first close can belong to I, VI, or IV; the f of the second, to I, V, or III; the c of the third, to V or II (VII will, of course, be omitted here); the $e\flat$ of the fourth and fifth, to IV or II. The final chord of the whole chorale, of the sixth line, must naturally be I. The question, which of the degrees should have preference, is to be decided according to the following considerations. Above all, the key is to be expressed. As we know, the tonic does that most clearly, then the dominant and the subdominant. Therefore, the pupil will

[NOTE As he indicated below (p. 296), Schoenberg quoted here the chorale melody ('In dich hab ich gehoffet, Herr') stripped of Bach's nonharmonic tones. Bach's harmonization in the *St. Matthew Passion* (Part II) is given in its entirety in Example 228. Cf. another harmonization in Bach's *Christmas Oratorio* (Part V).]

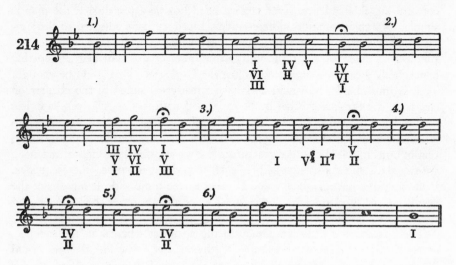

try, wherever possible, to close the first line with the tonic. If he cannot, then V or IV are next in line for consideration, and after these, III, VI, or II. For the other phrase endings he should choose those degrees which provide a good contrast with the first, the melody permitting: if I was first, then for the others, V, IV, III, VI, or II. All the same, the pupil does not absolutely have to avoid all repetition of a degree, especially of I; for sometimes the melody aims directly at such a repetition, quite apart from exact or slightly varied repetition of sections. Whenever possible, he should strive to vary such repetitions by means of a different harmonization. Wherever the repetition of a degree would be bad, a deceptive cadence could solve the problem. (More of that later.) But this solution will only occasionally be necessary. The closing tone is not enough by itself to determine the choice of cadence. One must also take into account the preceding tone, indeed, frequently two or three of the preceding tones. Since many a phrase consists of little more than six to eight melody tones, one might decide to start with the closing tone, with the cadence, and work backwards toward the beginning. This procedure is only partly correct; for the beginning has to be taken into account, too, both for its own sake and, in particular, for the sake of its relation to the preceding cadence. This relation should make it seem as if no interruption had taken place at the fermata, as if the harmony flowed on unbroken through the fermata. Accordingly, the two chords to be sought have to be related to one another as a progression, the second as a continuation of the first; and the first chord of the new phrase cannot be chosen without considering the last chord of the old. The pupil will first have to determine whether the two or three melody tones directly before the closing tone will admit those degrees necessary for a cadence to the degree selected. Because, a cadence it should be. Even if it is only a close in the middle, no definitive close, it is still a close, and the harmony should make that clear. For the moment we know no means for closing other than the cadence.*

Now let us examine the first phrase. From the figures under the last three melody tones we can see that the cadence to I is quite feasible. We can choose for the *c*, V, for the *e♭*, II or IV, and for the *d*, I, VI, or III. From these we can construct the following cadences [Example 215]: I – IV – V – I, VI – IV – V – I, even III – IV – V – I. The last requires some caution, because there is no such direct relation between III and IV. The progression III–IV is in fact like the deceptive cadence; and the deceptive-cadence progression, the 'superstrong' progression, if it is to be used in a manner consistent with its character, must have sufficient reason for its 'superstrong' action. It evokes a *change of direction* (and the same is true here of the actual deceptive cadence). Hence, we should first look to see whether the situation requires such, whether the deceptive cadence is a necessary solution, as in the following situation: by going straight ahead we run into the danger of going too far afield; a sharp turn in the other direction restores the middle course.

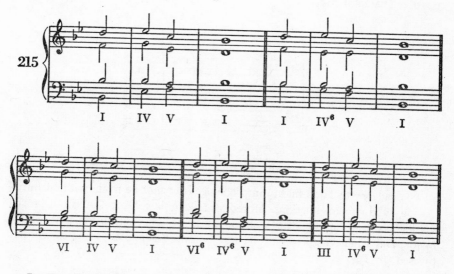

or I – II – V – I, VI – II – V – I, III – II – V – I

* In the chorales the pupil will be inclined to use everything he has previously learned. At first glance one would say this is not good, because it is inconsistent with the style to attach complicated harmony to so simple a melody. Theoretically, this seems correct. However, if we look at the Chorale Preludes of Bach, where, around such simple melodies, his parts unite in complicated harmonies, then we may well say that it is not stylistically inconsistent. Otherwise Bach would not have done it so. Hence, the theory is wrong; for the living example is right. Or perhaps stylistic authenticity is not essential to artistic effectiveness. In other words, it is of course possible

All these cadences are usable. And since the one to the Ist degree works so well and in so many different ways, we may well assume it is the one appropriate for this melody. Nevertheless, a cadence to the VIth degree would also be possible (Example 217).

The cadence to IV is highly improbable. It cannot be made without introducing subdominant relations. Moreover (Example 218), it would not be advisable because the key of the phrase could be too easily interpreted as $E\flat$ major; and whenever possible, the key is indeed supposed to be clearly expressed (by I).

---

to give a melody harmonies other than those that correspond to its style. And in this sense the chorale arrangements of Reger or the folksong arrangements of Richard Strauss may be completely blameless. However that may be, the pupil should restrict his attempts to simple harmonies: he should not use the more remote key relations; of the vagrant chords he should use at most the diminished seventh chord, but only occasionally, and then without enharmonic reinterpretation, as a ninth chord on a degree within the key. Secondary dominants may be included, since they also appear in the church modes. I have no objection if, in later exercises, the pupil wishes to try more elaborate means.

The VIth degree, while it will work, is also to be chosen only in case of necessity: if, say, the same phrase is repeated in place of the third phrase. It is generally preferred in chorales to assume that the root (octave) or the fifth of a [closing] chord is in the melody, rather than the third. There are historical reasons for this assumption: the third was discovered later than the others, was then at first only sparingly allowed, and was perhaps for a long time afterwards strictly avoided at exposed places. If now the pupil does give preference to the root or fifth, he does not therefore have to avoid the third. In Bach's music the closing tone is often the third of the chord.

If the pupil now examines the succeeding phrase endings in the same manner, he will find, among others, the possibilities shown below: For the second phrase:

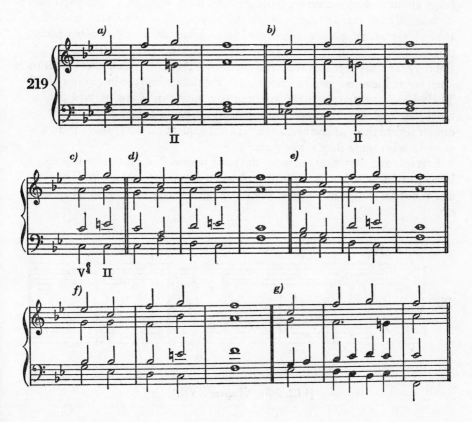

The II appears here, of course, as (secondary) dominant of V. Why the chord before this II cannot be a six-four chord on V (Example 219c) is clear, if we consider that none of the chords admitted by the preceding melody note *c* has a good connection with V. For the same reason the phrase will not close on III, although it could be easier here to find a way. The turn to V itself poses a problem, namely, the 'unresolved' *e♭* (that does not go to *d*!) just before the *c*. Since the *e♭* is left by skip, since it is thus not 'disposed of' before the region admitting *e* is entered, one should see to it that the *e♭* is 'resolved' in another voice, best of all in the bass, by going to *d*. Hence it will be good if the chord harmonizing *c* of the melody also contains the *e♭*, as in 219b, *e*, and *f*. But then there remains so little time for turning that the cadence may easily lack force. However that may be, if in the chord under the *c* of the melody *e♭* does appear, then the six-four chord of V cannot appear with the *f*, because the *e♭* would then not be disposed of. The cadence could of course go to I; but that was our final chord in the previous phrase, and besides, it would be reached by a plagal cadence (as also in Example 218), which has not yet occurred in all our previous cadences. (The plagal cadence will be discussed later.) It will not be at all easy for the pupil to find other harmonies for this cadence, in this [half-note] movement. In Bach's *St. Matthew Passion*, from which this chorale is taken (simplified here by omission of changing and passing tones), this line is harmonized as in Example 219g. By using two chords to every half note Bach was able to bring about a clearer cadence, with greater variety of chords. The pupil may occasionally use quarter notes – *but for this purpose exclusively*: to make possible, *through the use of quarter notes, a richer harmonization and clearer cadence*, particularly if without quarter notes a cadence could not be made strong enough. But only for this purpose! (We write the chorale melodies in half notes, whereas Bach wrote them in quarters; I have given the quotation here in our notation.) The widespread practice of 'decorating' by means of changing and passing tones the pupil should completely avoid. In the present stage of our study we cannot regard them as harmonic events; a subsequent examination of them will show in what sense they actually are.[1]

Example 220 shows cadences for the third phrase. Not much else is possible here. The forms *a, b, e, f, g*, possibly also *c*, will be relatively useful. The form at *d* is not absolutely impossible. But it will sound somewhat harsh on account

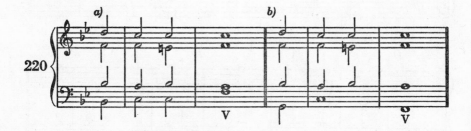

[1 Cf. *infra*, Chapter XVII.]

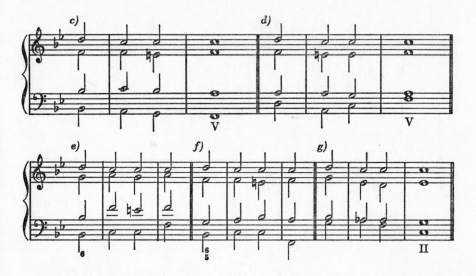

of the virtually unprepared *e*. This *e* is disturbing in the chord on *a*, because this chord to which the *e* is entrusted is indecisive. It is 'as if there were no point to it'. In itself the form at *g* (plagal cadence) is good. But consideration of the key makes it questionable, as becomes especially evident if we think of it together with the harmonization of the first phrase in Example 218.

The fourth and fifth phrases are of particular interest (Example 221). In our simplification the same melody notes appear both times (Bach varied them by using ornaments [Example 223]). Here it will be necessary to harmonize the two sections differently and to make sure the repetition is at once an intensification. As the degree for the closing tone, II or IV are to be considered. Thus we have an explicit turn to the subdominant region.

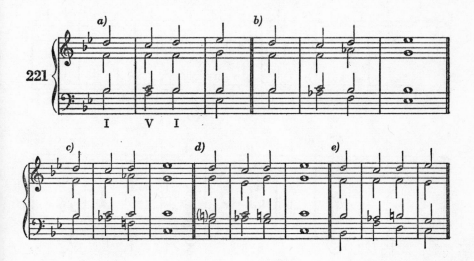

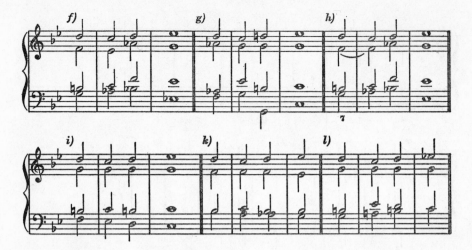

Example 221 shows a number of possible harmonizations, and in Example 222 pairs of possible harmonizations are variously connected to make a progression.

The simplest form is of course Example 221*a*, but the pupil does not have to avoid it at all cost. The other forms cooperate with the subdominant region by preparing in diverse ways now the leading tone upward, *b*, now the leading tone downward, *a♭*. The harmonization in Example 221*i* would be too simple, since it includes only II and its dominant (secondary dominant). Generally, this tonic-dominant harmonization is seldom used in chorales. But here and there it is unavoidable; then the pupil should prefer this simplicity, rather than write something more complicated, whose effect would perhaps be unnatural. The chorale melody was perhaps invented with just such simple harmony, and any other harmony would then be unsuitable. But here such simplicity is unnecessary, for there are plenty of appropriate and rich harmonizations. Example 221*k* shows another progression that the pupil should use infrequently. It does appear in Bach, but, all in all, seldom; and then never from want of anything else, as the pupil would perhaps do, but for the sake of an effect that the pupil does not presently have the means to achieve. To determine the sequence of the two forms we must decide whether it is more favorable to go first to *E♭* and then to close on *C*, or vice versa. Bach uses this form:

first II, then IV. The opposite order, however, is usually quite telling and more common; thus the decision depends on the context. In general it is definitely better to put II *after* IV, because one can then go through V to I. That is consistent with our knowledge of the strong root progressions, which can be extended this way from progressions of individual chords to [the succession of whole] phrases. Only, this order is not absolutely stronger. For if we put first II, then IV, the (imperfect) minor chord (II) is followed by the (perfect) major chord, the 'tentative' by the 'definitive' so to speak, a convincing arrangement. Bach's harmonization after this IV makes no more use of either the IV or the II (except that at the very end he uses II again, but now as a secondary dominant, where it actually almost belongs to the region of the dominant), but goes toward I with clear preference for VI and the chords pertaining to VI. Perhaps we cannot say categorically that this conclusion is the necessary consequence of the arrangement II–IV, but the tendency is noticeable.

Example 224 now shows a few harmonic possibilities for the last phrase. There are not many; the conclusion is quite clear-cut.

Many chorales, as well as individual phrases here and there, begin (without upbeat) on the strong beat of the measure and then have a 'feminine' ending, that is, they end on the second beat. In such endings the same tone usually appears on both one and two. If so the cadence is to be completed on the first beat with a repetition of the same chord on two. On occasion one or more voices can then be 'suspended' on the first beat and resolved on two to maintain some motion. If the note on one is different from that on two, we should first find out whether or not both (e.g. if they form the interval of a third) belong to the same chord (the final chord, which is then to a certain extent predetermined). If so, then this progression will be accomplished merely by a change of spacing in the same harmony. The rare instance where this treatment does not apply is somewhat more difficult. Then I recommend increasing the two last notes to whole notes. The first whole note then usually gives opportunity for cadencing.

Once the pupil has worked out the cadences (wherever possible, once he is more practiced, without writing them down, just by noting and remembering them, so that there is at least some room for invention), then he must decide which cadence degrees he will use. In deciding he should consider the following: (1) The final phrase must lead to the tonic. (2) Wherever possible, the first phrase should also end on the tonic, or if not the first, then certainly the second. One of the two will, if possible, go to V. If it absolutely will not work any other way, both phrases could of course go to V, or both to I; but then the key should be clear and there should be sufficient variety (different positions of the soprano and bass, close instead of open position; different progression of the harmony, etc.). (3) Generally, the IIIrd or VIth degrees are to be considered more for the middle parts, the IVth and the IInd most often toward the close, because the ascent from the subdominant to the dominant region is quite forceful. All the same, other treatment does often appear. (4) To put it bluntly, to exaggerate, we should like to require that no degree be repeated except for the necessary repetition of I (at the beginning and at the end). As I say, such a requirement would be exaggerated and almost never practicable; but we should, as far as possible, work toward that end. (5) Since what was just said is not easily attainable, care should be taken to separate cadences on the same degree by means of intervening cadences on different degrees. To say even this is to go much too far (as does everything in laws of art). Here, too, the contrary can be good, and repetition can be effective as reinforcement. (6) Most important of all, however, is to harmonize every phrase in such a way that no violence is done to the melody. That is a matter of *feeling*, of *talent*. Nevertheless, we do know many things that can help here. For example, we should pay attention to such characteristics of a melody as those shown in my discussion of the second phrase, where the e♭ is first to be neutralized before the e can appear.

Once we have determined the cadences, then we choose the chords that will begin each phrase. Most important for this choice is that the beginning of a phrase relates well to the preceding cadence. As I said earlier, these should connect, wherever possible, as if there were *no* fermata. Next, the beginning should also prepare for the degree that will close the phrase. That is best done by going at once, with the first chords, into at least the neighborhood of the key corresponding to the degree chosen for the cadence. This kind of preparation is almost always good, but not always possible. If such a preparation is not possible, it can then as well take place gradually, in the course of a phrase, even if the cadences are quite remotely related. Moreover, a sudden turn in the middle can often be exceedingly forceful.

For example, in another chorale from the *St. Matthew Passion* ('Was mein Gott will . . .'), in *b* minor, right after the cadence on *b* (I of *b* minor) Bach turns on the upbeat to the dominant, *E*, of the next cadential chord *A* (Example 225*d*). Examples 225*a*, *b*, and *c*, on the other hand, take time and veer toward the subdominant region of the cadence tone *A* (or *f♯*), toward *e*, *D*, and *b*. But Examples 225*a* and *b* make the transition gradually, whereas 225*c* brings about the decision with a sudden turn. Generally, that method is preferable which indicates at once, with the first step, the direction the line will take, as Bach does here. He himself, however, often enough turns more abruptly: for example, the fourth phrase of the chorale (in *A♭* major), 'Ich bin's, ich sollte büssen', from the *St. Matthew Passion*, could quite easily turn to the dominant as in Example 226*b*.[1]

But, in spite of the *e♭*, which actually stands in his way at the beginning, Bach chooses a cadence on the major chord of III (dominant of the relative minor, as it were) and makes the cadence with a fairly surprising turn. A comparison of the two forms will show how much more interesting Bach's is, even though I could of course have found something better for mine; and so much the more interesting is Bach's when we put one, then the other into the context of the chorale. Then we see that in this chorale other degrees were chosen for the third and fourth cadences because these two phrases are just repetitions of the first two. These are the grounds upon which a good draftsman writes abrupt turns. Variation is in this style one of the most important requirements.

In Example 227 attempts were made to harmonize the first phrase [of our chorale]. This melody is not easy to work out. It is fairly long, but does not have much variety of degrees, as the pupil can readily see once he writes down the degrees underneath and looks for good connections. It will be particularly

[1 Schoenberg quotes here the *fifth* phrase, rather than the fourth. The following paragraph should then state that the *fourth* and *fifth* phrase, not the third and fourth, repeat the first two.]

difficult to avoid repeating II or IV (with their accessories [*Zubehör*]) on account of the repeated *e♭* and *c* of the melody. Perhaps the best of these solutions is that in Example 227*b*, although it is rather modest and the repetition of the *f* in the bass (toward the end of the phrase) is not felicitous. Bach's solution is wonderful (Example 228). True, it would hardly be possible without the passing tones and changing tones, which therefore are not *ornamental* here, but *structural*; they are not incidentals, not non-harmonic, they are rather necessities, they are *chords*. In general the pupil must be particularly careful to avoid repeating chords, and more especially, what I called 'accessories': the dominant (or secondary dominant) of a degree or its substitute (a diminished triad, as quasi VII) will easily smuggle themselves in. As I said, it is not always possible to get around that repetition, and a good result is therefore not always easy to obtain. We can see clearly in Mendelssohn's chorale harmonizations how difficult it often is, even for a master, to make himself at home in a style not his own. Brahms is generally more successful, so successful in fact that his harmonizations are eminent masterpieces of style imitation. Nevertheless, the distinctions between a chorale harmonization by Bach and one by Brahms are quite conspicuous. For this reason I shall avoid putting in here any model harmonization of my own and offer instead the entire Bach chorale (Example 228). To be sure, I could produce something of a quality the pupil will not be able to match for some time. But to put it down as a model, as exemplary – I am not that presumptuous, even though I do have some regard for my ability.

If the pupil notices a number of things here that do not agree with the instructions I have given and the reasoning behind them, he should not worry;
art will never be entirely like the laws of art. Art is broad, the laws of art are
narrow. Yet I believe I have given the instructions broadly enough so that
there is still room for what actually occurs. It might be noted, for example, that
at $ the distance between the alto and the tenor (an eleventh) is greater than our
instructions allowed; but in establishing this point we spoke of an 'average'
euphony, and this expression means that there are also euphonious spacings
above and below the average, so that the octave interval continues to be the
average euphony. Or it might be noted that at † the alto does not first resolve
its e♭; what I said here was: 'it will be well to . . .', but not 'it should be . . .'.
Besides that – and this was also pointed out – the e♭ is resolved in the bass.

Let the pupil practice chorale harmonization with as many different melodies
as possible. At the same time I recommend, above all, that he work out each

chorale in at least two or three different ways. Naturally, he should strive for the smoothest possible writing. But he will not often achieve such ideal smoothness, if at all. The value of this exercise, then, consists only in handling and working through the material; it is a gymnastic exercise that strengthens specific muscles. As with all such training, the desired goal is not the beautiful execution of the individual exercise, rather, the schooling of certain faculties.

CADENCES (*Schlüsse*)[1]

In Example 218 a plagal cadence (*Schluss*) was used in place of an [authentic] cadence (*Kadenz*). Such is often necessary in harmonizing chorales, as is illustrated in Example 226a, where one must use a plagal cadence if the *g* is not to be the third of *eb*. The plagal cadence is a formula that is no doubt capable of ending even larger compositions, but it is less definitive and less emphatic than the authentic cadence. The most complete close is effected by means of the [authentic] cadence. But a close of such finality is not always desired; often, just for the sake of contrast, other kinds of closes must be used. And for yet another reason the exclusive use of [authentic perfect] cadences (*Kadenzschluss*) can be disturbing: the articulation can thereby become too definitive, or more precisely, too often definitive. As far as melodic requirements are concerned the need for a complete close arises hardly more than once or twice in the course of a piece; at the same time, the necessity for keeping individual phrases distinct but not too sharply separated gives occasion to introduce such incomplete closing formulas as half and deceptive cadences. Whereas the [authentic] cadence favors the ascending progressions or equivalent composites, the incomplete cadences can include descending progressions. We have a host of names for such cadences. Besides the authentic and plagal we may mention the perfect and half cadence, the complete and incomplete perfect and half cadence, the complete (or incomplete) authentic (or plagal) perfect (or half) cadence, and a mixture of all these elements. Example: incomplete authentic half cadence, union of plagal and authentic. . . . 'And those are only the names!'[2]

Since complete and perfect cadences can appear in the middle of a composition, just as well as half and imperfect cadences can appear at the end; since, moreover, cadences (*Schlüsse*) are not absolutely essential to articulation (for no formal effect depends solely on the harmony); since, still further, the great number of possibilities prohibits the naming of each one, names, after all, that would hardly characterize or define the potential uses: I think it is more practical to undertake the classification in such a way that the pupil is able to

[1 Cf. *supra*, 'Closes and Cadences', pp. 125–36.]

[2 In his revision, Schoenberg greatly expanded the remainder of this chapter, adding the following outline classification of cadences. (The outline form is Schoenberg's.)]

produce all or most of the possibilities himself through combination and variation.

I. To this end we shall divide up the cadences (*Schlüsse*) first into two groups:

A. Those in which the last three chords appear in the sequence IV (II)–V–I (*authentic cadence*). (The sequence VI–V–I, in which the overcoming of the subdominant region is superficially imitated by the strong root progression VI–V, is to be included in this category for lack of any better classification.)

B. Those in which this sequence is not adhered to.

II. In both groups one can make variations by:

(a) changing the positions of chord tones (inversions);

(b) use of the seventh or ninth chords, and the like, of the degree involved;

(c) substitution of nondiatonic tones for diatonic (secondary dominants, chords from the minor-subdominant region, etc.).

III. Important secondary forms emerge in both groups, if the principal triads (I, V, IV) are replaced by their substitutes; in these forms the same variations can be made that are indicated under IIa, b, c.

IV. We get an additional series of cadences by proportional transfer (transposition) of the forms introduced above to all degrees of the diatonic scale and, in the sense of extended tonality, to all degrees of the chromatic scale. We can transpose these cadences as follows:

1. inexactly:

(a) with diatonic scale tones exclusively;

(b) in part with nondiatonic tones;

2. exactly (degrees treated as if in another key).

NB. The cadence IV–I_4^6–V–I should be considered here only a special form of IV–V–I: IV–(I_4^6)–V–I.

I. The *perfect cadences* are the two forms from group A: IV–V–I and II–V–I (II as substitute for IV), but only

1. if they lead to the tonic;

2. if V is the dominant and consists of diatonic tones;

3. if I and V come in root position.

II. All transpositions of the authentic cadence to other degrees (whether diatonic or as if in another key) we shall describe as being *like perfect cadences*, but we shall group them with the half cadences. E.g.: V(♭)–VI(♯)–II(♯), VI–VII(♯♯)–III, V(♭)–I–IV, I–II(♯)–V, etc. (the penultimate chord in the form of a dominant).

III. All forms of the authentic-cadence arrangement that are distinct from the perfect cadences (because of inversions, etc.), as well as all cadences that arrange these degrees differently or use different degrees, thus producing different relationships – all these we shall call *half cadences*. Of these we shall point out first:

1. The *plagal cadence*, which is characterized by the total absence of the V (dominant) within the cadence proper. On the other hand the subdominant region (IV, II) is usually very broadly elaborated, so that the progression reads: IV (II)–I. This is usually regarded as a full or perfect cadence, and to do so seems justified, since it is frequently used as the final cadence of a piece. Yet, as is easily illustrated, many undisputed half cadences can be used to end a piece satisfactorily whenever supported by

all rhythmic, melodic, dynamic, and other cadential devices of compositional technique; hence they are, to that extent, equivalent to full cadences. This being so, it is more correct to regard the plagal cadence, too, as a half cadence.

2. The *deceptive cadence* (IV–V–VI, II–V–VI, VI–V–IV, etc.).

IV. The other half cadences that lead to the tonic we shall classify as:

1. those that replace characteristic degrees of the basic pattern, IV (II or VI)–V–I, with less characteristic degrees: e.g. IV–III–I, II–III–I, VI–III–I, IV–VII–I, II–VII–I, VI–VII–I, III–V–I, VII–III–I, etc.;

2. those that

(a) use a different sequence of the basic degrees: e.g. V(♭)–IV–I, V(♭)–II–I, V–VI–I;

(b) replace the characteristic degrees in these other patterns with less characteristic degrees: e.g. III($^7_6$)–IV–I, VII($_7$)–II($^7_{6♭}$)–I, III–VI–I, etc.; and

(c) use entirely different degrees (so far as this is not already included in the earlier categories).

V. Cadences leading to secondary degrees we shall classify as:

1. *Diatonic*, which, indicated here by the last two chords alone, are nothing else but transpositions of cadences previously shown to other degrees. These transpositions produce many unusable and uncommon forms.

(a) Commonly used are, in particular, those that lead to V; for, faintly recalling the incomplete methods of cadencing in the church modes, they have been used as incomplete cadences for punctuation, for pointing up the divisions in longer compositions: IV–V, VI–V, II–V, I–V, and even III–V as well. Why IV(II)–V is a half cadence can be explained by reference to IV(II)–V–I. The full cadence stops at the halfway point; it closes in midcourse.

(b) VI–V and I–V transposed to I yield II–I and IV–I: plagal cadences, hence, half cadences. Not all imitations of these patterns on other degrees are commonly used.

(c) The half-cadence character of VII–I, I–II, II–III, III–IV, and V–VI (this last familiar as a deceptive cadence), is readily apparent, patterned as they are after IV–V.

(d) One cadence that appears frequently is II–III, known as the *Phrygian cadence*, in which the II is usually a six chord and the III usually has the artificial, major third.

2. *Tonal* (*treated as if in another key*): Here one's resourcefulness in making combinations is given the widest latitude; for the techniques learned in the study of modulation, if applied sensibly and with regard for stylistic limitations, will insure smooth arrival at the goal.

The relations of the perfect-cadence type that belong here were already discussed and classified. Naturally, in our variation [of the cadences] the alterations of the IInd degree that we have learned get first consideration: secondary dominants, diminished seventh chord, augmented six-five and four-three chords, Neapolitan sixth, and the like. Moreover, the augmented triad, the artificial minor and diminished triads, as well as everything originating in the minor-subdominant relations may be used in the same manner as in the perfect cadences.

Example 229 contains merely examples of cadences and half cadences to secondary degrees, since everything of importance is already familiar from previously illustrated cadences.

The half cadence can be used often in chorale harmonization: principally, wherever melodic or harmonic characteristics require it, but then also for the sake of variety to secure softer contours. Occasionally, but not too often, the pupil may also write a deceptive cadence, as it is also found here and there in Bach's music. The phrase will then go clearly toward a I, but after the V it will turn to a VI or IV.

XVII 'NON-HARMONIC' TONES

I come now to one of the weakest points of the old harmonic system, to the point where it suddenly abandons its usual procedure and, as I said in Chapter I, is patched up with another system, which is not a system, in order somehow to include the most familiar harmonic events. It is remarkable that this point has not yet occurred to anyone: *Harmony, its theory, its pedagogy, is concerned with non-harmonic tones*![1] But non-harmonic matters have just as little place in a textbook of harmony as do non-medical matters in a textbook of medicine. (Significantly, the word *medizinfremd* is not used.) Whatever belongs in such a textbook is there precisely because it is not non-medical: if it were, it would not be there. The expression, 'non-harmonic' tones, I can interpret only to mean that a number of tones are declared unsuitable, or under certain conditions unsuitable, for forming harmonies; that such tones, because they intrinsically lack the ability to form harmonies, i.e. chords (*Zusammenklänge*), are designated as having nothing to do with music and consequently are thrown out of the art and out of its theory. For the theory and pedagogy of harmony can deal only with harmonies, tones sounding together (*Zusammenklänge*), and could say nothing about what is non-harmonic, or nothing more than that it does not deal with non-harmonic matters. Either there is no such thing as non-harmonic tones, or they are not non-harmonic.

Nevertheless, the non-harmonic tones (as we can see, the name, at least, is wrong) are said to be casual[2] accessories to the chords of the system: the harmony created by them is not supposed to be conceived as a chord because it is impossible to find a root for it. A second characteristic of non-harmonic tones is that they produce more or less dissonant sounds, hence something that requires a resolution or other justification through melodic means. The essential characteristic of non-harmonic tones, however, is said to be that they appear by chance, accidentally, that they are only isolated phenomena, occurring less often than the other sounds [i.e. the harmonies accepted as chords].

Before anything else, then, [let us affirm that] the non-harmonic tones do form chords (*Zusammenklänge*), hence are not non-harmonic; the musical phenomena they help to create are harmonies, as is everything that sounds simultaneously.

Yet, they are said to be chance harmonies; that is, such as do not happen of necessity, such as appear, not according to the laws of musical logic but, just contrary to that logic, when one would least expect and want them – according to that logic. Hence, they would be similar to, say, a meteor or shooting star,

[1 'Harmoniefremde Töne', that is, tones foreign to harmony; 'medizinfremd' (in the next sentence): non-medical, foreign to medicine.]

[2 The adjective (or adverb) 'zufällig' and its noun 'Zufall' appear repeatedly in this chapter. They are variously translated here: 'casual', 'chance', 'accident(al)', 'incident(al)'.]

which exists to be sure, but whose existence is apparently accidental since we did not know beforehand the moment of its appearance and cannot understand [why it appeared at just] that moment.

But this accident surely happens too often for us to regard it as really independent of law. Every melody must continually produce such sounds, in so far as it does not consist merely of tones from the chord under it (such a melody is relatively rare), and if only it moves somewhat faster than the harmonies under it. And something that occurs so often simply cannot be ascribed to chance; we ought rather to try to discover its regularity, the laws to which it conforms. We can dismiss as accidental the fact that such and such a man was passing below when a tile fell from the roof (although even that is not necessarily accidental, but can be predetermined). However, we can no longer dismiss as accidental the fact that he who is passing just at the decisive moment is the one hit by the tile; for if the tile falls (perhaps by chance) and someone is passing below (perhaps again by chance), then it is no longer by chance, it is rather entirely in conformity with law that he will be hit, and no one can expect it to be otherwise. Hence, the cooperation of two chance occurrences can produce something completely predictable, completely in conformity with law. Now we should consider yet another point: that the tile fell is accidental only, if at all, relative to the misfortune it produced. But not in itself. For its falling was the necessary consequence of two causes: on the one hand, the carelessness of the person who should have made it secure, and on the other, the law of gravity. Moreover, the fact that the man was passing below is no accident: he had to go this way for some reason; and, since he was walking at a certain tempo, he who previously was so far away from the scene of the future misfortune had to be there just at the decisive moment. What is accidental about it is only (perhaps!) the coincidence of the two circumstances; for this we know no law. It depends then upon the point of view one chooses, whether or not one ascribes something to chance.

Perhaps that is true here as well. Perhaps here, too, what we should view as incalculable chance is merely the circumstance that, through the movement of a voice against sustained harmony, chords are formed that we cannot categorize: chords that the composer, so to speak, did not intend, from which he expects no harmonic effect; chords that are without significance for the basic harmony and without influence on the future course of the harmony. That may be so; but he must then have intended his melody and his harmony to be independent of each other, not to be heard together, although he did not write them that way. All the same, we should not really speak of accidental harmonic structures. For, in spite of all arguments to the contrary, they are not accidental – because the two agents (*Ursachen*) that produce them both move along according to law; because it is not accidental, but necessary, that these two agents operate simultaneously; and because we can not only predict the occurrence of such harmonies from the nature of the whole, we can even calculate in advance precisely what they will be.

Perhaps we could speak, however, of unessential, inconsequential harmonic structures. Such they are, at least so far as they apparently have no influence on the further development of the harmony. To be sure, that is not completely correct either; for it is improbable that in a well-constructed organism, such as a work of art, anything will happen that exerts absolutely no influence anywhere in the organism. Let us examine the most rudimentary type of music, the waltz. Its harmonic development, if we may call it that, can hardly be influenced by such harmonies anyway, because the harmonic scheme generally antedates the melody that creates those harmonies. Yet, even in the waltz I find some things that make it unjust, to say the least, to set these harmonies apart in a class of their own. First, any other chord can also get into situations where it apparently has no influence on what follows, as is seen in recitatives where a chord is often followed by something that is not appropriate for it, something that becomes comprehensible largely through the intervening, unaccompanied singing voice. Or, in this waltz scheme itself, where the repetition of tonic and dominant is followed one time by cadential chords but another time not, the following cadence cannot then from any point of view be regarded as produced by the preceding harmony. On the other hand, if one does not jump to the conclusion that the harmonic scheme of the waltz really existed prior to the melody, then one must admit that these little occurrences added together determine at least the particular moment in which a harmonic change is to take place. We can surely call this an influence these harmonies have on the harmonic course of a piece, even if not in the usual sense.

Other harmonies besides these accidental ones can then also apparently be without influence on the succeeding harmonic development; conversely, it has not been proved that these accidental harmonies are really without influence. Another point should be emphasized here: it is *not their nature* alone; it is no more their nature [to lack influence] than it is *to have* influence. Their influence depends only on how they are used. We can write them on one occasion in such a way that they appear entirely unrelated to anything else, but on another occasion in such a way that everything seems to emanate from them. It should then be possible to turn these [accidental] harmonies to other uses. And even if someone should succeed in proving what is now their merely apparent lack of influence, it would nevertheless be wrong to conclude that they must then always be without influence; on the contrary, it would be more correct to try to find out what artistic means made it possible to paralyze their influence. But that [paralysis] testifies by no means against their capacity for forming chords (*Akkorde*) that are as significant as the other [recognized] chords.

What does all this mean?

Let us examine first of all the nature of those chords that are not designated as accidental or inconsequential harmonic forms, whose justification and whose possibilities for independent treatment are acknowledged. The following is generally accepted as the first characteristic: A chord is a composite sound (*Zusammenklang*) consisting of at least three different tones, hence, also of four, five, six, etc. This 'etc.', however, does not hold; for theory hardly acknowledges five tones – even the ninth chords arouse 'doubt in the hearts' of the theorists, instead of thought in their brains.[1] Here, then, there is supposed to

[1 Cf. Schenker, *Harmony*, pp. 190ff.]

be a limit. What it is, by whom and why it is set, we cannot learn, although we can read between the lines what is meant. Moreover, no one will say just what those composites are that contain more than five tones. That they are not chords is accepted without question; the most anyone will say is: accidental harmonies. This implies that the others are not accidental. Now I have already shown that these inconsequential harmonies are accidents only when observation is superficial and the wrong point of view is chosen. But what if I should now show, with still another example, that even those recognized by the system can be called accidental if one is uncritical enough to see no more than that in them. That they [too] can be without influence, I have already suggested. To prove my point I will not take examples from more modern compositions and will not appeal for support to *Leitmotive*, based on one or two chords, that are set down (impressionistically) without any harmonic consequences. Nor will I appeal to older examples, say, the 'thrice reiterated chord' from the *Magic Flute*; these are all genuine examples of lack of influence, examples which one could also call incidental if one wished to maintain imprecise description. I want, rather, to speak of counterpoint, of polyphony, concerning which it is said: Chords are formed merely as *accidents of the voice leading*, and they have no structural significance since responsibility for the harmony is borne by the melodic lines. There you have it!

That is of course only half true, for these chords are not really without influence; they are relatively uninfluential, just as are the chance harmonic forms produced by non-harmonic phenomena.

If then chance occurrence or lack of influence characterize, not the nature of these things, rather, at most, the mode of treatment, there is no argument left over from this first definition that will exclude the composite sounds of more than five tones, except that it is not their occurrence but their constitution that is accidental. To explain the constitution of the major triads we may cite the prototype in the overtone series. Even if we accept, however, the inversion of the idea of the triad and the undertones as an explanation of the minor triads, all such reasoning becomes inapplicable when we think of diminished and augmented triads and seventh chords, all such combinations that are [nevertheless] recognized as chords. These and the triads that are [satisfactorily] explained have nothing more in common than the superimposed thirds of their structure; and such is surely inadequate [as explanation]. The idea of alteration is no explanation, either, only an affirmation of the facts: that tones in the chords can be altered – or better, replaced by others – is of course a correct observation; but a uniform, general idea that could even only superficially explain the functions is entirely missing.

Thus it is most unclear what such a chord might be in reality, since the faculty for producing coherence, for evoking progressions, is given as a possibility of our technique rather than of the nature of the chord itself. And the prototype of the first overtones explains, at most, the major triad, but nothing else. And our harmonic system contains quite a bit more than major triads. What is the seventh chord, the ninth chord, etc.?

It is apparent that we shall get no farther this way. These are neither definitions nor explanations. Not once has the nature of the chord been described with adequate precision. How then shall we know what is not a chord?

I mean *generally*, so that no doubt remains. That a number of composite sounds, for whose relation to the natural no definite, direct formula, no simple, thoroughly applicable law is given, are designated as chords, while the great majority of composite sounds are not, even though they occur just as frequently – such cannot be considered a system.

But there are still some aspects to be mentioned by which to distinguish these two groups, aspects that have not been thoroughly considered, and one that, while it is indeed kept quiet, nevertheless plays the leading role in the secret society of theorists and aestheticians. This last is beauty, the limits of beauty. I will come back to it later on. The others are: (1) the historical origin; (2) the treatment found in works of art; and (3) a ridiculous aspect, but one that has had greater influence than we would like to admit: the appearance of the notes on paper.

The historical origin. Whether the chords were created through voice leading, or voice leading became possible only through our recognition of chords, is of no consequence here; for – whichever was first – they both spring from *one* impulse: to bring the natural material, the tone, into proper relation with the organ of perception [the ear] and with all secondary and tertiary functions contributing to perception, both associative and physical. This means, since the natural, inanimate material does not change, so to adapt the organ of perception to what is given in nature that the knowledge and the penetration of its essence is, wherever possible, complete. Both procedures [polyphonic and chordal] are consistent with this impulse; they both fulfil the purpose, even if by different routes, of creating the truest possible imitations of the [natural] material. These imitations are the more complete, the more the perceptive faculty (the intuitive and aural, or the reasoning and analyzing) succeeds in observing and distinguishing all characteristics. Thus we see composers of all periods continually learning new secrets, bringing forth ever more faithful reproductions [of nature]. Every innovation, every step attained opens the way to further penetration. The primitive ear hears the tone as irreducible, but physics recognizes it to be complex. In the meantime, however, musicians discovered that it is *capable of continuation*, i.e. that *movement is latent in it*. That problems are concealed in it, problems that clash with one another, that the tone lives and seeks to propagate itself. They had heard in it, and extracted from it, the octave, the fifth, and the third.

Here they would have stopped, had the will and talents of the theorists prevailed! But they did not stop: they had discovered the scale; true, they did not understand how to find its fundamental tone, but they did what men have to do if they want to find out: they reflected upon it, they organized what they had discovered (*kombinierten*). What they did led them onto all the wrong paths, but perhaps also to a number of truths; they did what men always should and must do when intuition will give no more help: they took up crutches to walk, put on spectacles to see, enlisted the aid of *mathematics and inference* (*Kombination*). Thus emerged a marvellous system; measured by our intellectual and spiritual powers it is marvellous, but compared with nature, which works with a higher mathematics, it is child's play.

Here they did actually stop. That ought not to have happened; for, shortly before, they had been on the right track, i.e. they had been under way, they had been moving. No longer did the natural prototype beget the new; instead, the laws spawned by inbreeding and incest those forms which inherited the paleness of the ideas, of their fathers and mothers, as token of their frailty. Until a short time before [musicians] had been on the right track, as, following the dictates of the material, they imitated the overtones. But then they tempered the system, and the system tempered the burning urgency to search. They had concluded a truce. But they did not rest (*rasten*) in order to rearm and regroup (*rüsten*); they rested in order to rust (*rosten*). The tempered system was an emergency measure, and an ingenious one, for the emergency was grave and the measure ample. It was an ingenious simplification, but it was a makeshift. No one, having wings, would rather fly in an airplane. The airplane is also an ingenious makeshift; but if we could fly merely by an act of will, we should gladly do without the machine. We ought never to forget that the tempered system was only a truce, which should not last any longer than the imperfection of our instruments requires. We ought not to forget that we still must account for the tones actually sounding, again and again, and shall have no rest from them nor from ourselves – especially from ourselves, for we are the searchers, the restless, who will not tire before we have found out – we shall have no rest, as long as we have not solved the problems that are contained in tones. We may indeed always be barred from actual attainment of this goal. But more certainly, we shall have no rest before we do; the searching spirit will not stop pursuing these problems until it has solved them, solved them in a way that comes as close as anyone can to actual solution. I think, then, contrary to the point of view of those who take indolent pride in the attainments of others and hold our system to be the ultimate, the definitive musical system – contrary to that point of view, I think we stand only at the beginning. We must go ahead!

The historical evolution can then, after a certain time, give very little help in explaining the actual significance of the phenomena. Namely, from that moment at which it neglects in part the natural prototype by putting in place of the real tones the artificial, the tempered ones. From that moment at which it dismisses nature from art by calling the overtones unmusical, by telling the choir singer who sings a [natural] major third correctly in tune that his intonation is musically wrong. Of course, at that same moment all those chords that make up our present system do become possible. As I showed previously, however, these chords also carry within themselves that which will eventually overthrow the system. This point was in fact mentioned in the discussion of diminished seventh chords. But the historical evolution, even in its earlier stages, can give no really unambiguous explanation; for even in these earlier stages it presents no unbroken line. Sometimes it arrives at chords by way of part writing; at other times it makes the part evolve over chords. Now if we are short-sighted enough – and we are – always to regard only the momentary result as the goal, to consider now the chord, now the melody the *Motor* that produces musical movement, then the possibility of perceiving and comprehending the whole vanishes. And instead of seeing that both serve only one purpose, that is, penetration into what is given in nature, we take now the one, now the other to be the essence of music; whereas, in reality, this essence is not even the third [possibility], but rather some fourth [possibility] that cannot be more closely examined here.[1]

Therefore, if the historical evolution of those composite sounds that are called accidental harmonies merely shows the way composers first used such sounds, then there are four reasons why it does not support the conclusion that these harmonies are accidental:

1. The historical evolution is different from the natural evolution it might have been. According to a natural evolution structures would exist that correspond to the laws of nature.

2. It is true, nevertheless, that the historical evolution has followed, somehow, the will of nature, even if by troublesome detours; for our minds (*Geist*) can produce nothing that is completely different from nature. And if we assume that nature has laws, then even this human creation cannot be accidental, but must rather conform to laws.

3. The historical evolution, after all, tells only in what order and by what route those harmonies broke into music, but not how they relate to the principal aim of our activity. Thus, whereas these harmonies may of course have arisen as accidental harmonic structures, they could be, nevertheless, just as legitimate and basic as the others, whose fundamental character we have already recognized.

4. Actually, all the other chords of our system came into being in a manner similar to that in which these harmonies emerged. That is, those too were first used sparingly, and with caution, as inconspicuously as possible; but then, as soon as they were familiar to the ear, they became everyday, self-evident events in every harmonic composition. They were freed from the context in which they ordinarily appeared and were used as independent chords, as I have shown with the diminished triad and the seventh chord.

And with this we have reached the second aspect that I suggested above to distinguish these uninfluential harmonies from the others: the treatment observable in works of art. From this, however, we shall not be able to draw any conclusions other than those we drew from the preceding, because in the treatment we find more how something came about, than what it means. That would not have to be so if artists always had the courage to go back to the primary source. But it is so. And since it is, one must, and can, understand it without being unjust and with full respect for those great spirits who have travelled this way. [One can understand] by becoming aware that their work was necessary, just the way they did it, and that, as I said,[2] art is in reality a fourth [dimension] which these great ones have always given [to us], even when

[1 That is, the essence of music is not (1) the chord, nor (2) counterpoint, nor (3) chords in conjunction with counterpoint, but (4) something different.]

[2 See the preceding footnote and corresponding text.]

with respect to the material they were deficient in their service to the ultimate aim of nature.

The treatment of these accidental harmonies in music is distinguished from that of the recognized chords as follows: The recognized chords are either consonances or dissonances. As consonances they are completely free, subject at most to the necessities of the root progressions. As dissonances they are supposed to be prepared and resolved; but it has been characteristic of the evolution of dissonances that both conditions are more and more disregarded. Should we assume, though, that resolution were still an actual requirement, and that nonresolution were only apparent or only a stylistic spiciness, presupposing resolution as the norm, then the following distinction would in fact hold: Dissonant chords are resolved, i.e. they are followed by a new chord that complements their dissonant character and the tendency of the root; but the accidental harmonic structures reveal something different in their resolution. A tone, *d*, for example, that appears as a suspension or passing tone against the chord, *c–e–g*, is resolved; but the chord beneath, *c–e–g*, is sustained, does not change. Now the sound, *c–e–g*, really looks as if it is the important thing, the constant, whereas the tone, *d*, looks as if it is actually an unessential, incidental, and variable addition. Even in the event of no parallel case being found in all harmony, [such singularity] would still not necessarily prove that *c–e–g–d* is not a chord. I think that [treatment] only reflects the historical origin of this composite sound and proves only that such was its earliest appearance and the way it was first handled. And I have often shown already that the mode of treatment changed once the singular instance became general and familiar. Moreover, I have only to think of the rule that says: at the same time a suspension is resolved, the harmony can also change, so that a new chord catches the tone of resolution (Example 244, p. 334) – I have only to think of this instance and it becomes apparent that what was given above is not even necessarily characteristic of the treatment of a non-harmonic tone.

There are, however, parallel cases. For example, when the seventh chord, *d–f–a–c*, resolves by the descent of *c* to *d–f–a–b*. Whoever objects that *d–f–a–b* is also a seventh chord, can think of it this way, that *d–f–c* (seventh chord with omitted fifth, which does occur!) resolves to *d–f–b♭*. Here the harmony beneath does not change. But, someone will say, the root changes, and this was not the case with the suspension. First, let us again be reminded that this has only to be a distinction in the mode of treatment, which is not binding on the harmonic significance. Then I should ask, however: How does one prove that with the resolution of the suspension the root does not also change? We have often seen how the old theory assumes a lower, tacit root to explain simpler situations, and we have accepted this explanation because it is really necessary if we want to retain the [system of] roots. Perhaps here, too, we should assume a tacit root that makes a progression. And if we believe in such a root at other times, then we may do so here as well. There can be many reasons why we cannot determine such a root here. Foremost among them is, perhaps, that it has not yet been tried. But then, if I were to try it, if I were to give the structure, *c–e–g–d*, a fundamental, for example *A* or *F*, then there would be a progression of voices that must be new to us, new because we have not yet tried such interpretations; [we cannot determine the root,] that is, because our conception of roots is probably too narrow and this case has too little similarity to the other objects of this conception. But is the similarity really so slight? Are there not also undisputed root progressions closely resembling the ones we do not wish to acknowledge here?

Do not Examples 230*a* and *b* look very similar to 230*c* and *d*? Yet here we do see the roots! And these (230*a* and *b*) are indeed *chords*! Not suspensions!

I do not believe it necessary to carry this any further, although much could yet be said on the subject. It is enough to understand that the first mode of treatment means only that it was formerly done that way. Yet it must at the same time be clear to everyone that, just for that reason, it will be done differently later. The former is the preliminary work, only by virtue of which the real accomplishment, the subsequent treatment, becomes possible.

Now there is one more distinguishing feature of the uninfluential harmonies, the discussion of which could seem to be a joke, but unfortunately is not. I maintain, namely, that the system of triads was extended to chords of four and five tones only because and wherever the image of superimposed thirds allowed extension, addition of thirds on top of thirds. Actually, then, [this extension grew] out of the graphic representation of the sounds, out of the *visual* impression: point, space, point, space, point, space. . . . Only the sounds that could be traced back to this image [notation] were incorporated into the system; for it is obvious that a seventh chord is a more complicated tone combination than such a chord as *c–e–g–d*, as I will show later [p. 320]. In spite of that, the seventh chord is a chord and *c–e–g–d* is not! It must be admitted that a musician may discover a seventh chord, especially if prompted by the graphic image, before he discovers the sound, *c–e–g–d*, although the latter ought to be more obvious to him; for the sequence of the ideas that occur to one does not necessarily depend on the degree to which they are related to the prototype. Yet it is by no means certain that the seventh chord was perceived earlier. It was only adopted by the system earlier than the other. And that, if it is not disgraceful, is still laughable.

I believe now I have shown that these combinations are neither any more accidental nor necessarily any less influential than the chords of the system, that neither the historical evolution nor the treatment observable in the literature determines their harmonic significance. I have also shown that they would

not belong in the study of harmony if they were non-harmonic, and I can now
surely come to the conclusion that:

   There are no non-harmonic tones, for harmony means tones sounding together
(*Zusammenklang*). Non-harmonic tones are merely those that the theorists
could not fit into their system of harmony. And that [they could not] results
from the arbitrary assumption of the theorists that the ear can attend only to the
first five overtones. Thus, for example, Heinrich Schenker, a first-rate mind, a
man of insight and imagination. I have not read his book;[1] I have merely
browsed in it. But, alongside the honest endeavor to know and understand, an
endeavor enhanced by unusual talent and learning, I found errors throughout,
though interesting ones.[2] The source of his errors, that tacit but fundamental
assumption of school historians that the 'golden age' of music is past, leads
Schenker into unbecomingly vigorous polemics against modern artists. Such
and such from the past is good, and he can often support his point beautifully;
but for him it follows, therefore, that such and such that is new is bad, and he
does not bother to inquire whether or not the new is, in principle, like the old.
Yet unripe but ripening apples he judges as one who knows only the dead ripe:
The golden age is past! However great his merits, he proves himself particularly feeble at those points where he makes the positive attempt to draw a clear
boundary. Just at such points he becomes nebulous, as when he speaks of the
'mysterious number five',[3] beyond which (if I remember correctly) we are not
to go. A poetic thought, certainly, yet somewhat too poetic in the bad sense,
since the real poet recognizes the truth; for that five is already far behind us. But
this fact does not bother him. He wants the number five to remain mysterious.
Holding to this aim, he is not only blinded to reality, he also lets pass false and
inexact observations; for otherwise this 'mysteriousness' cannot be maintained.
The number five is of course, in itself, no less mysterious than all other numbers,
nor is it any more mysterious. And, after all, such secrets as we uncover are
either not secrets, or we have not uncovered them. Whatever nature wants to
hide from us, she conceals better than that. Aside from all that, however: the
number five is supposed to be remarkable in that it shows up everywhere in
music as a kind of boundary, for example (I don't remember everything), as the
fifth overtone, and as the fifth tone of the scale, as the *Quint*. Yes, but who says
then that the *Quint* has anything at all to do with five. Because we have given
it the name, *Quint*? It is not really five on that account. In the overtone series,
for example, it is the second tone. In the triad it is the third tone, and in the
chromatic scale it comes in seventh place. That we name the interval *c – g*,
five, does not mean that *c – g* is actually, in every context, five; our usage comes
from the fact that in our present scale – *our* scale – exactly three tones come
between *c* and *g*. But what if there had been four or two? And there could have

[1 *Supra*, pp. 95 and 119, footnotes.]
[2 In the next few sentences ('The source . . . nebulous') Schoenberg elaborated
what was but a brief parenthetical remark in the first edition (p. 356). There he had
written that Schenker's 'overwrought and unjust' polemics against modern artists had
hurt him (Schoenberg) deeply.]
[3 Schenker, *Harmony*, pp. vii–viii, 25f., *et passim*.]

been, and it would have been right, too; for nature lends herself to a far greater variety of interpretations than [do] our secrets.

Such errors result whenever one merely searches out reasons enough to explain what is known, instead of providing a surplus of reasons to embrace cases that do not yet exist. Such errors result whenever one takes the *known* phenomena to be the *only ones* there are, to be the ultimate and immutable manifestations of nature, and *explains only these*, instead of contemplating nature comprehensively in its relation to our feelings and perceptions. If the latter viewpoint is taken, these phenomena will reveal that they are not conclusive, not final, not definitive; rather that they are a small part of an immense, incalculable whole, in which the number five is just as interesting as, but no more mysterious than, all other numbers, be they prime numbers, products, or powers.[1] And their secret is not kept from us through their magnitude; their secret, their mystery consists rather in that we do not know whether, why, and which phenomena are based upon them. We make guesses, to be sure, but we do not know. It should not be overlooked, however, that these mysteries are simply annoying to the ignorant, that the only one who justifiably takes on their dreadful burden is the one who is blessed with ideas for their solution, and that the mysterious in itself possesses no more truth than does what is entertaining in the movies.

There are no non-harmonic tones whenever one discovers such principles. For the natural prototype, the tone, can be used to explain, as chords, still other harmonic combinations entirely different from these simple ones. And our relation to this prototype is that of the analyst, of the seeker; in imitating it we discover more or fewer of its truths. The creative spirit strives for more, more and more; those who merely seek enjoyment are satisfied with fewer. Between this More and this Fewer the battles of art are fought. Here, truth, the search – there, aesthetics, that which has presumably been found, the reduction of what is worth striving for to what is within reach. What is worth striving for is to discover everything that lies within the natural tone, to attain thereby everything of which the human brain with its powers of association and its ability to systematize is capable. What is within reach has its temporary boundaries wherever our nature and the instruments we have invented have their temporary boundaries. What is attainable with the phenomenon outside ourselves, as far as the tone itself is concerned, theoretically speaking, has no boundaries. What has not yet been attained is what is worth striving for. What has already been attained is a system that was able to accommodate some overtones with considerable exactness, some others rather inexactly. What has been attained is the almost exhaustive combination of all possibilities of this system by the unconscious ear of the creative musician, by his intuition. Still absolutely missing is the correct identification of the relation between what has been attained and what is still to strive for. We must yet strive for everything that is left over: the precise accommodation of all overtones, the relation to

[1 Schoenberg added the following remarks (up to the end of the paragraph) in the revised edition.]

roots, eventually the formation of a new system, the thorough combination of resulting relationships, the invention of instruments that can bring that music into being, . . . and so forth.

Not merely the accidental chords but also the fundamental ones were discovered because the natural prototype, by allowing these discoveries, evoked them. The major consonances are direct imitations of the prototype, the other consonances, indirect. Both the latter and the former are contained in the overtone series, as overtones more or less close to the fundamental. The dissonances, corresponding to the remote overtones, are likewise in part direct imitations of nature (even if *inexact*, as the tempered system), in part indirect or inferred. The sounding tone vindicates the exact and the inexact imitations. It permits approximations, as the tempered system does in fact show. This system is a system of approximations: the complete system of an incomplete matter. The dissonances were always cautiously introduced: preparation, resolution, passing [tones], *Manieren* (ornaments),[1] and so on. The ornaments are only preliminary stages for the ultimate free usage. Restricted usage is the first means, free usage the next goal. And then, on to the next! For we are only at the beginning. We still do not notate, even now, all ornaments. Apparently we still do not sense that certain ornaments are preparing the future shape of music, and we do not know what they might be. But, as someone finally dared to notate the seventh chord, someone will also dare to fix these ornaments [in notation]. And then, on to the next! As someone finally used the seventh chord freely, wrote it even where an ornament no longer introduced it, adopted it into the system, carried it over to the other degrees, altered it, formed new chords from the degrees so constructed, thus here, too, someone will one day systematize, set up approximations, and then consider them definitive.

But we are not yet that far advanced. We do not have to go that far at all [here]. Our only concern is whether individual chords, even some whose use is permitted, belong in the system or not. I say they belong in it, even though the system is too narrow for them, even though this system has set up limits it should not have. For example, if we play a *C*-major triad in a lower register of the piano, the following, more immediate overtones are part of the sound: of *C*, *c–e–g*, of *G*, *g–b–d*, of E, *e–g♯–b*; thus, altogether, *b, c, e, d, g, g♯*. And these are only the more immediate overtones! Yet a *d* in a *c–e–g* chord is supposed to be non-harmonic, foreign to this sonority; i.e. if a *d* sounds, then it is a special case, not really the everyday thing. And if we do with the *d* the same that was done with the *e* and *g*, [the result] is not a harmony like *c–e–g*; rather, the *d* is non-harmonic and we have then an accidental harmonic structure. That is to say, if we have this *d* sung, this *d* that sounds as an overtone anyhow, justifying it the same way we justify putting *e* and *g* down as actual tones to be sung – these, too, are indeed realized simply on account of their 'sounding anyhow' – if we do have this *d also* sung by an actual voice, then [the result] is alleged to be an accidental harmonic structure, whereas the former [*c–e–g*] is a chord, although there is no distinction between them. Naturally. It is hard for

[1 *Supra*, p. 47.]

the *d* to find a place in the system because even the most advanced theorists maintain that the ninth chords, if there are such things in the first place, are not susceptible to inversion. Yes, even though the ninth chords are themselves a proof of just how precisely the harmony *c–e–g–d* does agree with nature. Moreover, this *c–e–g–d* shows that the ninth chord is more immediate than a seventh chord. For the seventh chord on *C* would have to use either the fourth overtone of *G* or the sixth of *C*, the latter being, however, out of tune. And, since in the chord actually sounding the *G* has almost equal rights with the *C*, the purer fourth overtone of *G* is more immediate than the out-of-tune sixth of *C*. But the *second* overtone of *G*, the *d*, is yet more immediate than its *fourth* overtone, the *b*. And so, if the fourth overtone of *G* can on occasion be given preference over the sixth of *C* (that does happen in the seventh chord, *c–e–g–b*, which, as a 'recognized' chord, may cite nature as precedent), then the second of *G* must certainly be yet more justified than the fourth. The chord, *c–e–g–d*, is then surely more immediate than *c–e–g–b* (or *b♭*). But what then can we do with the *g♯*? How is that to find a place in the system? As if the system had to be built up by thirds alone! Why not by fifths, which are indeed more immediate than thirds? Why built 'up' in the first place? Perhaps sounds, too, have three dimensions, perhaps even more! All right! Build it up, but don't expect me to take your system for more than it is: a system for presenting events, not one that explains them. A junk dealer, having bought up a lot of old odds and ends, brings about some order as a by-product of picking out and sorting the better items. But the trash, which he can no longer sort, he leaves in a pile and says to a customer: 'I have a number of things here that are better; over there are some more that I really don't know what to do with. Pick out what you can use.' Now, this junk man is going about his business just the way these 'building-up' theorists go about theirs. For in that trash that the junk man really did not know what to do with, over which he gave preference to his old trousers and patched jackets, it was generally in just such trash that old works of art, valuable paintings, rare violins, and the like, were found. 'I don't know what to do with it' – that doesn't bother me. You simply have to admit it! I shall be satisfied with that, and you may go right on building up. But that the system is false, or at least inadequate, because it cannot accommodate phenomena that do exist, or labels them trash, exceptions, accidental harmonic structures, piles of rejects – that had to be said. And yet the system would arrogate to itself the status of a natural system, whereas it will scarcely do as a system of presentation. Confess: 'because I don't know what to do with it!' Then we shall be good friends. But the pretense must stop.

There are, then, no non-harmonic tones, no tones foreign to harmony, but merely tones foreign to the harmonic system. Passing tones, changing tones, suspensions, etc., are, like sevenths and ninths, nothing else but attempts to include in the possibilities of tones sounding together – these are of course, by definition, harmonies – something that sounds similar to the more remote overtones. Whoever gives rules for their use is describing, at best, the ways in which they are most generally used. He does not have the right, though, to claim that he has then precisely separated those possibilities in which they sound good from those in which they sound bad. There are no such possibilities in which they [necessarily] sound bad. Proof: the whole of music literature. There are no limits to the possibilities of tones sounding together, to harmonic possibilities; [the limits are] at most to the possibilities of fitting the harmonies into a system that will establish their aesthetic valence. At present; even that may eventually be attained [i.e. a system embracing all phenomena, establishing the value of each].

Now an example. Against a sustained harmony, *c–e–g*, two voices execute a *C*-major scale in contrary motion.

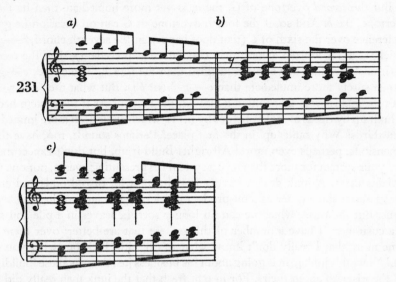

What harmonies are produced here (Example 231*a*)? I have notated separately the individual groupings that are particularly conspicuous (231*b*). Or, against a sustained triad, *c–e–g*, two [pairs of] voices in thirds move in contrary motion (231*c*). These are of course harsh sounds; and the theorists, who are forever confirming the blackest suspicion one can have against them, seem to have stayed away from these harsh sounds principally because such sounds are beyond the ken of a theory that would construct the beautiful instead of searching for truth – the theorists seem to have kept away from these sounds on account of their harshness, their ugliness. For should one receive these sounds into the system as members with equal rights and privileges, then there would surely be the danger that they might make more and more extensive claims, as the other harmonies have done; and there the theorists would have to start thinking. That would really be terrible! But these sounds do turn up often enough in reality. And just as often, we find chromatic scales moving in thirds; but there is no need to consider these, nor the many other things that appear in what is today called *Geräuschmusik*, 'noise music' (behind which lurks perhaps an 'ornament'). The example given is enough to make the point clear.

I maintain that these are chords: not of the system, but of music. Somebody will object: Yes, but they just happen by virtue of passing tones. I shall reply:

The seventh chord and the ninth chord likewise just happened by virtue of passing tones before they were accepted into the system. He will say: The seventh chord and the ninth chord were not such harsh dissonances as these. I shall ask: How does he know that? Who was there as the aestheticians, the unproductive, were aroused by the first seventh and ninth chords?[1] But that they were aroused by the first thirds that someone dared add to the empty fifths, that *I do know*. And our dissonances here do not really seem all too harsh, otherwise surely no one would dare write them. But there are those who dare. Somebody will counter: They dare only because the dissonances go by so fast, because the resolution is already there before we become conscious of the dissonance. My reply: What is fast, anyway? What is slow to one person is fast to another. The speed can only be expressed as proportionate to the capacity for perception. If one can make distinctions, then it may indeed be fast, but not too fast. And one does make distinctions! One who is sensitive to dissonances knows at least that he could not stop at such a dangerous spot. Thus, in this way at least, one does become conscious of the dissonance. But what if it just stayed in the unconscious. Does anyone believe that it is not the same process here as that which took place with the other, emancipated dissonances? Does anyone really believe that such simple processes of the subconscious do not finally enter the consciousness of artists who year-in and year-out consciously write and play such harmonies? But, apart from that, does not the *Kapellmeister* hear a wrong note in such harmonies, when the figure is not all too hidden? If there is then enough consciousness to verify that the harmonies [heard] agree with the score, and if the ear does then analyze them quickly enough, why should it not be able to acknowledge them as well when they appear disconnected from the context, when they sound for more time, where the ear has indeed more time to analyze them, more time to get acquainted with them by learning and acknowledging their drives and tendencies? And granted that heretofore such harmonies appear more often by virtue of passing notes than they do freely. Do they not also appear often enough as free suspensions? And how is a free suspension essentially different from a chord? What else is the appoggiatura but an embarrassed concession that the ear, with its sharp perception, makes to the slow-witted eye. Here something is supposed to sound whose notation the eye cannot tolerate. [Is it] that a suspension must be resolved? A seventh chord must be resolved, too. But a free suspension is more often left by leap, without resolution, than is a seventh. Then the free suspension would surely be a less sensitive dissonance than the seventh. And perhaps that is not far from correct. In general the free suspensions do indeed appear far less often for the sake of harmony than as a result of the melodic elaboration of parts. The melody, the motive, is then responsible for them, if one does not wish to regard the whole composite as a chord. One's inability to regard it as a chord does not mean it is not a chord, but rather that it is not like any of those that appear in the system.

But now comes an objection capable of knocking down everything I have

[1 Perhaps Schoenberg meant: Who can certify that the aestheticians were *not* aroused by the first sevenths and ninths?]

established: namely, 'such harmonies are not beautiful'. And to that I have to reply: Yes, unfortunately, it is true; they are not beautiful. The unhappy truth is that the great masters themselves have not shied away from writing passages of which the least among aestheticians can so easily declare: They are not beautiful. This has often much troubled me. And then I found recently in none other than Bach's music the following four chords, which an aesthetician could never like, should he notice them:

Bach, Motets.

232

[NOTE Schoenberg documented this reference below (p. 327) and cited these measures in full (Example 234). Another example, accessible even to Schoenberg's 'theorists' and 'aestheticians', may be found in the *a*-minor Fugue (measure 24) of the *Well-Tempered Clavier*, I.]

And, naturally, the rascal hid them in motets, which are written in the old clefs where a theorist cannot easily read them, and as passing tones where an aesthetician cannot easily hear them. The old gentleman should have been somewhat more closely watched and compelled to show his colors, that gray color on the shield of our theorists. And these examples are all the more remarkable when we consider that this Bach had himself reflected on theoretical matters and as a teacher even had to make them his business. Yes, he was even suspected of having inherited, as a family secret, a formula for the invention of fugue subjects. Surely, no one but a man with imagination can behave in a manner so improper for his station. And yet it is incomprehensible that a man of undoubted learning writes such things.

And it is really incomprehensible that musicians, who indeed always know more than the theorists, have written things that are not allowed by aesthetics. There is, for a similar case, 'that fellow, Mozart', who writes the following chord in the *G*-minor Symphony (Example 233*a*).[1] In this context (233*b*), of course, but still with no preparation whatsoever.

a)   b)

233

But the theorists told Mozart during his lifetime what a dissonance chaser

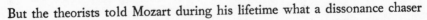

[1] First movement, measures 150 and 152. Cf. *infra*, p. 367.]

he was, and how all too often he gave in to the passion to write something ugly, and how with his talent such writing really wasn't necessary.

It seems, though, that [composers] do find it necessary. That they find it necessary to write just what the aestheticians do not like, just what these people declare to be ugly. Otherwise we should not see that happening over and over throughout history. But if it is really ugly, then who is right? The aesthetician or the artist? History leaves no doubt whatsoever about it, that he is right who will always be right: he who creates; even when it is ugly. Where, then, is the connection with beauty?

It is found this way: Beauty exists only from that moment in which the unproductive begin to miss it. Before that it does not exist, for the artist does not need it. To him integrity is enough. To him it is enough to have expressed himself. To have said what had to be said; according to the laws of *his* nature. The laws native to the genius, however, are the laws of future generations. The mediocre resist them simply because these laws are good. In the unproductive man the resistance to the good is such a strong urge that, to cover its nakedness, it desperately needs the beauty that geniuses unintentionally afford it. But beauty, if it exists at all, is intangible; for it is present only where someone whose perceptive power (*Anschauungskraft*) alone is capable of creating it does create it, through this power alone, and creates it anew each time as often as he perceives. With this perception beauty exists; as soon as the perception is over, it is gone again. Everything else is idle talk. The other beauty, that which one can possess in strict rules and strict forms, that is the beauty the unproductive yearn for. To the artist it is of little interest, like every fulfilment; to the artist the yearning itself is enough, whereas the mediocre want to possess beauty. Nevertheless, beauty does give of itself to the artist without his having sought it; for he was indeed striving only for integrity. Just integrity! Try for that, if you can, you who are unproductive! But the artist attains it, for it is in him and he merely expresses it, he merely extracts it from himself. And beauty is in the world only by virtue of one thing: by virtue of the congenial excitement in the nature of the nongenius, by virtue of the ability to suffer, to sympathize with what greatness experiences. As an accompaniment of that great capacity for sympathy that arouses the average person, as a by-product of the accomplishment of those necessary tasks that the genius performs in his penetration of nature – as such beauty may very well exist.

Hence, these chords are really not beautiful. Naturally not, for nothing is beautiful in itself, not even the tone. Of course it is not ugly, either. It becomes beautiful or ugly according to who is handling it, and how. Even so, it is perhaps more correct to say these chords are not beautiful than to call other chords beautiful. These chords are not beautiful, at least not at first; of course they will never become beautiful, either; if however they do not appeal to one immediately, one should first become familiar with them. Then they, too, will very likely release sensations of beauty like those that are long familiar. The ear is often slow-witted, but it must adapt itself. Adaptation to the new is not generally easy; and it must be said that precisely those persons who have acquired some sophisticated notion of beauty are the very ones who, because they presume to know what they like, defend themselves most vigorously against the new, against something new that would be accepted as beautiful. As a matter of fact, it would only be accepted as true and truthful, but that is what one calls beautiful.

I could be suspected of equating the idea of the beautiful with that of truth and integrity.[1] Indeed, so to interpret it could be an advantage; for we should at least be rid of those purely formal investigations, those experiments, that would reduce beauty to an arithmetical problem. Whereas that which beauty should be, if it were something real, could satisfy us only if it did *not* admit of representation by an arithmetical problem; if all the magic were revealed, not as something very simple, but as something very complex; if its many-sidedness actually sprang from a seed that burst because it could not withstand the power of germination within it. But [such satisfying, many-sided beauty would] not [issue] from a tidy formula, where to the left of the equals sign stands an improbability, which, although it does balance what is on the right, still cannot hide its improbability just because the equation balances. Life is not symbolized that way, for life is: activity. But then there is indeed the danger that the dry enthusiasm of formalism might be replaced by the dripping enthusiasm of over-wrought sentimentality and moral daydreaming. Let that danger arise! *From it* let there come for awhile that vagueness about the nature of things which, previously, formalism afforded us in such a satisfying way. I should really be satisfied just with change, with a differently colored glass. The new will be found here, and even if it is no more right, essentially, than what was formerly found, *even so it is at least new*; and the new, even if it is not the true, is at least the beautiful. The great anxiety of the philistines, who do not believe in beauty if they cannot verify it by applying rules, who have not experienced it but have only learned about it second-hand, I do not share their anxiety. Whoever is sensitive to humanity and to human endeavor will, without aesthetics, recognize the genius by those immediate signs that our instinct so unerringly distinguishes, just as it senses who is friend, who is foe, as it senses which person is congenial and which uncongenial. Integrity is perhaps also expressible in mathematical terms, perhaps even more so than beauty. With the latter the formula ultimately fails; sensations of beauty must be explained by the sense of beauty. Integrity is a ratio that indicates the relationship of the artist to his work. Their relativity one to the other is expressed by this ratio. It follows that there is only one perfect integrity, namely, when this fraction equals one, when therefore all activity stops; hence, all intermediate stages [of integrity] are at hand. That [imperfection] is in accord with life itself; for it reveals the goal toward which one strives and the criterion by which to judge one's efforts. In it error has a place, too; error is as much a part of integrity as is truth. In fact error would deserve a place of honor; for because of it activity does not stop, the perfection is not attained. Integrity, truthfulness never turns into truth; for it would hardly be bearable if we knew truth.

Moreover, the purely affective sources of beauty and the effects that are sub-

[1 *Das Wahre, das Wahrhaftige.*]

ject only to the control of the feelings will probably ultimately require of the intellect (*Verstand*) that it recognize their laws. But that does not mean it should prescribe these laws for them and require that they conform to these laws, as is the case with the laws of beauty. And so at least this advantage would be won, that reason (*Vernunft*) is prevented from undertaking the simplification of things one can judge only by feeling, that simplification which, although it suits reason, is too restricted for the feelings.

By the time the reader gets through what the quotations from Bach* and Mozart have prompted me to say, he will have forgotten my previously refuting the argument that these 'discords' occur only because of passing tones. I am predicting this because I know how the friendly reader thinks whenever he intends to refute, and I ask therefore that he recall that earlier passage [pp. 322–4]. The quotations from Bach are to be found in the Motet No. 4 (Peters Edition, pages 56 and 59),[1] with the following setting:

It will be recalled that I already stated my position on the question of the speed and transitoriness of passing tones; and whoever was able to follow my argument will have to admit that this idea is relative, cannot be an absolute standard. But assuming it were, and assuming Bach really aspired to beauty, what could we then conclude? Harmonies like those at ∮ between the two basses (N.B.: this is not a fast tempo!!!), or the progressions in seconds at + between second soprano and first alto, or the free entry of the tenor at ▣ (also of interest,

---

* A misunderstanding by a person who agrees with me has brought it to my attention that the chords cited here could be taken for isolated ones, just occasionally appearing in Bach's music. But it is not so. On the contrary, they appear regularly. They must, not only because of the urge to use the more remote overtones but, above all, because of the eight-part writing, which compels such usage.

[1 These quotations, like that on p. 334, are from the Motet No. 5, *Komm, Jesu, komm*. Cf. Peters 'New Urtext Edition' (1958), measures 14 and 41–3. In view of Schoenberg's remarks in the next paragraph below concerning the first tenor at ▣, it should be noted that this edition has a dotted half note g^1 instead of *c*, and no rest.]

incidentally, are the hidden octaves between second soprano and first alto in Example 234a) – these are still very harsh sounds. It is not to be assumed that a master like Bach, had his sense of beauty forbidden it, would have been unable to avoid such harmonies. It is also out of the question that they occur unintentionally or even by oversight; for they are found not only in this but in every other work of Bach. Hence, there is no doubt he must have considered them beautiful. Or at least they did not bother him, whether he indeed aspired to write something beautiful or not. It is then certain that harsh harmonies, since they appear in Bach and thus surely cannot be aesthetic flaws, are actually requirements of beauty, if beauty is itself a requirement. And granted that he could allow them only as passing tones because his ear would not yet tolerate them if written freely – he did write them nevertheless, and did more thereby than just nibble at the tree of knowledge. He followed his urge to accommodate more complicated harmonies, wherever he thought he could do it without danger to the intelligibility of the whole. But the essential thing, the urge to write harsh harmonies, which I find identical with the urge to include more remote overtones – this urge was there. He wrote them as passing phenomena so that we can use them freely; he used a life-belt so that we learn to swim freely. Just as he swam freely where his predecessors had found the life-belt necessary.

It will be asked, why I explained and analyzed every detail of a system so thoroughly in the earlier parts of this book, why I took the trouble to weed out minor errors, why I gave laws a different form, and so on, if I now produce evidence that testifies to the inadequacy of that system. It will be asked,[1] whether I can then build a new system or extend and improve the old one. And now, inasmuch as I can formulate no system – as I have said from the outset – an inconsistency will be found in the fact that such subtle distinctions were previously pursued, as for example with the six-four chord, whereas here such a great number of harmonies are not examined, organized, nor evaluated at all, not even collectively, let alone individually. It will be concluded that the pupil, who was previously under such strict guidance, faces here suddenly and without preparation a freedom he cannot cope with.

First of all: as for that inconsistency, perhaps it is even greater here than in other textbooks; but that is only because in the first half of the book I described more precisely than do the others, whereas in the second half I still say just as much. My attempts to explain the problems psychologically, or on practical grounds, or by the overtones, will at least be of use to a future theorist, even if he builds on principles different from mine. For, since my attempts never depend on the ephemeral aesthetic judgment; since I never say beautiful nor ugly but seek rather to find causes and principles that one may consider unchanging, or of which one knows that they have changed, and how, and why, so, the future theorist will find a relatively clean slate. He will not have to stop to investigate whether, for example, forbidden fifths really have any basis in

[1 This sentence and the following remark, that he could formulate no system, Schoenberg added in the revised edition. He reorganized and rewrote the remainder of this section of the chapter (to p. 331).]

nature; he will find clarification of the role played by the six-four chord in the older works, and the reasons for it; and the distinction between what is given in nature and what was produced 'artificially' through the activity of artists, remarks on the formation of harmonies through the influence of melodic elements, and the explanation of many a detail will be guideposts for him. For these reasons, therefore, I believe my presentation was not too detailed. If now the laws of the older harmony (the *real* ones, not the exaggerations of orthodoxy) are also those of the future – of this I am convinced – then I did not say too much in the first half. The inconsistency proves, however, to be even more trifling because I do not leave the old system as abruptly as do the theorists, who are also forced to leave it but are unaware of doing so. As long as it will work, they go the way of roots, they refer chords to degrees; they arrange the chords [into progressions] with no consideration of their origin. This procedure is made possible by judgment of the valence of the chords and their capacity for connection. Then, however, the theorists spring abruptly over to a different mode of presentation, the historical, where events are arranged and judged only according to their origins. Yet I have shown even of chords referred to degrees that many did not originate harmonically, and at those places I shifted to melodic justification. And, although from the outset I have aspired only to a system of presentation, not a natural system, still I have found *one* point of view, at least one, afforded by the systematic contemplation of the older harmony that also permits a glance into the future: the principle, namely, that dissonances are the more remote consonances of the overtone series. This principle alone implies that the harmonies produced by non-harmonic tones are chords too, just like the others. This principle is broad enough to embrace all harmonic occurrences and does not necessitate exceptions. The harmonies held to be accidental are chords; it is clear that they are usable as such, and had the system not been abandoned here, then this mode of presentation could have been continued. This continuation had to be denied those theorists because they did not recognize these harmonies as chords.

Now, as for the pupil and the reproach that, undirected and unprepared, he suddenly faces a freedom he cannot cope with, I have this to say: that, incidentally, the rigorous preparation itself that he has received in the earlier chapters, that fact alone can more likely enable him to acquit himself well when faced with freedom than a less rigorous course could have done; but, quite apart from that, I have no intention of giving a pupil this freedom. To what end, anyway? One does not give freedom, the other takes it. And only the master can take it: one, that is, who has it anyhow. What the pupil might take, even though the teacher does not want to grant it, is not that freedom. What he gets in that case is the same that he already had before he came to the teacher: a groundless freedom that still recognizes no responsibility. Thus, I cannot give him freedom; consequently, I ought either to set up a system myself to regulate the use of such chords, or I ought to prohibit the use of non-harmonic tones.

I have not succeeded in finding a system nor in extending the old one to include these phenomena. If that is perhaps denied me, owing to the limits of my talents, then let my accomplishment consist in having disclosed the flaw in the method used to date. Perhaps, however, it is at present not yet possible to set up a system because there is still too little material and because we are' still too close to the older system. If we disregard the experiments of a few younger composers who have the courage to follow their ear – there are many today who indeed have the courage, but instead of the ear they have an eye for what will immediately succeed: these we may confidently ignore – then, up to now such harmonies have been used almost exclusively where they can be explained as passing tones and the like. That is natural, too, and in no way contradicts my findings. For these laws really form part of the musician's constitution, not only because he was schooled in them but also because they actually indicate the way these harmonies came into being. I have pointed out often enough that most of the dissonances probably gained entry into harmony through melodic treatment. What my polemic would call attention to is in fact something else: (1) that they are henceforth chords, just like all the other dissonances that came about the same way; and (2) that they are only superficially annexed to the old system, that they are judged according to a different principle, according to their origin, and are not referred to roots.

On the other hand, instances like this one from Mahler (Example 235)[1] as well as numerous other passages in his music and in that of Strauss[2] are too isolated, and, more important, all that is still too close to us. We must be at some distance from an object if we are to see it as a whole; up close we see just individual features, only distance reveals the general ones. It would not in fact be too difficult to figure out all conceivable harmonies of from two to twelve tones in relation to a root, to connect them with one another, and to illustrate their potential use with examples. Even names could be found. For example, one could designate a C-major triad with a 'non-harmonic' d♭ as a 'minor-two-one major triad', one with a non-harmonic d as a 'major-two-one major triad', one with e♭ as a 'double-third triad', one with f as a 'minor' and with f♯ as a 'major-four-three major triad'. One could apply the familiar rules of resolution to these chords and add to these rules the ones arising from the treatment of non-harmonic tones. But whether all that would amount to much is questionable, because without description and evaluation of effect we have no practical application. Should we evaluate, however, then we should again get a

[1 Sixth Symphony, last movement, measure 387.]
[2 Cf. p. 372 of the first edition: '. . . isolated passages from the "Widersachern" in Strauss's *Ein Heldenleben* . . .'.]

system that deals in aesthetics; moreover, unlike the old system, it would be one that cannot appeal for confirmation to an imposing series of works of art, one that would rather go ahead of the works, prescribing a path for them that they will perhaps never take. Only the ear may take the lead, the ear, sensitivity to tone, the creative urge, the imagination, nothing else; never mathematics, calculation (*Kombination*), aesthetics. Hence, since I can give no system, and if it were merely a matter of superficial logic, I should prohibit the use of non-harmonic tones. So much the more since I have said from the outset that matters of voice leading belong in the study of harmony only so far as they are necessary for presenting harmonies. If it is borne in mind, however, that the interpenetration of the two disciplines, harmony and counterpoint, is as complete as their separation is incomplete, because every occurrence in voice leading can become harmony and every chord can become the basis for voice leading; and that, therefore, the fusion of the two courses of study into a single course would be of the greatest advantage, were the material not too vast – so, the attitude that I am to take towards these chords then becomes obvious. It is as follows:

Only a pedagogical consideration keeps me from giving the pupil a completely free hand with these chords: up to now I have told him exactly when he can rely upon this or that harmony to be effective, according to traditional experience; and I should like to continue that way. There are no traditional experiences upon which to base the free use of these chords; instead, in the rules of voice leading, we have tested and approved methods for controlling them. Consequently, I will take the same position here that I took, for example, with forbidden fifths: the master is free; but the pupil stays under restrictions until he has become free. Hence, I shall present the non-harmonic tones, briefly, in a manner similar to the usual one. Only, the pupil will know – and this is an essential distinction – that he is dealing with chords, chords that are dissonant like all the other [dissonant chords]. And he will know that the directions he gets for their use mean no more than did those which recommended that he introduce vagrant chords chromatically; no more than this: the simplest way is the one patterned after the historical evolution, but the as yet non-historical future will bring something different.

SUSPENSION, DOUBLE SUSPENSION, ETC., PASSING TONES, CHANGING TONES, ANTICIPATIONS

All these so-called non-harmonic tones – suspensions, passing tones, changing tones, anticipations – are to be presented in our exercises in such a way that they emerge through melodic events. Their appearance and the dissonances that they inevitably produce are thus justified by the impetus of a motive or of

a rhythm associated with the motive; quite frequently, however, they are justified by certain established formulas, the oft-mentioned ornaments (*Manieren*).[1]
Whether or not these are consistent with the fundamental intuition that any
harmonic combination of tones is possible, we see here again how the familiar
effect of certain established, cliché-like figures, whose satisfying resolution is
promised by the memory and anticipated by the ear, makes possible the fulfilment of necessity outside the excessively narrow rules. The cliché permits the
use of the figures because we have become familiar with the cliché; gradual
familiarization favors freer usage. New clichés come into being. Thus, the
method makes use of habit to produce new methods in turn, through habit.
One of these ornaments, for example, appears as follows:

236

If this *g* clashes with some tone or other, then the ear expects a resolution,
because such is its habit. But the voice now leaps away from the dissonance to
c. Even that is familiar; for we know that the *c* will then spring back to *f*, the
tone of resolution – as in a comedy, when the situation becomes momentarily
quite grave. But one has read 'Comedy' in the playbill and knows the situation
will not become too dangerous. Love will eventually triumph. This effect is
thus based on the recollection of similar forms. Example: that motive has appeared often in a piece; hence one knows that after the big leap upward a leap
downward will restore the balance. Such can be applied to other melodic
occurrences as well, besides those of the ornaments. Any well-defined motive
that appears in a piece often enough can on occasion be set with a dissonance, if
only the final tone clearly gives the satisfying, consonant resolution. Such a form
appears frequently in the counterpoint of Mahler and Strauss. As can be seen,
it is entirely justified, even though one need not go as far as I do [to justify it];
for it is based on the same principle as the ornaments. The actual execution of
such experiments belongs of course not in harmony, but in counterpoint. But
I should not like to proceed with this discussion without having affirmed this
point of view; it is important to me to have shown right here the similarity of
the ornaments, the motivic cliché, and the free motive to one another. If then
even the complicated phenomena are easy to explain in such manner, although
the explanation is outside the system, hence is not a musical, but a psychological
explanation, then the simple ones can naturally be disposed of with a few directions. I believe it is enough to describe what they are, to mention a few examples
and a few possibilities, and the pupil must then know how he can use them.

The suspension and the passing tone are to be referred back to the simplest
melodic form, to the scale, to the scale segment.

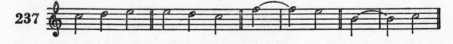

237

Suspension means delaying a step of a second in a voice while the harmony changes. If the suspension is to be typical, it is usually required that the suspended tone form a dissonance. But this does not seem to be absolutely necessary; for the *a* in Example 238 is without doubt a suspension, once the approaching I actually enters as the goal, as in a final cadence.

The more frequent form is of course that in which it actually creates a dissonance; only then is the suspension conspicuous enough. Besides, [this chapter] does indeed have to do with dissonances, with methods for introducing more remote overtones. The suspension can come with or without preparation. The pupil should prepare it at first; later he can also introduce it without preparation, as a 'free suspension'. The preparation takes place just as it does with every other dissonance: the tone that is to be dissonant appears in the preceding chord in the same voice. If the suspension is to be dissonant, then in the chord in which it occurs it can be a second, seventh, ninth, or fourth in relation to the root. The resolution of the suspension, as a melodic event that is ultimately to produce a step of a second, can be upward or downward.

An ascending leading tone will generally not be used as a suspension resolving downward, and a descending leading tone rarely as a suspension going upward. Nevertheless, these resolutions do occur.

There is a rule requiring that the tone to which a suspension resolves does not appear simultaneously with the suspension.

It happens, however, so often, that today we can raise no serious objection to it. It is not well suited to piano music in close position. But in choral writing Bach used it countless times (and of course also in his keyboard writing, etc.): [for example, in this passage]

from the Motet, *Komm Jesu, komm* [measures 6–7] (soprano I and alto II, ♭). An exception, even to the strictest form of this rule, was allowed in the bass of Examples 241c, d, e.

Two or more voices can also be suspended.

Moreover, during the resolution of the suspension the harmony can move on, so that there is a harmony with the tone of resolution different from that

accompanying the suspension. Obviously, nothing should happen by virtue of the suspension that would otherwise be prohibited; hence, no parallel octaves or fifths! One can, however, leave the suspension by leap: in the form of the so-called interrupted resolution, in which the tone of resolution comes only after one or more intervening tones. Without knowing all the common ornaments, one can safely use for this purpose any formula that one remembers.

These intervening tones will, in general, circumscribe the resolving tone, play around it, keeping melodically to neighboring tones, or they will be tones consonant with the resolving chord, or a mixture of both (Example 245c).

I should like to call attention to a few very familiar formulas because they suspend, in part, the pivot-tone rules in minor (245d, e, f). As can be seen, they interrupt the progression of the seventh tone to the eighth by going backward to the sixth.

The free suspension is very nearly a changing-tone figure. For the prepared suspension, there was at first the rule that it should come on the strong beat of the measure. As an exception (!) it could also come on the weak. Ultimately, however, the exception was almost more often manifest than the rule. Obviously, the free suspension can also be put on the weak beat. Then it is scarcely anything else but a changing-tone figure. What is important in both cases is the resolution. But even in the most rudimentary dance music we find instances like that in Example 246, where, for example, *d* leaps straight to *b♭*.

The *d* and the *b♭* are changing tones that circumscribe *c*; but *c* is itself 'non-harmonic'. One is of course at liberty to leap away from suspended notes. Thus, the dissonances in Schumann's 'Ich grolle nicht' (Example 247 +, †, ⊕) are either unresolved seventh chords or suspensions. They can be interpreted

either way. But it is enough to interpret them as sevenths. The pupil will do well at least to hint at the resolution, in the manner of the interrupted resolution.

The passing tone we have already frequently mentioned. It is the melodic connection wherein a melodic interval of at least a third is filled in with the intervening scale tones; hence, with the interval of a fourth there are two passing tones.

Most important here is that the initial and final tones of the figure should be consonant. Should passing tones connect a fifth, then of course not all three tones can be dissonant.

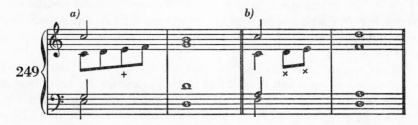

The *e* (249*a*) is consonant. Both passing tones connecting a fourth can be dissonant (249*b*). The passing tones, too, can appear in more than one voice at the same time.

Parallel octaves and fifths created by passing tones are to be judged precisely as before.

The older theory holds that the parallels are not cancelled by the passing tone and are not hidden by the suspension. And that is right; they are not better, and not worse, than unhidden parallels. The pupil is often inclined to attach a suspension to a passing tone. Even that is not allowed in strict, all too strict, composition. But there is really no reason to object to such a combination; it is in fact a common occurrence in the masterworks.

Passing tones in several voices at once often produce complete new chords that could be considered either independent or passing chords. In reality they are independent; only, the theory of passing harmony, which would impose its accidental harmonies, explains them as dependent.

The passing tones can of course also be borrowed from the chromatic scale. That cannot cause the pupil any difficulty, if he thinks of our secondary dominants and keeps in mind the sense of passing tones as a simple melodic form (scale segment).

The passing tone performs outstanding services with vagrant chords, where, for example, a reinterpretation brought about by a passing tone allows two modulations such as those in Examples 255*a* and *b* to be joined in one phrase (255*c*).

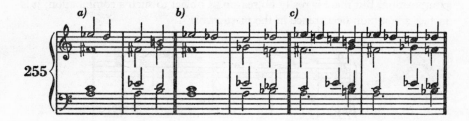

An excellent way of modulating; or Example 256*a*.

That will work without vagrant chords, too (256*b*); here the transition from major to minor is greatly facilitated by the chromatic introduction of the *e♭* and by the passing *b♭* and *a♭*.

The following passing harmony also appears frequently.

And even these:

Obviously, the closer the pupil stays to the prototype, the scale, especially the chromatic, the bolder the combinations he can write.

Whenever altered or vagrant chords are involved, the effect will most often in fact be rather mild. Frequently, vagrant chords can go through passing tones to unaltered chords and vice versa, unaltered to vagrant, a useful technique for modulating as well as for enriching the cadence.

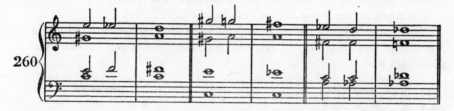

Here, and in many other examples, we see how passing tones may create chords, chords that are familiar, well-established forms. Thus, it is again apparent how unjustified is that classification which assumes accidental harmonic structures. How it simply makes a virtue out of necessity by not acknowledging as chords those chords that it cannot accommodate in the system. We can again recognize the correctness of this statement by remembering that those chords already accommodated also sprang from none other than just such melodic requirements. That happens only out of necessity. But the virtue is therefore correspondingly meager.

To list everything that can appear is naturally impossible. The pupil will do best, as I said before, to produce first the prototype of the passing tones, the scalewise melodic segment. Also, of course, chromatic scale segments. There is a certain exercise which, as it is given in almost all textbooks, I have to reject: in it the pupil is to add decorative suspensions and passing tones to a phrase already sketched out in half or whole notes. This assignment is ridiculous, inartistic to the highest degree. This decoration with ornaments, 'tattooing', as Adolf Loos says, is a childish activity. I have no objection if the pupil undertakes an occasional correction in a piece he has completed, in which there are already passing tones and suspensions *that occurred to him simultaneously with the melody, as harmony*. He might, for example, improve a stiff-sounding connection with a passing tone or a faltering rhythm with a suspension. There is little to criticize in such corrections. But what the pupil must strive for is the ability *to invent* these non-harmonic tones *together with the rest of the harmony*. That is not at all as difficult as it appears; [as] an incidental, separate exercise [the writing of non-harmonic tones is] quite superfluous. The pupil must indeed not overuse passing tones or changing tones, so long as they still do not come to him spontaneously. Of course the pedagogical purpose that the commonly used exercise can serve is not to be discarded: the pupil is compelled thereby to keep the basic harmonies constantly in mind and not to lose sight of them among the non-harmonic tones. Nevertheless, I could not bring myself to assign this exercise; for it is too mechanical for the pupil who at this stage must already possess considerable harmonic skill. The actual accomplishment, even with successful solutions, is too trifling; but even more disturbing is the deceit lurking behind this procedure: an insignificant idea is superficially enriched by means of embellishments that do not suit it. I would rather recommend that the pupil experiment often at the piano or on paper, looking for figures and connections, and then work out what he finds in a little piece. Working out, elaborating – that is a better exercise than decorating, for it fosters the ability to introduce something correctly and to continue it correctly.

The changing tone (*Wechselnote*) can best be explained as a notated ornament (*Manier*) or as a motive. Usually, at least in its simplest forms, it belongs to a figure that consists of one or more non-harmonic tones and circumscribes a consonant tone.

We might say we already have such a changing tone in the trill, or the trill with turn. Written out it appears as follows:

In the conventional ornaments – I have taken those quoted here from Heinrich Schenker's work, *Ein Beitrag zur Ornamentik*[1] – the pupil will find numerous models for such standard formulas which, played slowly, are unquestionably changing tones, even if one will not acknowledge them as such when played more rapidly. Of course in almost all of the ornaments a tone is circumscribed by its *neighbor* tones. The changing tone, however, does not have to be so, as is shown by the interrupted suspension, which springs from a fusion of suspension and changing tone. Usual forms of the changing tone are, among others, the following:

Of course chromaticism can also enter into the formation of changing tones; at first it should perhaps be used with some caution.

The basic idea of the anticipation is just the reverse of that of the suspension. Whereas with the latter one or more voices are delayed during a change of harmony, with the former it is just the other way around: these voices get there early, so to speak.

In 265*a* and *b*, where *a* illustrates suspension, *b* anticipation, both are notated

[1] (*neue revidierte und vermehrte Auflage*; Vienna: Universal-Edition, n.d. [1954?]), pp. 34, 38, 45, and 54. Schenker's 'Contribution to the Study of Ornamentation' was first published in 1908.]

side by side for comparison. The anticipation, like the suspension, can take place either in a single voice or in several. Nothing more need be said on this subject.

Once the pupil has become familiar with non-harmonic tones in the way previously recommended, he should have no protracted difficulties in exploiting the possibilities they afford; and he does not need the exercise that I have proscribed: he does not need to make a semblance of flesh and blood by hanging rags here and there on a skeleton. On the contrary, by following the recommended way he will acquire the ability to introduce those sonorities (*Zusammenklänge*), those created by 'non-harmonic' tones, with the same foresight he gives to his harmonies (*Harmonien*). They will thus cease to be accident and begin to be [to manifest] law – only, law that he cannot put into words. That a real master has never done something so inartistic, not even under the pretext of the harmonic sketch to be worked out later, ought to be clear to anyone who takes a close look at a Bach Chorale. I give here [in full] the one previously cited from the *St. Matthew Passion*:[1]

[[1] *Supra*, Example 225*d*, p. 301.]

I think the first glance ought to show that Bach was not merely hanging ornaments onto an otherwise deficient or uninteresting harmony to give it luster. Just take out each individual voice and look at it by itself. You will find that they are nothing less than melodies, which are often just as beautiful as the chorale melody itself. And this is an aim entirely different from that external [adornment]! Then, try to leave out what might be considered accidental changing tones. Generally, it is almost impossible, or the result is at least so clumsy that, although it could be by an ornament lover, it is not by Bach. Perhaps [such deletion of 'ornaments' is] not always entirely impossible; for, even though what one considers ornament was conceived along with everything else, there is still enough left over that is good. One can of course go on living if the little toe is lost; but it is no longer a well-constructed foot.

[Consider], for example, in the very first phrase, the passing tones in the bass, tenor, and alto. It is clear that they form chords; for their harmonic purpose is to harmonize a melody that comes three times (note the repeat sign and the penultimate phrase) in such a way that the harmonization, which could easily turn out to be deficient in chord changes, defines in vigorous strokes the chief features of the key (I, IV, V) without becoming so rich that a later repetition cannot be still richer and surprising. Hence, the degrees from the subdominant region are disposed of on the weak beats and are consequently less binding; but their pace is faster and they come twice, whereby their relative weakness is compensated. Thus, unequal forces are held in balance by applying them to unequal arms of a lever.

Or [consider] how in the second phrase the principal key is hesitantly introduced. Even at the very next to the last moment (*) an *a* in the bass acts as if the major key is to come. The reason is clear: the chorale wavers between *D* major and *b* minor, as the cadences make plain; a too definite *b* minor at the beginning would hardly be advantageous. The decision comes later. The purpose of the *a* is, then, to postpone! Thus, it is no ornament!!

The third phrase: the eighth notes, which came at the beginning as imitation of the first four notes of the melody, turn here into a little independent motive that dominates the figuration of the entire middle part. Hence, this motive is no mere ornament; it is rather a structural component, even if of secondary importance.

In the next phrases the music becomes so rich that I prefer to make no attempt to describe or explain what happens. Here one can no longer speak briefly. The relation of chords to one another in a true work of art is so definite, so well grounded in structural necessity – no matter whether their fundamental meaning is more or less obvious, whether they appear in a more imposing manner or are only carried along by the 'ornamental' movement of voices – this relation, I say, is so definite, so necessary, that these voices constituting the chords can never be seriously interpreted as aimless decoration, however much they may contribute incidentally to the ornamentation of the whole, however mobile and interlaced their lines may be. One could no more omit them than one could omit something similar in a construction of steel. An *Ornamentierer*, a decorator, should first try out his bold scheme – not adding what he supposes is merely beautiful until later – should first submit it to a practical test in a steel construction before he recommends it to a pupil. And he should stand underneath during the construction; he will never again recommend it. Only in art do we find such lack of conscience,* where there is no steel beam to fall on one's head and give the minimal intelligence its due. One could object that it is only a matter here of assigned exercises; of course the pupil will stop doing it that way later on. But those are immoral assignments, and one cannot learn morality by practicing immorality. One would then simply have to regard the example the teacher sets as an example of what not to do. But that is too much to expect of the pupil and too little of the teacher.

* In other crafts as well, understanding of the structural and other purposes of ornaments unfortunately seems slight; this lack of understanding leads some to thoughtless omission, others to senseless inclusion. Thus I had to drop a new watch several times before it occurred to me, why I kept dropping it. It slipped through my fingers because, although it was modern, it was too smooth. Then I understood that the casing of my old watch was engraved so that, because of its fairly rough surface, it would be easier to hold on to. As a contrast to this hatred of ornament, note the book-binders' love of ornament. They apparently consider the binding nothing more than a decoration of the book; and perhaps they like it, they think it is 'artistic', only when they can regard most of what they produce as decoration, hence, as senseless. Thus, for example, they glue onto the ends of the book a 'ready-woven' headband, which looks 'more beautiful' than the sewn, 'hand-stitched' ones but does not fulfil its purpose, does not hold the book together at top and bottom. The purpose is unclear to them, hence unimportant. And that is by no means the end of this nonsense; just consider the specially coined word 'aufkaschieren'. To protect the edges of the paper and cloth and the ends of the threads from wearing out, they were hidden (*kaschiert*, from *cacher* – to hide) by means of one or more layers of paper glued on. Whenever now a sheet of paper is stuck onto the cardboard, which easily becomes frayed from rubbing, this is called '*aufkaschieren*'! [This footnote was added in the revised edition.]

XVIII A FEW REMARKS CONCERNING NINTH CHORDS

The ninth chord is the stepchild of the system. Although it is at least as legitimate a product of the system as the seventh chord, it nonetheless comes repeatedly under question.[1] Why it is questioned is obscure. The system begins to be artificial as soon as it fashions the minor triad after the major triad. Thus, the formation of a seventh chord by adding the seventh is of course not a necessary consequence of this initial organization, but it is a possible consequence. If it is possible, however, then ninth chords, eleventh chords, etc., are also possible; and at least one advantage could be gained from this possibility in that the system of superimposed thirds could be extended. The further advantage would surely follow that much of what today lies outside the system, in the sphere of the accidental harmonies, could still be brought into it without losing the control provided by the root progressions. I could do that myself; why I do not, I shall say later.[2]

As far as I know the most important objection to the ninth chords is that their inversions are not supposed to be practicable. I suspect also this silly hindrance, that the ninth chord is not easy to represent in four-part writing; for the sake of the ninth chord we should need five or six voices. One could of course disregard the analogy with the inversions of seventh chords, or at least disregard it temporarily, and use at least what there is; but theory has the tendency, whenever it has no example for something, to declare it bad, or at least [to dismiss it as] impossible. Theory too willingly says: ninth chords do not appear in inversions, hence, they are bad; or: ninth chords do not appear in inversions, hence, they just don't exist. Of course, the other way would not be right, either: namely, that the theorists should invent the inversions of ninth chords rather than wait for the composers to do so. Theory cannot and may not take the lead; it should affirm, describe, compare, and organize. Therefore, I will restrict myself to giving composers and future theorists a few incentives toward further expansion of the system, and will refrain from systematizing (*kombinieren*) forms which are certainly, to some extent, already appearing in modern works, but with a usage that is fundamentally different from what should take place here. Theory was on the right path when it affirmed the existence of ninth chords. Then it should have mentioned that inversions of ninth chords do not appear, but it could just as well have suppressed its opinion that they are bad or even impossible. To affirm the fact should have satisfied the theorist in such cases. He has done enough by supplying 'data for harmonic theory'; he does not have to make himself vulnerable and indulge in aesthetics, for then he makes a fool of himself. What is still not used today is not on that account ugly; for it may be used tomorrow, and then it will be beautiful. In my Sextet,

[1 Cf. Schenker, *Harmony*, p. 190.]   [2 Chapter XXI.]

Verklärte Nacht [measures 41–2], in the following context, I wrote the inversion of a ninth chord, the one in Example 267a at ✗, without then knowing theoretically what I was doing – I was merely following my ear.

What's worse, I see now that it is none other than that particular inversion which the theorists condemned most resolutely of all; for, since the ninth is in the bass, its simplest resolution goes to a six-four chord, and the so-called '*böse Sieben*' [bad seventh], the forbidden resolution of a seventh to an octave, occurs between two of the voices (267c). But the six-four chord could surely occur as a passing chord, or it could also have been absolutely forbidden (the old theory certainly did not shrink from such cruelties in other matters); and the 'bad seventh' could be avoided if (as in 267d) the tenor skipped to *d*♭. Only now do I understand the objection, at that time beyond my comprehension, of that concert society which refused to perform my Sextet on account of this chord (its refusal was actually so explained). Naturally: inversions of ninth chords just don't exist; hence, no performance, either, for how can one perform something that does not exist. And I had to wait a few years. To be sure, when it was then actually performed, nobody noticed anymore that a ninth chord occurs there in the fourth inversion. Today, of course, that sort of thing disturbs no man who is to be taken seriously. In *Salome* yet other, quite different ninth chords occur. Just to name *one* work that is not only performed but is today highly esteemed even by such as at that time could not tolerate my ninth chord.

Therefore, as I said, the ninth chord and its inversions exist today, or at least they can exist. The pupil will easily find examples in the literature. It is not necessary to set up special laws for its treatment. If one wants to be careful, one will be able to use the laws that pertain to the seventh chords: that is, dissonances resolve by step downward, the root leaps a fourth upward.

II III IV VI VII

Watch out for fifths!

But even the deceptive-cadence resolution must actually work as well here as it does with the seventh chord. For, if the seventh can be sustained, the ninth can surely also be sustained while the root ascends.

269

V IV   V VI   I II   II III   II I

III IV III II IV V IV III VI V VII I VII VI

All that does occur, at least as phenomena of voice leading, hence is already justified thereby (for example, as passing harmony); and it surely follows from

270

my presentations that the system of dissonances completes its task satisfactorily once it accommodates the things that occur in the voice leading. Should one try also to leave the dissonance by skip one would advance still further.

To prove the existence of the ninth chord, apart from its occurrence as a suspension, it should really be enough to mention the dominant-seventh-ninth chords with major or minor ninth, chords that are not disputed by anyone. If one does not wish to accept the ninth chords erected on the secondary triads, one must nevertheless at least acknowledge that in the sense of the secondary dominants major and minor ninth chords can be made on every degree, even if all cannot be used immediately and unconditionally as diatonic chords.

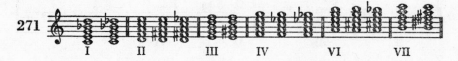

271

I   II   III   IV   VI   VII

As long as they have minor ninths it is no more difficult to relate them to the key than it is the diminished seventh chords that are derived from them; and those with major ninths are certainly no more difficult than the corresponding seventh chords. Obviously one could apply to them all those alterations that are customary with seventh chords, for example (272):

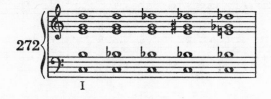

272

I

The possibility of using them is unquestionable when we regard them as vagrant chords or connect them with vagrant chords, as in the example from my Sextet or in Example 273a.

273

The resolutions in 273a are taken from the *Harmonielehre* by A[ugust] Halm (*Sammlung Göschen*),[1] an otherwise very fine little work. There are plenty of first-rate things in it; yet he calls these connections 'outrageous' and declines to 'ascribe any undeserved, fundamental value to them'. For he puts them in root position (273b), because, as he says, the ninth chord is not invertible (particularly with the authentic resolution, root progression a fourth upward).

273

[1 (Leipzig: G. J. Göschen'sche Verlagshandlung, 1902), pp. 118–19 and Example 97c.]

However, one could still at least try to invert it, with a different resolution; no parallel fifths appear then, if these are what is outrageous. It is remarkable that such a sensible fellow does not hit upon that, when he is so very close. The blinders of the system! We have reason to be astounded at all the things man is capable of inventing. We could wonder, though, with equally good reason, at how much he has not invented even though he was close to it. Somewhat more outrageousness in thinking and less fear of outrages in aesthetics, and it would go better, far better! The pupil will do well, in using ninth chords, to try again at first the very simplest application. Then he can of course try out variants after the manner of secondary dominants and in the sense of the suggestions given here, later the connection with vagrant chords, as well. Of course it will be best for him here to impose the strictest laws upon himself. The more he finds in this way that is admissible, the greater his advantage. As for freedom – one can see to that for oneself.[1]

[1 *Die Freiheit 'kann man schon allein'*. Cf. Schoenberg's remarks on 'Freedom' on pp. 329, 331, 395 and 396.]

XIX SOME ADDITIONS AND SCHEMATIC PRESENTATIONS TO ROUND OUT THE SYSTEM

1. ALTERATIONS OF TRIADS, SEVENTH CHORDS, AND NINTH CHORDS

The most important chromatic modifications that may be undertaken with triads were already made possible for the pupil in what was said about secondary dominants, about the relations to the minor subdominant, about the Neapolitan sixth, the augmented six-five chord, etc. The following generalizations repeat what was already shown and fill in what is still missing. Not, of course, with any claim to completeness. Thus, upward alterations of a major third remain unmentioned here. Not because I consider them impossible, for I do include them among the alterations of the seventh chords. Rather, because it is not my intention to include everything that is possible, no matter whether it appears in the literature or not. Hence, here I have not proceeded systematically but have mentioned for the most part only those things for which I had an example in mind or those for which I thought an example could surely be found; yes, sometimes even those for which I gave in to the temptation to invent one myself.

Every tone of a triad is altered* chromatically, upward or downward. The alteration can involve one tone, two, or all three. I cannot readily accept the idea of an altered root; I prefer the assumption that a new root is introduced. I have already set forth my reasons for this view in my discussion of the Neapolitan sixth.[1]

Lowering the third in major triads and raising the third in minor triads, we get the forms already familiar to us:

274

* The derivation of the word *alterieren* from [Latin] *alter* (other) allows it to be interpreted as *verändern* [to change or exchange]; it is probably better, however, to assume: whenever one alters (*alteriert*) a tone, one uses the *other* tone, in place of the diatonic. This points toward the substitution, often mentioned here, of the chromatic scale for major and minor. Language usage in technical matters of music, by its inclination to abbreviate expressions, spoils so much so thoroughly that the restoration of the original meaning is almost impossible. Such is the case, I think, with the expression: 'in the fourth circle of fifths upward' or 'into the fourth circle of fifths upward', which is apparently short for: 'In the circle of fifths four steps (or segments or degrees) upward.' It does not especially have to be said that I use such abbreviations only with great reluctance, yet my courage fails me when I think of introducing the correct, old usage as an innovation.
[This footnote was added in the revised edition.]
[1 *Supra*, pp. 234–5.]

By raising and lowering the fifth in the major and the minor triad:

275

By raising the fifth and lowering the third in the major triad:

276

By lowering third and fifth in the major triad, of fifth alone in the minor:

277

By lowering the fifth and raising the third in the minor triad:

278

By lowering the root in the major or minor triad:

279

By lowering root and third in the major triad:

280

By raising the fifth and lowering the root in the major and minor triad (with, at the same time, enharmonic change);

281

By raising the fifth, lowering third and root in the major triad, raising fifth and third, lowering the root (enharmonic change) in the minor:

282

By lowering the third and raising the root in the major triad, or raising the root in the minor: Example 283*a*; lowered fifth and raised root in the major triad, lowered fifth, raised third and root in the minor triad: Example 283*b*; lowered third and fifth, raised root in the major triad, lowered fifth and raised root in the minor triad: Example 283*c*.

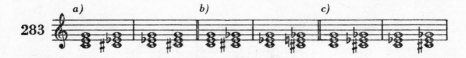

When the root is altered, these alterations produce, in some cases, chords that are to be referred to another fundamental, as has been said. In other cases it is appropriate, if one does not wish to enter the current, idle strife over orthography, to make enharmonic changes, for example, to write *c–eb–ab* instead of *c–eb–g♯*, even though the rule for alteration is usually given as follows: the upward alteration is expressed by ♯ and × (or ♮), the downward by ♭, ♭♭, or ♮; or, more generally: the alteration is expressed by putting the appropriate accidental in front of the same note.

In place of a complicated notation that often results from this pedantic exactness, I prefer to write the symbol that gives a familiar chord. Such will be possible with the majority of these chords. In other cases one may concentrate on the individual voice leading and notate *that*, at least, simply. Consequently, I would substitute Example 284*c* for 284*b* (as in 284*d*, from the Scherzo of the Piano Sonata, Op. 26, by Beethoven).

The sonorities resulting from these alterations are chords in their own right. Whoever so desires may regard them as passing phenomena. One can do that so much the more easily since, after all, if one thinks about tonality, [one can see that] everything, with the exception of the first degree, [the tonic], is so to speak passing, or at least going – everything is in motion.

Example 285 illustrates simpler instances, 286, more complicated.

Perhaps one or other of these chords is harsh. For example, the one from Example 283c[1], that appears in 286 at † (also on other degrees). It sounds like an incomplete dominant seventh chord; that the third is missing makes it unwieldy. Yet, it is not wholly unusable. The fact that one which is certainly harsh occurs in 'classical' music will perhaps appease even those who are sensitive, if they consider that here their sensitivity to harsh chords is analogous to the sensitivity of Figaro. Let us not forget that Figaro did not sprain his toe: this pain was merely his excuse.

In a similar fashion one can undertake alterations of seventh and ninth chords. The alteration of the root can be absolutely disregarded here. The alteration of the seventh or ninth will in the majority of cases produce no new forms. Nevertheless, it will be possible to refer certain connections back to such derivation and to write them only where they emerge chromatically. If one just wants to! If one would not just be content to acknowledge that, although the melodic occurrence of passing tones (etc.) did evoke the harmonic occurrence of altered chords, the recollection of this their origin still does not absolutely have to be spelled out in composing. Unlike the snail with its shell, a composition does not have to drag around with it forever, wherever it goes, a

[1 For Schoenberg's incorrect citing of Example 283c, read Example 283b, of which the second chord is shown at first dagger in Example 286 above. The second dagger shows the same chord standing on another degree. The notation is, of course, enharmonic in both cases (in the first, G♭ stands for F♯; in the second, G♯ stands for A♭).]

motivic etymology, an exact, legal proof of its right to exist. Such a chord could very likely be a phenomenon produced by voice leading, but it is not used in a certain place on account of this qualification; it is there because it is a chord, like any other.

I shall restrict myself to suggesting possibilities of altering the seventh chords and to showing a few connections.

For the present the pupil should still abide by the view that (let us once again be reminded) a tone is altered primarily to create a leading tone. The alteration upward will readily continue by yet another half step upward, the alteration downward, which produces a descending leading tone, by another half step downward. But it can happen that an altered tone is sustained, occasionally also that it sets off in the direction contrary to that indicated by its leading-tone tendency. The [recommendation above] will at least serve as a guide in judging such phenomena as that in Example 287 at ⌀, whose feasibility may be called into question. The alterations were shown here from the dominant seventh chord only. To work through the secondary seventh and ninth chords the same way is to some extent superfluous because many forms are duplicated; moreover, the discussion of all these chords would far overstep the limits of this book. The pupil can easily try all that out himself. The other chords only lead of course to other degrees of the tonality, but beyond that there is no difference. To the questions, how they are to be introduced, and whether the pupil should use them, I have indeed already given my answers.

As we can see, even those alterations whose possible applications are not evident at first glance can produce good effects. Naturally, a melodic voice leading is responsible for part of this effect, and one will be inclined to consider the alterations as chromatic passing tones. But one should not, for the reference to roots is always a more appropriate aid to harmonic analysis than is melodic justification. The latter says something only about the origin of the chord. The former, however, gives a uniform account of its uses and its tendencies.

The 'aesthetic' justification of these connections is indisputable. Their harmonic effect is good here in itself; once the power of the motive, the melody, is added, then their possibilities for use become substantially richer.

Example 289 presents alterations of the ninth chord, Example 290 a few possibilities for the use of such alterations. Here I have kept to the practice of having the altered tone continue in the direction of the alteration. As the seventh chord can be resolved by a deceptive progression, so can of course also the ninth chord and the altered ninth chord. And, since even very circumspect theorists assume that the seventh of the seventh chord can ascend, as proved by Example 291, which appears in almost every textbook, then one will surely have to

concede that the ninth of the ninth chord can also ascend, chromatically at least.

That naturally increases the possibilities for handling the ninth chord.

Example 292 shows two ascending ninths. The pupil can search out others for himself.

2. ABBREVIATION OF SET PATTERNS THROUGH OMISSION OF INTERMEDIATE STEPS

The principle expressed here is only relatively new to us. Nevertheless, I should not like to neglect giving it here in this form, because it can clarify a number of things. We have often spoken about the effect of the cliché, of the formula, which is characterized this way: frequently recurring usages become fixed patterns with one explicit, unmistakable meaning. So unmistakable that once we hear the very beginning we immediately and automatically expect the usual continuation: the formula is obliged to lead to a predetermined conclusion. Assuming this, we can now even omit the middle parts of the formula, set beginning and end right together, 'abbreviate', so to speak, the whole pattern, set it down merely as premise and conclusion.[1] Perhaps the cadential progression IV–V is already such an abbreviation; indeed, I did mention that it is best construed as standing for IV–II–V. That treatment of the Neapolitan sixth where it goes directly to V is the same sort of abbreviation.

For it should actually progress as follows:

Perhaps the plagal cadences are the same sort of thing. Perhaps they sound incomplete just because something is omitted. Namely: instead of IV–V–I or II–V–I we have IV–I and II–I. The same principle is evident in the progression in Example 295*a*, which comes from that in 295*b* and occurs in cadences or half cadences.

[1 That is, the intermediate 'reasoning' is omitted as self-evident.]

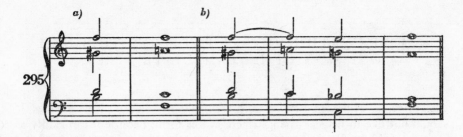

Such abbreviations can in general be undertaken only with progressions that have a definite function, hence, primarily in cadences. For example:

3. TRIADS CONNECTED WITH ALL OTHER TRIADS AND SEVENTH CHORDS; ALSO, ALL SEVENTH CHORDS WITH ONE ANOTHER

In the following schematic presentation a major and a minor triad are connected with all other major, minor, and diminished triads. The majority of these progressions are already familiar. A few less common ones are presented in little phrases in Example 298. There the diminished triad is not considered.

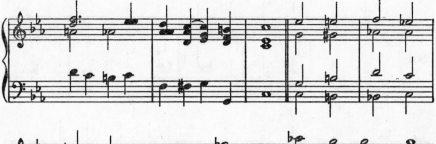

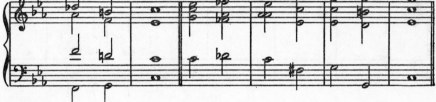

Example 299 shows the same thing with a triad and the dominant seventh chords, Example 300, one dominant seventh chord with the others.

In Examples 301 and 302 there are some connections that are not immediately comprehensible. It is evident that under certain conditions their effect can be quite good. The same could of course be shown of ninth chords, as well. I shall leave it to the pupil who wants to make it his business to put together such connections himself. Everything can turn out well if it comes at the right place. The melodic line of the soprano and that of the bass will be especially useful for improving the effect. But the rhythm is not to be entirely disregarded, either. Sometimes a progression will be greatly enhanced if its chords are connected by means of passing tones. Nevertheless, the use of passing tones, changing tones, and suspensions, since it introduces quarter notes – if not quicker note values as well – means increased motion, which will not be entirely without influence on what follows. I recommend the following: if, once the pupil has the ability to invent passing tones, changing tones, and suspensions along with the harmony, he then sometimes gets himself into quarter-note movement, he will best continue it to the end, because this procedure will probably be most consistent with his ability to handle rhythm. It is not impossible to make the quarters disappear – by avoiding them first on the strong beat, later on the weak, or in the melody and then in the middle voices. But it is by no means easy.

4. SOME OTHER DETAILS: POSSIBILITIES OF THE ASCENDING SEVENTH; BASSES FOR THE DIMINISHED SEVENTH CHORD; A CHORD OF MOZART; AN EIGHT-PART CHORD

If we assume that the seventh can also ascend, it becomes possible to use the diatonic seventh chord on the 1st degree of minor [a–c–e–g♯].

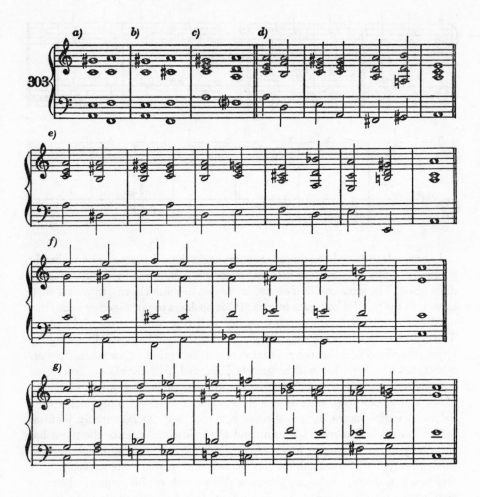

This chord can be transposed to other degrees of a key, where, especially in connection with vagrant chords, it can produce good results (Example 303*e*, *f*, *g*).

Another matter that is not for fastidious ears, but that does often occur in modern music, especially in that of R. Strauss: different bass tones for a diminished seventh chord. This treatment is based on the fact that one diminished seventh chord can be interpreted as four different ninth chords. If after each of the four (Example 304*a*) we imagine a sufficiently long pause or an event that makes the reinterpretation possible, then nothing stands in the way of connecting these four chords within one progression. And in fact that happens even in classical music. If we think it faster, however, or imagine the reinterpretation as direct, with no intermediary, then we will see how it is possible (304*b*) to play together with one diminished seventh chord a voice that consists of the four tones of a different diminished seventh chord. (This 'thinking faster' plays a leading role in fomenting evolution – in every sense: just as thinking too slowly, which easily becomes identical with 'not thinking at all', effects the contrary!) Here it may be at least helpful if (304c), whenever one writes a scale against the diminished seventh chord, the principal notes on the quarters of the measure also have these tones. But such a scale can also read as that in Example 304d, because each moment does indeed allow reinterpretation (when one

304

thinks fast). Here on the weak eighths of the bass appear the four tones that constitute the third diminished seventh chord: *e, g, b♭, d♭*. The five-part dissonant sounds there have an analogy in the pedal-point form, Example 304e; they prove to be transpositions of this *g–f♯–a–c–e♭* to three other bass tones. Hence, by the combination of the two forms 304d and e, it is explained how, in 304g, the third diminished seventh chord, too, can be written against *f♯–a–c–e♭*: each individual instance can be interpreted in itself like 304e. Since 304f is obvious, since it has just been shown upon what grounds the other eight tones can appear against one diminished seventh chord; since, therefore, for all twelve tones possible harmonic combination with the diminished seventh chord was demonstrated, it follows that every melody could be harmonized with a diminished seventh chord. We will not do so because it would not be interesting, and besides, it would be contrived. Better just to invent a new and characteristic harmony. But it would work! Naturally, that is not for fastidious ears, rather only for good ones! For those with quick perception!

I mentioned before [p. 324] a chord of Mozart that, as he uses it, goes by quickly, as passing harmony. Of course this chord can also pass slowly, for then we understand it still better. Then even fastidious ears should be able to grasp it and – notice it. This chord (Example 305a) would make an attractive sequence (305b):

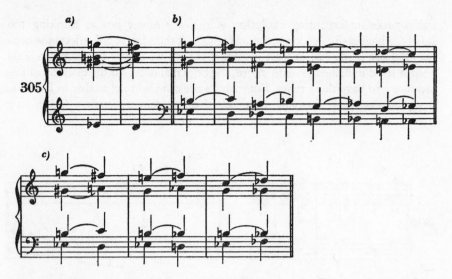

With inversions (305c) it becomes still more attractive. One can have nothing against this; it is, after all, by Mozart!

But now I should like to point out still another chord which, it is true, does not occur in Mozart's music, yet could almost appear in Bach's. The leap from the *e* in Example 306a surely needs no explanation. The way it appears at 306b, over the pedal point, can also surely occur. The same holds for the figures in 306c and *d*, which are not unusual. If we write them all to sound simultaneously, we obtain a chord made up of eight different tones (306e †). This chord could occur as shown in 306f. I do not know whether it does occur or not; but I think, in view of the example I presented from the eight-part motets of Bach [p. 327] – in which occurs a six-part chord that could hardly please fastidious ears any more than our present eight-part chord – in view of that, one can

surely say: should there be twelve-part choral writing by Bach, then perhaps this chord would occur after all! Or at least could occur – although ninth chords do not exist!

5. ADDITIONAL SCHEMES FOR MODULATING

In principle, I have used the old modulatory schemes. Nevertheless, by virtue of the systematic introduction of secondary dominants, diminished seventh chords, and the vagrant chords, the results are essentially different from what is usually achieved here. But I have used all these stronger means only to make the modulations richer and have expressly prohibited the use of these chords as actual means of modulation. My reasoning should be recalled: We have time to modulate! Also my contention that, in the works of art that use simple means for modulating, the modulation either takes place gradually or it seldom goes very far [otherwise]. When, however, a sudden and remote digression from the key does take place, it is really a different sort of thing: it then has to do with a particularly pointed contrast that is to be judged more as dynamics than as harmony. Of course it is also a harmonic matter, namely, an excursion into a harmony of the future. And in this sense it is no exception, either, but corresponds to a law, which could be formulated thus: Everything alive contains the future within it. Living means begetting and giving birth. Everything that now is strives toward what is to come.

Now that we have got to know modulation of the past and have enlarged our foundation with the means of the present, we have reached the point where we can also try out the effects of the new means that have attained independence in the meantime. Obviously new laws could be given here, if such were our aim, since new forms are at hand. On the contrary: we ought to apply the earlier laws correctly or extend them. That would not be difficult for us. For we recognized that, when the tone (or the tonic) is the power center of the harmonic events, it is a prototype rich enough to include even the most complicated phenomena under its name. It allows us to speak of it as the progenitor, even if it does perhaps carry within itself only the possibilities, not the fulfilments. For this reason I preferred to use the more complicated harmonic devices in cadences rather than in modulations. To show that the key does not necessarily have to break down by virtue of their appearance, that they do not have to modulate, was more important than to show the contrary, that they can modulate. Even the simplest chord *can* modulate. I have shown that tonality does not spring from any inevitable requirement of the fundamental tone. As long as we speak of modulations, however, tonality is presupposed just as the curved line presupposes the straight. The one is inconceivable without the other. Hence, it is more to the point to regard tonality as the large region in whose outlying districts less dependent forces resist domination by the central power. If this central power endures, however (this can depend on the will of the composer), it then forces the rebels to stay within the circle of its sovereignty, and all activity is for its benefit, for the benefit of the central power. All activity, all movement leads back to it; everything turns within the circle. This conception is actually confirmed by the facts of art. For the one musical art form that does not have such a central power, opera, is merely a proof of the other possibility: suspended tonality. But all rounded symphonic forms of the older art, all forms for which tonality is fundamental, show that digressions lead back to the key. Thus, tonality can be suspended, to be sure. But if it is present, then modulations are digressions from the principal tone, scarcely different in essence from any chord that is other than the tonic. They are just episodes of a large cadence; hence, my method of introducing the vagrant chords primarily in cadences agrees with the facts of art.

Modulations are only episodes. But such an episode, which in a cadence is presented only in concentrated form, can also be set apart and given individual treatment. Then one can present it more expansively; it can be less concentrated, more richly elaborated with greater independence of movement and clearer tendencies. That is just what we did in the earlier modulations where, for that very reason, we acquired the habit of shaping modulations broadly and gradually. Meanwhile, through the more complicated devices for modulation, we have learned possibilities for extending our efforts. Now if we have mastered the difficult task of making these devices serve the purposes of a key, then it must be that much easier to exploit them in modulating. Since I have been at all times more concerned with developing the pupil's sense of form than with stuffing him full of indigestible information, I should not like to neglect mentioning something that now seems to me worthy of attention, especially now that I am going on to recommend to him modulation by 'fast' means. I believe that harmonic richness does not come about by going through a great many keys, but by making the *richest possible use of the degrees*. In this sense a chorale of Bach is harmonically richer than most modern compositions. There was a pupil who thought he was writing something 'modern' when, in the fourth measure, he modulated from G major to Db major, then two or three measures later to B major. But within Db major and B major he behaved just as tamely as in G major, where he used scarcely more than tonic and dominant. I showed him his error by transposing everything back to G major, uncovering for him the unimportance, the monotony, and the harmonic wretchedness of his melody in its true form. He caught on when I asked him if he considered it especially reckless to carry the same philistine behavior from G major to Db and B.

Rich, varied use of the degrees (*Stufenreichtum*) is thus the most essential feature of the harmonic art. Aside from that, it is relatively unimportant which particular devices we employ. But one thing is clear: if we use vagrant chords, and especially if we use them for modulations, they must be consistent with the other harmonic events. Otherwise formal smoothness could hardly be achieved. They must fit the surroundings; hence, the surroundings should be such as require something of this nature. In a progression of pure triads, for example, the sudden reinterpretation of one of these triads as a Neapolitan sixth would hardly be consistent; and, on the other hand, it is just as unlikely that such a sudden turn would come to a satisfying close with a simple IV–V–I cadence. In the work of art, naturally, all that is quite different; and I hope the reader knows already that I am not criticizing works of art, only harmony exercises. And he remembers, I hope, what I think concerning the relation of our manual exercises to the work of art: that they have scarcely anything in common. Therefore, even my examples always turn out relatively stiff: they lack the creative impulse, the impulse that makes us the gift of form, even where it only intended expression. My exercises merely exploit a possibility; they do not spring from any inescapable necessity. Here the application of laws forms the basis of competent criticism. Here, as distinct from what may be done with works of art, a procedure like the one in question may be censured as unsuitable; the exploitation of an accidental, isolated, 'fast' means of modulation may be designated as immoral; here, it must be said: Something of that sort [a simple cadence] is not used when a sound introduced as a dominant seventh chord proceeds as an augmented four-three chord. That is repulsive; for the effect is as when one chops up an enemy even though he had already fallen and broken a leg, or, if he is already dead, shoots him still deader. And the satisfaction obtained from closing such a modulation with a simple cadence undoubtedly springs from the same sort of deceitfulness as does the excuse a man gives when, having stumbled, he pretends he was actually jumping. Once one has made a sudden turn by one of the fast means toward a remote region, then one should use it only as an allusion to the goal, a suggestion, an initial advance in that direction. And after that turn a long cadence should, so to speak, search out the middle ground between point of departure and goal, to create balance. As I asked earlier for clarity of goal, so here the phrase should indicate, by virtue of its being 'in motion', that it seeks a goal already alluded to.

If the pupil does what I recommend here, his work will perhaps not turn out any better than if he neglects to do it. He does not have to follow me here, then, if he lays greatest importance on the smoothness of his product. If he tries it nevertheless, he is sure to spoil many things, but he will have undergone something that makes all the difference. He will have made it difficult for himself. Yet it is more moral to fail in following this way, than it is to succeed in following an easy one. For success means nothing, or, at most, that one made it too easy for oneself.

With these ideas in mind I shall now place at the pupil's disposal some more schemes for modulating.

A major key can be turned by simple means into the parallel minor key, and conversely the minor into the parallel major.

There are naturally numerous means that can be used. Here mainly the Neapolitan sixth and the augmented six-five (four-three, two) chords were used.

This scheme can be used with a modulation that is to go to a major key by setting it up to go to the parallel minor key and then turning that minor into its parallel major. And conversely, if minor is the goal, first to the parallel major which is then changed to minor.

These will easily recall the methods used in the third and fourth circles of fifths [Chapter XII], methods that rest on similar principles. They can of course also be done with different means.

Another kind:

One steers toward a vagrant chord, a Neapolitan sixth, an augmented six-five chord, an augmented triad, etc., and thereby takes the first step toward modulation.

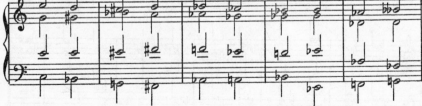

i) C—A

That can be said differently. Namely: every major triad can be interpreted as a Neapolitan sixth chord, every dominant seventh chord as an augmented six-five chord. Naturally, such should not be the sole means of modulation.

Example 310 shows something that the pupil should practice. A progression of two chords (+ +) is continued in different ways. With this practice, what is important is not so much that the whole thing should aim at a definite modulation, but that the pupil explore the pivotal possibilities of such a chord.

a) C—F♯

310

b) a—f

In Example 311 the same thing is tried with another chord progression
(++).

Example 312 shows how one can work toward a key by very roundabout
ways. It is essential in such modulations that the goal should always be suggested at the outset.

I myself do *not* consider these examples very good, most of all because no motive is present. By adding richer movement, changing tones, passing tones, and suspensions, the examples can be readily improved, particularly if, as in Example 313, individual details actually develop gradually into a motive. But even here I must repeat once again: Let the pupil try this only when he invents the quicker notes simultaneously, right along with the others.

In these last exercises I have deliberately retained, in general, the sort of orthography customarily prescribed. I wanted to show thereby how inadequate it is even for clarifying derivation, yet how heavily it taxes readability. Only in those places where I myself should not be able to get through it at all did I make enharmonic changes. I shall have to be pardoned for treating this question so lightly, for I am proud of [my attitude]. I am proud that I have not devoted a moment of serious reflection to that which generally makes up the why and wherefore of the academicians, but have gone directly over from ignorance of such matters to [first-hand] knowledge. To the knowledge that here lies an insoluble problem whose existence is to be blamed on the inadequacy of our notational system.

6. SOME ADDITIONAL DETAILS

Something similar to what was shown in the fourth section of this chapter, concerning the diminished seventh chord: There we saw the possibility of putting any melody over *a single* diminished seventh chord. Here we shall see, conversely, how a melody can be put over any diminished seventh chord (or over the corresponding ninth chord). This is nothing new; such can be found even in the music of the classical composers.

The suspension in Example 314*a* and the 'returning' passing tone (a changing tone) over a diminished seventh chord are very familiar phenomena. The *e♭* suspended before a ninth chord is nothing new either (314*b*). Every time this diminished seventh chord is referred to a different root (314*c*), this melody then acquires a different meaning (different spelling). It can be set without question over three of the roots (*c*, *f♯*, and *e♭*); consequently, the melody also appears over the fourth (in classical works), so that Example 314*d* becomes possible. Combination of the preceding gives 314*e*, where the melody appears with all four ninth chords. The same procedure can be applied also to the figure 314*f*, thereby making possible 314*g* and leading in turn to 314*h*; then in 314*i* the respective ninth chords are resolved by progression a fourth upward. Out of the two figures one can put together 314*k* or 314*l*, and the same possibilities are seen to hold with this melody, too (314*m*). Obviously one can treat 314*n* in the same manner, and of course one can try similar things with other figures and over other vagrant chords. One of these possibilities I will show in the next chapter, with the augmented triad. Perhaps no one will have much interest in putting these four figures, as they are here, directly next to one another. But that it could be done admits their use for something better: for harmonic variation, which opens up another route along which a phrase [or composition] may continue.

Something else: A connection that is also not infrequent and is best conceived as imitation of the diminished seventh chord (Example 315*a*):

It reminds us very much of Example 315*b* and is familiar to us as 315*c*, as one of the resolutions of the augmented six-five (four-three) chord. Moreover, it occurs also with the lowered fifth (*d♭* – 315*d*) or as a kind of ninth chord (315*e*). Indeed, even 315*f* is nothing uncommon. This progression can give valuable assistance with modulations. The first chord has dominant character here, so to speak, in spite of the descending bass progression [quasi IV–I?].

Another observation is to be made concerning the six-four chord, particularly as used in the cadence. Today, it is of course handled rather freely. In general, if it is used at all, its character is customarily preserved, either by introducing or resolving it in a manner similar to that of older music. Most frequently of all, its characteristic [effect] is preserved by putting it at suitably accentuated places, whereby it arouses the usual expectations. But the departure from the six-four even Brahms treated more freely. I do not mean so much instances like that in the third bar of the 'Sapphic Ode', where the six-four chord enters in such a way that the bass melody appears to be going farther (it did in fact introduce the chord before [in the first bar]; the bass melody is, after all, made up of the chord tones of the tonic triad); nor am I referring to the instance in the penultimate bar of the same song, where a six-four chord emerges by virtue of the anticipation in the bass.[1] I mean, rather, something of the order of the one in 'Botschaft', measures 14–19, where Brahms leaves the six-four chord freely by leap.[2]

Brahms conceives the six-four chord here simply as another position of the triad (like the six chord), which can go immediately to a different position, to

[1 There is nothing of the sort in the penultimate bar of the 'Sapphic Ode'. Perhaps Schoenberg had in mind the six-four chord in the fourth bar from the end.]

[2 Measures 18–19 are quoted in Example 316. When this same passage returns (nine measures from the end), the six-four chord resolves normally: I_4^6–V_2.]

the root position. More recent music naturally takes even more liberties with it; and thus we see here how the development of art actually confirms the principle mentioned at the outset: one no longer takes great pains with dissonances, once the ear has become familiar with them.

7. CONCERNING FLUCTUATING AND SUSPENDED TONALITY[1]

Now, before closing this chapter, I should like to keep a promise I made earlier: to speak of fluctuating and suspended tonality. Such is not readily illustrated by little phrases because it most surely involves the articulation (*Gliederung*) of distinct parts of a composition. Whoever wants to take a look at it will find many examples in the music of Mahler and others. Actually, one does not even have to look farther than the last movement of Beethoven's *E*-minor Quartet (Op. 59, No. 2) to find an example of fluctuating tonality. (Other examples: the last movements of Op. 127 and Op. 130, and the finale of Schumann's Piano Quintet.) Beethoven begins in a sort of *C* major which, however, keeps reaching over toward *e* minor. Indeed (because *C* is somewhat distant), it reaches over for the most part even as far as the dominant of the dominant ($f\sharp-a\sharp-c\sharp$), which can almost be construed as the dominant itself. Since, then, there are good classical models, I do not have to be ashamed of producing something of this sort myself. Two pregnant examples of fluctuating tonality from my own compositions are: *Orchesterlied*, Op. 8, No. 5, 'Voll jener Süsse', which wavers principally between *D♭* and *B* major; and Op. 6, No. 7 (*Lied*), 'Lockung', which expresses an *E♭*-major tonality without once in the course of the piece giving an *E♭*-major triad in such a way that one could regard it as a pure tonic.[2] The one time it does appear, it has a tendency, at least, toward the subdominant. Neither of these was at all contrived; they were invented! Hence, nothing for imitation.[3] But if one takes a look at them, one will know what I

[1 *Schwebend*: fluctuating (suspended, not yet decided); *aufgehoben*: suspended (not in effect, cancelled). In his *Structural Functions of Harmony* (p. 111), Schoenberg explicitly translated *schwebende Tonalität* as 'suspended tonality'. There is no mention in that work of the term *aufgehobene Tonalität*. What Schoenberg called 'roving harmony' in his later book (pp. 3 and 164–5) conforms to his description here of *aufgehobene Tonalität*.

Here he tried to make the following distinction: Tonality is ambiguous, it fluctuates; or tonality is (at least momentarily) lost, suspended.]

[2 Cf. Schoenberg's analysis of 'Lockung' in his *Structural Functions of Harmony*, pp. 111–13.]

[3 That is, these songs are not mere examples for exercises. Cf. his remarks at the end of the following paragraph.]

mean [by the term *schwebende Tonalität*] and what rich resources must be at hand to bring it about.

Yet, to show what is involved, I shall try to say something more about it. If the key is to fluctuate, it will have to be established somewhere. But not too firmly; it should be loose enough to yield. Therefore, it is advantageous to select two keys that have some chords in common, for example, the Neapolitan sixth or the augmented six-five chord. *C* major and *D*♭ major or *a* minor and *B*♭ major are pairs of keys so related. If we add the relative minor keys, by fluctuating between *C* major and *a* minor, *D*♭ major and *b*♭ minor, then new relations appear: *a* minor and *D*♭ major, *C* major and *b*♭ minor; the dominant of *b*♭ minor is the augmented six-five chord of *a* minor, etc. It is evident that vagrant chords will play a leading role here: diminished and augmented seventh chords, Neapolitan sixth, augmented triad. I have tried repeatedly to put examples together, but I cannot bring it off 'in a vacuum'. I think the pupil will find out how to do it sooner than I [how to make such examples]. And even if not: he at least does not have to produce a model!

Further documentation is to be found in Wagner. For example, the Prelude to *Tristan*. Note that *a* minor, although it is to be inferred from every passage, is scarcely ever sounded in the whole piece. It is always expressed in circuitous ways; it is constantly avoided by means of deceptive cadences.

As for suspended (*aufgehoben*) tonality, the theme is undoubtedly the crux of the matter. It must give opportunity for such harmonic looseness through its characteristic figurations. The purely harmonic aspect will involve almost exclusive use of explicitly vagrant chords. Every major or minor triad could be interpreted as a key, even if only in passing. The classical development sections are not too far removed from this. There, to be sure, at any particular moment, a key may be unmistakably expressed, yet so lacking in support that it can be lost at any time. Examples from the literature are easy to find in the works of modern composers, as well as in sections of Bruckner's and Hugo Wolf's music.

8. THE CHROMATIC SCALE AS A BASIS FOR TONALITY

I am writing this chapter after completing the book, because of some objections and criticisms raised by Dr. Robert Neumann[1] (a young philosopher, whose keen understanding makes me extremely curious about his own work). His criticisms were twofold: First, that the principle by which dominants are constructed on secondary degrees is nowhere made explicit, and that one can therefore conclude that the secondary dominants were introduced only because

[1 Cf. *supra*, p. 25.]

they can be extracted from the church modes. Secondly, that I established no relationship between the key and certain minor chords, but just introduced them generally in a schematic presentation (pp. 36off. [Example 297]). The first criticism I find in part unwarranted; the second gives me an idea.

Concerning the first:

It is not incorrect that the principles of my presentation are nowhere drawn together and stated continuously. It is questionable whether that is absolutely necessary, since they are after all applied again and again at the appropriate places. Nevertheless, I shall recapitulate them here. It will then be evident how uniform my presentation is, although it does fall short of being a system.

Most essential is the following psychological assumption: The development of the harmonic resources is explained primarily through the conscious or unconscious imitation of a prototype; every imitation so produced can then itself become a prototype that can in turn be imitated.

On the basis of this assumption are explained: the scale as horizontal, the chords as vertical imitations (more or less faithful) of the natural prototype, the tone. The faithful, but incomplete, vertical imitation, the major triad, produces jointly with the scale another, a more remote imitation, the minor triad. The other diatonic chords are explained then as imitation of the idea 1–3–5 of the triad, regulated and limited by the requirements of the scale. The secondary dominants are transpositions of the basic (major) triad to secondary degrees, influenced by the prototype of the scale, whose seventh tone, the leading tone, is the third of a major triad. This conception follows also from another principle that is applied throughout the book, which affirms that a bass tone strives to impose its own overtones, thus has the tendency to become the root of a major triad; and this conception has the advantage that it allows the transfer (imitation) of all functions manifested by the basic triad to the new secondary dominants. Foremost among these functions, as the one that proves to be the strongest tendency of every root, is the drive toward resolution on a root a fifth below. It is necessary to express it this way, because it can also be erroneously stated that the secondary dominant exists only for the sake of this resolution. This error is evident in the idea of Dr. Schenker, who speaks of the tonicalization process;[1] such a secondary dominant can, however, also appear strictly for its own sake, with no intention of going to a secondary tonic. Once the diminished seventh chord was conceived as a ninth chord on a Vth degree, then this idea, too, could be transposed to the secondary degrees, to the secondary dominants. And the same [conception] was manifest as functions and variations of the IInd degree were explained: the Neapolitan sixth, the augmented six-five, four-three and two chord, and other vagrant chords were imitated on secondary degrees. Likewise, the augmented triad, carried over from minor to major.

Then came the minor-subdominant relations. If one conceives tonality, as I do, to be a possibility of the fundamental tone, which in its vertical aspect alone makes available to the analyzing ear an unbelievable body of apparently

[1 Cf. *infra*, Appendix, p. 428.]

foreign harmonies (*Zusammenklängen*), then there is the possibility of under-standing everything that happens in a modulation to the third and fourth circles of fifths as being tied together by the tonality:[1] Hence, imitation of a modulatory process permits the introduction of these nondiatonic occurrences even into the key itself. Here I could perhaps have gone one step further, had I recommended imitating those connections from all other degrees on which they do not appear through this relationship. But we should still not reach all triads that way, as one can easily confirm. How this does nevertheless become possible, I will show in a moment.

We cannot speak of the principles of my presentation without recalling certain ideas reached by way of polemics and used for polemical ends; for these ideas, even if they are negative, even if they do not themselves lay any founda-tions, are all the same no less fruitful than positive principles: If they do not themselves form the foundation, they have at least cleared the ground for a foundation. These ideas are: (1) The proof that instruction in musical composi-tion does enough if it is purely instruction in the handicraft without regard for a natural system or for aesthetics. (2) The recognition of the merely gradual distinction between consonance and dissonance. (3) The proof that the three alleged laws of dissonance treatment – descend, ascend, or sustain – were long ago overtaken by the hoary reality of a fourth law: skip away from the disson-ance. (4) The thesis: There are no such things as non-harmonic tones, tones foreign to harmony, but just tones foreign to the harmonic system.

All of this together yields, even if not in a closed, systematic presentation, that which the art has already achieved: the possibility of conceiving more re-mote (multipartite) tone combinations as harmonic resources of art. This far I have come. That I cannot go farther, I know and say often enough in this book.

Now for the second criticism.

It is justified; for I have in fact not shown any key relationship for a series of minor chords: namely, in *C* major, the minor chords on *d♭, e♭, f♯ (g♭), a♭,* and *b.* Now of course I do not believe that a direct, immediate relationship of these chords with *C* major can be demonstrated. Nevertheless, some ways in which to show indirect relationships have occurred to me, thanks to this criti-cism.

First to be considered would be the possibility, already shown with the intro-duction of secondary dominants, of substituting on occasion the triad *g–b♭–d* for *g–b–d,* a minor triad for a major. Now the major triads on the tones *d♭, e♭,* and *a♭* were introduced through the minor subdominant. The one on *g♭* al-ready occurred as imitation of the Neapolitan sixth on V of major and minor, and the one on *b* is the secondary dominant on VII (*b–d–f♯* could, moreover, be patterned after II of *a* minor). Hence, minor-for-major substitution would be one way to produce this relationship. And as a matter of fact, I construe the sixth chord in Example 290 (at NB), *e♮ (or f♭)–a♭–d♭,* as a passing chord going to the Neapolitan sixth.

A second way would be to exploit the minor-subdominant function of IV

[1 *Supra,* Chapters XII and XIII.]

[that is, in *C* major, *b♭* minor]. I have an objection to that (though not a very weighty one). Namely, it disturbs me that that would then be the function two fifths removed, which, since two fifths above oppose it, is not very compelling. Since it all has to do with more remote relationships, however, this objection does not carry any great weight. Moreover, this reference would of course not yield everything that is missing, only some of it: the minor chord on *e♭* and the major chord on *g♭*. But in conjunction with the way first mentioned [i.e. substituting minor for major], this way does give *d♭*, *a♭*, and *g♭* as minor chords, and this double reference can *only benefit* these more remote relationships of the key.

A third and more significant way, however, would be to work out an idea already mentioned in this book: to base our thought, not on the seven tones of the major scale, rather, on the twelve of the chromatic scale.[1] Such a theory could begin as follows:

I. The raw material of all forms (*Gestalten*) produced by the connecting of tones is a series of twelve tones. (That there are twenty-one note names here, and that their presentation begins with *c*, is consistent with and derives from our imperfect notation; a more adequate notation will recognize only twelve note names and give an independent symbol for each.)

c		d		e		f		g		a		b	
c♭	c♯	d♭	d♯	e♭	e♯	f♭	f♯	g♭	g♯	a♭	a♯	b♭	b♯
(c♭) c c♯		(d♭) d d♯		(e♭) e (e♯)		(f♭) f f♯		(g♭) g g♯		(a♭) a (a♯)		b♭ b (b♯)	

II. From these twelve tones different scales may be formed ([listed here] in historical and pedagogical order):

1. twelve times seven church modes;

2. twelve major and twelve minor modes;

3. a number of exotic modes (and the like) that are not used in European art music, or very rarely at least; it is best to include here also the two whole-tone scales, which can be referred to any one of the twelve tones as fundamental;

[1 After this sentence in the first edition (p. 434), Schoenberg brought this chapter to an abrupt close, as follows:

'A future theory will undoubtedly follow that course; it would thereby reach the only correct solution to this otherwise difficult problem.

'I will add here only one small detail. Somewhere I remarked that, in a certain sense, all chords can be vagrant. Little is left to say about that here, for in the schematic presentation we found a multitude of such possibilities, by virtue of which ordinary major, minor, and dominant seventh chords were used in progressions where we should least expect them. Even so, it should not be forgotten that these chords do after all have multiple meanings, merely because they appear in various keys. Besides, every major chord is identical with a Neapolitan sixth, every dominant seventh chord with an augmented six-five chord.'

In the revised edition, Schoenberg added the outline that follows here. (For further comments, see *supra*, Translator's Preface, p. xvii.)]

4. twelve chromatic modes;

5. one chromatic mode.

III. For the sake of stylistic and formal completeness (*Geschlossenheit*) the characteristics that derive from the conditions peculiar to each scale are clearly worked out: Laws of tonality.

IV. Tonality is extended as follows:

(a) through *imitating* and *copying from* each other the keys become more similar to one another;

(b) similar things are considered *related* and are under certain conditions treated as identical (for example, chords over the same root).

V. The reduction of the eighty-four church modes to twenty-four major and minor keys and the development of the relationship of these twenty-four keys to one another takes place as follows:

1. Horizontally.

(a) Relationship, resting on identically and similarly constituted chords, divides the church modes into those like major and those like minor.

(b) The mutual imitation of cadences allows the major to incorporate everything from the major-like church modes and the minor everything from the minor-like modes, and later also allows major and minor to approach one another so closely that they resemble one another from beginning to end.[1]

(c) Of the seven times eighty-four, i.e. 588, triads of the church modes, in part different, in part just differently related, a great many duplicate one another, hence are referred to a smaller number of keys, whereby seven times twelve, i.e. eighty-four, chords are left, chords referred to two types of key (major and minor); each chord, however, is found in several major and minor keys;

(d) the chord relationship mentioned under (a) and

(e) that through common roots bring about closer ties with the keys that lie one, three, and four steps away in the circle of fifths;

(f) by virtue of the smaller number of boundaries and the simplified character of the keys; by virtue of the multiple meaning of chords and scale segments and the extensive implications of this ambiguity; by virtue of the diminished triads that emerged from the necessities of the scale together with the corresponding seventh chords (free imitation of the natural triad) and their imitation on other degrees – by virtue of all that the more remote keys are also made more accessible (those two, five, and six steps removed in the circle of fifths).

2. Vertically.

The vertical aspect assumes some of the burden of the horizontal by the use of four and five-part chords. A seventh chord, since it introduces four tones of the scale, contributes a third[2] more to the key definition than a triad, a ninth chord two thirds more.*

[1 *bis auf Anfang und Schluss* could also be translated as 'except at the beginning and end'.]

[2 One might suppose Schoenberg meant the interval of a third, *Terz*; but the word he used in this sentence is *Drittel*, the fraction.]

* Multipartite chords and real polyphony, rightly understood, do not serve to make an otherwise uninteresting piece modern, rather, to hasten the pace of presentation.

VI. Transition from twelve major and twelve minor keys to twelve chromatic keys.

This transition is fully accomplished in the music of Wagner, the harmonic significance of which has not yet by any means been theoretically formulated.

VII. The polytonal chromatic scale.

Up to and including point V this outline corresponds to the course of my book. For a number of reasons, stated at various places, I shall go no farther. Here I should like to add yet another reason. I believe that continued evolution of the theory of harmony is not to be expected at present. Modern music that uses chords of six or more parts seems to be at a stage corresponding to the first epoch of polyphonic music. Accordingly, one might reach conclusions concerning the constitution of chords through a procedure similar to figured bass more easily than one could clarify their function by the methods of reference to degrees. For it is apparent, and will probably become increasingly clear, that we are turning to a new epoch of polyphonic style, and as in the earlier epochs, harmonies will be a product of the voice leading: justified solely by the melodic lines!

The literary art takes pains to express ideas clearly and comprehensively with the smallest number of words consistent with its content, selected, considered, and set down according to that content. In music, along with the content of its smallest components (tone, tone progressions, motive, *Gestalt* [pattern, figure], phrase, etc.), there is an additional means of economy available, the possibility of sounding simultaneously. Perhaps for this reason it says more to everyone than do the other arts. Anyway, the value of our present-day musical achievements is, so considered, unmistakable and independent of the taste of the times. The method can change; the goal is constant.

XX THE WHOLE-TONE SCALE AND RELATED FIVE AND SIX-PART CHORDS[1]

For about the last ten years[2] a scale consisting of six tones equidistant from one another has been appearing more and more frequently in works of modern composers: the whole-tone scale.

317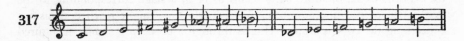

It is said that the modern Russians or the French (Debussy and others) were the first to use it. I do not know for sure, but it seems that Liszt was the first. This year (1910) I heard the *Don Juan Phantasie*, with which I was not previously familiar, and to my great surprise I heard the whole-tone scale. One thing I do know, however: I was acquainted neither with the Russians, nor with Debussy, nor with this composition of Liszt when I wrote it for the first time; and long before that my music showed tendencies that had to lead to the whole-tone scale. Some think the whole-tone scale arose from the influence of exotic music. That would be the music of exotic peoples in which scales of this and other types appear. As for myself, however, I have never been acquainted with exotic music. My connection with these peoples could only be telepathic, at most; for I have made no use of the other media of cultural exchange. Nor do I believe that the Russians or the French, who have perhaps greater access by sea to the Japanese, have taken advantage of that access expressly to import this raw product duty free. I believe, on the contrary, that the whole-tone scale has occurred to all contemporary musicians quite of its own accord, as a natural consequence of the most recent events in music.

In Vienna there used to be an old composition teacher who was employed to administer teacher-certification examinations. Year in and year out he is supposed to have asked the candidate the following question: 'What can you say about the augmented triad?' If the examinee was to escape this trap safely, he had to answer: 'The augmented triad is a favorite device of recent German music.'

Terrible as this fact was to the old professor, his observation was correct. The new German music did in fact favor the augmented triad, and what is more, made abundant use of it. It came about this way: The 'Walkürenmotif' and some other usages in Wagner's music provided the point of departure; some altered seventh and ninth chords provided further impetus; and in this way, I think, we can show the origin of the whole-tone scale, a way that is far less complicated than that of the international spiritual kinship. In works of modern composers,

[1 Cf. *supra*, Chapter XIV, the section entitled 'The Augmented Triad'.]
[2 This sentence remained unchanged from the first edition; hence, Schoenberg meant since about 1900.]

as well as in mine, two forerunners of the deliberate use of the whole-tone scale can be determined.

The one: over an augmented triad the melody steps from chord tone to chord tone, using a passing tone that produces two whole steps, thus dividing the major third into two equal parts. This progression can of course start from each of the chord tones (Examples 318*a*, *b*, *c*), and the result is the whole-tone scale (318*d*).

The same result is produced by passing tones over a dominant seventh chord with augmented (319*a*, *b*) or omitted (319*c*) fifth.

The two derivations are quite similar to each other; for the altered seventh chord is essentially nothing more than an augmented triad with added seventh, and the omitted fifth is identical with the augmented.

Likewise, Example 320*a* is only an expansion of the augmented seventh chord to a ninth chord. Of the six tones of the whole-tone scale this chord contains five; it is easy to understand that one can risk the same successively, in melody, as simultaneously, in harmony, as in Example 320*b*, where nothing more than the *c♯* is needed to complete the whole-tone scale.

Example 321 presents a *chord* that contains all six tones of the whole-tone scale.

Its resolution is this:

Its derivation, this:

By simultaneously raising and lowering the fifth of the ninth chord, we get two tones, which together with the other four make six.

This derivation reflects the way in which our ear draws analogies (*kombiniert*): it connects like things, it sets widely separated events adjacent to one another and adjacent events over one another. Once the three figures of three tones shown in Examples 318*a*, *b*, and *c* are actually used, they soon move closer to one another (318*d*) and finally sound together at the same time (321). Such concentration, however much it at first taxes the faculty of perception, promotes succinct presentation.

Every modern composer has at one time or other written three corresponding scale tones above an augmented triad or above a seventh chord with augmented fifth – or, better expressed: two motives or motivic segments one above the other (in the age of *leit*-motivic writing, a frequent occurrence), of which one is on the augmented triad, while the other forms a three to six-tone scale segment. Every modern composer has undoubtedly written such; hence, it is clear that neither Strauss nor Debussy, Pfitzner nor I, nor any other modern was the first, from whom 'the others got it', rather, that each discovered it for himself, independently of the others. For example, I use the whole-tone chords in my symphonic poem *Pelleas und Melisande* – composed in 1902, at about the same time as Debussy's opera *Pelléas et Mélisande* (in which, as I have heard, he also uses the whole-tone chords and scale for the first time[1]), but at least three or four years before I became acquainted with his music. In my work these chords appear as follows:[2]

324

Through progression of augmented triads in contrary motion, chords emerge of which one is always an augmented triad, the other (at *) a whole-tone chord. But even before, in my *Gurrelieder* [1900–01] and *Sextet* [*Verklärte Nacht* – 1899], there are places that suggest the whole-tone scale (in the Sextet it is found in a middle voice, as someone recently brought to my attention); and then, in the following work [i.e. *Pelleas*], I wrote it as a whole-tone scale, without having become acquainted with anything else in the meantime.

Debussy uses this chord and scale more in the sense of impressionistic expressive devices, somewhat as a tone color (so does Strauss in *Salome*); but they entered my work more for the sake of their harmonic and melodic possibilities: the chords for the sake of their connection with other chords, the scale for the sake of its peculiar influence on the melody. I have never overestimated the value of the whole-tone chords and the whole-tone scale. As enticing as it seemed, that two such scales (there can only be two, because the third would be a repetition of the first) could displace the twelve major and twelve minor scales in a manner similar to the displacement in their time of the eighty-four church modes, I nevertheless sensed immediately that the exclusive use of this

325

[1 Debussy's opera was first performed in 1902, but he began work on it nine or ten years earlier. Other works composed during the same period include the *Prélude à l'Après-midi d'un faune*, whose measures 32–3 and 35–6 contain little else but the two whole-tone scales. In the light of Schoenberg's remarks at the beginning of this chapter and in this same paragraph, it would scarcely be surprising to find Debussy's very first use of these scales or chords in yet an earlier piece.]

[2 Three measures before rehearsal number 32, in the woodwinds.]

scale would bring about an emasculation of expression, erasing all individuality (*Charakteristik*).* That there would then be only three scales, the pair of whole-tone scales and the chromatic scale, would be a quite enticing prospect, as I have said. But at the very time this idea had its chance to make its mark on the evolution of music, it had even then already been left behind. The recognition that it is contrary to nature and superfluous to become attached to such scales had to be the undoing of that idea. Anyone who regards tonality as an indispensable requirement of music disregards *ipso facto* all such scales. At least that is how it ought to be; for if the harmonic possibilities that were shown here are used in modern works, not just occasionally but almost exclusively, then reference to a fundamental tone can only be designated as disturbingly unsymmetrical. And if tonality is in other cases a technique that attains an appropriate effect, here it could easily become an illusion that ill conceals a thoroughly inappropriate effect. I believe it will not work: to flirt with freedom while retaining one's bonds. Vagrant chords, relationship with all keys, whole-tone scales, and everything else that is particularly favored – all that is supposed to occur, the bonds of the key are supposed to be loosened, its affirmative elements suppressed, those that destroy it supported; and yet, in spite of all, it is supposed to turn up suddenly at the end, or if occasion arises, somewhere else, and make everyone believe it is the sovereign over all that occurred! There again one has 'taken a prisoner who won't free the captor'. I should not wish to sit on that throne from which tonality's luster of sovereignty emanates. No, I believe this kind of thing really cannot succeed. If tonality is to be attained, then one must work toward it with all suitable means; then one must maintain certain proportions in the modulations as the classicists did in fact maintain them; then elements that will not be bound [to tonality] must be omitted, and only such as willingly fit in may be used.** Thus: for one who believes in tonality, who be-

* I am not unaware that in giving this opinion I may perhaps be saying something just as nonsensical as the statement of our Viennese professor who found *Tristan* dull because so many diminished seventh chords occur in it. Since I believe what I say, however, I feel that the wrong in not saying it is greater than the advantage I should get from shrewdly keeping quiet. There is a small distinction here: I was not talking about finished compositions but about unwritten ones. And yet another: the old professor was not bored with *Tristan* because of the diminished seventh chords, but because he did not at all understand it. Whenever one does not understand something, self-esteem takes over, becomes self-conceit, and shifts the cause from the subject, where it really belongs, onto the object. And there is yet another distinction [between his statement and mine]: in *Tristan* there are not all that many diminished seventh chords; but I am attacking here the *exclusive* use of a scale, I am attacking something that I have already seen with students and of which I can definitely say, it was bad. In the music of masters I have not found it as yet. Should it occur, then I shall retract this judgment in good time.

** What I say here is only apparently contradictory to what I said previously about tonality: it depends, namely, on the composer, whether he creates tonality or not. For, that one *can* create it, I consider possible. Only, whether one *must* still work for it, indeed, whether one *ought* to work for it any more at all, I doubt. For this reason I have called attention to the formal possibilities of fluctuating and suspended tonality;

lieves in scales (*Tonreihen*), that sort of new scale must be excluded as a matter of course. But what other purpose should the formulation of a scale have if not to create a tonality, a specific tonality? Is it for the sake of melody? Does melody need certification by a particular scale? Is not the chromatic scale enough? And as for the chords – what service should a scale render them? After all, these scales were not formulated until long after the chords had come into being! The scale would then never explain the origin of the chord; it would even exclude many a chord. There is much that one could not do without departing from the scale. The old modes, however, and our major and minor *were consistent with at least the average of what happened in a piece of music*. To accommodate the average of what is created to the bondage of new scales can only be the wish of one who would prove himself a master within a restricted sphere[1] because what he can do is too meager for him to attain mastery of freedom.

And even the experiments of Busoni and Georg Capellen, otherwise ingenious, as it seems, would be subject to the same criticism. I do not yet know Capellen's book, but I will certainly read it.[2] I like the lovely tunes that he published in the August 1910 edition of *Die Musik*.[3] They are expressive, interesting, and warmly conceived. But I do not believe one has to set up special scales to arrive at these and other sorts of melodic figures, that one has to prefabricate what ought to be invented, because I know for sure that it can be done differently, and because I firmly believe that one must not compose that way. Invention, but not calculation! One may compose by taking thought, but one must not deliberately observe how one is thinking. One can create freely within a tonality (*Tonart*) only if there is the feeling for this tonality in the unconscious. I do not understand why a man who can invent such lovely melodies in spite of a [self-imposed] handicap does not rather depend on his native powers, which even the handicap cannot entirely paralyze, instead of hanging on to theories, which do not thrive in the same soil that nourishes the creative act.

And Busoni, that noble and courageous artist – I value and respect him highly. But he could spare himself the affliction of figuring out hundreds of scales.[4] It was a toilsome and troublesome task for me to memorize the names of the seven church modes; and those were 'only the names'! I shall not be able to remember five of his keys. But how then could I compose in them – if I cannot

---

whereas these do admit the assumption of an effectual [tonal] center, they show how it is not necessary to help this center attain externally a power that it has, at most, internally.

[1 An allusion to a famous line by Goethe. Cf. *infra*, p. 396.]

[2 Schoenberg added here (in 1911) a last-minute footnote, identifying and commenting on Capellen's book. See Appendix, p. 431.]

[3 IX, 22. Capellen's 'tunes', settings of Japanese texts, accompanied his article 'Die Akkordzither und die Exotik' (pp. 228–32). Through the use of exotic scales, Capellen thought to expand traditional major-minor tonality and thereby develop a 'new, exotic musical style'.]

[4 Cf. *Sketch of a New Esthetic of Music* in *Three Classics . . .*, pp. 92–3.]

even keep them in mind. Ought I to do as Weingartner does, who keeps them written down over his desk? No. I should not like to do anything at all the way Weingartner does it![1]

What I said before about tonality is not by any means to be interpreted as criticism of a masterwork. In the works of Mahler and Strauss, for example, I find that tonality is still quite homogeneous with the character of their thematic material. It is important to me, therefore, to say here that I consider Mahler's work immortal and that I rank it beside that of the greatest masters.[2] Aside from that, however, theoretic considerations like these could not bring me to doubt the power I felt. And at different places in this book I have shown that the artist has something to say other than his technique; and what he says to me is above all this Something Other. I have always first understood [a work] this way, not analyzing until later. My arguments were meant to refute the belief in the necessity of tonality, but not the belief in the power of a work of art whose author believes in tonality. What a composer believes in theoretically he may indeed express in the external aspects of his work. With luck, only in the external. But internally, where the instincts take over, all theory will with luck fail, and there he will express something better than his theory and mine. And if Goethe's sentence, 'In der Beschränkung zeigt sich [erst] der Meister,'[3] has any meaning at all – it certainly does not mean what the Philistines of art always intend it to mean; and even if Goethe himself should have meant it that way, it applies least of all to him; he himself was much too great for the narrowness of this unfortunate saying – if it then has any meaning at all, it can only be this: the narrowness of our powers of imagination and conceptualization would impose restrictions upon our true spiritual and instinctual nature; given these restrictions, the master proves his mastery by breaking through the barriers and becoming free – even where he thought he was not free because external pressure made him want restrictions to keep him artificially balanced. My criticism

[1 Felix Weingartner, the conductor, composed a number of operas and symphonies, as well as chamber, piano, and vocal music.

In his 'Handexemplar . . .' (see *supra*, Translator's Preface, p. xvi), Schoenberg repudiated this attack on Weingartner in a marginal note, dated 29 May 1923: 'I have been punished for this attack in familiar and predictable ways. But I wanted to delete it long ago. For the attack is uglier than I realized at the time, and unjust. It is by no means impossible to compose that way. However, the [musical] result is more important; that alone is to be judged, and not how it was achieved. If the result is good, then the method must have been correct.' (The attack on Weingartner appeared in the original edition of 1911 and remained in the revised edition of 1921/22. It was finally deleted in the seventh edition of 1966.)]

[2 Cf. *supra*, pp. 4–5.]

[3 This the penultimate line from the sonnet 'Natur und Kunst' has become an oft-quoted German proverb. The last three lines of the poem may be paraphrased as follows:

He who would achieve greatness must exercise restraint.
It is only within restrictions that the master proves his mastery,
And law alone can give us freedom.]

thus does not apply, even if I had so intended it, to the master himself who strives for tonality, but only to his belief, only to the superstition that over-estimates the significance and the theoretic necessity of tonality.

The whole-tone scale is a device famous for its coloristic effect. Debussy is of course completely justified in using the whole-tone chords in this sense; for his work is effective and beautiful. But still I should not neglect to point out the harmonic and structural possibilities of this harmony. The whole-tone chords, regarded as vagrant chords, have at least the same possibilities for connection as the augmented triad. Depending on the degrees to which they are referred, they can be used for modulations and modulatory episodes.

Each tone can be the root of a dominant; there are then six resolutions to major triads.

Obviously, for any other type of resolution shown, there will also always be six transpositions (one on each of the six tones). Hence, six times the resolution to a dominant seventh chord (Example 327a), to a secondary seventh chord (327b), to a diminished seventh chord (327c), to two augmented triads (327d and e), to a seventh chord with lowered fifth (327f), to a minor ninth chord with lowered fifth (327g), to a major ninth chord (327h), to a minor ninth chord (327i), and finally to the other whole-tone chord (327k).

That makes more than sixty resolutions already, even though we gave prefer-ence here to chromatic progressions or sustained tones. Resolution, then, entirely in the sense of strict dissonance treatment. Many other resolutions may certainly be found in the same manner. If one replaces the strict resolution with the free, as we have indeed often done, then the number of possibilities must greatly increase.

I shall not give any examples here in phrase form; for a reason already stated, they could hardly turn out well. The use of such chords will hardly be possible, unless the melodies exhibit influence of this sort of harmony. But such melodies, if one wants to *invent* them, cannot fail to surpass in every respect what is merely adequate to produce a model for practice. They would surely be melodies with motivic power, with expression, rhythm, and the like. I do not think such can be achieved in the sterile manner of the exercise. The pupil may of course try it. I prefer not to do it, so as not to contribute unnecessarily, where I do not have to, to those examples of what not to do that are customary in other harmony texts. If the pupil looks at modern music, he will find what he needs. If he understands the sort of harmony being considered and has the motivation to use it, the rest will come of its own accord, or never.

I have often said that certain things are to be permitted later. This would be the place for it. But I still do not want to give this permission without recommending to the pupil that he make no use of it. In the last chapter I will discuss in detail the reasons why I advocate such restraint. They are not so much pedagogical considerations – certainly those, too – as, far more, artistic ones. Let the pupil wait until he knows his talent!

XXI CHORDS CONSTRUCTED IN FOURTHS

I have shown that the system of tertian harmony has a rupture and that chords that do not fit in the system have been grouped together under the heading 'non-harmonic tones'. I have exposed this classification as the poorly disguised attempt to plug up the hole in the system with an imposing heap of unexamined scrap material, a heap so big that neither the hole nor the system itself is big enough to accommodate it. If we now speak of chords constructed in fourths, it is in no way meant to suggest replacement of the old tertian system by one based on quartal construction.[1] True, the quartal system, since it is identical with a system built on fifths, would perhaps be no less defensible on natural grounds, and would be able to accommodate all conceivable chords more uniformly than the tertian system. It must be observed, however, that the contradiction to the reality of present-day music would not be insignificant: a major triad is a simple form in the old system, in the new it is complex. In the latter a triad would read, *d–g–c*, or *c–g–d*, and surely has natural justification; for *c* (the root) has as its first overtone [after the octave], *g*, whose first overtone is, in turn, *d*. Yet this harmony is certainly not as natural as *c–e–g*.[2] True, the will of the tone is fulfilled nowhere else the way it is in the fourth chords; for they imply that the resolution to the tone a fifth lower actually symbolizes the unity of everything that sounds simultaneously, indeed, everything that sounds. Even so, the quartal system would find itself forced to look for a number of explanations apart from nature – without being at all inferior on that account to the old system, which can get along far less well without artificial help. Nevertheless, I believe an exploration [of quartal harmony], filling out the tertian system more or less temporarily, ought to open up certain new prospects for the theorist. Whether everything would thereby become simpler than it was before is not within my power to determine. I shall therefore guard against going into much detail: that would only bring new confusion into the old disorder; and I shall restrict myself to explaining why I speak of fourth chords: because they do appear in the literature, although, as far as I know, they appear largely as superimposed fourths [rather than as full-fledged chords].

The fourth chords make their first appearance in music as an impressionistic means of expression, as does apparently everything that later becomes a commonly used technical means. Consider, for example, the effect of the violin tremolo the first time it was used; it then becomes clear that such did not come about as a dispassionate technical experiment, rather as a sudden inspiration

[1 The adjective 'quartal' appears in the *Harvard Dictionary of Music* (Cambridge, Mass.: Harvard University Press, 1953), p. 619, thus apparently has currency among musicians. Consistency would require 'quartan', by analogy with 'tertian', and 'quartan' is the form listed in Webster's *Third International Dictionary*.]

[2 Because, as Schoenberg explained in the original edition (p. 446), *e* and *g* are *both* among the first overtones of the fundamental *c*.]

evoked by a powerful expressive urge. That which is new and unusual about a new harmony occurs to the true composer only for such reasons: he must give expression to something that moves him, something new, something previously unheard-of. His successors, who continue working with it, think of it as merely a new sound, a technical device; but it is far more than that: a new sound is a symbol, discovered involuntarily, a symbol proclaiming the new man who so asserts his individuality. Such a new sound, which later becomes characteristic for the entire work of an artist, often appears very early. Take Wagner's music as an example and note how in *Lohengrin* and *Tannhäuser* those chords that later became highly significant for his harmonic style had already occurred. In the youthful works, however, they turn up only as isolated phenomena, assigned to exposed spots, to places with an often strangely new expression. It is expected of them that they accomplish *everything*, the *utmost*; that they represent a world, giving expression to a new world of feeling; that *they tell in a new way what it is that is new: a new man!* With Wagner that is easy to trace; for he is still close enough to us that we can remember what was new about him, and yet already far enough removed that we can to some extent view his work as a whole and understand his development and the development of what was new about him. Starting wholly from within the bounds of what everyone of his time understood music to be, his music follows at first the one necessity just to express himself somehow or other, with not the slightest concern for beauty and novelty or for style and art. But without his noticing it, traits that point toward his future development insinuate themselves. One time it is merely that he does not accomplish something that any musical craftsman would have done faultlessly. Here there are obstacles in the way which will cause his stream to find a new course. Another time it is something positive: an inspiration, some direct, unconscious, often brutal, sometimes almost childish assertion of his own nature. But the young artist does not know himself; he does not yet sense wherein he is different from the others, different above all from the literature. He still adheres generally to the precepts of his education and is not able to break through it everywhere in favor of his own inclinations. He does not [consciously] break through; where there is a breakthrough, he does not know it. He believes that his work is at no point distinguishable from what is generally found to be good in art; and all of a sudden he is violently awakened from his dream, when the harsh reality of criticism makes him aware that somehow he is not really so normal after all, as a true artist should never be normal: he lacks perfect agreement with those average people who were educable, who could submit wholly to the *Kultur*. He begins to notice what he likes that is different from the [norm]; he begins to notice what is hateful to him. *The artist who has courage submits wholly to his own inclinations. And he alone who submits to his own inclinations has courage, and he alone who has courage is an artist.* The literature is thrown out, the results of education are shaken off, the inclinations come forward, the obstacle turns the stream into a new course, the one hue that earlier was only a subordinate color in the total picture spreads out, a personage is born. A new man! This is a model for the development of the artist, for the development of art.

That is called revolution;[1] and artists, those who submit to such necessities and cherish them, are accused of all possible crimes that can be culled from the rubbish of the political vocabulary. At the same time, however, it is forgotten that one may call it revolution, if at all, only in a comparative sense, and that this comparison has to hold only with respect to the *points compared*, i.e. *points of similarity*, but not in every respect. An artist who has a good, new idea is not to be confused with an arsonist or a bomb thrower. Any similarity between the advent of the new in the spiritual and intellectual sphere and in political revolutions consists at most in this: the successful will prevail for a period of time, and in the light of this prospect, the older will feel under threat from what is new. But the fundamental distinctions are greater: the consequences, the spiritual and intellectual consequences of an idea endure, since they are spiritual and intellectual; but the consequences of revolutions that run their course in material matters are transient. Besides: it has never been the purpose and effect of new art to suppress the old, its predecessor, certainly not to destroy it. Quite the contrary: no one loves his predecessors more deeply, more fervently, more respectfully, than the artist who gives us something truly new; for respect is awareness of one's station and love is a sense of community. Does anyone have to be reminded that Mendelssohn – even he was once new – unearthed Bach, that Schumann discovered Schubert, and that Wagner, with work, word, and deed, awakened the first real understanding of Beethoven? The appearance of the new can far better be compared with the flowering of a tree: it is the natural growth (*Werden*) of the tree of life. But if there were trees that had an interest in preventing the flowering, then they would surely call it revolution. And conservatives of winter would fight against each spring, even if they had experienced it a hundred times and could affirm that it did become, after all, *their* spring too. Short memory and meager insight suffice to confuse growth with overthrow; they suffice for believing that when the new shoots emerge from what was once new the destruction of the old is at hand.

This is the explanation, for me, of the impressionistic quality that characterizes new devices of art at their first appearance: youthful sounds of that which is growing; pure feeling, with no trace of an awareness, still firmly attached to the germ cell, which is more intimately connected with the universe than is our awareness; yet, already marks of a singularity that later will bring forth a singular being, one who singles himself out from the others because he is singularly organized. [Those youthful sounds are] an omen of possibilities that later will become certainties, a presentiment, enveloped by a mysterious luster. And as these are a part of that [germ cell] which connects us with *the universe, with nature*, so they almost always appear *first as an expression of a mood of nature* (*Naturstimmung*).[2] The brook reminds us of its source.

It is remarkable that such a happy discovery never quite loses its effect, even if it represents only the point of departure of a development that will leave the form of its first appearance far behind. The subsequent development may even

[1 This paragraph is new in the revised edition.]
[2 Cf. *infra*, p. 403, paragraph on Debussy's music.]

bring it to the pinnacle of its artistic exploitation, yet it will never again produce
an impression just like that made by its first appearance. I am thinking of the
horn passage from the last movement of the *Pastoral Symphony* and of the
sound of the distant hunting horns at the beginning of the second act of *Tristan*.
These will surely never lose the charm they have for us all, although their basic
idea has subsequently evolved far beyond them.

In the Beethoven we have no ordinary pedal point and [not merely] a melody
that avoids the third; in the Wagner it is not merely the use of the horns' open
tones, for he has the remaining horns playing other than open tones as well.
One senses this, of course, without its being explained. And that Beethoven
quite certainly sensed this singularity is proved by his sense of form, which
pressed him to answer this singularity with another, congruent singularity, to
resolve as it were this singularity: with the *rhythmically remarkable entry* of the
tonic harmony on the second half of the measure (𝄋).

I believe everything that modern composers have written in the sphere of
quartal harmonies is implied in and emanates from these two passages. Certain
quartal progressions in Mahler, the 'Jochanaan Theme' of *Salome*, the fourth
chords of Debussy and Dukas can all be attributed to the peculiar freshness
that emanates from these chords. Perhaps the future of our music speaks
through this freshness. It is heard only by those who are highly sensitive to
impressions, the impressionists. The impressionist's organ [of perception] is a
mechanism of extraordinarily fine tuning, a seismograph, which registers the
slightest motion. The most delicate stimuli can arouse his sensibility, whereas
crudeness shatters it. To pursue these most delicate stimuli, which the coarser
nature never perceives because he hears only what is loud, is a powerful temptation to the true impressionist. What is soft, scarcely audible, hence mysterious,
attracts the impressionist, arouses his curiosity to savor what was never tried

before. Thus, the tendency of something unheard-of to reveal itself to the searcher is just as great as is the tendency of the searcher himself to find something unheard-of. And in this sense every truly great artist is an impressionist: ultrafine reaction to the slightest stimuli reveals to him the unheard-of, the new.

This is particularly striking in Debussy's music.[1] His impressionism writes the fourth chords, as well as everything else, with such great power that they seem bound up inseparably with the newness that he is expressing; and they can be rightfully considered his spiritual property, even though it can be shown that similar things had been written before and were being written by contemporaries. Perhaps a part of [their power] is also that they express moods of nature; for it does indeed sound as if nature would speak that way. And it is clear that before her language all else gives way.

As many other composers apparently did, I, too, wrote fourth chords without having heard Debussy's music. Perhaps even earlier, but certainly at the same time as he. As far as I know, [I wrote them] for the first time in my symphonic poem previously mentioned, *Pelleas und Melisande* [1902–03].

[NOTE Cf. the third and fourth measures before rehearsal number 9.]

Quite isolated, they appear there just once, as expression of a mood whose singularity caused me against my will to find what was to me a new means of expression. Against my will – I still remember, even today, that I hesitated to notate this sound. The clarity with which it forced itself upon me, however, made it impossible for me to dismiss it. Then, not until long afterwards, in my *Kammersymphonie* [1906], did I take up fourth chords again, without recalling the previous case, and without having got to know in the meantime the music of Debussy or Dukas. Here the fourths, springing from an entirely different expressive urge (stormy jubilation), shape themselves into a definite horn theme (Example 331), spread themselves out architectonically over the whole

[NOTE Measures 5 and 6 of the *Kammersymphonie*.]

[1 This idea, expressed in a single sentence in the first edition, was expanded to form this paragraph in the revised edition.]

piece, and place their stamp on everything that happens. Thus it turns out that they do not appear here merely as melody or as a purely impressionistic chord effect; their character permeates the total harmonic structure, and they are chords like all others.

I shall have to be pardoned for dealing so particularly with my own work. I have to do so, for I do not know whether any composer before me ever used these chords in this sense, in this harmonic sense.* Of course their use as an impressionistic expressive device is included in this harmonic sense. I am talking to the point when I talk about myself, as Karl Kraus[1] says.

Not all forms of fourth chords appear in this work or in my later works. Here, then, are some possibilities.[2]

One can obtain three, four, five, six-part chords, and so on. All of them admit of manifold usage.

The four-part fourth chord can even be produced by alteration within the tertian system (Examples 333*b* and *c*).

---

* It is possible, it is indeed probable, that others besides me have written these chords. Perhaps Mahler, Strauss, or Pfitzner. But I do not know. They have never come to my attention. Maybe I simply have not noticed them. It is by no means my intention to secure here a priority for myself. To do so is of too little importance to me, for I know too well that is not what matters.

[1 'Ich rede also von der Sache, wenn ich von mir rede.' – Karl Kraus, the Viennese polemicist and satirist, founded, edited, and largely wrote the polemical magazine, *Die Fackel* (1899 to 1936), which was avidly read by Schoenberg and his disciples. The profound influence exerted by Kraus upon Schoenberg's thought and literary style merits study. (An estimate of Kraus as social critic and writer is to be found in Erich Heller's *The Disinherited Mind*.)]

[2 In the first edition (p. 451), this sentence reads: 'I shall list them here theoretically.']

Likewise the five-part chord. This chord and the four-part chord can be substitutes for a dominant, from which they are derived by lowering the root (if one wishes to admit such), the seventh, and the fifth for the four-part quartal chord, and by raising and lowering the root (a♮ to a or b♭♭, and to g),

raising and lowering the fifth (e♭ to e, e♭ to e♭♭), and sustaining the third for the five-part quartal chord. Here inversions were used. But if one does not shy away from fifths, one can of course write the chords in root position as well.

Example 335 presents some connections [of the five-part chord] with common chords. The six-part quartal chord contains a minor ninth (from the bass note), and is thus the first 'rather sharp' dissonance among the fourth chords. One will therefore tend first to dispose of this ninth, to resolve it in some way or other. I include here only such connections as produce a resolution of the ninth.

Please note: only resolutions to the most common chords are given, omitting even such less common chords, whose use could hardly arouse opposition, as that in Example 337*a*.

Example 337*b* shows how by lowering three tones (*b* to *b♭*, *a* to *a♭*, *g* to *f♯*) we obtain the six-part whole-tone chord (a connection that also appears in my *Kammersymphonie*), and how the latter goes on again to a six-part fourth chord, if we lower the remaining three tones (*c* to *b*, *d* to *c♯*, *e* to *e♭*).

Obviously, it is possible also to adduce fourth chords of seven, eight, nine, or more parts. Since I am not familiar with them as fourth chords [in the musical literature], even though I have certainly already written them myself, I decline to present them theoretically. Indeed, theory could perhaps provide some initiative here, but it should never, as has often been said, anticipate what will happen [in actual composition]. There is one consideration that could induce me to elaborate this system: the construction of chords by superimposing fourths can lead to a chord that contains all the twelve tones of the chromatic

scale; hence, such construction does manifest a possibility for dealing systematically with those harmonic phenomena that already exist in the works of
some of us: seven, eight, nine, ten, eleven, and twelve-part chords.

Besides myself, my pupils Dr. Anton von Webern and Alban Berg have
written such harmonies. But the Hungarian Béla Bartók, and the Viennese
Franz Schreker, both of whom are following a path more similar to that of
Debussy, Dukas, and perhaps also Puccini, are probably not far [from writing
such chords]. However much it seems, then, as if the most talented of our young
composers are tending to go in this direction, toward the use of such chords,[1]
there would be little value in formulating a system right now; for our lack of
distance from these events gives us only a bewildering view of them. But the
quartal construction makes possible, as I said, accommodation of all phenomena
of harmony; thus, if we assume that on occasion tones may also be omitted from
the middle [of the twelve-part chord], that a chord could consist, for example,
of the first, second, fourth, and tenth tones, then we can also produce the chords
of the tertian system. The tertian construction, however, no matter whether we
juxtapose only thirds of equal size or choose a certain pattern of unequal
thirds, will not produce this result [i.e. all twelve tones], because tones are repeated too soon. Alternating a major with a minor third (major chord), we get
at the ninth tone a repetition of the second tone (Example 339a). Minor chords
produce repetition at the eighth tone (339b). Exclusively minor thirds give only
four different tones (339c), exclusively major only three (339d). Were we to set

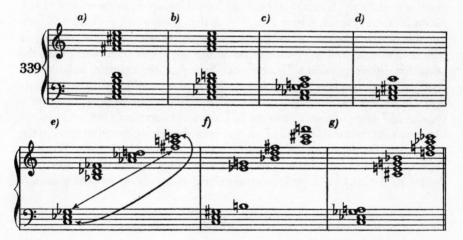

up a pattern of two minor thirds and one major, then we would get ten different
tones. The tenth and the twelfth are repetitions of previous tones of this construction, and only the eleventh is again new (339e). Besides, a system of that

[1 Schoenberg wrote a new footnote for the revised edition (transferred here to the
Appendix, p. 432), examining – and rejecting – the word 'atonal', together with
'atonalists'. (The word appears only twice in his *Theory of Harmony*: in this footnote
and on page 128.) The long footnote on pages 454–6 of the first edition was added, as
text, to the end of the chapter (see *infra*, pp. 408–10).]

sort would be far less in accord with natural models than the quartal system; for its basis, two minor thirds, has nothing more in common with the idea of a major triad than the principle of tertian construction. The same objection applies to the two attempts in Examples 339*f* and *g*. These do now produce all the tones, it is true. But the augmented triad, basis of the one, and the diminished seventh chord, basis of the other, are without doubt artificial products of the system.[1]

That the fundamental thesis of the gradual nature of dissonances leads me to reject non-harmonic tones, and, moreover, makes me bold enough to designate the system of tertian construction as inadequate and to consider the possibility of a quartal system, will enrage the defenders of the older music (which is not at all under attack here; apparently, I understand it better and revere it more fervently than they), enrage even more the textbook writers who cling to an outmoded, because misunderstood, aesthetic. Thus, I learned that just such a person, whose attention was drawn through an indiscretion to a few sheets of the manuscript and to some accounts of the contents of this book, called it a great defense of modern music. I am not really unhappy about that, but I have to deny it, because it is not true. For modern music has greater need for performance than for defense.[2] Our interest in warding off attacks wanes the more we see how the attackers only annihilate themselves whenever they marshal their criticism against the work of art, their impotence against power, their sterility against productivity. Their inactivity in the creative sphere robs them of any good hope for the future; but it turns into outrage when they assume a creative posture and lay claim, though with cracking voice, to the utmost recognition for their systems, setting these higher than the musical works themselves. Let this not be taken to mean disrespect for the systems. On the contrary, I admire in others, with an almost unjust lack of envy, this talent that I lack, the talent for devising systems. Dr. Heinrich Schenker, for example, although he breaks through nowhere to complete clarity, is in my opinion worthy of attention and respect just because he is one of the few who are really striving for a system; still more, of course, because he loves and understands the works of the older art with the same fervor as I, so that even though we are miles apart in the present and future of our art we are so much the closer in its past. When he speaks, however, (as I have heard) in a new counterpoint book[3] about the decline of the art of composition, maintaining that nobody can compose any

[1] The remainder of this chapter represents the re-working and expansion of a long footnote in the first edition (pp. 454–6). The footnote was appended to the fourth sentence of this paragraph.]

[2] Cf. edition of 1911 (p. 454, footnote): 'The conclusions I draw from the development of my views concerning the gradual nature of dissonances – that the tertian system is inadequate and that a system based on fourths is desirable – will be welcomed by my opponents as cause to call my book a great defense for modern music. It is not, however; for, although modern music should perhaps be defended, the attacks are not worthy of such serious attention.']

[3] *Neue Musikalische Theorien und Phantasien*, Band II: *Kontrapunkt* (*Erster Halbband*) (Stuttgart: J. G. Cotta'sche Buchhandlung Nachfolger, 1910), pp. vii–xxiii, *et passim*.]

more, then that is not much better than the grumbling of the aged and infirm in their nostalgia for 'the good old days'. Certainly we must not be satisfied with our time. But not because it is no longer the good old times, gone forever, but because it is not yet the better, the new times of the future. Accordingly, unfounded attacks like this are not such as require any defense of our art against them. The vehemence that breaks out here is psychologically interesting; for it shows that those noted defenders of the old art are quite uneasy over the outcome of their defense and of our struggle. They suspect and fear that the old art will again be victorious and will win for the new, for the younger sister, a place of honor at her right hand.[1]

If, moreover, according to good old military wisdom, every problem of defense is solved offensively, if then a good defense is hardly distinguishable from an attack: Whoever seeks theoretic knowledge, but *bases it on received aesthetic judgments without examining this aesthetic and these judgments to see if they are correct*, exposes his theories as nothing but attempts to drag up proofs for these judgments, hence, as worthless. Here I am attacking, openly and honorably, with the will to annihilate; I am not on the defensive, they are. For (this is the greatest difference between us) I have asked myself that question and not built upon air as does, for example, Riemann, who is proud that his theory succeeds in sharper and stricter formulation of the rules, and who has no inkling that, for this very reason, he will swiftly be left behind.

Mayrhofer, too – whose book, *Der Kunstklang*,[2] I would perhaps have read long ago if it were not so ponderously written – seems to stop at the same frontier. He too is on the verge of giving a theory; that would indeed be an accomplishment, since up to now we do not have a theory. Yet, he calls the dissonance the necessary complement of the consonance, hence, emphasizes the antithetical relation; for this reason I doubt whether he will get as far as he perhaps would have got without this compromise between aesthetics and his own direct perception of the phenomena. That would be a shame, for it appears to me as if he were capable of greater understanding (except for his intricate terminology, which gives names without awakening ideas). Nevertheless,

---

[1] Schoenberg added this sentence in the revised edition; and the following paragraph represents a significant reduction of the analogous passage in the first edition (p. 455, continuation of the footnote). The first few sentences of the original version of this passage are given below to amplify, to clarify what is perhaps an over-reduction:

'But I would not have decided to write a book just because of such attacks. I decided to write it because I believed I had something to say that is not yet known. It should be obvious to anyone who reads this book that it deals with some basic principles. Above all, the most important characteristic of my method in contrast to those of other writers: The others have accepted aesthetic judgments as given and erected their theories accordingly, by trying to drag up proofs for those judgments. But they have forgotten to ask themselves the most important question, *whether these aesthetic judgments are even right*! I believe that is the greatest difference between me and the others, that I have always first asked myself this question . . .']

[2] Robert Mayrhofer, *Der Kunstklang*, Band I: *Das Problem der Durdiatonik* (Vienna: Universal-Edition, 1910). Cf. 'Über Konsonanz-Dissonanz', pp. 239–47.]

although he too starts with aesthetics, by forming a pact with aesthetics, it is still possible that he will find what is correct.

Of course I had it easier in a certain respect than those theorists, who are not composers. I could not accept their aesthetics simply because my imagination, my ear, and my sense of form insisted upon a different aesthetics. Because for me those prohibitions and commandments that they take pains to justify were annulled at the outset by my musical inspiration (*Einfall*), which testified to the contrary. Hence, words were put into my mouth, so to speak, when I asked whether the [traditional] aesthetics was right. And it was not first my deliberation that decided against it, it was rather my musical intuition (*Gefühl*). And when I then arrived at other conclusions through deliberation as well, I did not do so for the sake of defending anything. I felt, rather, as if I were only recounting, as if I were only reporting, describing what creative activity in art is really like. My ear had said: yes; and the ear is, after all, a musician's whole understanding!

Perhaps I have invented much that was already given; but I invented it and did not learn it from reading. I found it out for myself (that is, after all, what 'invention' means) because I experienced it. It has been my experience that my way of understanding has made it impossible for me to correct a bad inspiration; and I told myself: that can be no accident, there must be a law here. This law is: Inspiration (*Der Einfall*). Hence, I began to reflect on the relation of handicraft to art. And upon reflection I saw that art and handicraft have as much to do with one another as wine with water. In wine there is of course water, but he who begins with the water is an adulterator. One can indeed consider the water apart from the wine; but then there is a clear distinction. This led me to regard instruction in composition solely as instruction in the handicraft, and nothing more. Thereby, the problem is solved [i.e. the problem arising from aesthetics and its prescriptions], since the necessities of a handicraft are not binding on art. Therefore, I could place instruction in the craft on a purely practical basis, giving definite means to serve definite ends (*Zweckmässigkeit*); for in art, as I see it, the absence of [preconceived] ends (*Zwecklosigkeit*) is, alongside expression, of supreme importance. [Practicality, means-toward-ends,] is appropriate for the handicraft, is indeed unavoidable. In art it has no place. But the two actually have nothing to do with one another.

I do not recommend that the pupil use the harmonies presented here in his attempts to compose, so far as they do not also appear in other, older texts. His efforts, regardless of whether he uses modern or unmodern means, will be good or bad depending on how his innate talent for having something to express relates to his ability to express it. The teacher has influence only on one component of this relation, on the ability to express. Perhaps not even on that; I doubt whether even this ability can be increased by imparting technical devices. The pupil does not learn to express *himself* when he imitates the techniques of models. Actually, the real artist is unteachable in the first place. If we show him 'how he must do it', and base what we say on the fact that others have also done it that way, then that may be instruction in art, but it is not instruction of the artist. Ability to express oneself certainly does not depend on the kind and number of means placed at one's command. But inability depends on that. Inability can develop only by way of techniques; for it does not exist through what it produces of itself, but thrives on what others have produced. The work of the truly gifted, however, ultimately manifests very little external relationship with the literature that was once his model. Because he esteems himself; because, through this self-esteem, he evolves away from his preliminary conditions, from his models, which perhaps at the beginning did serve as props, crutches he used in his first efforts to walk. Because ultimately he will not write what is *artistically acceptable (Kunstgemäss)*, but rather what is *acceptable to him, the artist (Künstlergemäss)*.

The following consideration seems to contradict this view: That there are essential distinctions between Mozart's style and that of Beethoven, for example, is today still clear to everyone; nevertheless, the distinctions are not so great as to justify a contention that the laws applicable to the one do not hold for the other. On the contrary, there are passages, even movements, by Mozart that could almost be by Beethoven, and some by Beethoven that could almost be by Mozart. If we go even farther back, say into the sixteenth or seventeenth century, then the distinctions become so subtle to our eyes [and ears?] that we can easily mistake the music of one composer for that of another. Distance from a group of objects equalizes them to such a great extent that it erases the individual distinctions. Stylistically, perhaps even in content, one artist can hardly be distinguished clearly from the other; we only perceive common traits, from which we can abstract the artistically acceptable. There is a certain distance, however, from which we can really detect only the spirit (*Geist*) of the century. He who can set himself far enough apart, will detect the spirit of mankind. Individualities disappear at this distance, but what they express – mankind, the best that is in it – becomes visible. The highest pinnacles, which are most accessible to the observer, into which the capillaries lift the finest and best from the depths, these alone set forth the spirit of mankind. Thus, increasing distance, initially reductive, once again magnifies: the individuals, the pinnacles, become visible again, even if in a different way. One sees that they are related and how they are related, that they are coherent among themselves; one no longer sees what proximity revealed, one no longer sees that they were sharply separate; *but the relationships are not those of art, not those of the techniques of art; they are rather deeper ones.*

Naturally, observing from a moderate distance, we can, as I said, even find a line revealing the path of the techniques and of the artistically acceptable. And if we admit that the smallest part of a curve may be viewed as an infinitely small straight line, then such an optical illusion is surely also allowed with the vascular network that designates the way the techniques of art developed. Discounting the little deviations, that can surely be a line. Even must be, perhaps, for the ultimate goal is common to all. And something else is common to all: our ultimate limits.

The eye that will occupy itself with the contemplation of art must be able to focus on all these distances. The images revealed by distance are as important as those seen close at hand. But from a distance we can only contemplate the past. If we could look at the present from afar, then all our struggles would be over. But the struggle will not release us, even though its outcome is predetermined. Its goal we know. We know who will be victorious. As with maneuvers, where in fact the victor is determined in advance. The struggle must be carried on, nevertheless, just as seriously as if one could change the outcome. We must fight just as passionately as if we did not know which idea would conquer. Although this idea would conquer anyway, even if we did not fight, since its victory is predestined. Perhaps our struggle itself is predestined; anyway, the passion is justified.

Proximity, the present, which we do indeed sense most strongly, most directly, reveals the living personality poised for the struggle, in vigorous conflict with its environment. The personalities differ sharply from each other; it looks almost as if they had nothing in common, as if they would fall completely out of the line of evolution, as if nothing connected them with the rest of mankind. And, as in maneuvers the one marked for defeat must try to turn every previously known situation to his advantage, so the idea that will succumb struggles for every inch of its property. And as the predestined conqueror in maneuvers may not simply fold his hands in his lap, but must operate as if he could otherwise be defeated, so the conquering idea acts with the same vigor, even though it would win anyway, even if it did nothing. Battle position, all muscles taut, every movement has a reason and a goal. This is the state, as we see it up close, of the personality that is striving.

If proximity teaches us diversity, so distance teaches us the general. If the present shows us the divergencies of individuals, so the median distance shows the similarity of means; but the great distance in turn cancels out both, shows the individuals as different, but even so also shows what really connects them. It shows what is most important about the individual, that most profound introspection into and absorption with his own nature, that which leads him to express: the nature of mankind.

What really matters, the ability to listen to oneself, to look deep into oneself, that can hardly be acquired; certainly it cannot be taught. The average person seems to possess this ability only in a few sublime moments, and to live the rest of the time, not according to his own inclinations, but according to principles. He who really has principles, principles of humanity, lives according to his own inclinations. These correspond of course to the principles of humanity, without his knowing it; but perhaps he senses it is so.

And that which is considered the means of art, which is considered style, all those characteristics of which the mediocre believe it is only necessary that they imitate them and they too will become artists – all these things turn out to be secondary matters, whose value is at most that of symptoms. True, the stylistic similarity of masterworks of a time already remote from us can be explained by our external distance from them, and that similarity disappears whenever we draw nearer. And the straight line of the evolution of means shows, upon closer inspection, manifold complexity. Everything that makes up style, however, is at most characteristic for the time in which the person is still alive and struggling with his contemporaries. It is merely a symptom by which the contemporaries are supposed to recognize which are the significant individuals. But it is inconsequential in relation to what distance reveals.

Thus, instruction that is supposed to educate an artist could consist at most in helping him to listen to himself. Technique, the means of art, will not help him. This ought to be, wherever possible, occult knowledge, to which he alone has access who finds the way himself. He who listens to himself acquires this technique. By a route different from that of the curriculum, by roundabout ways perhaps, but with unerring certainty. For he hears that which is common to all, and what it is that sets him apart from the others is perhaps not how he hears it, but *that* he does in fact hear it. And the 'how' of the means is more likely to separate one from the 'what' of art than to bring one closer.

Therefore, I do not recommend to the pupil that he use modern techniques. Of course he should practice them so that he will have the ability to accomplish whatever the spirit should eventually demand. The older means will also do here. The newer will of course cause no harm. But there is perhaps still a copyright on them, a quite arrogant right of ownership, that refuses to open the road to those who will not make the effort themselves. Those who themselves make the effort find it anyway, find it in a way that gives them the right of use. To them the road is open; to the others, who only want to try their hand at it, may it remain closed. Ultimately, the newer techniques will be in the public domain; but then those who use them will at least no longer be wanting to learn 'how to represent a personal style'.

Precisely because I am not recommending these harmonies, it is not necessary for me to give an aesthetic evaluation of them. Besides, whoever comes to them on his own will have no need for a guide. His ear and his sense of integrity will lead him more dependably than any law of art could ever do. There is yet another reason, however, why I may easily omit such an evaluation, without hiding behind a procedure like that in other textbooks. The older theories give a system, and in it appears that which experience can designate as beautiful.

But other things also appear in it, other things that are not recommended, that are even forbidden. The method is as follows: one sets up a number of possible combinations and excludes as exceptions those one considers unfit. A system with exceptions, however, is no system, or at least an inadequate one. Besides, I have proved that the arguments for these exceptions are mostly wrong and – this would be to me the most important thing anyone could learn from this book – that these exceptions are solely the expression of a certain taste in art, which relates to what is natural only in that the taste lags behind what is natural. [I have proved] that these exceptions are only imperfect adaptations to the natural, whereas a more adequate adaptation has to lead to what this book has set as its goal. Yet certainly to more than that, certainly beyond that. [I have proved] then that the rules indicate at best only the degree of penetration into what is naturally given, hence, that they are not eternal laws, but only such that the next achievement always flushes them away. And now, should I also give laws, myself carry out an evaluation of that kind and make exceptions? No one could require that of me, no one who has followed and agreed with what I have said.

I suspect the following question will be put to me: how does one distinguish between the skilful and the bungler, if there is nothing to establish what is good and what is bad? First, I have to say, I do not consider it very important to make any essential distinction between this skill that is meant and bungling. There is little that is impressive about this skill that really consists only in carefully noting and obeying all laws. It is truly difficult to distinguish from bungling, but [to make that distinction is] just as superfluous. The skill of the artist, however, has nothing to do with that. The artist does nothing [so] that others will consider [it] beautiful; he does, rather, only what is necessary for him to do. If others want to apply aesthetic laws to his works, then it is their affair – if they just cannot live without aesthetic laws – to find such as are applicable. But are they really necessary? Can one really not enjoy works of art without aesthetic laws? And then, what about the artistic sensitivity of the layman, who knows nothing of the code (*Tabulatur*)? Schopenhauer explains the respect of the mediocre for the great work of art as belief in authority.[1] Certainly, as far as the respect shown by the broad masses is concerned. But among laymen I have found people whose organs of perception were much more sensitive than those of most professionals. And I know for sure that there are musicians who are more receptive to painting than many painters, and painters who are more receptive to music than most musicians. Whoever does not agree will still at least have to see that – if there is any sense at all in disseminating art – the receptiveness, the sensitivity, the powers of discrimination of the layman are absolutely prerequisite. If he responds sensitively to art, then he must surely be able to evaluate it also – if that is necessary! And if he can evaluate for himself,

[1 Cf. *Sämtliche Werke: Parerga und Paralipomena, zweiter Band* (Zweite Auflage; Wiesbaden: Eberhard Brockhaus Verlag, 1947), pp. 489–90. Masterworks, wrote Schopenhauer, can be enjoyed only by those who have a correspondingly high intellectual and spiritual capacity. Those without such capacity can only accept the judgments of those who have the capacity to judge.]

then for him the aesthetic laws are superfluous. For whom, then, do they exist? For the critic? He who can distinguish a good fruit from a bad with his palate does not have to be able to express the distinction through the chemical formula and does not need the formula to recognize the distinction. But should someone who has no palate pass judgment on foods? And would the chemical formula then be of use to him? Moreover: would he understand how to apply it, and if so: for what purposes would he apply it? Does the pupil have need for the laws, so that he can know how far he may go? I have indeed just said how far he may go: as far as his nature drives him; and he must strive to hear his nature precisely if he wants to be an artist! If he only wants to be a craftsman, then a barrier will appear somewhere all of its own accord; the same barrier that keeps him from artistry will also keep him from going all too far. And suppose a young man should err and go farther than his talent pushes him! Whether he does not become anything special because he went too far or because he did not go far enough, let that be as it may. But fools are always afraid that they will be taken for fools, that is: recognized. They fear they will be duped. This, their uncertainty, is what demands protection. Since the aesthetic laws, in this form at least, cannot be ends in themselves, it seems to me almost as if their sole purpose were to protect the inferior from being taken for fools. Or, perhaps also, secretly, to protect the inferior against being overwhelmed by a new beauty. The mediocre person fears nothing else so much as he fears being compelled to change his view, his philosophy, of life. And he has also set up an ideal for himself, which expresses this fear: character. The man of character, that's the one (to paraphrase a saying of Karl Kraus) whose hardening of the arteries comes from his view of the world.

In another form, however, the aesthetic laws could be an end in themselves. As precise description of those effects that are common to the greatest possible number of works. As attempts to reduce the greatest possible number of effects to the fewest possible common causes. As attempts to organize the phenomena to give perspective. That could be an end in itself, but one would have to be content with it so; and, above all, one should never draw the conclusion: that is true of most works of art, hence it must be true of all others. Enough would have been accomplished, more than one dares require, but the utmost that may be allowed.

Someone will ask why I am writing a textbook of harmony, if I wish technique to be occult knowledge. I could answer: people want to study, to learn, and I want to teach, to disseminate what I hold to be good; thus, I teach. But I think that a person should study. The artist, perhaps, only so that he will get into errors from which he must free himself. The surge of energy that washes away the error then cleanses him also of whatever other inhibitions were soiling him. A catarrh of the eye is healed by provoking inflammation of the eye. The healing process heals not only this inflammation but also the actual illness. But the artist should also study because not everyone has to begin at the beginning, not everyone has to experience first-hand all the errors that accompany the progress of human knowledge. One must and may to a certain degree depend upon one's predecessors. Their experiences and observations they have recorded in part in the [literature of the various] sciences; but another part – I do not know whether it is the most dependable or not – lies in the unconscious, in instinct.[1] It is our right and duty to doubt. But to make ourselves independent of instinct is as difficult as it is dangerous. For, alongside [the knowledge of] what is right and what is wrong, alongside the inherited experiences and observations of our ancestors, alongside that which we owe to their and our past, there is in the instinct perhaps a faculty that is only now being developed: a knowledge of the future; perhaps also other faculties, which man will one day consciously possess, but which at present he can at most only sense and yearn for but cannot translate into action. The artist's creative activity is instinctive. Consciousness has little influence on it. He feels as if what he does were dictated to him. As if he did it only according to the will of some power or other within him, whose laws he does not know. He is merely the instrument of a will hidden from him, of instinct, of his unconscious. Whether it is new or old, good or bad, beautiful or ugly, he does not know. He feels only the instinctual compulsion, which he must obey. And in this instinct the old may find expression, and the new. Such as depends on the past, and such as points out paths to the future. Old truths or new errors. [It is] his musical nature, as he inherited it from a musical ancestor or acquired it through the literature, but [it is] perhaps also the outflow of an energy that is seeking new paths. Right or wrong, new or old, beautiful or ugly – how does one know who only senses the instinctual urge? Who would dare to differentiate right from wrong in the instinct, in the unconscious, to keep separate the knowledge inherited from predecessors and the intuitive power granted by the spirit? The artist must study, must learn, whether he wants to or not; for he has learned already, before he became capable of wanting to. In his instinct, in his unconscious lies a wealth of old knowledge, which he will resurrect whether he wants to or not. The true artist will be as little harmed by what he learns from the teacher as by what he learned this way prior to his time of awareness.

And the person of ordinary talents, who is not actually productive in that highest sense – he, above all, should study. For him study and learning is an end in itself. His task is to take for knowledge what is in reality only belief. Knowledge makes him strong; for the others, belief is enough. He does not discover for himself from the beginning, nor would he know how to advance on his own beyond the middle. If he will really remain the ordinary person, as he was born, then he must always keep equal the distance above and below himself; and since those above him push forward, he must move along at a suitable interval behind. What he does not have to discover because it was already discovered, and is not able to discover because otherwise he would be superior, that he must learn. To protect him from errors is just as little necessary as it is possible. But instruction can lead him as far as he must go if he wants to be a good average. Since he cannot himself produce something of value, he can at least be made capable of appreciating properly the values others create;

[1 The impact of Sigmund Freud's work (and that of Jung and Adler) on his Viennese contemporary, Schoenberg, and on other artists of the period, invites investigation and speculation.]

and that is an end that would make teaching worthwhile. 'There are relatively enough people who know how to produce, but relatively few who know how to be consumers,' says Adolf Loos. It could indeed even be the purpose of teaching to cultivate consumers. Not through aesthetic rules, of course, but through enlargement of their field of vision.

But there is yet another reason [for my writing this book], perhaps the most compelling: the formulation of a course of study [a theory or doctrine – *Lehre*] can be an end in itself. Without being directed at an actual pupil it can speak to an imaginary one. Perhaps the pupil is only an outward projection of the teacher. The teacher speaks to himself when he speaks to that pupil. 'Mit mir nur rat ich, red ich zu dir' ('I am only deliberating with myself when I speak to you').[1] He instructs himself, is his own teacher, his own pupil. That he allows the public to listen in, when his intention is actually to make things clear to himself, by removing the rubble of old errors and setting up in their place new errors, perhaps, but at least more farsighted ones – that here he allows the public to listen in is analogous to the work of art that he creates and turns over to the public. He comes to terms with himself, and the public listens; for the people know: it concerns them.

Hence, I can just as well abstain from giving an aesthetic evaluation of these new harmonies. It will come sometime; perhaps it will not. Perhaps it will be good, though probably not. I hope it will be intelligent enough to affirm: these are the things that up to now are considered good; the others have for the time being still not found favor, but probably sometime later they, too, will be accepted. I should not fail to mention, however, a few little experiences and observations that have come to me from the contemplation of actual compositions. Obviously, I can do that only by intuition; this intuition, moreover, is dependent upon preconditions, upon the influence of my inborn and acquired *Kultur*. Therefore, I do not exclude what I do not happen to mention. Possibly, I have not noticed it yet; probably, I do not know it yet. And if I do not write everything that must be considered possible by association or inference (*Kombination*), perhaps it is because inhibitions of my earlier education stand in my way. In composing I make decisions only according to feeling, according to the feeling for form. This tells me what I must write; everything else is excluded. Every chord I put down corresponds to a necessity, to a necessity of my urge to expression; perhaps, however, also to the necessity of an inexorable but unconscious logic in the harmonic structure. I am firmly convinced that logic is present here, too, at least as much so as in the previously cultivated fields of harmony. And as proof of this I can cite the fact that corrections of the inspiration, the idea (*Einfall*), out of external formal considerations, to which the alert consciousness is only too often disposed, have generally spoiled the idea. This proves to me that the idea was obligatory, that it had necessity, that the harmonies present in it are components of the idea, in which one may change nothing.

Generally, in the use of chords with six or more tones, there will appear the

[1 Wotan, to Brünnhilde, *Die Walküre*, Act II, Scene 2.]

tendency to soften the dissonances through wide spacing of the individual chord tones. That such is a softening is obvious. For the image of what the dissonances actually are, more remote overtones, is imitated in a satisfying way. It is in this sense that the following quotation from my monodrama, *Erwartung*,[1] is to be understood.

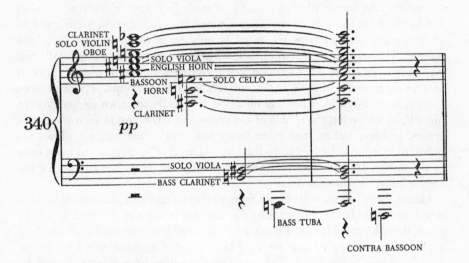

Eleven different tones appear in this chord. But the gentle instrumentation and the fact that the dissonances are widely spaced make this sound quite delicate. Perhaps there is something else besides: the individual groups of tones are so arranged that one could easily refer them to previously known forms. For example, in the first group I believe the ear expects the following resolution:

That is does not come can do no more damage here than when the resolution is omitted in simple harmonies. The second chord may be resolved as in Example 342*a*; this resolution may be combined (342*b*) with that of the first chord (341), and this combination may be interpreted as in 342*c*. [It is] an addition of two chords that have a diminished seventh chord in common; by virtue of two different bass tones this diminished seventh chord is turned into two different ninth chords.

[1] Measures 382–3.]

Such a derivation, however, will not always apply; the reference to older forms will not always work, or, if so, only by very broad interpretation. For on a different occasion I write such a chord in much closer position. And in a string quartet by my pupil, Anton von Webern,[1] there is the following:

Franz Schreker, in his opera, *Der ferne Klang*, writes, among many other things, the following:[2]

where, although of course many of the individual sonorities are to be attributed to moving voices, the similarity with the samples previously given still holds: namely, that the chord-building capacity of dissonances does not depend on possibilities of or tendencies toward resolution. The Hungarian composer, Béla Bartók, also comes close in some of his piano pieces to these acoustical sensations (*Klangempfindungen*), as the following passage demonstrates:[3]

[1] *Fünf Sätze für Streichquartett*, Op. 5, first movement, fifth measure.]
[2] Act I, scene 7, measure 36.]
[3] *Fourteen Bagatelles*, Op. 6, X, measures 36–7. (New York: Boosey and Hawkes, New Version, 1950. In this edition the *b♭* and the *a♭* in the treble of these measures recur, unraised.)]

The following, from a composition by my pupil, Alban Berg,[1] is also an interesting example:

Why it is that way and why it is correct, I cannot yet explain in any detail. In general, it is self-evident to those who accept my view concerning the nature of dissonance. But that it is correct, I firmly believe, and a number of others believe it too. It seems that the progression of such chords can be justified by the chromatic scale. The chord progression seems to be regulated by the tendency to include in the second chord tones that were missing in the first, generally those a half step higher or lower. Nevertheless, the voices seldom move by half step. Then, I have noticed that tone doublings, octaves, seldom appear. The explanation for that is, perhaps, that the tone doubled would acquire a predominance over the others and would thereby turn into a kind of root, which it should scarcely be. There is perhaps also an instinctive (possibly exaggerated) aversion to recalling even remotely the traditional chords. For the same reason, apparently, the simple chords of the earlier harmony do not appear successfully in this environment. I believe, however, that there is another reason for their absence here. I believe they would sound too cold, too dry, expressionless. Or, perhaps, what I mentioned on an earlier occasion applies here. Namely, that these simple chords, which are imperfect imitations of nature, seem to us too primitive. That they lack something, which, for example, Japanese painting lacks when compared with ours: perspective, depth. Perspective and depth of sound could be what we find wanting in the simple three and four-part harmonies. And as in a picture one section can hardly show regard for perspective while another disregards it, without impairing the effect, so perhaps, analogously, these somewhat empty sounds cannot appear alongside those full,

[1 *Vier Lieder*, Op. 2, No. 4: 'Warm die Lüfte', fourth measure before the end.]

sumptuous sounds; whereas the exclusive use of the one *or* the other assures coherence, hence the right effect.

It is striking, and suggestive of conclusions, that I and those who write in a similar vein distinguish precisely when a five or six-part chord should appear, when a chord of yet more parts. It would not be possible without impairing the effect to omit a tone in an eight-part chord, or to add one to a five-part chord. Even the spacing is obligatory; as soon as a tone is misplaced the meaning changes, the logic and utility is lost, coherence seems destroyed. Laws apparently prevail here. What they are, I do not know. Perhaps I shall know in a few years. Perhaps someone after me will find them. For the present the most we can do is describe.

I will forgo any further description in favor of yet another idea I want to mention in closing. In a musical sound (*Klang*) three characteristics are recognized: its pitch, color [timbre], and volume. Up to now it has been measured in only one of the three dimensions in which it operates, in the one we call 'pitch'. Attempts at measurement in the other dimensions have scarcely been undertaken to date; organization of their results into a system has not yet been attempted at all. The evaluation of tone color (*Klangfarbe*), the second dimension of tone, is thus in a still much less cultivated, much less organized state than is the aesthetic evaluation of these last-named harmonies. Nevertheless, we go right on boldly connecting the sounds with one another, contrasting them with one another, simply by feeling; and it has never yet occurred to anyone to require here of a theory that it should determine laws by which one may do that sort of thing. Such just cannot be done at present. And, as is evident, we can also get along without such laws. Perhaps we should differentiate still more precisely, if attempts at measurement in this second dimension had already achieved a palpable result. Again, perhaps not. Anyway, our attention to tone colors is becoming more and more active, is moving closer and closer to the possibility of describing and organizing them. At the same time, probably, to restrictive theories, as well. For the present we judge the artistic effect of these relationships only by feeling. How all that relates to the essence of natural sound we do not know, perhaps we can hardly guess at it yet; but we do write progressions of tone colors without a worry, and they do somehow satisfy the sense of beauty. What system underlies these progressions?

The distinction between tone color and pitch, as it is usually expressed, I cannot accept without reservations. I think the tone becomes perceptible by virtue of tone color, of which one dimension is pitch. Tone color is, thus, the main topic, pitch a subdivision. Pitch is nothing else but tone color measured in one direction. Now, if it is possible to create patterns out of tone colors that are differentiated according to pitch, patterns we call 'melodies', progressions, whose coherence (*Zusammenhang*) evokes an effect analogous to thought processes, then it must also be possible to make such progressions out of the tone colors of the other dimension, out of that which we call simply 'tone color', progressions whose relations with one another work with a kind of logic entirely equivalent to that logic which satisfies us in the melody of pitches. That has the appearance of a futuristic fantasy and is probably just that. But it is one which, I firmly believe, will be realized. I firmly believe it is capable of heightening in an unprecedented manner the sensory, intellectual, and spiritual pleasures offered by art. I firmly believe that it will bring us closer to the illusory stuff of our dreams; that it will expand our relationships to that which seems to us today inanimate as we give life from our life to that which is temporarily dead for us, but dead only by virtue of the slight connection we have with it.

Tone-color melodies! How acute the senses that would be able to perceive them! How high the development of spirit that could find pleasure in such subtle things!

In such a domain, who dares ask for theory!

APPENDIX

AUTHOR'S FOOTNOTE FROM PAGE 25

Concerning his calculations, Dr. Robert Neumann has informed me as follows (in part):

As more and more of the possible combinations of our twelve tempered scale degrees are felt and used as harmony, the stock of unused possibilities is being gradually exhausted; and the continuing need for new harmonic (and melodic) vocabulary will finally break through the boundaries of the system. Then new systems of temperament with smaller intervals might come about, later perhaps even complete independence and freedom in the use of all conceivable intervals, all conceivable frequencies and combinations. Now the division of the octave into 53 equal parts would be an example of a new temperament that could come under practical consideration: specifically, whenever music has advanced so far that there is need for a system with about four times as many tones as we now have; and when there is need (or more correctly, when there is again need) for the purest possible intonation of the basic intervals – those determined by the first overtones – but at the same time, no wish to do without the convenience of a temperament. As intermediate stages between the 12 and the 53-part division of the octave only multiples of 12 could be considered, thus, division into 24, 36, and 48 parts; for with any other number of parts there would be no sufficiently pure fifth. The first step, anyway, is to divide every semi-tone into two equal parts, whereby the octave would be divided into 24 parts. Dividing again by 2, one could then obtain 48 parts. A 48th of an octave and a 53rd are almost the same size; the 53-part temperament, however, is preferable to the 48-part because of the much greater purity of the consonances. The 48-part system has of course the same basic intervals as appear in our 12-part temperament, from which it is derived. Now our tempered fifth is indeed already pure, but that of the 53-part system is about 28 2/3 times purer; the third of the 53-part system is about 9 times purer than ours and is even purer than our fifth, which is only 7 times purer than the third.

The average musician will laugh at such speculations and will not be inclined to see their point. It is clear that, just as the overtones led to the 12-part division of the simplest consonance, the octave, so they will eventually bring about the further differentiation of this interval. To future generations music like ours will seem incomplete, since it has not yet fully exploited everything latent in sound, just as a sort of music that did not yet differentiate within the octave would seem incomplete to us. Or, to cite an analogy – which one has only to think through completely to see how very relevant it is: The sound of our music will at that time seem to have no depth, no perspective, just as Japanese painting, for example, affects us as primitive compared with our own, because without perspective it lacks depth.[1] That [change] will come, if not in the manner that some believe, and if not as soon. It will not come through reasoning (*aus Gründen*), but from elemental sources (*Ursachen*); it will not come from without, but from within. It will not come through imitation of some prototype, and not as technical accomplishment; for it is far more a matter of mind and spirit (*Geist*) than of material, and the *Geist* must be ready.

The fashion of recent years to set off the culture of older, oriental, and exotic peoples against that of Europe seems disposed to encroach also on music. Whether or not the achievements of these peoples are in themselves just as great or greater than ours, they represent, nevertheless, either the higher stage of development of a lower cultural level or the lower stage of development of a higher cultural level. The true relation of these cultures to European culture, and vice versa, can be compared to the relation of the pony express to visual telegraphy and of the latter to wireless telegraphy. As the most primitive form of the second surpasses in speed the highest form of the first, so the most primitive of the third has the advantage over the highest of the second. Nevertheless, whereas technical achievements can almost always be transferred directly [from one culture to another], spiritual and cultural achievements perhaps sometimes, in the field of music the first difficulty to be encountered is the question of the criteria for determining the higher culture. One may assume that *finer subdivision of the octave into scale degrees* (*Mehrstufigkeit*) indicates a higher level of development. Then, the greater number of available scale degrees yields so many more melodic possibilities that, even with its greater age, music embodying such has probably not yet had time to advance much beyond the elaboration of monophonic combinations. Hence, there all polyphony is probably at best in its early, tentative stage, comparable to the initial stage of polyphony in our music several centuries ago. In the meantime our music has rather exhaustively exploited the possible relations of seven tones, not just in one voice, but in several voices, and with the concurrent refinement of motivic logic besides. And now our music is about to attempt the same with twelve tones. Let it be freely admitted that the same [ideas, feelings?] can be expressed with more primitive as well as with more advanced combinations. But that must then also hold for us, and our music could then advance only by widening the circle of our thought, of our ideas. It should of course not be overlooked that a progression of tones is in itself, to a certain extent, a musical idea and that the number of such ideas increases with the number of available tones. Never-

[1 In the first edition Schoenberg's footnote ended here. Amplifying his footnote *c*. 1920–21, he looked forward to an immediate musical future of 'twelve tones squared by . . . polyphony'. This was apparently one of the steps 'closer to the truth' that he mentioned in the Preface to the revised edition (*supra*, p. 4).

Schoenberg's venture in this footnote into biased cultural comparisons can detract our attention from his main point: i.e. that the proposals of Robert Neumann, Busoni, and the rest of the microtone enthusiasts are mere theoretical formulations that correspond to no musical or cultural necessity. Essential musical change must come from deep within a culture and be expressed first in new music, not in theory. Musical styles and techniques are not to be changed by theory alone.]

theless, twelve tones squared by the second dimension, polyphony, presumably yield just as many combinations as twenty-four tones that are combined mono-phonically, in only one dimension. There are enough possibilities, at least, to postpone for some time any necessity for further subdivision of the octave.

It is a different matter if one considers as the criterion for the more advanced stage, not the finer subdivision of the octave (*Mehrstufigkeit*), but polyphony (*Mehrstimmigkeit*): the use of several voices to present the idea and its ramifi-cations. It has to be admitted that such a presentation is at least more concen-trated; for it transfers a part – at least – of what is to be presented to space, by virtue of simultaneous sound, whereas monophonic presentation also needs time [i.e. in polyphonic writing more happens in a given time].

If we consider, however, that next to the lofty requirements of elegance, uniqueness, and integrity, only intensity can serve as a criterion of true art, then it becomes clear that we can easily disregard those who have recommended to painters and sculptors the imitation of exotic and primitive art – even going as far as Negro carvings and children's drawings. And we can most especially disregard those who, since they themselves are barren of understanding and ideas, also want to reduce the language [of music] in its ideational content to a quarter-tone art. They are modern, indeed (for they do not know what matters), but they are not prophetic of the future. To predict or influence the future, even more than to be modern, a sense of timing is important. Whoever predicts rain and misses the time is a bad prophet. And a doctor who has a patient buried before he is dead, a woman who bears a child before it can live – these are ahead of their time, but not in a very exemplary fashion. It is not merely tone that makes music, but timing (*das Zeitmass*) as well; and it is typical of dilettantes of all fields and tendencies that they are devoid of all feeling for at least one or the other – tone or timing.

AUTHOR'S FOOTNOTE FROM PAGE 97

These sentences, written ten years ago, may today – 1920 – serve as en-couragement to all who, in losing the war, suffered loss of their self-esteem. Since we lost a war, there was little else for the others to do but to win it: it was more to our credit that we lost it than it was to theirs that they won it. We were fully active. It is not that the war *was lost*, rather that *we lost it*. We set ourselves back a few notches: that is their war reparations. We do not need any; otherwise we should receive them, too. We are not only capable of continuing to exist without war reparations, as they think they cannot do, but they themselves consider our strength still great enough that we can even pay reparations. In light of that, who can claim that we are decadent!

The alleged 'extinction' ('*Untergang*')[1] of a civilization (that of an entire section of the world is fortunately an impossibility, at least linguistically) is

[1 The first volume of Oswald Spengler's *Untergang des Abendlandes* (*Decline of the West*) was published in 1918. Whether or not Schoenberg had read that work, he was attacking that widespread pessimism of which Spengler was a noted spokesman.]

strictly a historicism not founded upon any coherent thought. A good man grows old gracefully, and if he was not much worse than average, he possesses wisdom. Thus a nation, too, whose achievements are esteemed by posterity, is not contemptible from the moment in which posterity's interest turns – for unknown reasons – to other nations. Whoever sees in the old man nothing more than a cadaver to be gobbled up shortly by worms; whoever does not believe in the immortality of the soul; whoever does not sense that the soul of an old man is about to be elevated to a new plateau (as yet unrecognized by historians) – only such can forget what sort of greybeards Goethe, Wagner, Schopenhauer, Kant may well have been. But neither does a nation by any means have to be decadent at the moment of its defeat, yes, even annihilation. Hector slays Patroclus and Achilles Hector: *at least two* of these would be *decadent*. The better is the enemy of the good: the 1920 model of a typewriter can be replaced by the 1921 model, if 1921 is better than 1920. Yet the older model does not therefore write *worse than before* (in principle, naturally), but *just as well*.

AUTHOR'S FOOTNOTE FROM PAGE 154

At certain places on the circle of fifths a so-called enharmonic change has to occur. This stems from the circumstance that in our system of notation, as everyone knows, every pitch can be expressed by two or more symbols. Thus, $c\sharp$ equals $d\flat$, $f\sharp$ equals $g\flat$, f equals $e\sharp$ or $g\flat\flat$, etc. The same is true of chords ($d\sharp-f\times-a\sharp$ equals $e\flat-g-b\flat$, $b-d\sharp-f\sharp$ equals $c\flat-e\flat-g\flat$, etc.), of whole keys ($G\flat$ major equals $F\sharp$ major, $a\flat$ minor equals $g\sharp$ minor, $D\flat$ major equals $C\sharp$ major, etc.), and also of tone progressions (a succession of tones, $d\sharp-f\sharp-e-c\sharp-d\sharp$, for example, enharmonically changed, reads $e\flat-g\flat-f\flat-d\flat-e\flat$). The purpose of these enharmonic changes is, first of all, to promote legibility by means of the simplest possible notation and only subsequently [involves] the so-called spelling. Wherever in the course of a composition an excessively complicated notation makes its appearance (the necessity for such cannot arise here for the time being), it will be best to choose a point for the enharmonic change where a chord with multiple meanings permits a different notation. I think we must not be too anxious about the so-called spelling. Most essential, it seems to me, is simple notation. When it is asserted that the purpose and sense of the spelling is to show the derivation of chords, I counter by saying that in simple passages the derivation will be clear even without any intricate notation; but in complicated ones where the sense of the passage is more accessible to the reader than to the performer, I find that consideration for the performer is of more importance and, consequently, I still give absolute preference to the simple notation. The performer has no time; he has to keep in tempo! Now the [visual] impression becomes just as confusing [as the question of derivation] when, along with rapid harmonic changes, flats, sharps, double flats, and double sharps appear too close to one another and with too frequent changes. For that reason it is well to rely, wherever possible, on the key signature most appropriate for the particular segment of the piece, if possible, the key signature given at the outset for the whole piece. Above all, let us prefer that notation which contains fewer sharps or flats, and where possible no double flats and double sharps. In very complicated writing it is often hardly possible to devise any really simple notation. That is so because of the inadequacy of our notational system, which is oriented in the C-major, diatonic scale, rather than in the chromatic scale. In C major c♯ (d♭) is not regarded as an independent tone, but as a tone derived from c (or d); hence it has no place of its own on the staff and no name of its own.

Of course these difficulties will not arise here for some time yet. I mention them only because I just read somewhere that the expression, circle of fifths, is not entirely adequate. Allegedly, the names of the keys should actually be written on a spiral because C♭ major and B major are not the same, neither according to their origins not according to their frequencies; the line should consequently not return exactly to itself. That is remarkable. In that whole book hardly an observation is made that is really founded on the natural tone, or at least it is never thought through to the correct conclusion (true, I have not read the book from cover to cover – too dull an undertaking for me – but have only browsed through it). But just here, just where we are concerned with the *musical* relationship of keys – if you please, with the *musical* relationship, hence, relationship of the *tempered* keys; indeed, strictly speaking, not even with these, but merely with their notation on paper! – should, just at this point, the question of the natural tone be raised? After all, in the tempered scale the octaves are perfect, above all the octaves, and B major is thus really assumed to be identical with C♭ major. That way it is easy to be a theorist! Although I do indeed know how to compose, I am no theorist; I only teach the handicraft of composition.

AUTHOR'S FOOTNOTE FROM PAGE 175

I see in Riemann's *Vereinfachte Harmonielehre*[1] that this inventive, fertile thinker also hit upon the notion of opening up the wealth of the old church modes; for he introduces such terms as 'Dorian sixth', 'Lydian fourth', etc. But by virtue of his giving names to the individual phenomena he turns them into special cases and in so doing deprives them of further development. They are then merely antiquarian reminiscences of the church modes, through whose use certain singular effects are created, as in Brahms's music. In my view the notion of secondary dominants etc. embraces all this [wealth from the church modes], and I therefore stand on the premise that the major and minor keys only accidentally lost this characteristic, the inclusion of nondiatonic chords, during a short period of music. For if we sum up the characteristics of the church modes, we get major and minor plus a number of nondiatonic phenomena. And the way in which the nondiatonic events of one church mode were carried over to the other modes I conceive as the process by which our two present-day modes

[1 Hugo Riemann, *Harmony Simplified: or the Theory of the Tonal Functions of Chords* (trans. Rev. H. Beverunge; London: Augener and Company [1895]), pp. 88–97.]

crystallized out of the church modes. Accordingly, major and minor contain all those nondiatonic possibilities inherently, by virtue of this historical synthesis. Only, in the period of homophonic music, when composers restricted themselves on the average to three or four degrees, those possibilities were merely used less or not at all and were forgotten. But they are inherent, thus do not have to be introduced only as special cases; they have merely to be drawn out.

Heinrich Schenker (*Neue musikalische Phantasien und Theorien*) makes decidedly a far more systematic attempt to elucidate these harmonies by speaking of a tonicalization process (*Tonikalisierungsprozess*).[1] He means the wish of a secondary degree to become [a] tonic, or its potential to do so. This wish would imply that a dominant should precede that degree. His conception is in fact rather similar to mine. Yet I find it inexpedient and incorrect to present the matter this way.[2] Inexpedient, because there is much that either could not be explained thereby or only in a very complicated manner. Here may be the reason why Schenker does not arrive at so inclusive a synthesis as I. According to my presentation, for example, a deceptive cadence from a secondary dominant is easily explainable, as will be seen. Since we cannot speak of tonicalization here, because the second chord (e.g. III–IV) is not the tonic of the first and the first is not the dominant of the second, we should have to speak, according to Schenker's conception, of tonicalization deferred by a deceptive cadence. That explanation would indeed be valid, even though it is complicated; but it does have a shortcoming, in that this tonic that gives the whole process its name may not appear at all.[3] Nevertheless – not even taking into account that these chords are actually the dominants of the old church modes, although strictly speaking we must take that into account; and although Schenker is certainly thinking about the center tones of the old church modes – I consider it incorrect to associate these secondary degrees with the word, tonic, thus lending them a meaning they do not have: within a given key there is only one tonic; *f–a–c* is in *C major* nothing more than a form of the IVth degree and can be conceived as tonicalized only by one who unjustifiably calls it *F major*. That such a meaning cannot be accorded all these degrees is shown by the example opposite.

Here, in *a*), the chords between the beginning and the end without doubt function as secondary triads. The variation-like elaboration in *b*), where secondary-dominant sevenths and the like are used, changes nothing at all in the function of these triads. That is still more easily seen in four-part composition (*vierstimmigen Satz*), where the occurrence of a leading tone need have noth-

[1 *Harmony*, pp. 256–301.]
[2 Schoenberg rewrote the remainder of this footnote, adding the (unnumbered) example below. The essential change is the addition of the remark that a key has only one tonic. This remark defines 'monotonality', as he developed that idea here and in his later book, *Structural Functions of Harmony*.]
[3 The 'tonic' may not appear, but it is expected. A 'deceptive cadence' leads us to expect a 'tonic', then betrays our expectation.]

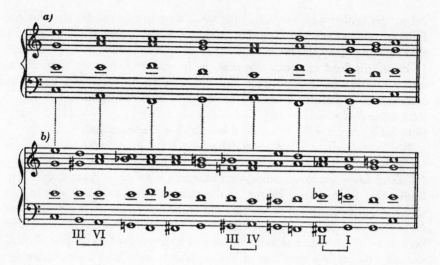

ing at all to do with a tonic; the leading tone can go just as well to other degrees.[1]

AUTHOR'S FOOTNOTE FROM PAGE 180

An explanation might be found as follows: *Wechseldominante* has a counterpart in the word *Wechselbalg* (changeling). This word is of course understood to mean a child that has been exchanged for another. Since, however, it invariably has to do with a misshapen child that was substituted by witches or the devil for the real child, I hit upon the idea that *Wechselbalg* is related to *vexieren* (to vex): i.e. to torment, to fool, to tease. A *Vexierbalg* would then be a child substituted with intent to torment, fool, tease. If we look for more synonyms we find: to annoy, delude, deceive, the last of which, in the sense of illusion, appears in connection with ghosts or apparitions (*Spuk*). Accordingly, one might think *wechseln* and *vexieren* are in fact the same word. Whether then *Wechsler* (money changers, bankers) and *Wechsel* (money changing, banking) may be [inherently] fraudulent; or whether the creditor, by virtue of his having the promissory note (*Wechsel*), has the right to vex (*vexieren*) the debtor, to torment him by demanding payment – we may be indifferent to these questions since torment as well as deceit could be correct translations [of the word *Wechsel*], and the word could have gained its double meaning from the relationship of the two. [We may] similarly [ignore] the question, whether one calls the exchange (*Umtauschen*) of the money of one country for that of another *Wechseln* because of the loss suffered in the transaction, or, as I assume: because the broker from whom one bought drafts (*Wechsel*) for payment of foreign

[1 This sentence does not appear in the first edition nor in the revised edition of 1922. Schoenberg added it in his 'Handexemplar . . .', and it is included (in italics) in the seventh edition, p. 208 (see *supra*, Translator's Preface, p. xvi).]

debts, the broker who converted (*umtauschte*) money into drafts, who confounded (*verwechselte*) [money and drafts], was also called *Wechsler* when he sold foreign money, *Wechsler*, whether he converted [one's money] into drafts (*Wechsel*) or hard currency. Because, as is well known, only forgetfulness assuages unavoidable annoyance and vexation, so the vexatious deceit that accompanies exchange (*Wechseln*) could finally be best forgotten, and the objectionable (*bedenklich*) word [*Wechseln*] could become a synonym of the unobjectionable (*unbedenklich* – 'not to think about it') '*umtauschen*'.

Now the *Fux'sche Wechselnote* (changing tone) contradicts the foregoing, for in Italian it is called *cambiata* (from *cambiare*); moreover, *Cambia Valute* (*Wechselstube* – exchange office) and *changer* (*Wechseln* – change, exchange) testify that in Romance languages the same notion, *wechseln*, and in both meanings, is used without the implication of *vexieren* (annoy, deceive, torment). Nevertheless, even if many German words do stem from Latin and Italian, because as we learned an activity we learned its name, even so the first *Wechsler* was not necessarily a merchant of Venice; he may have been from Nuremberg. He may even have been from Holland; it is certainly not impossible, for Amsterdam indeed still serves as the world money market. And even the *Fux'sche Wechselnote* may have come from the Netherlands, from the period of the Dutch hegemony: The Romance languages, unaware of the deceit in *Wechseln*, may then have learned to use this expression as a musical term from the Germanic languages.

What interests us in the relations among the verbs *vexieren*, annoy, torment, and *wechseln* is, in particular, the connotation of *deceit*. Then our *Wechseldominante* would be called *Vexierdominante* and would then be a *deceptive dominant*, that is, one that executes a *deceptive progression* (II–I).

AUTHOR'S FOOTNOTE FROM PAGE 203

To what extent men lose their awareness of sense can be witnessed in the two examples, picked out at random, that follow. The one: *Strasse* (road, highway, street) is the connection across the countryside of two separate, distinct localities. But since the *Wege* (paths, roads) in the city have been lengthened and widened to accommodate the traffic, their designation as *Gasse* (lane, street) is disappearing more and more, and soon this word will no longer appear in the German dictionary. – The other example: New cities are criticized for laying out their *Strassen* – properly, *Gassen* – in straight lines at right angles with one another: that layout is not considered beautiful. But it is not the purpose of *Gassen* to be beautiful; they are rather the interconnected spaces between rows of houses and serve to connect each house with all other houses and to give access to every house. Wherever it can be done – in level terrain – *Gassen* are laid out in straight lines; for the straight line is the shortest distance between two points in our terrestrial geometry. This way saves time, money, and work. Where it cannot be done – in undulating, hilly terrain, and if the community does not raise the money for levelling – the *Gasse* follows not so much the former footpaths, rather, the carriage roads (*Fahrstrassen*) and reaches the top by making large and gradual curves around every significant hill, as is necessary for the lungs of men and horses. This is the way the beauty of the old cityscape came into being. I would no sooner impugn this beauty than I would the contrasting beauty of the new cities. Both are beautiful for the same reason; those who laid them out and built them completely fulfilled their obligation by doing what was practical, without any other consideration. In return for that the good Lord gave the beholder the ability to forget sense and purpose and to find the practical beautiful. But, with all the enjoyment of this beauty: how far may forgetfulness go? In a large German city I had often and in great haste to visit the centrally-situated house of a young colleague,[1] and saw my patience put to a severe test: this house could be reached only by circuitous routes. The *Gassen* (which, naturally, were called *Strassen*) were laid out somewhat like the paths in a park from the period of Louis XIV. The *Kultur* to which the second generation has risen, through much reading and with the help of the money of the first, is certainly noteworthy; but I fear that the first, which read less, must have complained every time that, thanks to the many circuitous routes, they arrived just a few minutes too late at the stock exchange.[2]

AUTHOR'S FOOTNOTE FROM PAGE 395

Just now (1911), while engaged in correcting the proofs, I am leafing through his book, *Ein neuer exotischer Musikstil* (*A New Exotic Style in Music*), and I find that, armed with a quotation from Riemann, he attacks the 'dogma' of independent voice leading, the forbidden parallels. Then he cites Professor Stumpf, who says it is conceivable and probable 'that the [intervallic] relations 4:7, 7:8, 5:7, and the like will be raised gradually to the status of consonances'. – At such moments I regret that I know so little. I have to guess at all of it. If I had only had an inkling that a scholar with the reputation of Stumpf represents the same view as I! I am ignorant of all these sources and have to depend on a single source: on thinking. Then one progresses more slowly! But one can get along, nevertheless. And I was right when I instinctively resisted the 'back-to-nature' movement and was puzzled that a Debussy would hope to find nature behind the pathways of art, on the stretches already travelled – in that hinterland that is becoming a place aloof from art by harboring stragglers and

[1 '. . . eines jungen Cottages'. Apparently, 'Cottage' is a misprint for 'Kollege'.]
[2 These remarks may be interpreted as follows:
The layout of the streets may have facilitated their construction; but they do not, for that reason, necessarily fulfil their purpose – to connect houses – in the most exemplary fashion. Something 'practical' may be, or come to be, considered 'beautiful'. It is then imitated without regard for its original meaning, practicality, or even necessity, and without regard for its appropriateness under different conditions. – Schoenberg's intent, at least, is clear: he will have no gratuitous counterpoint in harmony exercises.]

marauders; [I was puzzled] that a Debussy would not sense that whoever wants
to get to nature must go, not backward, but *forward*: ahead to nature! Had I a
maxim, it could perhaps be this. I think, however, there is something even
loftier than nature.

[Georg Capellen's book was not available for collation.]

AUTHOR'S FOOTNOTE FROM PAGE 407

The list of those who use such resources today (1921) would probably be
extensive. I do not wish, however, to diminish the value of my book by embracing current events just to bring it up to date. Moreover, the quantity and
quality of the fellow combatants does not entirely please me. For them, there is
once again a new 'Direction', naturally, and they call themselves 'atonalists'.
I have to dissociate myself from that, however, for I am a musician and have
nothing to do with things atonal. The word 'atonal' could only signify something entirely inconsistent with the nature of tone. Even the word 'tonal' is
incorrectly used if it is intended in an exclusive rather than inclusive sense. It
can be valid only in the following sense: Everything implied by a series of
tones (*Tonreihe*) constitutes tonality, whether it be brought together by means
of direct reference to a single fundamental or by more complicated connections.
That from this single correct definition no reasonable opposite corresponding
to the word 'atonality' can be formed, must be evident. Where could the nega-
tion be introduced? Is it that *not all* implications of a series of tones, or *not any*,
should characterize atonality? [I.e. does atonality exclude only certain implications or all of them?] A piece of music will always have to be tonal, at least in
so far as a relation has to exist from tone to tone by virtue of which the tones,
placed next to or above one another, yield a perceptible continuity. The
tonality [itself] may then perhaps be neither perceptible nor provable; these relations may be obscure and difficult to comprehend, even incomprehensible.
Nevertheless, to call any relation of tones atonal is just as farfetched as it would
be to designate a relation of colors aspectral or acomplementary. There is no
such antithesis. Besides, there has been no investigation at all of the question
whether the way these new sounds go together is not actually the tonality of a
twelve-tone series. It is indeed probably just that, hence would be a phenomenon
paralleling the situation that led to the church modes, of which I say (page 25):
'The effect of a fundamental tone was felt, but since no one knew which tone
it was, all of them were tried.' Here we do not yet even feel the fundamental;
nevertheless, it is therefore [?] probably present. If one insists on looking for
names, 'polytonal' or 'pantonal'[1] could be considered. Yet, before anything
else, we should determine whether it is not again simply 'tonal'. This is all then
a piece of nonsense; and as certain as it is that among the atonalists there are

[1 Cf. Rudolph Reti, *Tonality in Modern Music* (New York: Collier Books, 1962).
This work originally bore the title *Tonality, Atonality, Pantonality*. On pages 54–9
appears a critique of Schoenberg's *Theory of Harmony*.]

many who could more appropriately occupy themselves with something really atonal, rather than with this manufacture of bad compositions, I believe, nevertheless, that these same people would not succeed even in anything atonal – at least not in anything with tones. (Excepted here is the Viennese, Josef Hauer.[1] His theories are profound and original, even where I find them extravagant. His compositions betray creative talent, even where they seem to me more like 'examples' than compositions. But his attitude, his courage and self-sacrifice, makes him in every way worthy of respect.) The sad part is just that the idea, 'one may write anything today', keeps so many young people from first learning something accepted and respectable, from first understanding the classics, from first acquiring *Kultur*. For in former times, too, one could write anything; only – it was not good. Masters are the only ones who may never write just anything, but must rather do what is necessary: fulfil their mission. To prepare for this mission with all diligence, laboring under a thousand doubts whether one is adequate, with a thousand scruples whether one correctly understood the bidding of a higher power, all that is reserved for those who have the courage and the zeal to shoulder the consequences as well as the burden which was loaded upon them against their will. That is far removed from the wantonness of a 'Direction'. And bolder.[2]

[1 Cf. Schoenberg, *Letters*, pp. 103–7. In two long letters written to Hauer in December, 1923, Schoenberg outlined his ideas concerning 'twelve-note composition'. Furthermore, he proposed conferences with Hauer (to compare views) and even collaboration (in disseminating their views).]

[2 In his letter of thanks to well-wishers following his seventy-fifth birthday (1949), Schoenberg wrote: 'Once, in the army, I was asked if I was really the composer A.S. "Somebody had to be," I said, "and nobody else wanted to, so I took it on, myself".' (*Letters*, p. 290).]

TOPICAL INDEX

[Prepared by Alban Berg for the first edition (*supra*, p. 3), this index was enlarged in the third, revised edition with additional page references and topics.] (Numbers in italics indicate pages where the topic, as a chapter heading or subheading, also appears in the Table of Contents.)